The Writings of
CHARLES DE KONINCK

Charles De Koninck, University of Laval, Quebec.

The Writings of
CHARLES DE KONINCK

VOLUME ONE

Edited and Translated by

Ralph McInerny

with a biography by Thomas De Koninck
and an introduction by Leslie Armour

University of Notre Dame Press
Notre Dame, Indiana

University of Notre Dame Press
Notre Dame, Indiana 46556
www.undpress.nd.edu

Published in the United States of America

Paperback edition published in 2016

Library of Congress Cataloging-in-Publication Data

Koninck, Charles de, d. 1965.
[Works. English. 2008]
The writings of Charles De Koninck / edited and translated by Ralph McInerny ; with a biography by Thomas De Koninck ; and an introduction by Leslie Armour.
p. cm.
Includes bibliographical references and index.
ISBN-13: 978-0-268-02595-3 (cloth : alk. paper) — ISBN-10: 0-268-02595-9 (cloth : alk. paper) — ISBN-13: 978-0-268-02622-6 (pbk : alk. paper) — ISBN-10: 0-268-02622-X (pbk : alk. paper)
1. Koninck, Charles de, d. 1965. 2. Science—Philosophy.
I. McInerny, Ralph M. II. Title.
Q175.K664 2008
149'.91—dc22

2008010161

∞ *The paper in this book meets the guidelines for permanence and durability of the Committee on Production Guidelines for Book Longevity of the Council on Library Resources.*

Contents

Works by Charles De Koninck

Preface

A few years ago, David Quackenbush, a tutor at Thomas Aquinas College in California, conceived the idea of photocopying the Charles De Koninck archives at the University of Laval. Thomas De Koninck gave the open sesame, and I arranged to have two photocopies made, one for Thomas Aquinas College, the other for the Jacques Maritain Center at the University of Notre Dame of which I was then director.

I had the great good fortune of studying under Charles De Koninck and receiving both my licentiate and doctorate under his direction. During the summer of 1950, I followed his courses at Laval. After receiving my M.A. from the University of Minnesota in 1952, I decided to complete my graduate studies at Laval in order to study under De Koninck. As it happens, when Quackenbush made his proposal, I already had a good number of De Koninck's papers. In the summer of 1953, I was hired by Laval to be De Koninck's assistant and each day I would appear at his home on the Rue Ste-Genevieve, settle down in his study, and rummage through his files. The idea was that I should introduce order into them. The assignment was largely a ruse designed to provide me with much needed financial support. I soon discovered that the files were filled not only with holographs in De Koninck's distinctive and elegant hand, but also typescripts, ribbon copies, and carbons. Might I appropriate such carbon copies? I was told to go ahead, and of course I did. I also typed out a number of things for myself of which there were no carbons, notably courses given in the late 1930s on scientific methodology. There were several copies of the page proofs of *Le Cosmos*, and I was allowed to have one. And there were off-prints of printed articles. Precious as this collection was, it was as nothing compared to the complete De Koninck papers.

During the early 1960s De Koninck divided his academic year between Laval and Notre Dame, and thus I became the colleague of my mentor. Later, as director of the Maritain Center, I was impressed by the fact that such figures as Maritain and Etienne Gilson continued to be read and to exert their influence. They had never ceased being household names.[1] But there were other figures, on the next level of the Thomistic Revival initiated by Leo XIII, whose posthumous reputation was less assured. Yves Simon, thanks to the dedication of his wife Paule and son Tony, has enjoyed a long and deserved continuing influence. Simon died young. So, too, did Charles De Koninck. (By contrast, Gilson and Maritain lived into advanced old age and were publishing almost to the end.) When Quackenbush's initiative made the De Koninck papers available to the Maritain Center, I formed the idea of collecting the papers of as many North American Thomists as I could. It had already been brought home to me that many of the great figures I had the privilege to know, some more intimately than others, and, more importantly, who had defined Catholic philosophy in the middle quarters of the twentieth century, had become historical figures for a new generation. I and the dwindling number of my coevals could invoke personal memories, contemporary gossip. The gossip of one generation becomes history for later ones, and it seemed important to gather as many materials as possible to facilitate that historical re-creation of the twentieth century which is already under way. This project is now under the capable direction of my successor in the Maritain Center, John O'Callaghan.

It would be disingenuous of me to suggest that the writings of Charles De Koninck are for me simply an important trove of materials in the Thomistic Revival. A year or two ago, for quite accidental reasons, I began to reread Charles De Koninck. I was overwhelmed. One night, having finished an essay of his on the Eucharist, I sat back and said aloud, "Thank God that I studied under this man." Soon I began to see the desirability of bringing out the collected works of Charles De Koninck. Thomas De Koninck was enthusiastic, but pointed out that a French edition of his father's works was in the planning. No matter, I had in mind an English edition. And so it began.

This first volume contains writings ranging from De Koninck's 1934 dissertation at Louvain (written under the direction of Fernand Renoirte) through two remarkable early essays on indeterminism and the unpublished book called *The Cosmos*.[2] Students of the Thomistic Revival will be interested in the criticisms of Jacques Maritain's philosophy of science to be found in the 1934 dissertation. De Koninck was here following the lead of his director Fernand Renoirte. The two long pieces on indeterminism flow nicely from the dissertation. I have no idea why *Le Cosmos* was never published. There it is, in page proofs, all but ready to go. It is a great *tour de force* but perhaps DeKoninck thought it premature. The article from *Culture* comes almost as a surprise, since in it appears for the first time De Koninck's own distinctive view on the relation between philosophy of nature and the experimental sciences. It is possible to see that view slowly forming itself in the courses De Koninck gave on scientific methodology.

All the translations from the French in this volume are my own. Mr. Raymond Hain was of inestimable help in restoring the quotations from Eddington in the 1934 dissertation to the original English from the translations I had unwisely made of De Koninck's citing of French translations. Eddington was a notable stylist and must be allowed to speak for himself.

Ralph McInerny, Notre Dame

NOTES

1. For all that, the Maritain Center, in conjunction with the University of Notre Dame Press, began bringing out the writings of Jacques Maritain, in English, which is projected at twenty volumes, a third of which have appeared.

2. The dissertation is translated from the typescript found in the De Koninck papers. Advantage has been taken of later written comments in the typescript by De Koninck. "Le problème de l'indéterminisme" is a paper read to the Academie Canadienne Saint-Thomas d'Aquin at its meeting of October 9–10, 1935. It appeared in the printed proceedings of that session in 1937, pp. 65–159. It is from that printed version that the translation has been made. "Réflexions sur le problème de l'indeterminisme" appeared in *Revue Thomiste* (1937) in two installments, pp. 227–52 and 393–409. "Les sciences expèrimentales sont-elles distinctes de la philosophie de la nature?" appeared in *Culture* 4 (1941): 465–76.

The Philosophy of Charles De Koninck

Leslie Armour

Charles De Koninck devoted his philosophical career to answering three of the questions which have most exercised contemporary men and women: How can we understand the growing chasm between our scientific world pictures and the world as it appears to common sense? How can we understand the power of modern science and accept its insights while maintaining our most central and traditional religious beliefs? And how can we maintain the responsibility and dignity of the individual without undermining the communities in which we live and without denying the scientific accounts of human nature?

Many philosophers have tackled these questions, but De Koninck was one of the relatively few to do so while denying himself the right to change the terms of reference. He wanted, that is, to retain his religious faith and not, as perhaps Whitehead did, to create a new religion. He wanted to accept science as it really is and not insist on redefining its functions and practices. And he wanted to maintain commonsense notions of human responsibility and to defend human dignity as it was understood by ordinary men and women around him.

A priori, there is no reason why the philosopher should not, if he deems it wise, question the terms of reference and propose new religions or new tasks for scientists. De Koninck's significance lies partly in the fact that he did try to answer the very questions which intelligent men and women were asking and continue to ask. It seemed clear to him in any case that any intelligent enquirer would conclude that science was one of the great human achievements. And his religion was to him a matter of unshakeable faith. Both religion and science were to be enquired into, but each had claims which a philosopher was unlikely to overturn. Human responsibility and the dignity that went with it seemed to him beyond reasonable question. The problem, therefore, was to understand both of these so that religion and science did not destroy one another in a fruitless war and so that human freedom was not bought at the expense of the community and the community was not sustained at the cost of human dignity. I think, within his terms of reference, that he came as close as anyone has to answering these questions and that, while his philosophy has many loose ends, it is capable of substantial development.

1. The Structure of Charles De Koninck's Philosophy

It is a commonplace that Charles De Koninck was a philosopher of science and a religious man, but it would be almost as true to say that he was a philosopher of religion and a man of science. For, despite his long and complex involvement with ecclesiastical affairs in Quebec and despite the fact that bishops in Quebec and senior church bureaucrats in Rome both sought his advice and took it seriously, he was by no means a figure of conventional piety. If he had a quarrel with contemporary science, it was that mathematical physics, in pursuit of its legitimate policy of abstraction, sometimes forgets the richness of the facts of experience on which it is founded. De Koninck came to Laval University in Quebec in 1934 from Louvain, where he had written a doctoral dissertation in the philosophy of science, and he came as Professor of the Philosophy of Nature. He was to become Dean of the Faculty of Philosophy, and would write on moral, political, and social theory as well as religious meditations. But science and its relation to nature remained always at the centre of his thought. Students find it curious—even paradoxical—that a man who not only devoted himself to the study of the intellectual foundations of modern science but whose writings show all the usual marks of a "man of science" should also have played an important part in the discussions which led up to the promulgation of the dogma of the bodily assumption of the Virgin Mary. That promulgation, which took place in 1950, was seen as an embarrassment to many Catholic intellectuals; even those who welcomed it often did not relish the thought of explaining it to outsiders. But De Koninck (though he once said in print that he understood their embarrassment) felt no unease whatever.

The problems posed by this dogma both illustrate and are symbolic of the tension between science and religion in the last half of the twentieth century. They illustrate the tensions because the idea expressed in the common understanding of the dogma seems so clearly to run counter to our whole scientific world picture. The problems are symbolic because the case became, for a time, notorious: it seemed to many non-Catholics to be a case of the Church deliberately challenging science and urging the faithful to choose between one and the other. Understandably, then, when students read De Koninck they are startled. How can anyone be on both sides?

Hopefully, those who read the writings of De Koninck will see for themselves how someone could be—and was—on both sides. De Koninck's writings are, however, fragmentary. Even the apparently complete works are, in a sense, occasional and unfinished. *The Hollow Universe* was a set of public lectures given at what was then still quite strongly a Baptist institution, McMaster University, intended both to whet the appetites of philosophers and members of a general public who did not share all of De Koninck's presuppositions and convictions, and intended as well to open rather than close a discussion about our contemporary world picture. Equally, *De la Primauté du bien commun, contre les personnalistes* was produced under the difficult conditions of a world war. It was intended partly to deal with some current controversies which had become pressing (compiled in part from previously published articles) and opened more questions than it finally settled. De Koninck did not want it published again as it stood and did not live to rework its contents.

He died at the age of fifty-eight and at a moment in his career when he might have begun the rounding off and tidying up of what was already a distinctive philosophical position. He left behind not only one extensive unfinished manuscript but many published fragments whose ultimate intentions had to be inferred by his readers. Yet De Koninck himself surely saw his work as a unity which made sense against the issues which dominated his time and place and which made sense, equally, within the long and richly developed philosophical tradition to which he belonged, and many of his contemporaries would have seen it as he did—though some of the controversies in which he became involved show clearly enough that not all of them did so. The contemporary reader most likely finds himself in a different position. The specific issues which dominated the 1930s, 40s, and 50s have, in some cases, faded from view. The Quebec in which De Koninck lived and worked has been transformed by social forces and by changes in religious outlook so much that many propositions about the social order which in De Koninck's time would have been taken for clichés are now actually false.

Finally, the Thomistic philosophy which De Koninck very often used as a fundamental model—though he was never its slave—has fallen on hard times. Those who have followed its adventures over the centuries may well suppose that its story is not yet over, but reaction against this philosophy began to gather momentum less than a year after De Koninck's death. The Vatican Council, which was widely taken to have opened the doors to other kinds of philosophising within the Church, was part of the explanation, but the Council itself was the product of forces which had long been at work. Some were obvious and deplored by few. For instance, non-Thomistic strands in the Catholic tradition had always claimed attention, and another Quebec philosopher, the Franciscan Ephraim Longer, played an important part in opening the way for the revival of the Augustinian and neo-Platonic traditions. In England the philosophy of John Henry Newman claimed attention as well. But the "mainstream" philosophers usually called "Thomist," including Jacques Maritain and De Koninck himself, had always maintained that philosophy, in the end, had to stand on its own feet, and that Thomism must stand or fall on its intellectual credentials and could not depend forever on the fiat of the Church or simply be defended by scholars of mediaeval thought who devoted themselves to finding out what St. Thomas had said. De Koninck said that he hoped to know enough of St. Thomas not to have to remain forever just a disciple who has faith in his master. One had to be intellectually convinced and, for that, one needed to develop the Thomistic system so that it could solve the live and pressing problems of the day. Too often the dead hand of rote belief and the formulae of the manuals got in the way. More importantly, no doubt, in France, in Italy, and in northern and western Europe generally, competing philosophies—philosophies of the enlightenment, the philosophies which developed from Hegel (and from Marx) and the phenomenological and existentialist movements—provided stiff competition for the minds (and hearts) of Catholic intellectuals; even the most creative thinkers who worked with the Thomistic tradition could make only limited gains. Louvain, where De Koninck was educated, and the Quebec universities, where he taught, formed, along with the American Catholic universities and the Catholic universities in Rome itself, the heartland of a Thomism which was always under siege.

When the official defences were lifted, the besieging forces moved so quickly and the change was so rapid that Quebec Thomism was swept out of sight before anyone really had a chance to make a scholarly estimate of its condition and of its achievements. Both those who look back to the period of its dominance in Quebec as a golden age and those who look back on that period as one in which philosophy was the unhappy prisoner of the Church are alike apt to make false assumptions about the way it was understood by De Koninck and his contemporaries. The reader who comes afresh to De Koninck's work therefore has a good deal of reconstructing to do. In the absence of De Koninck's own gathering-together of his philosophical system, the reader must decide for himself or herself in what framework the work ought to be read and, cut off as he is from De Koninck's time by a kind of temporal fault line along which there has been a minor earthquake, he must decide how to position himself so as to understand what is being said.

The justification for this introduction is simply that few readers will have the time or the inclination to do all the work for themselves. De Koninck's philosophy is thus likely to molder on the shelves or, worse, perhaps, to become a grab-bag out of which anyone with a cause of his own can pluck stray bits of ammunition. All past philosophy is, of course, an idea-mine from which anyone may legitimately draw whatever is needed, but it is important to distinguish, if we can, what the philosopher wanted to demonstrate from what we want to demonstrate. Respect for our predecessors is important, but it is not the central point. Rather, the point is that the history of philosophy has a certain logic: in seeing how ideas are pushed this way and that by the force of argument, we may gradually be able to chart the direction of a development which leads on to the truth. If we obscure the past too much, we have no such hope.

To begin with, I think, we must accept the fact that De Koninck himself might never have "rounded off" or "tidied up" his philosophy even had he lived several more decades. He was, by nature, a man who loved arguments and he was, therefore, a natural controversialist. He died as he often lived, in the midst of controversy. And the controversies tended to occupy his time. If these controversies sometimes gave his philosophy the look of being dominated by particular occasions, it is important to see that the controversies themselves generally had their own unity and almost always served to express the essence of De Koninck's own philosophy.

The controversy in the midst of which De Koninck died is a perfect example. It was characteristically a mixture of theological and scientific issues—the question of whether or not the use of drugs to control fertility for the purpose of birth control was or was not a violation of natural law. De Koninck believed, on philosophical grounds, that it was not necessarily so, though he had doubts in the end about whether or not those in use should be approved. On moral grounds, he believed that there was a serious question involved about the nature of motherhood and about the rights and duties of women. Since it is natural for human beings to be educated—we are not born with enough instincts to govern our lives without education—it is also natural for women both to have the time to learn enough and to have the time to impart enough to their children. Too many children, therefore, can threaten the highest notion of natural motherhood. It can also threaten the humanity of women. The example makes it easy to see how scientific, theological, and moral issues merge to form a philosophical question and this merging of issues was central to all of De Koninck's thinking.

If this is so, we must start, I think, by seeing De Koninck's philosophy as a response to a series of tensions. The nature of these tensions is not always so obvious as one might think, but, basically it seems to me they are the growing tension between science and experience, the tension between science and religion, the tensions created by the fragmentation of knowledge—especially the divisions between philosophy and science and the division between factual and moral knowledge—and the tension between the individual, the community, and the human relation to the universe at large. Growing out of these is an ever more pressing tension between theory and practice.

De Koninck had other continuing concerns. One of them was to show that wisdom is not a special state given only to those with special experience or extraordinary talents but simply the right outcome of the application of natural human reason. But this, it will turn out, is a problem associated with the fragmentation of knowledge. Another of his concerns was to prevent the encroachment of "le grand État" on the real basis of community and on the responsible life of the individual. But this has to do with the balance which he believed must be developed in order to master the tensions between individual, community, and universe. A third and growing concern was with the relation of time to eternity.

I propose, therefore, to organize this discussion around the basic tensions.

2. Science and Experience

De Koninck's first extended work *Le Cosmos,* his most popular book *The Hollow Universe,* his last major series of articles "Abstraction from Matter," and his one remaining substantial unfinished manuscript, a study of the philosophy of nature, all point to the major preoccupation of his life: the relation of science to experience.

It was De Koninck's contention that the objects available to us in experience are much richer than those described in modern mathematical physics and that, without in the least denigrating physics and its attainments, it is important to philosophise about the difference. In De Koninck's theorizing, concepts and world pictures derived from the Aristotelian tradition are developed in various ways as he develops his critique of modern thought. Questions about the nature of experience, the concept of matter, and the difference between names and symbols all concerned him. But, basically, his position is this: the external "objective" world is a collection of objects which can be sensed in a variety of ways. In particular, they can be seen and touched. They are actually unique individuals. We know about the world because we make use of a "common sense," i.e., we have a facility for putting together these elements in a way which assures us of the existence of the ordinary, solid world around us. The natural world is indeed, in De Koninck's view, above all a solid world. Though our most sophisticated information comes to us through the sense of sight, it is the sense of touch on which we rely more than anything else for our assurance that the world is really there as it seems to be. Our scientific picture of the world is, however, rather of a world stripped down from this rich environment and it is this simplified world to which the various facets of the human intellect are peculiarly well adapted. Mathematical physics deals, literally, with abstractions and there is a tendency to take these abstractions for the whole of reality. The result is what De Koninck meant by the expression "hollow universe."

It is important, however, to be very careful about this. It is not a mistake of mathematical physics that it deals in these abstractions. That is its function. There is important knowledge to be gained in this way which cannot be gained in any other way. Mathematical physics is not flawed because of its abstractive method. On the contrary, it would be flawed if it did something else. But mathematical physics also presents us with a puzzle. Its great powers of prediction and the power it bestows on us to control nature present us with difficulties. For, if we are not careful we are apt to read our most advanced sciences as if they were reductionist in essence. Without understanding what we are saying, we may say things like: "Within the realm of physics—which includes everything that can be talked about rationally—there is nothing special about life. Living things are just collections of molecules whose behaviour is chemical, and molecules are just collections of atoms whose behaviour is described by physics." And all this is true. Only it doesn't mean what we may think it means. We may think it means something like: "Only atoms are real. To believe that life is something over and above them is just a remnant of a superstition."

Curiously, we are more likely to try to dispose of life ("life is only a kind of atomic behaviour") than to dispose of molecules; the molecular sciences and the atomic sciences still retain a kind of distinction and, indeed, some British universities have replaced the old disciplines called chemistry and physics with new ones called molecular and atomic science. If we think about this example for a moment we begin to see something of the point De Koninck strove all his life to make. Each of these sciences confronts the material world. The material world, for De Koninck, is what is revealed by the normal functioning of the human intellect within its proper context of rationality. Its correct analysis is a matter for philosophical physics. Early on, in *Le Cosmos,* he had distinguished, as did Jacques Maritain, between the philosophy of nature and natural science; later, for reasons which will become apparent, he abandoned that distinction. What I am here calling "Philosophical Physics" (the term is my own, but expresses De Koninck's intentions) is something in which both philosophy and physics have a part to play. How these parts are to be understood is explained, for instance, in De Koninck's papers published as "Abstraction from Matter." Other versions can be found scattered in various discussions, but the claim is basically this: human knowledge proceeds by taking elements from what is presented and by doing so in a consistent way at a given level of abstraction. Thus chemistry, in its most traditional modes, made its fortune, as it were, by discovering that things which look quite different—bits of glass and bits of stone for instance—might nonetheless be made of the same basic stuff. The molecules in these different objects were of the same sort. Physics, by generalizing further so as to find elements common amongst molecules, proceeds to a level at which we find that molecules are in their turn composed of atoms. But along the way something is lost. Ordinary objects are coloured. Chemists, even, are interested in the fact that certain chemically treated papers change colour when exposed to acids. But in physics colour has disappeared. It is not sensible to ask: What colour is a hydrogen atom? The abstracting activities of each of the sciences are necessary and normal. And the ease with which properties "disappear" in these various analyses is furthered, De Koninck thought, by changing from names which designate particular entities found in experience to symbols which do not designate anything in this way. But it does not follow that the importance or unimportance of these disappearances is something for science alone to pass judgement upon. It is also not, in De Koninck's view, just a matter for the philosopher to decide upon. For everything depends on just how it is to be done. The questions involved are philosophical, but the answers depend on an understanding of how the sciences work. If we are to understand what is at issue here and also understand just what De Koninck's discussions amount to, we must look for a moment at the period of the rise of modern science and the philosophies which, in science's name, reacted to (and against) certain elements of sixteenth- and seventeenth-century scholasticism. De Koninck's discussions do not consist in a simple reversion to the scholasticism of the early modern period. Nor are they Aristotle restated. De Koninck does make use of doctrines found in Aristotle and in St. Thomas, but he puts them to new ends and he develops them in new ways. And we need to see exactly how this comes about.

At the heart of the problem which De Koninck faced in the middle of the twentieth century was the situation created by the fact that one of the central features of the rise of modern science was the growing conviction that reality is not directly revealed in our experience. We are apt to forget this obvious truth for a number of reasons. One of them is that we associate the rise of science with the Renaissance concern for experienced reality. Another is that we confuse the use of selected experiences as the test of scientific hypotheses with a concern for experience as a whole. A third is that we tend to contrast "empirical science" with the "rationalist metaphysics" of the seventeenth century in a way which would not have occurred to the thinkers of that era.

Modern physics had many of its roots in the physics of optics which, in turn, had its roots in the art of the Florentine Renaissance. The desire to paint things as they were—to portray nature and the human form in all its perspectives—was a departure from the main lines of mediaeval art which used symbols to convey a reality more fundamental than that of immediate experience. This concern with painting things "realistically" stimulated interest in the processes of vision and we therefore tend to think of Renaissance science as an exploration of the structure of experience. There is, though, more to it than this. Concern with the physics of optics did influence the development of the telescope which, in turn, played a part in the development of astronomy. But the great advances in the science of the time—and of the succeeding centuries—were essentially conceptual. It is said that the great shock provided by "science" was the growing realization that the earth revolves around the sun. The displacement of the geocentric universe was supposed to shock people because it displaced the earth from the centre of the universe. I suspect that this shock has been greatly exaggerated, but another, greater, shock is less often noticed. The heliocentric universe forced us to believe that the senses deceive us: the earth seems to stand still and the sun certainly appears to move. What led to this change was, initially, nothing more than the discovery that the calculations of the whereabouts of the planets are much simpler if one assumes that the planets move and the sun "stands still." The growing interconnection between science and "calculation" was one of De Koninck's persistent interests.

Much later the bits fell into place with Newton's theory of gravitation. This, too, was a conceptual discovery. The "facts" about falling bodies, moving planets, and the tides had all long been known and, as far as the observations go, even the calculations about planetary movements were not possible in detail until the invention of very large computers. Newtonian science was neo-Platonic. Newton (who had learned from the neo-Platonists at Cambridge) surmised that there were standard patterns, which he expressed in the form of his laws of motion, and that what had to be explained were observed deviations from them. Newton supposed, for instance, that, if nothing got in the way, bodies would move in a uniform direction at a uniform velocity—and would continue to do so for ever. We have never observed anything but deviations from this rule. But the deviations are explicable. Science did, of course, progress in an important way by "observation." But observations increasingly came to be made by instruments which replaced human observers. I feel hot and you feel cold. But the "temperature" is given by reading a thermometer. It does not matter what either of us feels. And, though different observers will all very likely report different sensations of heat and cold, all of them will almost certainly report that they read the same numbers. Physicists, as De Koninck realized, when they boast of their experiments, talk of getting "good numbers." But notice that the humble thermometer reading as much as the grand theses of astrophysics teaches us that the world may not be—usually is not—quite the way it seems to be. The selective use of experience breeds the distrust of ordinary experience. Just as it is easy to suppose that, because the physics of optics grew out of a concern for the immediacies of experience, the astrophysics which was stimulated by the physics of optics must be "empirical," so it is easy to suppose that data derived from instruments intended, as much as possible, to replace the senses must still be "empirical data" just because, at some point in the process, the senses continue to play a role. The sense which functions in instrument reading is, of course, sight. But it is not important as sight. It would be all right if the machine spoke its numbers—or whistled them. Anything which can convey numbers will do. De Koninck was concerned by the fact that touch, which normally plays a vital part in our determinations of what is "real" and what is not, plays no part in these processes. Finally, because there came to be a tendency to distinguish certain metaphysical questions on which no experience seems to bear from "scientific" questions (on which some experience always bears), there came to be a tendency to think of science as "empirical." But this is not, itself, an easy issue to determine. No experience provided evidence for the proposition that the earth revolves around the sun. The issue was a matter of convenience of calculations and, indeed, questions about what moves are always questions which are, in a sense, arbitrary. One thing moves in relation to another. It makes no practical difference whether you say that your aeroplane starts over Montreal but stands still and the earth rotates under it until you are over Chicago, or say that the aeroplane moves while the earth stands still. For many practical reasons we talk about "air speed" and "ground speed" and assume a little of each, but our reasons for doing so have nothing to do with any experience about what seems to move. Experience does play a role. We leave Montreal and find ourselves in Chicago, and so there is something to explain. The problem is given by some experience, but the solution is not. And so it is perhaps with even the most abstruse metaphysical questions.

The problem posed by the question "Why is there something rather than nothing?" is given by the surprising fact that there is anything at all. The surprise is given (as St. Thomas suggests) by the fact we know full well that whatever we find in existence might not have existed. In reality, of course, the gradual opening of the gulf between the world of the physicist and the ordinary, experienced world posed serious philosophical problems. In the seventeenth century, philosophers responded by developing the "way of ideas."

The "way of ideas" took many ingenious forms which, alas, cannot occupy us here, but, after Descartes, one common version had it that what the mind confronts in experience is not itself the primary reality but only something that represents that reality. From these "representatives" we can infer the world, but the world differs from our experiences essentially because there are some properties—primary qualities—which can be "objectified," in that they can be read by anyone from the instruments of science, and others—secondary qualities—which cannot be so objectified. Thus anyone can tell the wave length of light rays given the right instrument, and we can all agree upon the answer but no two people perhaps will see the same shade of blue or of green. Light rays therefore, it came to be said, were out there "in the real world." But things in the real world are not blue or green. Light rays are made up of particles called "photons" or of wave patterns (depending on what one needs to talk about). Photons are not blue or green. Nor are light waves. Indeed, the final conclusion is interesting: photons enable you to see other things. Therefore you cannot, in principle, see photons. If you could, you could not see anything else.

This story leads us to take reality as more and more abstract. Wave lengths are given numerically. In the end everything is expressed in a formula by substituting numbers for the values of the variables.

The tendency is then to claim that what is "real" is simply what is specified in scientific theories. Among scientific theories De Koninck thought we accept the theory which is simplest and the theory which lends itself best to calculations from which we can predict the future. De Koninck noticed that, in the end, we tend to think of the world as a single giant Turing machine. A Turing machine is a machine which can calculate anything whatsoever. If whatever is can be calculated, and if the universe runs by the rules of such calculations, the world must be such a machine.

Ideally, perhaps, we might think of such a world as consisting only of calculations. Indeed, Willard Quine, the Harvard logician and logical ontologist, once suggested that perhaps all we need in our ontologies is the set of natural numbers. This would be the result of taking the strong form of the

Löwenheim-Skolem theorem very seriously. This theorem specifies, innocently enough we might think, that all acceptable theories have denumerable ontologies. Then suppose we add Quine's further claim that "one ontology is always reducible to another when we are given a proxy function *f* that is one to one." Then we get the result that all we need are the natural numbers. A "proxy function" is a relation that is true whenever the original function is true. So, if the number "13" designates Percy the pig, then we need merely say that whatever is true of Percy is true of "13." If our universe is denumerable, then there is one natural number for each and every entity specified in any intelligible theory.

Quine is a wise as well as a witty man and he quickly pointed out that this "Blanket Pythagoreanism . . . is unattractive for it merely offers new and obscurer accounts of old moves and old problems." What Quine means is that such an ontology is always relative, and it is only intelligible as he says repeatedly in terms of some "background theory."

We can see this in various ways. For instance, Quine's most consistent expression of his own view is expressed in the curious phrase "to be is to be the value of a bound variable." If we say "one of the things which exist is the pig, Percy," we express this in logical terms by saying "there is an x such that x is Percy the pig." The general form of this expression is (x) $(fx$ and $gx)$. "Pig" and "Percy" are ways of filling in the blanks. They are "values" of f and g. Thus $(x)(x$ is a pig and x is Percy). The "values" of these variables are what exists. The rest of the formulae consist after all of bits and pieces of logical apparatus.

When someone says "all the values of the variables are natural numbers," what is being said is that a choice has been made. But such a choice always implies some theory in terms of which it has been made. This is the "background theory" of which Quine speaks. It makes no sense to make such a choice unless one has the appropriate theory.

The "Blanket Pythagoreanism" which Quine in fact derides does not suggest only that the background theory involves some claim like "everything that exists would be described by an ideal and complete science of physics or at least by the basic natural sciences." If this is taken together with the further theory that what matters in such theories is their references to natural numbers, one will get "Blanket Pythagoreanism." Quine, of course, thinks the real is what is described in the sciences, but sees the absurdity in saying that the numbers are what matters.

But notice that the plausibility of the thesis about reality and science is less than obvious. One reason for thinking this is that its strongest partisans (Quine, for instance) long ago abandoned the "way of ideas" so that it is no longer actually claimed that one can infer one's way back to reality. The objects in such theories are all "ideas" in the Cartesian sense. No one ever actually sees, tastes, or touches an electron or a photon. (Photons are particles of light which actuate our optical apparatus. If you could see them, you couldn't see anything else. Electrons are "used" in electron microscopes to enable us to see other things, but we cannot see them.) Thus these things are known to the mind and not to the senses. "Ideas" in the very special sense which governs the way in which this particular post-Cartesian theory is usually taken are mental entities and science cannot get at them. Quine, indeed, says "there is no place in science for ideas." The result is that those who think this way take all beliefs about reality to be purely pragmatic. Quine calls himself a logical pragmatist.

It is convenient to believe in science, in short, because science gives us power over nature—and over one another. The theory, taken in this way, undercuts science as a discipline which gives us insight into reality and turns science into an instrument of the power brokers. It is this thought, above all, I think, which always horrified De Koninck. Not only did he think better of science than that, he thought, for reasons which will emerge as we go along, that the view that knowledge is primarily a form of power was ultimately dehumanizing. His alternative has four basic elements. One element is the concept of experience as something which is richer than all our abstractions from it. His claim here centres on the notion that science departs from experience not because what we experience is not there in reality but because science uses experience selectively. Philosophy must, therefore, consider the nature of experience itself, but it must do so in the light of science. Part of what we know about experience, after all, is what science abstracts from it and this, in itself, may contain important information about the original situation.

The second element has to do with the fundamental concepts which one should use to grasp the original situation. How should we look at a state of affairs which can reveal itself in a set of successive abstractions? We should not look at it as an onion which appears when one peels off the successive layers but rather as a set of abstractions each of which may make some claim to be the whole object. It is here that De Koninck used the Aristotelian concept of matter which he was still, as the reader will see, struggling to make clear toward the end of his life when he wrote the papers called "Abstraction from Matter."

The third element has to do with the way in which the human intellect works together with the senses. Though the senses bring us fragments of information they do so in an orderly way so that one sense can confirm—frequently—what another suggests. We think something is there because when we touch it, it feels as it ought if it is what it looks like. Doubting Thomas is convinced by touching Jesus. The problem of the "common sense," the ability to put things together, fascinated De Koninck because the workings of the human system of knowledge-finding do enable us to move toward an idea of the real. This is so, at least in De Koninck's view, because the intellect is so designed as both to receive characteristics from reality and to be able, by appropriate rational activity, to assemble them in a way which displays the origins of the successive abstractions. The intellect is not like a camera which simply records, all at once, the object presented. Rather, the intellect is analytical and can display the data in various logical orders.

The fourth and final element of De Koninck's theses about the world and knowledge is his insistence that the objects of immediate experience are unique individuals—particulars which are quite different in kind from the sorts of things which can be designated by scientific symbols. Let us look briefly at the contentious facets of these claims. The first claim is not easy to state with absolute clarity, but I think its essence lies in the belief that experience always outruns or extends beyond any attempt which we make to analyze it into specific components. And this seems to be true as a matter of psychological fact. Look at any object. Make a list of what you see. You can always add something to it. There seems no limit to the range of discriminations which are possible. If this is so, no science can claim to have grasped the whole of experience, but every science can claim to have added something to what we know about experience. This is true even of mathematics as mathematical physics so clearly shows. A vast array of mathematical theories reveal to us ways of ordering which in turn have led us to look for unsuspected elements and connections in experience.

The further claim which De Koninck makes is that experience reveals to us a solid and substantial world on which science works and that the best evidence about this world of concrete objects (concrete in the literal sense of bringing together the elements of form and matter) is not in any abstraction taken alone but in the whole considered as the potential from which the abstraction arises. It is evident that this is a more contentious claim and it depends on two things: one is the Aristotelian theory of matter; the other is the theory of the intellect and the senses which De Koninck uses. This is the part of his theory which derives most clearly from the Thomistic-Aristotelian tradition, though his lifelong struggles with it do not suggest that he believed that it was simply "there" to be read off the page like a set of do-it-yourself instructions from Sears Roebuck.

"Matter" is a curious expression. The most common modern view held by people on the street approximates to the view held by the Greek atomists Democritus and Leucippus and their successor Epicurus. On this view, matter consists of bits of ultimate hard stuff which do not come into being or go out of being but which combine in different ways to make up the things of the world. The Aristotelian view was, of course, quite different and so, no doubt, is the view commonly held by contemporary physicists, though it is not easy to say what it is that physicists (or philosophers who claim to be guided by them) actually mean. Indeed, contemporary philosophers who claim to be guided by physics to the extent of believing that the world ultimately contains all and only the things described by physicists usually do not call themselves "materialists," but "physicalists." Chiefly, however, matter is best described as sets of fields and forces which determine the forms which visible and tangible objects take when confronted by human brains. The word "matter" usually is a technical term with an agreed-upon meaning among its users. But it is one of the more casual of such terms, and it is not something on which editors of physics journals greatly rely. The entities described in such journals are often discontinuous in space and time or, more exactly, define only space-time systems in which the identifiable entities exhibit discontinuity.

In many senses the Aristotelian notion of matter is, in fact, closer to the accounts which physicists use than is the view of the Greek atomists, but the comparison of conceptual systems so different from one another is a task of great magnitude whose outcome may, in any case, prove at best uncertain and at worst misleading. It is as well, therefore, simply to look for a moment at what De Koninck was theorizing about and to ask what advantages (and disadvantages) might accrue to the conceptual system which he chose. He tells us a good deal about the problem in *The Hollow Universe,* though in "Abstraction from Matter" he may appear to be less forthcoming than we might hope. *The Hollow Universe* was written for a general audience and therefore tends to give the kinds of reasons which an audience with many different commitments might expect whereas the articles which formed the "Abstraction from Matter" series were part of a project from which it was at one time hoped to generate a philosophy of nature text for Catholic colleges, and it assumes, without much question, that the issues are to be posed, broadly, in the Aristotelian-Thomistic tradition. The reader should not assume that De Koninck made this assumption for himself as a matter of course, but only that the project in question demanded that assumption. *The Hollow Universe* text makes clear that he was quite prepared, as a serious philosopher, to begin without prior commitments or, at least, to justify his prior commitments on philosophical grounds. The difficulty, however, is that *The Hollow Universe* lectures deliberately avoided certain technicalities and the "Abstraction from Matter" series deliberately avoided questions about the basic framework of the discussion.

Despite this, it is not unduly difficult to establish De Koninck's general position. To begin with, we can see that the view of science as a succession of abstractions naturally provokes the question "Abstraction from what?" If one conceives the abstractions as successive identifications of forms, then the natural answer is simply "abstraction from whatever it is that the forms inform." As I said, the simplest and most traditional definition of Aristotelian matter was "matter is the capacity to take on form." If matter is the capacity to take on form, then abstraction, if it concerns forms, must be, by definition, "abstraction from matter." The basic reason, historically, for the Aristotelian theory was epistemological, and it is certainly the case that De Koninck always saw these problems in the context of the theory of knowledge. Even when he was concerned with the ontological nature of man he tended to use epistemological expressions. He spoke of the "Sapientia" nature of man. Following St. Thomas, indeed, he thought that the most informative account of the nature of man was in terms of man's capacities as a knowing being. (So much for those who have suggested that Descartes gave philosophy a wrong turning by overemphasising epistemology at the expense of ontology. De Koninck had other objections to Descartes, some of which, no doubt, concerned the precise relation between the two enquiries, but he would not have suggested that ontology and epistemology can really be separated.)

The reason that epistemological problems suggest the Aristotelian view is a simple one: if I know something, there must be something of the thing in the knowledge. But it must not be the thing itself which is possessed "in knowledge." One does not get to know about pigs by becoming a pig. On the contrary, pigs have a limited capacity for knowledge—even for knowledge of pigs or of piggishness itself. But if the thing known is not present in some way in knowledge, then the skeptic must win the ancient battle. The Aristotelian theory proposed a straightforward account. The form which informs the thing can also inform the human intellect—though the object which is the knowledge will be ontologically quite different from the object which is the thing. This view, as I have suggested, came to grief with the rise of modern science because it seemed that nothing of the object was actually in the intellect, and skeptics like Simon Foucher taunted the Cartesians with the claim that even "ideas" could not fill this gap. They could not "fill the gap" because, if they were to fill the gap, they would have to resemble the objects in the world. To do this they would have to have some property in common with the things in question. And this would bring back the scholastic (Aristotelian) theory.

There are many possible answers to the questions thus posed. In order to understand the force of De Koninck's solution, however, we must look briefly at two of the most interesting of them. By means of some transformations of the distinction between formal and objective reality in ideas (a distinction which Descartes developed from Suarez) one can generate effective ways of distinguishing the referring powers of ideas from the forms embodied in them. In order to refer effectively to lions one need only, for instance, have an idea which, whether it has anything to do with lionhood or not, infallibly enables one to identify lion-containing situations. You might have a trip wire which only a lion-sized thing would activate and your idea of lion might be only "the thing which rings the bell." This would do if there were no other things in the environment with the same capacity to trip the wire. This principle is used extensively in physics, for instance, in cloud chambers which enable one to identify particles by reference to the vapour trails which they make as they pass by.

A second way of dealing with the relation of ideas to reality is to follow the eighteenth-century neo-Platonists (Malebranche, for instance) and hold that ideas are themselves efficacious. If ideas tend to have instances—in the manner of the emanations of Plotinus—then we can infer from the idea that we have that reality will have certain properties unless more powerful ideas (those closer to the One) interfere. This idea sounds curious to the modern ear but, as I suggested, it is the principle of Newtonian physics. According to Newton, there are master patterns which hold unless something compels deviations from them. Our ideas give us the master patterns. Our experience shows us deviations. Our reason connects the two by generating scientific laws. It is still true that our experience does not show us ultimate reality; but it does play a role along with reason.

De Koninck chose neither of these. But he certainly knew that he could not simply go back to the "scholastic" view that the properties of things are in some simple way just transferred to the intellect. For this would be to suppose that the modern crisis which one might call the separation of the intelligible and the sensible had never occurred.

De Koninck's answer was to develop the theory of abstraction. Science works by developing particular abstractions which are not necessarily—or even often—apparent in the immediate confrontations which we have with the things in question. When you look at a glass of water, you are not aware of its molecular structure. Much less are you are aware of its atomic structure. Water is composed of molecules which, in their turn, are composed of atoms of hydrogen and oxygen. None of this is apparent to the "naked eye." But the distinction can, rather easily, enter into experience. If you separate the oxygen from the hydrogen you can quite readily blow yourself up. Now notice that these abstractions which yield knowledge do not work by separating some parts of the glass of water from others. The whole glass of water consists of molecules. The whole of every molecule consists of atoms. There is nothing in the water "in addition to" the atoms. But, in talking about the atoms, for instance, one does ignore certain properties of the glass of water. The atoms are not wet. They are not even a liquid. Rather one attends to certain features of the whole and one makes a series of transformations in the types of concepts which one employs. One moves to different levels of generality and these involve different types of discourse.

The glass of water is a distinct and unique object. This is what I designated as the all-important fourth element in De Koninck's account of science: the objects from which the abstractions are made are quite different from the objects that nuclear physics are talking about. A glass of water is this glass of water and not any other. But any hydrogen atom can do as the replacement for any other. A glass of water is the glass which is here and no other. It makes no sense to talk about the atoms in quite this way. Geography has problems as a science because every point on the surface of the earth is unique. Physics has no such problems because every hydrogen atom in its standard form—even one which is an isotope or a member of some other subclass must be exactly like every other member of that sub-class. If one needs to identify them one must do so by some extrinsic reference—by means of the path of the particle through space and time, for instance.

As a consequence one changes one's way of talking; just as when we replace talk about our feelings of being hot or cold with talk about the measurements of a column of mercury, we no longer talk about a particular state of affairs—Susie's sensations of approaching frost bite or John's complaints about the cold—but rather about something universal, a reading of –27 Celsius or +89 Fahrenheit. De Koninck's distinction between names and symbols may sometimes seem puzzling. In some passages they are actually difficult notions, for he was struggling with complex ideas. But in these cases, it is quite clear what is going on. It is perfectly comprehensible that "John's sensation" is actually the name of something which can be directly encountered in experience as part of our transactions with the ordinary world. So one may name one's dog Fido. But the element marked out by the thermometer is not in the same sense an element in the world, for 89 degrees Fahrenheit does not name the state of the mercury column; rather, it refers to something else, the temperature of the air which surrounds the thermometer. Nor does one name Fido's atoms, for each atom is not distinct in the way that Fido is.

The symbols, in the end, are traceable back to interconnections with the world. If the issue belongs to chemistry, then a particular chemist in a particular laboratory made the discoveries and wrote a particular paper which was published in ink on paper in a particular chemistry journal. And, of course, it is the actual concrete world which will be explained by his theory.

Are atoms real in the way that dogs are real? The answer will depend, inevitably, on what you mean, and here we come to a difficulty. I have been writing as if the transformation of feelings about heat and cold into temperature readings and the transformation of descriptions of glasses of water into theories about atoms of oxygen and hydrogen were transformations of much the same kind. But there is a difference. The numbers on the thermometer symbolize feelings rather indirectly for there are not things in the nonliving world which are hot and cold in just the way that there are hot and cold feet amongst pedestrians in Quebec City. There are, on the other hand, complex structures within a glass of water which correspond in a more direct way to the things which physicists or atomic chemists like to talk about. In fact, hot and cold feet are part of a whole universe which, in De Koninck's view, represents a causal system. Our symbolizing of temperatures skews our picture because it throws the weight of the description onto an "objective" element, the column of mercury. Our symbolizing of the glass of water does not have this effect but, like all such transformations, it may skew our picture, too, however different the process may be. We may think of glasses of water as being built up out of atoms of hydrogen and oxygen, whereas the truth, more exactly, is that we can analyze the glass of water into atoms of hydrogen and oxygen. It is the whole glass of water—cold and wet—which is real. We can, when we have learned about molecules and atoms, separate the hydrogen from the oxygen. But we should remember that what we will have is another whole concrete object—a cylinder full of hydrogen or a gas-filled balloon which will spin off into the sky if we let it go.

De Koninck's concerns about the way in which science influences civilization had first of all to do with the effects of misunderstanding the priorities. The misunderstandings are not, primarily, the work of physicists or chemists or of "scientists" in general. Presumably, they are no more and no less prone to philosophical confusion than the rest of us. The principal misunderstanding results from the fact that it looks, when we read the physics books, as if what must be being said is that "all reality consists of atoms" or "all reality consists of physical forces and fields." The notions of force and field, in turn, would have to be understood through mathematical formulae. But what is being said is only that reality, conceptualized in a certain way at a certain level of abstraction, is to be understood as a set of forces and fields.

This misunderstanding arises in part at least because of the way in which knowledge has been subdivided. The physicist does not, when writing an article for *The Physical Review* (or even for *Scientific American*) explain just what methodology produces the level of abstraction at which he works. No one does so because it would be necessary to say the same thing in every writing and the physicist supposes that everyone already knows the writing is a specimen of physics, not a prose poem modelled after the philosophies of Coleridge and Wordsworth.

The prestige of physics and the consequent prestige of its particular level of abstraction derive from something else: our power over nature comes, above all, from applying knowledge obtained at this level. A poem by Wordsworth may well give deeper insights into nature than a dozen issues of *The Physical Review* or a whole year's issues of *Nature,* but it adds nothing to our power. In De Koninck's view, if we ignore the concrete reality of nature we distort, as we shall see, our relation to the universe as a whole. But the immediate effect of distancing ourselves from concrete reality is more devastating. We become preoccupied with the shells of things and with the aspects of them through which we can manipulate them. The title of *The Hollow Universe* is to be taken literally. It describes the universe as seen by science. We forget that things have insides, that they have a perspective which is their own.

For nonliving things, we have no way of approaching them from the "inside" except in the special sense that their inner essence is given by their place in the divine scheme of things. We must not, De Koninck thinks, forget that the things of the world have being, that their being comes from God, and that, therefore, in one sense, what they "really are" can be understood only if we see them as expressions of the divine intellect and will. But for living things, we can grasp that their inner nature is given in part by the kind of consciousness they have.

When in *The Hollow Universe* De Koninck talks about the "lifeless world of biology," he is talking about living creatures seen as abstractions. Their inner life is, after all, what makes them alive. But even unconscious living things have a form of organization which focuses their environment in a way which makes it sensible to talk of their point-of-view as understood "from the inside." De Koninck reminds us that we like to go to the zoo to see the animals. We would not have the same attitude to a collection of stuffed animals, no matter how "lifelike" the taxidermist had made them.

What is being developed in *The Hollow Universe* is an incipient natural theology, and more of its nature will emerge as we go along, but here it is worthwhile to notice the mainspring of its development: the inner being of the objects of nature is evidently determined by their relation to the ultimate reality or being-as-such, that is, to God and to providence. When that inner reality becomes aware at the different levels appropriate to different kinds of living things, it is, of course, the eternal being itself which is being expressed through it just as it is the eternal being itself which is expressed through every act of creation. If man is made in the "image of God" it is because the inner being of man is expressed through knowledge and because, in knowledge, we, in our turn, can reproduce the whole universe. But "reproduce" is the right word. Nature is not our creation. It may seem to be if we mistake our own abstractions for the concrete reality. But what we cannot do is to create the concrete world for ourselves. The concrete world is given, and the evidence that it is given is in the fact that the original matter from which abstraction produces science is always richer than the abstractions.

These considerations, inevitably, bring us to the third element in De Koninck's nature philosophy: the workings of the human intellect. It is not just that the given is never exhausted by our abstractions from it. In addition, our place as knowing beings suggests to De Koninck that nature and knowing beings are so designed as to go together, and so designed as to be unintelligible without one another.

Sir Arthur Eddington, about whom De Koninck wrote a dissertation, had been surprised to find that "God mathematicises"—to find, that is, that our mathematical formulae are able to grip reality. De Koninck was not so surprised by this. Mathematics itself is the result both of abstractions from experience and of transformations within the logical apparatus with which we confront reality. That it should give us power over nature may be surprising, but that it should grip nature is not surprising unless either our experience is delusory or our logic is not itself a natural order. (This last possibility is a vexed one which, however, seems not to have troubled De Koninck himself unduly, probably because he accepted that physics had anyhow proved that mathematics does grip reality.)

The explanation for the good terms on which intellect and reality find themselves lies, for De Koninck, at a deeper level. Curiously, for instance, there are properties of things which are genuinely discovered only by a combination of our senses. What did doubting Thomas learn by touching the Jesus whom he saw? Nothing, we might think. And yet it is characteristic of the real as opposed to the illusory world that touch confirms what we see. We do not touch what we see or see what we touch. Rather the property of being an extended, solid thing is the property of having a certain appearance together with a certain feel. We act in the world and learn about it in a way which is quite different from introspectively imagining it. But this involves a combination of sense and intellect—of grasping characteristics and of ordering them intelligibly. The sensible and the intelligible do come linked according to De Koninck, despite the enlightenment philosophers. It is just that the abstractive function was not clearly understood by those philosophers.

To make all this work De Koninck used a good deal of the traditional Thomistic and Aristotelian apparatus. He regarded the senses as recipients of actual qualities in the world, and the intellect as providing a foundation for their intelligibility as well as an activity which enters in different ways into knowing and doing. Intellectual activity enters in different ways into knowing and doing, but does not itself, on his view, distort reality. De Koninck's justification for it, ultimately, is just that it all seems to make the system fit together intelligibly—and, finally, that it enables us to keep the insights of the sciences while not dehumanizing ourselves. De Koninck keeps the notion of the concrete object as something prior to and not finally dissolved by the sciences—though something the sciences can and do throw much light on. Thus he preserves the natural world as the arena within which the traditional Christian dramas of life, death, resurrection, and confrontation—even miraculous confrontation—with God can still take place.

3. Science and Religion

Students find it curious—even paradoxical—that a man who devoted himself to the study of the intellectual foundations of modern science should also have played an important part in the discussions which led up to the promulgation in 1950 of the dogma of the bodily assumption of the Virgin Mary. De Koninck, though he once said in print that he understood the embarrassment of those Catholic intellectuals who found the promulgation disturbing, felt no unease whatever. He believed that a universe which works by divine providence can also be a universe which lends itself to explanation by scientific laws. These beliefs had both a negative and a positive aspect.

The negative aspect emphasises a certain kind of independence between science and theology. It is not unimportant in De Koninck's philosophy, but it does not account for its originality. Certainly, given that physical laws are widely regarded as probable rather than certain, given that at the level of the fundamental entities, observations inevitably influence what is observed, and given that alternative conceptualizations and the necessary use of models give science an ineradicable element of subjectivity, there are many ways in which one can evade claims about the collision of science and religion. De Koninck noted all of these elements and, more fundamentally, he argued that, since science necessarily abstracts selectively from a given reality which is invariably richer than the scientific descriptions which result, there is always a case to be made for the proposition that concrete reality has a natural priority over scientific description. But all that this shows is how the various orders of reality—especially the providential order and the order described in physics—can be understood as not conflicting with one another. De Koninck hoped for more than this.

He hoped that a positive thesis would emerge—one which would ultimately show that science and religion tie together so as to imply one another. His further efforts, both those found in religious meditations like *Ego Sapientia: La Sagesse qui est Marie,* and those found in *The Hollow Universe,* are suggestive, even tentative, and would, I think, have undergone further development had he lived longer. It is this line of thought which I want to develop.

There are two main lines of argument. One begins specifically with the idea of wisdom and with the relations which that notion demands between the concrete and the abstract in both religion and science. The second has to do with the idea of universal cause. The two are connected in a way which will become evident, but I will deal with each in turn.

The principle involved in the problem about wisdom is to be found most clearly in *Ego Sapientia.* Indeed, the argument bears directly on De Koninck's concerns about the special subject of that book. The argument which he puts forth begins in a neo-Platonic way, though there is a sense in which, in the end, he wants to stand Philo, in whom the argument has its roots, on his head. (Philo is not mentioned by name, but De Koninck would have expected his readers—or many of them—to recognize the source.)

De Koninck recalls the tradition that Mary said "I am wisdom." She did not say "I am wise," not even "I am the wisest of creatures." Here we have a philosophical curiosity. The issue is the predication of an abstract property upon a concrete being. It is only of God, he says, or of the transcendentals, that one can ordinarily do this. "He is goodness itself," we may say, but, unless we speak of God, we intend it metaphorically—unless, like Keats, we speak of the transcendentals. "Truth is beauty, beauty truth" is, at least, verbally possible. But "he is truth," and "he is beauty" will not do, as a rule, unless said of God. "He is truth" is, after all, a theological commonplace.

Still, there is a tradition about the Virgin Mary. She was early associated with Sophia, the traditional personification of Wisdom, and, in the Christian tradition, she took over this role from Sarah, whom Philo had identified in just this way with wisdom itself. In De Koninck's own tradition there is the further identification of Mary as "the mother of God" and so, as De Koninck says, as quite literally the "origin" of God. ("Origin," here, is a point of orientation: here God comes into our world.)

So tradition suggests that the rule against the predication of an abstract property on a concrete being has an exception in this case. Is this just a way of talking, a form of words making clear that the sacred is involved? De Koninck did not think so. And the reason is not so hard to find if one looks seriously at his whole discussion of the relation of the concrete and the abstract. What if one really had "wisdom"? Surely wisdom cannot itself be an abstraction. When we speak of a wise person we mean not just a man or a woman who knows a lot. There are autistic people—unfairly called idiot savants—who can calculate huge numbers without having any idea how they do it or knowing any theory of arithmetic. In some sense they know a lot. Nor do we mean to call attention simply to a man or a woman who has a knack for getting things done or for doing the right thing. There are many admirable people with "a lot of know-how," but we do not necessarily think of them as wise. Rather by someone who is "wise," we mean one who knows what to do and how do to it in the strongest sense of "knows"—someone who has real knowledge.

Wisdom is not, according to De Koninck, a special or unusual or mystical insight. It is the ordinary state of men and women carried to its ultimate development. The idea of wisdom, when it has instances, is not distinct from its concreteness. Now it is, of course, the essence of the claims about Mary in the Catholic traditions which De Koninck so strongly supported that it is through her, somehow, that God comes into our world as a concrete being. The perfection of our world is the existence of Jesus—a perfection which could not hold longer than it did because of the evils still latent in our world, and a perfection which can only return at the end of time when our world, in whatever way, has fulfilled itself.

Philo, in whom, as I said, the argument first takes root, believed in the power of ideas. In a very particular sense so did De Koninck. In Philo's neo-Platonic view of the world, wisdom, like all the ideas, tends to have as many instances as possible within the limits of the structure formed by the instantiation (or hypostatization as he more nearly said) of other ideas. The concrete world around us is always, for Philo, less real than the ideas which are its guiding forms. For De Koninck the concrete is most real. Science works by abstraction and, if taken for reality, seems to hollow out the world.

The idea of wisdom gives us a reason for starting with the concrete. Wisdom implies a merging of the theoretical and the practical. It, therefore, can only be in the world if there is a wise being. We may not be sure that there is such a being (who would be God in the ideal case), but we have a sense that wisdom is possible and worth struggling for.

God transcends our world and fits into it only by the ultimate miracle (one truly difficult to understand) which, for De Koninck, is the Incarnation. If God comes into our world, as religion demands, there has to be a way for him to come into it, one which, though no doubt created by God himself, also is the very origin of God in our world. This is personified in the Virgin Mary. It may, indeed, seem very odd to suppose that there is such a thing as concrete wisdom. De Koninck does not pursue the matter. But let us suppose what seems more likely at first glance. Let us suppose that there is no concrete wisdom.

To say that there is no wisdom is to say that there is no effective combination of concrete truth and right action. But science itself is not possible without some such identification. Science works, ideally, by methods which reveal the structure of the concrete through various kinds of manipulation. These manipulations are called controlled experiments. Even where we cannot perform controlled experiments—as in astronomy—we try to tie our theories to parts of physics which can be subjected to such controls. The truth is thus predicated upon a choice of right actions. And this is not just a game with words which plays on the different senses of "right."

Experiments can be manipulated themselves—scientific reputations can be and have been built on corrupt manipulation. The scientific community collapses unless its members work together on moral terms—unless, that is, they act wisely. They must therefore claim to know what wisdom is, but, were there no such thing in the concrete world, their claims would in the end be hollow.

We are shocked at the notion that scientists might play fast and loose with the evidence or design experiments which deliberately mislead their colleagues. Yet we are only shocked, on scientific grounds, because we believe that nature is so designed that it is more likely to reveal itself correctly to those who do not deliberately contrive to mislead than to those who do. That is, the faith which makes science feasible in De Koninck's universe is the same faith which leads him to believe that there is, really, a concrete wisdom. But if such a concrete wisdom existed in an ideal form, it would be a perfect whole. It could not be divided into body and soul as if it consisted of two unrelated elements which might exist apart. We do not always act on our knowledge because our minds do not always activate our bodies in the way that we wish. There is a disunity of body and soul. If we were really wise, there would be no such disunity.

So, argues De Koninck, it must have been with the Virgin Mary. But if there was no disunity, how could body and soul have been separated? The faithful, he argues, do not pray to the Virgin Mary as a disembodied spirit, but as a person. Yet a person is a unity of body and soul. Tradition, practice, and theory led De Koninck to the position of the bodily assumption. For most people, admittedly, the bodily assumption, however cleverly put, still seems to be a piece of nonsense.

But, within De Koninck's philosophy, it is not nonsense at all. If Mary's body and her soul were a genuine unity, they could not be separated. She would, therefore, not have been in space and time just as you and I are, though she would have seemed to have been to any casual observer. We are dispersed through space-time in a way which makes it possible for us to be fragmented. I am not quite the man I was twenty years ago, and we all know that our mind-body relations are often confused and puzzling.

It would have been otherwise with one who was truly wise. Since our space-time is fragmented and ourselves along with it, there could have come a time when we could no longer make contact with her in the usual ways, though Mary or wisdom might always have been available to the perception of the truly discerning or deserving, as De Koninck and the Church say. There need be no scientific discontinuities in this. When she was visible to ordinary mortals all of the time her body would have revealed the properties of ordinary visible things and, of course, when she is not visible, science does not discern her either. In either case, as befits her character, she does not discommode scientists or anyone else.

This view of the relation between science and religion, however, may well seem to founder on the rock of causality. It is all very well, one may say, to speak of the difference between the concrete world and the world described by the abstractions of science. But we think of our scientific laws as not merely predictive but also explanatory. It is this explanatory power, for instance, which is not quite dealt with by a simple regularity account of causality.

If, however, the "real" causal relations amongst things in the world are actually captured by science, then the very different relations which hold amongst things in the "concrete" world—supposing them to be, after all, such as to accommodate the events which figure in the religious descriptions of the world which De Koninck accepted—would still seem to conflict with our scientific view.

De Koninck proposed to solve this difficulty by recourse to the notion of "universal cause." He lays out his account of it in an essay entitled "The Immaculate Conception and the Divine Motherhood: Assumption and Coredemption." Though the words "universal cause" do not occur there, the notion of universal cause is derived from a passage in Book II, Section III of Aristotle's *Physics.* There are cases where one determining factor is logically prior to another of the same general type: "Health, for example, may be attributed both to the doctor and to [the more general term under which he falls, namely] the expert. An octave is determined both by the ratio of 2:1 and in a more abstract sense by number. This situation is found wherever one of the factors is more inclusive in meaning than the other which is subsumed under it." Aristotle warns about possible confusions. He reminds us that, in addition to the particular thing or event which is said to be the reason for something, we may sometimes say that the genus of that thing is the reason for it, but sometimes we may call attention to an incidental factor or attribute of the thing. Incidental factors can be confused with causes. Confusion can also result, as Aristotle notices, from using the words "the reason" (or as we might say "the cause") to denote these aspects singly or collectively. Distinctions of potentiality and actuality are also important. The expression "universal cause" is to be found later in St. Thomas, introduced explicitly in the sixth lecture of his *Commentary on Aristotle's Physics* when he is distinguishing between universals which are causes in some serious sense and universals which are mere common properties.

De Koninck refers to this development, though he returns to Aristotle himself in the development of his own ideas. His own ideas were something he continued always to wrestle with and his final accounts are to be found in a textbook on the philosophy of nature which remained unfinished at the end of his life. Basically, if I can put the issue in my own way, the notion is this: it is true that the doctor sometimes cures his patients. How? One answer is "by his expertise." Another is that it is the medicine which cures the patient. The medicine is, in the ordinary sense, the "efficient cause." But one could ask why it is that the doctor is able to prescribe this medicine. Then one gets the answer "because of his expertise." About the "expertise," in its turn, we can ask different questions. How did he get it? Well, his teachers spoke and he listened; other doctors wrote and he read what they said. His ears and his eyes brought about various appropriate changes in his brain. But the question "Why does the expertise work?" demands a different kind of answer. It works because the world is organized in a certain way: certain general principles are at work in the world. Similarly, when we say that—to return to Aristotle—"number" is the "cause" of the octave we mean, in part, that the world has certain general properties in virtue of which things are denumerable. This makes certain general principles applicable. It is these general principles with which we are concerned. In his unfinished textbook, De Koninck is concerned, as was St. Thomas, to distinguish these "universal causes" from mere universals of predication. Everything in the universe can be organized under an ascending set of general predicates.

The most general, perhaps, is "being," but it is somewhat odd to say that "being is the cause of Elvis Presley." Again, Ottawa is a city, but it is quite wrong to say that 'cityhood' is the cause of Ottawa. Some universal properties give rise to principles of explanation and some do not. Being a city is something which results from the workings of quite other causes. Population is, in a sense, the cause of being a city. In another sense, if we mean by a city something with the rudiments of civilization, then the conditions which make for a certain sort of civility are the causes of being a city, and some of these will turn out, in all likelihood, to be "universal causes." We might say that being is the cause of Elvis Presley if we have some notion of the principles of being such that they tend, according to some principle, to result in the occurrence of people. We do not usually do so, for we do not know the principles. Even so, we need more distinctions.

There are different kinds of universal causes and it is one special kind which figures most strongly in De Koninck's essay about the Immaculate

Conception. To say things like "he was cured by the medical art" is to call attention to the fact that there is involved not just what the doctor did which happened to be followed by a cure (something which happens when quacks cure patients, too), but that there is a rational body of knowledge which is being applied. This, too, has a history. The doctor learned it, in part, from other doctors and in part, no doubt, developed it for himself. But it is an objective state of affairs, there to be discovered, and it plays a causal role. Its history is the history of medicine. Without it there could be no history of medicine. Sometimes, too, we say things like "this painting exhibits real art" implying some sense in which one might claim, in part at least, that "art is the cause of this painting." "Art" in this sense is something that the painter has grasped and which works through him. We may analyze it in a historical context, showing how it develops from one age to another and from one painter to another. But we never quite analyze it away, for the earliest painting which we discuss nevertheless still must show it in a rudimentary way if we are able to discuss it at all.

What we are talking about, here, is what really should be called the universal efficient cause. Universal efficient causes enter into the world and are transmitted in a way which has a history. There are also, evidently, universal formal causes. In his unfinished textbook, De Koninck tries hard to make clear the distinction between universal causes, in general, and mere predications. He mentions the distinction between efficient causes and formal causes though it is not completely developed. We may make the distinction somewhat easier to understand in the following way: "goodness" like "redness" is a universal. So is "art" in the sense in which we were using it. Goodness is what all good things have in common. Redness is what all red things have in common. "Art" is what certain skilled acts of doctors have in common or, indeed, in another sense of the word, what all paintings of a certain sort have in common. Redness, however, as De Koninck is at pains to argue, is not really a "universal cause" because it is merely one of many more or less incidental properties of a thing and what we want to explain is how the thing got to be the way it is. "Art," on the contrary, is what explains how the properties of what the doctor does, or the properties of the painting, fit together to make them the kinds of things they are, because "art" is a kind of controlling property. It is the doctor's art or the painter's art which gives meaning to their actions or to their work. "Art" in all its senses is possible because the world is ordered in a certain way, because it has a certain form. In this sense "art" is a universal formal cause. But the art which is transmitted from one doctor to another or from teacher to pupil in the art school is a part of the particular explanation of how things take on the shapes which they presently exhibit. This is "art" as a universal efficient cause. When we come to "goodness" a further complexity becomes apparent. In a sense it is the controlling property par excellence. All things, Aristotle says, aim at the good, but goodness is not merely a "final cause" but also a universal cause in three different ways. It is a "universal final cause" in the sense that it is the final cause of everything and in the sense that it is the same cause, though it appears in many different things in demonstrably different ways.

If, as has usually been thought in the philosophical tradition which occupies us here, evil is always a negation, a lack of something, then goodness is the ultimate universal formal cause as well: it is in virtue of having some positive property (i.e., some goodness) that things can be at all. Again it is universal in that it is ubiquitous and universal in that it appears in different things. But goodness is also a universal efficient cause. A man's knowledge of the good, whether extensive or minimal, animates him to do what he does, for in general people do not act except for what they take to be the best. Even the bank robber thinks it better (in some sense of better) that the money be in his pocket than in that of the banker. Nothing is just good. Each thing always has some other properties through which goodness, we may say, is "expressed." "Goodness" cannot be created or destroyed, though good things can be. I may take credit for a good act, but not, literally, for the goodness which is in the act. Sometimes I may say that I have "grasped" the goodness (as the artist grasps the art). Sometimes my acts express a goodness which I do not grasp at all. We may picture this transmission of goodness, its communication as a universal to a series of particulars, in somewhat the way that we picture the history of art.

As we trace art on through its history, we find more and more of its intrinsic nature being expressed as the various possibilities unfold, even though, of course, later art is not necessarily better than earlier art. But "art" is never absent. From its first discernment, it must always be present in the examples through which we create our history. For, though a universal, art must be expressed through particulars. If there is a break, as there would be if a civilization broke down leaving no trace of itself, "art" would have to be communicated again to a first individual and the story would begin anew.

Christianity has it that, in the case of the human race, there was a break in the transmission of goodness with "the fall," and men and women stumbled about unable to save themselves. The damage had to be repaired, if at all, by a fresh act of divine grace. Such an act would be literally a new appearance of the divine goodness itself in the world. This new appearance was the Incarnation. According to De Koninck, this is an even more radical event than his philosophical and theological opponents would suppose. For in it God shows, he says, his ultimate humility. He comes as a man.

To come as a man (in the full and ordinary sense which orthodoxy ascribes to the Incarnation) he must have a mother and, if so, his mother must also be without sin, the first such person since the fall and, therefore the "new Eve." Otherwise the goodness cannot be communicated whole. But this permits her—indeed makes it necessary for her—to be in a wholly distinct position. The persons of the Trinity are, by nature, goodness itself. She is, rather, a first and crucial link in the chain through which goodness comes to us. But the creation of such a cause also shows God's sound judgement, indeed, his wisdom: for it is St. Thomas' view, and De Koninck's as well, that it is better, in a sense, to be the cause of causes than simply to be the cause.

Thus St. Thomas says in the *Summa theologica* first that God is to be understood as the "universal cause" and then specifically that the "divine wisdom" is the cause of the distinctness in things. Individual entities cannot be their own universal causes. In *Summa contra gentiles,* he argues that if God caused all the actions directly, then God's wisdom in creating things at all would be called into question, for creation would be useless. On the contrary, he believed that creation is the manner in which the divine attributes come to be distributed in the world. One of St. Thomas' problems is to reconcile the view that God is responsible for everything in a world which he creates ex nihilo with the view that creatures actually act in the world. The notion of universal cause is a key to this conundrum in that God acts through all things as their universal cause without, thereby, becoming literally identified with them—an identification which would divide his nature.

Obviously these propositions are linked to the questions about God and evil. It is because of his ultimate humility that God permits evil. He comes in all his weakness as a man. But this humility, in its turn, is linked to the problem of universal cause: How is goodness to be communicated to us except through this unbroken chain and how can the chain reach us unless God becomes man?

One may certainly ask just how wisdom in the sense De Koninck demands is connected to science. One may argue, indeed, that wisdom really has to do with practical reason and therefore has no obvious links to science, which depends upon theoretical reason.

But consider: science, I suggested, involves practical activities which must be governed by honesty and by the search for truth—that is to say that science depends on the supposition that honest enquiry is more likely to reveal the truth than other kinds of activity. We do not know by pragmatic means that this is really so, for all our scientific propositions are fallible, and all the ones we think we now have may well ultimately be proved false. Indeed, if science proceeds by abstraction as De Koninck thought, it will mislead us by taking things out of context unless we have some notion of what the concrete world from which the abstraction takes place is like. This is the message of *The Hollow Universe.* But it is religion, more than anything else, which gives us, as abstracting animals, at least a glimpse of what the concrete world might really be like. Thus we need to have faith in the nature of the concrete world in order to justify our continuance in it.

Not all human activities are of this kind. Advertising, for example, may succeed by destroying the rationality of its audience. Not too long ago, Paula Drillman, the executive vice-president of McCann Erickson, one of the largest advertising agencies in North America, was quoted as saying that advertisers are giving up emphasis on the "rational benefits" of their products and are instead trying to create emotional attachments because rational benefits can be emulated too easily by one's opponents.

What is special about science, then, from the point of view of its need for wisdom is that it proceeds by abstraction and therefore needs a complement, and that it is directed to the truth. When Monsignor L. A. Paquet spoke of "La culte de la vérité," he was speaking of something very important. Science fails, therefore, unless integrated into a larger reality. Partly, this larger reality is discovered through the philosophy of nature and through natural theology, but the nature of the concrete world is given to us in De Koninck's view only with the help of religious revelation. Hence, I think, in *his* view, we had best not keep them separate.

This may make the puzzles about the role of the Virgin Mary in Christian theology more intelligible, but does it help us when we return to science? It does not if, as the drift of thought from the sixteenth century through to the end of the nineteenth century seems to suggest, scientific theses tend to dispose of everything except particular efficient causes. But some of this appearance may vanish on closer analysis.

An older science tried to explain why things move at all. Part of Newton's innovation was to assume fixed laws of motion and to explain the deviation. These laws are, if you like, ideal forms and function, indeed, as the universal formal causes of events. The principle of the conservation of energy which came to be a bedrock of physical mechanics, by contrast, is the notion of a universal efficient cause, for no particular description, whether of particles in motion or of forces and fields, accounts for it. The strength of Hume's critique of scientific causality depended on an attack on particular efficient causes. Hume was undeniably right to suggest that nothing in the descriptions of such causes made it in the least likely that what had happened in the past would continue to happen in the future. The missing notions—not attacked by Hume because they had largely disappeared from view (if, indeed, anyone had ever had them quite straight)—were those of universal formal and universal efficient cause.

Certainly the principles embodied in the Newtonian laws of motion are universal formal causes. Newton himself appended to his *Principia* an argument for the existence of God.

Two rival interpretations of it developed. One was deistic according to which God simply made the world as a single machine and then abandoned it to its work. The other was a theistic one according to which God interfered continuously. Newton favoured the latter, partly because he wondered why gravity did not cause the world to collapse into itself and partly because he was concerned with the perturbations in planetary motions, but one of his concerns was with the conservation of energy.

In his book on eighteenth-century versions of the design argument, Professor Hurlbutt summarises the response to Query 39 of the *Optics* this way: "Newton begins with the belief that the amount and variety of motion in the universe is always decreasing, and he feels that this implies a need for its conservation and recruitment by active principles." Neither the literal description of the material bodies nor the description of the laws of motion guarantees this result. Some activity is required, but it is not the sort of activity which moves any particular body from here to there. Even when we think, as we now do, of the laws of thermodynamics as requiring that kinetic energy is transformed into thermal energy in exact proportion, the problem remains. Why shouldn't some of the energy simply be lost? We could still, like Newton, think of this balancing act as an activity, but, if so, it is the activity of a universal principle. It is, again, a universal activity, not simply the passive ordering of all-pervasive form. Its connection with God is, of course, another matter.

Perhaps, however, the case I want to make would be clearer if I referred to what I think was a still more important concern for Newton. Newton was strongly influenced by Henry More, the Cambridge Platonist. It was from More that he came to think of space as the sensorium of God, for instance. The questions of perturbation and gravitational collapse have disappeared, but the question of the structure of the sensorium of God is the question of how nature is organized so as to be intelligible. This is the question which arises when one considers universal efficient cause. In this sense, intelligibility and, indeed, intelligence itself (the working of the Aristotelian agent intellect), like art, can be a universal efficient cause. The question is alive again in physics because physicists like John Barrow of the University of Sussex have raised it in connection with the use of the anthropic principle. Unless one is prepared to take the view that science is justified only pragmatically by its ability to predict, or simply on the basis of a Humean natural belief or a Kantian account of the synthetic a priori in human experience, one must accept that, not only have universal formal and efficient causes played a role in science, they must necessarily do so.

Pragmatic acceptance of predictability is a circular notion in the sense that it would be reasonable if and only if we already had some ground for thinking that the future would resemble the past. Humean natural beliefs founder on just the question we are concerned with here. Why do some of our beliefs seem more natural and reasonable than others? Neither Hume nor the partisans of science and religion quite believe that all beliefs are equal. The Kantian proposal somehow forces a distinction between what may exist in a noumenal world and what seems to be the natural pattern of our minds. But the more that we know about the unity of knowledge, the less plausible all such separations may be.

By contrast, the strength of De Koninck's claim is that it shows how certain elements of science and certain elements of religion come together to make sense in a single unified pattern. Pragmatists can unify science and religion at the price of denying objectivity. Humeans and Kantians must keep them separate.

One may certainly raise questions about just how the relation of religion to science is to be construed in De Koninck's philosophy. The central question which critics usually pose about De Koninck is simply about whether his position can be made intelligible, and I have been trying to show clearly that it can be made intelligible and even acceptable to at least some of those who are committed to a scientific view of the world. But one can also raise questions from the perspective of faith and ask about faith's claims to independence, as well as raising important questions about the details of certain concepts or principles which, I suggested, played a part within science as well as within natural theology, the philosophy of nature, metaphysics, and religion.

De Koninck surely accepted the claims of faith. Christianity seemed to him to be the true religion. He believed that he accepted not only all the things required of a Catholic, but also that he accepted the things which Catholics usually accept even if they are not, in the strictest sense, formally required to do so.

He did not think that reason could demonstrate all these truths. By and large, the list of the doctrines he supposed to be known to the faith but not demonstrable by reason corresponded to St. Thomas' list. The doctrine which formed my central example—because it was so often De Koninck's own example—was the doctrine of the bodily assumption of the Virgin Mary. De Koninck believed that this had always been a Catholic belief, though it was not an official dogma until 1950. Not only would he not have said that it could not be demonstrated by reason, he would have added that, but for the traditions and teachings of the Church, it is unlikely that anyone would ever have heard of, much less discussed, the special status of the mother of Jesus.

Faith thus works to present doctrines. De Koninck believed that they must somehow be made intelligible. They are presented to the human understanding; they are truths to be reasoned about. They must be understood in some way which is at least not incompatible with the demands of reason.

There has been, certainly, debate about what this means. A minimalist interpretation, perhaps, would have it simply that dogmas must not contain formal contradictions. But there was a long rather particular scholastic tradition in Quebec which De Koninck followed and which demanded more than this. It seems to me that he adopted and made this tradition very much his own in a way which explains his influence within the Church in Quebec. Indeed, he developed this tradition to what may well prove to be its final clarity.

The rationalism which this tradition involved was Thomistic rationalism, though as Professor Watzlawik has shown, Thomism in Quebec, which dated from the 1840s and thus preceded the main body of the Thomistic revival, had some features of its own. Whether some of this was influenced by the mixture of Cartesianism and Augustinianism which was implanted in the Collège Jésuite in the seventeenth century and continued through to nineteenth-century thinkers like Jacques Odelin or whether it was founded wholly on a reading of St. Thomas is a question which cannot be settled here.

But the essence of what I think was the standard position in Quebec on the question of faith and reason was laid down by Monsignor Louis-Adolphe Paquet in 1890 in a book entitled *La Foi et la raison en elles-mêmes et dans leurs rapports.* In it he argues specifically that it is the function of reason to establish the credibility of the faith and to make the faith intelligible and provide the basis for its interpretation. Paquet went so far as to defend the geological theory of the history of the earth against the book of Genesis, implying a clear basis for the theory of evolution, a basis later developed by De Koninck, for whom the notion of universal cause provided a key to the problems which evolutionary theory set for a Christian philosopher. (In *The Hollow Universe,* De Koninck says that many people make evolution so trivial that they do not think there is a difference between two tons of elephant and two tons of coal. What is important is the kind of thing involved: "To produce a man from some ape-like creature no more destroys the kind of creature this was than a degenerative evolution of man into an ape-like creature could suppress what it is to be a man.") Paquet reminds us that St. Thomas says that not all passages in Scripture are of the same character or of the same importance. How are we to determine which are which? Surely only reason can do this.

The view that I have been suggesting as the natural outcome of what De Koninck says does not go further than this, and it does, in a sense, give a certain priority to faith. The concept of wisdom which is central to his concern about the Virgin Mary is one which is necessary for religion and for science alike. In its fullest and most developed form, it is only available to the religious man. The man of science with no religion is not thereby precluded from doing science but he is committed to the existence of a kind of wisdom which cannot, I think, be made fully intelligible within science alone. Thus religion and science complement one another. The essential link between them was emphasised again by Paquet in *La Culte de la vérité,* published thirty-seven years after *La Foi et la raison.*

De Koninck in his turn had still more than this in mind. I think the invocation of Philo is deliberate, even if Philo is not mentioned by name, and it illustrates the nature of De Koninck's ecumenical concerns. He believed that one would find the common ground by pressing one's own doctrines to their logical limits, not by retreating from them. Thus his thesis about the Virgin Mary reveals common ground with a Jewish tradition which he held, in any case, in high esteem. The suggestion is that there is a deep structure which reason can reach and which is the basis for religion and science alike, and is also the basis for an understanding of the likenesses and differences of religions.

It is true that De Koninck supposed that certain crucial truths of Christianity were available only by revelation, but the religions which preceded Christianity and those which are contemporaneous with it may nonetheless exhibit important truths which stem from the common ground available to reason.

4. The Fragmentation of Knowledge

From the discussion of science and religion we can see why the problem of the fragmentation of knowledge greatly occupied De Koninck. We can also sense what his solutions might be. But the issues deserve some further discussion.

In De Koninck's philosophy the fragmentation of man and the fragmentation of knowledge go together. His argument, constantly, is that human beings are to be seen as a unity, the fragmentation of which destroys the very notion of the person.

Mind and body are conceptually distinct; they can even be actually distinct. After death and before the resurrection to which Christians look forward, the soul will, De Koninck concedes, be separated from the body at least as we now know it. And what remains will not be a whole, complete, and natural person. The whole discussion about the bodily assumption of the Virgin Mary makes clear what De Koninck has in mind. The theoretical notions which underpin his view of the unity of man and the unity of knowledge need, however, some further exploration.

Between the two great traditions which animate western philosophy, one of which descends from Plato and the other from Aristotle, there was a long (and not always very enlightening) debate. Though individual Platonists held a number of distinct theories they believed that the soul was clearly differentiated from the body and that the natural home of the soul was in another realm, perhaps (though this is a matter of dispute) the eternal realm of the forms. The Aristotelians held that the soul is the form of the body. As such, to be efficacious, it needs a body to inform. In Aristotle's view, something did come to the human body "from outside" but it was not exactly the human soul. What came "from outside" (in Aristotle's account in one of his few references to the matter) was what came to be called the agent intellect, the power to reason correctly about any subject matter. The Arab philosophers of our Middle Ages—against whom St. Thomas argued—tended to the view that, since, insofar as we reason correctly, our agent intellect is the same for all of us, there must be only one of them which we all share. Distinctness of souls between persons comes from the passive intellect. The passive intellect is essentially the ability to receive sensations, though some of the Arab thinkers even held that since that capacity, too, is really the same in all of us, it will not serve to distinguish one "soul" from another.

On these views, then, individuality would have to come from the body and, up to a point, the Christian philosophers were not averse to such notions, for they believed in resurrection. But St. Thomas and others were concerned because Christian doctrine held that there was a period—perhaps a very long period—between death and resurrection and that the soul nevertheless lived on in some manner or other.

In addition, both views about man tended to fragment knowledge. Even on the Aristotelian views which brought soul and body together, there was a kind of knowledge appropriate to the passive intellect, and another appropriate to the agent intellect. Reason and experience became deeply separated. (This is part of the reason for the nature of Aristotelian logic about which Antoine Arnauld complained that it could only take us from one thing we already know explicitly to another which we already know implicitly, for the intellect which actively reasons can add no new facts.) The Platonic thesis also suggested that the real and true soul could know only what was appropriate to its nature, the eternal. About sensory matters, essentially alien to the soul, there could be at most "right opinion."

St. Thomas, too, was concerned to find a way of understanding these doctrines which would re-emphasise the natural unity of knowledge and he was concerned to provide a solution to the problem of disembodied souls. His picture was generally the Aristotelian one that the intellect worked by abstracting from matter, but the process was not really to be understood as two completely distinct activities, one of receiving data, as it were, and the other of processing them. The modern computer, in fact, supplies a reasonable analogy to what St. Thomas talks about. The computer receives data in the form which is necessary if its data processing systems are to work. The "processing" capability has to be built into the receiving capability if the system is to work at all. Thus though all reasoning is the same insofar as it is correct and though there is an ultimate "agent intellect" which St. Thomas likens to "the sun of Plato" (the form of the good), each of us has his own subsidiary agent intellect which St. Thomas likens to "the light of Aristotle."

This provides the somewhat slender thread on which the Thomistic weighty doctrine of disembodied immortality must hang—a thread which later "Thomists" like Cajetan feared might be too slender—but it also provides a notion of the unity of knowledge. The intellect which receives the data could not achieve intelligibility without the activity of the agent intellect.

The problem is the one which came to plague modern philosophy: How are we to tell whether or not what the intellect is capable of receiving as intelligible is what there is in reality? St. Thomas thought that, since all things were designed to work together, it was reasonable to suppose that the intellect was designed to receive whatever was real. That answer is much like Descartes': we can trust the world of experience because God is trustworthy. St. Thomas' thesis began to run into difficulty, as we saw, when modern science began to come to the conclusion that reality was not much like the sensory world.

De Koninck wanted to go further with the unification of knowledge. And his method of doing so was to understand the world as a set of concrete entities from which we abstract. When we abstract we do not, thereby, on his view, depart from the object; rather, we grasp facets of it which would be closed but for our intellectual activity. Thus our intellect, in fact, uncovers, if you will, new data—for, by permitting new points of view, it brings out from the object what was hidden in it. The object itself is never exhausted in this way, but this does not, as I understand De Koninck's position, constitute, for him, a concession to the skeptic. It is not that there are objects out there whose fullness we can never know, for we can know them as whole objects. The method for doing so is the ordinary perceptual one of assembling things through the use of the "common sense," the sense that enables us to grasp that some things emerge on the condition that we put together what we receive from more than one sense.

Touch is an essential ingredient in at least some determinations of reality. For instance, if a thing is what we think it is, then it will have a certain feel as well as a certain look. The human being is himself or herself such a unity. The truth about humanity is that persons are concrete entities whose nature cannot be grasped or exhausted simply by biochemistry or neurophysiology, but only in the usual ways that we have for coming to know people, ways which include talking to them. Christian theology generally sees man as a whole and not as a series of abstractions. According to De Koninck, it is this wholeness of human nature that must be proclaimed. The proclamation of the bodily assumption of the Virgin Mary was to De Koninck, therefore, an important affirmation of a truth which everyone knows but which, in the midst of the modern fascination for certain specimens of knowledge which give us power over nature, tends to get lost.

In a sense this forces De Koninck into a difficulty: the problem of the disembodied soul becomes rather pressing, but it does so only because of De Koninck's view of what it is to be a "concrete entity." His view is one which still retains, pretty much full-bodied, the Aristotelian distinctions of form and matter and makes of matter not primarily an appearance of things but a genuine stuff on which forms are impressed. His theory, however, only requires a more commonsensical view: there is a sense in which things are as they seem to be when they are made intelligible by the intellect acting on (and in and through) sensation. If the intellect is to become aware even of its own operations, it must manifest itself through some set of concrete activities.

De Koninck writes as though the only intelligible forum for this awareness is made of solid material substances. But there is a neo-Platonic as well as a Hegelian alternative. On the neo-Platonic alternative ideas are seen as active agents. The idea of redness, for instance, cannot itself be created or destroyed in the way that red cars and red balloons can be. But neither does it exist wholly independently of the world. What should we say of it? Is the idea of redness red or the idea of justice just? To say that they are seems absurd. To say that they are not seems to be a contradiction. But one can say that the idea of redness tends—when opportunity arises—to inform the world and so does the idea of justice. Ideas can be defined not as real in the way that socks and hats are but as tendencies toward reality. Ideas, on this view, are dominant. Material things approximate to them as in Newtonian physics forces approximate to ideal patterns. To be a material thing is, indeed, just to be an idea expressed under certain limitations—those of space and time for instance—which are themselves expressions of other powerful ideas. But this makes ideas predominant and, for De Koninck, it is concrete things which are predominant. On the Hegelian view, matter and form are just elements in a dialectic which demands that one have both or nothing, but this dialectic also, in Hegel's mind, leads to the dominance of the Idea, and De Koninck resisted all such doctrines.

Hegel can hold that God creates some means for the soul to express itself and discover the intelligible, but it does not seem clear to us how this branch of the divine economy works. All the same problems recur with angelology, and, indeed, De Koninck liked to talk about angels. Alas, he wrote little or nothing about angels and we certainly have nothing from him which even remotely resembles a treatise on angelology. Perhaps he might, in the end, have written about angels but perhaps he thought that, with God's help, angels could take care of themselves.

But to the great human problems of the fragmentation of knowledge, De Koninck does have a clear answer: man is not a simple material object, nor is he a purely psychological object. Knowledge of human beings must start on the immediate level of personal interaction. The most important lesson is the one which De Koninck used for the title of a collection of his essays and which now graces a building named after him at Laval: *Tout homme est mon prochain* (everyone is my neighbour).

5. The Individual, the Community, and the Universe

The main outlines of De Koninck's social and political philosophy are clear. Whether they are set out in *Le Bien commun,* in *Tout homme est mon prochain,* or in his submission to a Quebec royal commission on Canadian confederation, they carry the same message: The individual is distinct, ultimately valuable, and unique; yet individuals get their own meanings from the meaning which they add to the universe at large, and find their identities through their relation to a community.

Because De Koninck was first of all a philosopher of nature, it is the human relation to the natural order which immediately attracts his attention and, because the human being is a creature with a foot in each of two worlds, the relation to the supernatural seemed to De Koninck of even greater importance. The problem, therefore, of De Koninck's social and political philosophy is in large measure the relation of the natural to the supernatural.

In *La Primauté du bien commun contre les personnalistes* and in "In Defence of St. Thomas," his book-length reply to Father I. Th. Eschmann who had savaged the original book, De Koninck sets out the main lines of his thesis about human beings and the good. There are many ways of talking about the human good. There is the individual good of each of us. This good is related to, but not necessarily contrasted with the social good of the communities to which we belong. There is also goodness in and of itself—that ultimate which Plato called the form of the good and of which St. Thomas said, "In our religion, we call this God." It is this God for the sake of whom everything exists.

All of these claims about the good are important. The individual has duties to God, and God is described by De Koninck as "the extrinsic common good." That is to say that God is the end for which each individual exists and yet, since God transcends each and every thing in the universe, God is "extrinsic" to the whole. The community is an essential good, for the human individual does not live alone, but depends, as Aristotle insisted, on education to make up for what people lack in instinct. One can only realize one's own individuality within the context of a variegated society.

But the individual has rights as well, for individuals are unique and have the duty of deciding just how their own contributions to the whole are to be made. Otherwise, they would not be free beings. God intends, according to De Koninck and St. Thomas, to save each of us by our own free wills, and no social order can forget this simple fact. Yet these categories are not enough to make clear the situation about public duties and public morals—nor to bring out the full nature of individuality. The extrinsic common good, the social good, and the individual good are not enough if we are to take full account of the universe as the creation of God. Everything in it has a natural place and a function intended by God and watched over by providence.

De Koninck says that the question he wanted to answer was above all: "Why did God create the universe many?" This question has become of great importance and has been too little asked, in part, no doubt, because we have all busied ourselves with our own survival and so with the mastery of nature. Now, however, our mastery of nature risks becoming finally destructive, and we must understand that the common good involves the whole universe and not just ourselves.

Father Eschmann mistook De Koninck's purpose and supposed that De Koninck had in mind some authoritarian scheme in which each and every one of us would have his or her life determined by some celestial or mundane authority for the greater glory of some nameless end. But what De Koninck was saying was quite different. In fact, since each of us determines his or her own actuality (within the potentialities given by providence), the roles which we can play are partly self-determined, but they must work together for the mutual good of all like a Kantian kingdom of ends and, what is more, the optimal well-being of the universe is involved in every move we make. We must not thoughtlessly wipe out species and destroy that nature whose concrete richness was the object of De Koninck's philosophy of science and nature.

To understand this we must explore a little more De Koninck's notion of freedom and its function in the kind of universe in which he thinks we live. There is, for him, no possibility of a Calvinist account of the relations between divine providence and individual actions. Though we are creatures of God, it is our nature to be free creatures and, insofar as God acts through us, he makes use of our free actions. The issue, at bottom, is a simple one. We are creatures with certain potentialities; to have potentialities is to be able to be in one condition or in another. This is true of objects in the natural non-human world as well as of us. But we are creatures who have knowledge, and the possession of knowledge involves a measure of choice. The doctor who knows how to cure you could kill as well. If you want to demolish a bridge, consult the engineer who built it.

We might look at the formal structure of this situation: it is De Koninck's (and Aristotle's and St. Thomas') view of knowledge that it consists of the possession by the intellect of forms abstracted from matter. It is also the case that matter, as the capacity to take on form, can take on new forms—though, only of course, through some orderly causal sequence. But the intellect also multiplies forms, for all propositions, after all, have negations. To possess some knowledge is also to know how to negate it. The potentiality thus always exists (if the circumstances are right) for an act of human will to identify the possibility of a change of forms. In knowledge we are free.

Nothing follows from this as to whether or not God knows or does not know, and the various attempts to get over the seeming paradox that God might know what I will do even though I am free not to do it do not seem to have commended themselves to De Koninck. Freedom he took to be a natural concomitant of his metaphysical position.

The protection of all the natural opportunities to exercise this freedom—on the exercise of which, in his view, our salvation or damnation depends—was always to De Koninck a primary concern. *Le Bien commun* included a long, detailed, and devastating attack on the various totalitarianisms of the 1940s. The right-wing totalitarianism—fascism and Nazism—seemed to him (as the essays published later in *Tout homme est mon prochain* make particularly clear) especially horrifying not just for their denial of basic human rights but for their espousal of kinds of racism which denied his central premise about human beings—their ultimate unity as beings who, with God and the angels, possess the power to know and to reason.

The Marxist tyrannies which had emerged into the light of day with the Moscow purge trials of the 1930s struck him, however, as more interesting and more in need of explanation. Did Marx and his followers not begin by exalting the freedom of the human individual? Did they not begin by proclaiming the needs for equality and the kinds of social justice which reasonable men would be inclined to support? Did they not rightly denounce the greed and petty oppression of unbridled capitalism? If so, how could it be that they should turn so easily into tyrannies? Nazis and fascists were, after all, self-proclaimed tyrants almost from the beginning (if we ignore the anarchist strands in Mussolini's early thought), but Marxist tyranny was not what most people would have expected.

De Koninck's critique of Marxism comes as something of a surprise: he says that Marxism is not a modern form of the materialism of classical antiquity. Classical materialism had many elements. Among them was the claim that both the ultimate real and the chief good of man were material things or material states. Possession, physical well-being, pleasure, and the acceptance of oneself as a further extension of the underlying natural order were parts of its doctrine. A reform based on such a doctrine would hold that all material possessions should be shared equally or held in common, and even Thomas Aquinas, as De Koninck notes, was aware of the attractiveness of this ideal.

But Marx specifically rejected it. Marx was, indeed, a student of ancient history and he regarded all such notions as bourgeois fantasies. Rather, Marxism, says De Koninck, is a spiritual doctrine devoted to the maximization of liberty. Furthermore, it is not a doctrine which rejects the well-being of the individual in the name of a higher social good, but rather one which is directed to the well-being of the individual at the expense of all else. For the goal which Marx puts forward is not the satiation of material greed, and it is not the liberty of a communal order, but the liberty of the individual. His doctrine is that there is nothing outside man by which man can be judged. But human beings are all individuals. They may, on the Marxist theory of history, be controlled by social and economic forces, but these forces are to be dissolved as the Marxist progress toward history unfolds. It is the individual who is to emerge as free. De Koninck might well have noticed that it is individual well-being—the well-being of one who is free to do as he or she pleases, to write poetry or herd cattle or just be himself—which is described in the *German Ideology*, one of the very places in which Marx gives any details about the life of men and women under "communism" rather than simply under the transitional state of the "dictatorship of the proletariat."

The problem with making liberty the primary human end is that it supposes that there is nothing beyond and above the individual. There is no God. But there are also no replacements for God. There are no objective moral principles, for Marx thought of morality itself as a bourgeois notion. There is no ultimate judge.

Furthermore, Marxism is, says De Koninck, a tragic doctrine which breeds despair, for it holds that the human race is doomed. Matter will survive forever. Humanity in its concrete expression will not. The serious Marxist does not, to be sure, take the view that because we live on briefly and have no judge we ought to eat and drink and be merry, for the serious Marxist has spiritual aims for everyone. But these can only be the ultimate liberty of all individuals, for there is no test of goodness outside the individual person. Even the state is only, De Koninck quotes Lenin as saying, "an organized power capable of enforcing its norms." The community is not itself a distinct spiritual end. It is this combination of the pursuit of liberty and the recognition of tragedy, he thinks, which turns Marxism ugly. Is true liberty the power to do as one pleases? Then those who have it may now do as they please? Not quite. For they must work for the liberty of others. But what if the most effective way to do that is to have, for now, a tyranny? If men are only temporary beings and there is no outside authority, can they be sacrificed to the future? There is no Marxist reason why not; for men, who are merely matter reflecting on itself for a moment before the final darkness, do not have intrinsic value. The value of each person belongs to his or her evolutionary moment—his or her role in the introduction of the future when real liberty will exist.

In one important sense, Marxism is a principled philosophy. The pursuit of liberty is a noble goal. But the very idea of nobility leads us beyond it. What is noble is what leads us beyond ourselves. Morality is the practice of not acting on one's self-interest. The pursuit of liberty becomes a noble aim when it is seen within the whole pursuit of the common good, the good which is the good of the whole creation. For only when they are free can individuals creatively add, on De Koninck's view, to the meaning of the whole. De Koninck warns us not to be complacent. "It is hard to justify the indignation that some of our intellectuals, politicians and business men have acquired toward communism. . . . They find Stalin's realism displeasing, but they themselves have been operating on the same basis of expediency."

Not only fascism and Marxism were targets of *Le Bien commun* and of later works. *Le Bien commun* also took a swing at what has since been called "the cult of personality." God, in De Koninck's view, does not revel in a universe of "great personalities" and miscellaneous showoffs. God seems, in fact, to have a taste for the simple and the straightforward—at any rate for those who seek the glorification of the whole of creation and not of themselves.

The book was subtitled "contre les personnalistes." Who were "the personalists?" De Koninck does not say. But it is easy to find people who called themselves personalists whose philosophies were in conflict with De Koninck's. Emmanuel Mounier and some of his associates are examples. Some critics, wrongly, I am convinced, imagined that it was Jacques Maritain (who also was nowhere named in the text) that De Koninck was subjecting to attack. De Koninck did differ from Maritain in emphasis on these questions and they did differ about the nature of science and the relation of science to philosophy. De Koninck, however, never attacked Maritain by name in any of his other critical texts.

Nor did he ever attack Mounier, for it was not his style. But anyone who reads Mounier's own summary of his doctrines will notice the obvious conflict with much that De Koninck held dear. Mounier's *Le Personnalisme* was published six years after De Koninck's *Bien commun,* but it summarizes views which Mounier had been publishing since the mid-1930s. Mounier speaks of "popular sovereignty" which is not founded on the "authority of numbers" but on "direct pressure." Such "popular sovereignty" is attained, he insists, through "street marches, riots, spontaneous groups, clubs, strikes and boycotts." Such things he says are not illegal "but have a deep legality." He also insists that the human person should "not submit to nature" but "should transform it."

One might call this a political philosophy of planned disorder. De Koninck has been rightly called "a philosopher of order" by Ralph McInerny. De Koninck respected orderly democracy. Though he would have insisted that counting heads does not decide what is right, he would not have thought that street riots were an improvement. He had a natural respect for established authority, civil as well as ecclesiastical, though he insisted equally on the right to disagree with it in a peaceful and orderly manner—a combination which suggests the need for a system of law. This system of law, he thought, was also part of the natural order of things. What Mounier meant by "transforming nature" is less than clear, but De Koninck, again, would have wanted to distinguish between working with nature for orderly change while keeping a watchful eye on the totality and working against nature.

Finally, Mounier's own adventures and uncertainties suggest that the fear that "personalism" could turn into the "cult of personality" were not so far-fetched. Mounier had been closely attached to Jacques Chevalier, a philosopher who became Petain's Minister of Education in Vichy, and Mounier originally followed him to Vichy. Like many others, he eventually broke with the regime and later became involved in attempts to reconcile Marxism and Christianity, something De Koninck would have supposed impossible.

6. Theory and Practice

De Koninck's views about science and nature lead naturally to the most pressing problem about science in our age, one that is so obvious that philosophers and ordinary men alike are apt to yawn when it is mentioned: we have an enormous amount of knowledge about "nature" and we do not know what to do with it. Our machines, like those of Daedalus, are not within our control.

One thing which is immediately obvious from De Koninck's analysis is that we cannot simply sit back and let events take care of themselves. For science multiplies choices. You cannot have knowledge without coming face to face with the awesome fact of human experience. To know how to run an atomic generator is also to know how to blow up the world. The two go hand in hand. But what seems equally obvious is that science does not itself give us any guidance about how to make these choices.

Centuries of study of the processes of hydrogen fusion would not give you any clue as to what you ought to do with the atomic bomb. One popular escape from what seems a hopeless responsibility has been through the theory of history: perhaps our social processes—of which scientific investigation is itself one—are the products of inexorable historical forces. And perhaps it is "society" which will decide what to do with science. In a sense it is not "science" but technology which demands our attention. But there is a sense in which technology proceeds inevitably from science.

Indeed, it is De Koninck's contention that the one forces the other. Suppose we could destroy all the weapons in the world and then wipe out all the engineering data and diagrams along with them. Still, if we possessed the scientific knowledge, we should only face the same dilemmas over again. One cannot understand the way in which energy can be released through the process of fission and fusion without almost at once grasping what this might mean to the poor in places without energy. I say "almost at once," for Lord Rutherford who played so large a part in developing atomic theory is said to have remarked, when his pupil John Cockcroft split the first atom, that it would have no practical consequences. But to nearly everyone else, the truth was apparent. And one cannot have atomic reactors without imagining atomic bombs. But this, however true, does not, in De Koninck's view, make history inexorable.

It is in his essay "The Nature of Man and His Historical Being" that De Koninck lays down both his view about history and his view about theory and practice. In this essay, he tackles two great themes: the nature and character of human freedom and the nature of history. And here he gives his answer to the "historicists": humanity is not really driven by history because the human person considered concretely is a unique particular and can only be understood as a unique particular—that is to say that no general law describes such a being. This is true, as well, of the ordinary concrete things of nature. But the unique particular events in human lives include human actions—actions which De Koninck says are not even fully describable except in a way which points to concrete particulars. In a charmingly anachronistic example he imagines Socrates alighting from a streetcar while thinking of Henri Bergson's intuition of being. Socrates knocks over a rather bulky lady sending a great array of things rolling about the street. Now we have to describe the situation exactly in order to be sure that we have the right "explanation" and even then it will only be a sort of educated guess: "Absent-mindedness," we may say, "thinking about Bergson again."

We can extend De Koninck's example by imagining that Socrates knows something else which we cannot know. A small disturbance in his brain sent a tiny shudder through his frame, momentarily distracting him. Perhaps the mishap was not attributable to thinking about Bergson, after all. How are we to grasp the unity of this particular individual? Of course, in a sense, the whole universe can be taken as a unique particular. But that does not help us much. Indeed, De Koninck remarks in this paper that the particular which is the whole can only be grasped in the providential picture possessed by God. He says that the sufficient reasons for the particulars of this world are not, themselves, of this world: "None except the Maker of history could 'narrate' to us the life of Peter."

One should not misunderstand the point: there are, he notices at the beginning of the paper, two senses of history. We are here talking about history as the unfolding array of facts in time—facts especially involving human beings. There is also, though, the disciplinary sense of history. History may well, like any other enquiry, be a science.

Here, to avoid confusion, it is worthwhile to mention a distinction which De Koninck does not make—and to explain why he does not make it. The distinction is that between sciences and disciplines. Many people think it very important. History, like literary criticism, is more often called a "discipline" than a "science." The Latin origins of the two words suggest that discipline has to do with learners or enquirers. In the case of history, the enquiry is not distinct from other enquiries in terms of its subject matter as much as in terms of the way in which the subject matter is looked at. History assembles all the facts about everything. Even if we restrict it to "human" events, human events include what human beings do. One of those things is to study physics and so all the "facts" in "physics" will turn up in history also. History is thus a "discipline" in the sense that it concerns a certain way in which the student takes the facts—in this case historically.

The same kind of analysis might be given for physics, as well, however. Physics covers all events which involve the movements of objects in space and time. Some of these objects are historians writing history, and so history would become part of the "subject matter" of physics. But physicists do not usually get around to such arcane facts as those describing the movements of historians at university department meetings. Some kinds of historians do get around to the history of science, so we may think that it is more important to regard history as a "discipline" than to think of physics in this way. But De Koninck concedes that history, can, in a sense, like any other enquiry, be a science. For it can abstract from particulars just as physics does or chemistry does. But De Koninck thinks that "science" is not the whole narration of the particulars: Socrates knew what Socrates did in a way that no one else can—but even he did not finally know as God did. Just the same claim, however, can be made about physics. Physics does not exhaust the concrete thing. Even the physical analysis of steel balls does not give us an account of the subject matter being enquired into as a concrete thing in the world. The steel ball of physics is, as Sir Arthur Eddington liked to remind his audiences, a buzzing collection of tiny particles and is mostly empty space. The steel ball as concrete in the world can be felt and seen as solid—and can even give comfort to Captain Queeg as he rolls it in his hand while nervously pacing the bridge of his ship.

Eddington used to worry his audiences by telling them that the table in front of them was not really a solid thing. De Koninck would have replied "nonsense." It is because physics, as much as history, involves us in taking a point of view that physics yields something which is not a description of the object which we have named a steel ball. The distinction between sciences and disciplines, then, does not exist. Physics is a discipline and a science. So is history. So, no doubt, is literary criticism. The important distinction, according to De Koninck, is between the object of science—*objectum scientiae*—and the subject matter of science—*subjectum scientiae.* The object is what science sets out to attain. Physics and history have different objects. They have the same subject, the world.

De Koninck lays all this out in "Natural Science as Philosophy." This essay was re-created from a tape of his response to Mortimer Adler who had been laying down what De Koninck conceded to be pretty much the "received view" amongst Thomists about science and philosophy. Science and philosophy are, for De Koninck, like physics and history. They have different objects (meaning different goals).

Philosophy seeks to understand the whole as the whole. Science seeks consistent, intelligible—and no doubt useful—abstractive sets. But for De Koninck it is because science casts light on the nature of the perceived object in the process of abstracting from it that philosophy can come along and offer a cogent analysis of the relation of the unique, concrete, particular object. So, indeed, physics and history also illumine one another. The characters described by the historians lived in a universe governed by the same laws of physics and chemistry that we do. Sometimes even the "hard sciences" may provide a piece of crucial evidence for historians. The Romans had a taste for lead as a sweetener. Did lead poisoning help bring about the fall of the Roman Empire and account for some of the bizarre behaviour of the later emperors?

More importantly, though, once we have disentangled the relations of physics and history, the main issues begin to come clear. One is the nature of human responsibility; the other is the way in which theory and practice really come together. De Koninck's answer to the responsibility question is this: if what determines Socrates' actions is a whole complex of particular circumstances, dominant amongst which are his own knowledge and his own mental states, then the responsibility cannot be assigned to anything beyond him.

I do not know just what answer De Koninck would have to Galen Strawson's recent argument that we are, in any case, determined by our characters and do not, in any intelligible sense, choose our characters. But I think he would have said that a character, in any case, is something which involves, perhaps predominantly, a certain manner of making choices so that what one chooses is still a part of the story. The same kind of answer could be given to claims about psychological determinism. Psychology has its own goals, and abstracts from the concrete data so as to fulfil them. (There are, however, as I shall suggest in Section 8 of this essay, special problems about the "social sciences" as an abstractive subject matter.) In the process of abstraction, much is learned about the concrete subjects which psychology studies. But it does not dominate its subjects. One must make choices to choose the object of psychology. These choices can hardly be analyzed out of its conclusions without destroying the science. The psychologist must satisfy his colleagues that he made the right choices in the right way in accordance with the objects of scientific psychology or his researches do not count. The psychologist must stay responsible. But so then—in most cases—must the human subjects he studies. There will be exceptions. There are people who do not act responsibly and some of those people cannot act responsibly. But they cannot be the whole of humanity if psychology is to maintain its rationality.

As to theory and practice, it begins to come clear that every science has an object—an aim as well as a subject matter. Choosing to undertake a scientific study is, therefore, choosing a certain aim. That aim or object acts as a final cause of the science; it directs its progress and patterns. Physics gives no moral guidance because that is not its object. But one must ask what practical science makes it possible to have physics in any case. It is only in certain societies and within certain patterns of organization that science is even imaginable. Science is therefore, in a sense, subordinate to human well-being.

Furthermore, physics does not give us knowledge of the concrete subject matter. The only science which does this is theology, because only theology has for its goal the understanding of "the sufficient conditions of the things of this world." Yet physics, too, is dependent on this concrete subject with which it starts. To do physics without theology is therefore an act of folly. Are we now paying for that folly?

7. Thomism and Quebec

De Koninck spent virtually all his working life in Quebec and it was there, in the midst of particular philosophical, political, and ecclesiastical controversies that his writing was done. Quebec was and is a French-speaking island in English-speaking North America. Quebec is also overwhelmingly Catholic by religion and, in De Koninck's time, it was celebrated for the devoutness of its population, the number and variety of its religious orders, and the influence of the Church on its political and social life. Until the mid-1960s most of Quebec's social and educational services were provided by the Church. The lynch-pin of its educational system was a body of collèges classiques which stood between its high schools and its universities and provided the basis for a Latin culture which its elites shared.

Officially at least "Thomism" was the philosophy taught in its classical colleges and universities. But this can be very misleading both historically and in De Koninck's particular case.

As I have said, De Koninck worked within the Aristotelian and Thomist traditions. It was Aristotle and St. Thomas who provided the framework of his thought. But that does not mean that his philosophical opinions can be found in or deduced from the works of St. Thomas, though it would be fair to say that he believed constantly that what he wrote was Thomistic in spirit.

De Koninck was confronting the modern crisis which resulted from the fact that scientific doctrine could no longer be derived from elements which could be found immediately in experience. His solution was to dwell on the interplay of abstraction and understanding—to hold that we learn about hidden properties of things by abstracting and then by reflecting on our abstractions. He buttressed these reflections by making distinctions between names and symbols which allowed for an understanding of mathematical physics. Mathematical physics undoubtedly does go back to Thomas Bradwardine in the fourteenth century, but not to Thomas Aquinas in the thirteenth century, and so much of what De Koninck says could not, in the literal sense, be "Thomistic." Equally, however, there is no reason not to regard what he says as a legitimate development of Thomism.

De Koninck's moral and political theory is Thomistic in a fairly strict sense, though in applying his theories to modern democracy, he again extended them. Father Lawrence Dewan in his article in the *Oxford Companion to Canadian Literature* concluded that, in the dispute over the nature of the common good, St. Thomas would certainly have been on De Koninck's side.

De Koninck's critique of Marxism is new in the sense that it involves issues which would hardly have occurred to St. Thomas. Scarcely anyone in the thirteenth century thought that human beings stood alone as the measure of the universe. The view had been held by Protagoras and others in classical antiquity, but St. Thomas' opponents were, after all, chiefly, when they were not other Christians, Arab Muslims. De Koninck's critique may owe something to Dostoyevsky (though not, I think, consciously), but it is not St. Thomas'. St. Thomas, I suspect, would not have seen, at once, that Marxism was a spiritual doctrine nor have made the distinctions which gives De Koninck's critique its biting edge—the distinction between the pursuit of liberty for its own sake and the pursuit of liberty as the means through which the individual can make his own contribution to the well-being of the whole.

It is not, again, that such a distinction is not "Thomistic." On the contrary. It is just that it would not likely have occurred to St. Thomas that anyone would make the particular confusion involved. Curiously, I think that De Koninck's account of the bodily assumption of the Virgin Mary is also something which could not have been simply deduced from the pages of St. Thomas. Certainly De Koninck makes use of a concept of person which can be found in St. Thomas, though, as De Koninck himself pointed out, it can also be found in St. Bonaventure. But De Koninck's idea of what it is to be the incarnation of wisdom—his, at it were, inverted Philoism—suggests a notion which hangs very much on his own view of immediate, concrete objects, a notion which because it involves the interaction of our meetings with concrete objects and our understandings of abstraction is richer and more complex than anything St. Thomas needed to develop in the thirteenth century. In almost every area in which he wrote, then, De Koninck extended the writings of St. Thomas.

But in fact that was normal rather than exceptional in Quebec. Quebec was a special case in the Catholic world. In most of that world, Thomism had only a very precarious hold on the Catholic mind until August 4, 1879, when Pope Leo XIII signed the famous encyclical. Thomism, however, had captured the minds of a very large proportion of Quebec philosophers nearly forty years earlier. In the 1830s, in the period leading up to the rebellion of 1837, the main philosophical contenders had been Cartesians (led by Father Jacques Odelin) and a group of followers of Felicité de Lamennais who were especially influential at some of the centres of intellectual life which then included the celebrated college at St. Hyacinthe.

The tendency, however, was to reach back into the history of philosophy for supporting arguments, particularly into the Augustinian tradition which had been mixed with a kind of Cartesian Jansenism since philosophy first came to Quebec in the mid-seventeenth century. Cartesianism had come to Quebec in the mid-seventeenth century—brought in fact by young Jesuits, several of whom had like Descartes been at La Flèche. Founding a college and teaching philosophy in it must seem to us an odd thing for the young men from La Flèche to do when they arrived in Quebec. What is more surprising is that the instructors began to write their own texts. Plenty of those existed in France and, though copying was expensive, nothing was saved by writing one's own text, for copyists were always needed. The earliest we have survives only in the hand of a professional copyist.

But recent enquiry has shown that the concern to rethink the religious life in the new world was very strong, and that the young Jesuits had every reason to rethink their affairs for themselves. Out of this arose a particular and intellectually quite powerful version of Cartesianism, one which was communitarian (based on the commonality of innate ideas) rather than individualistic. It was also, like Descartes himself, dedicated not to iconoclastic enterprises but to expressing Christian orthodoxy in a way which would take hold in the intellectual climate of the time. It developed consistently for a century and a half and emerged early in the nineteenth century as a powerful political force in the public debates led by Jacques Odelin against a populist, sentimentalist version of Menaisianism.

Orthodox Thomism, though it came relatively early to Quebec, was, in these terms, rather a latecomer, an attempt to head off both these movements and one stimulated in some measure by the influx of conservative clergymen into Quebec after the French Revolution.

The Jesuit missionaries faced a double crisis, traces of which can be found in Quebec through to the time of De Koninck. Christianity had been made less plausible by the new scientific outlook which had replaced the rich complexities of everyday experience (within which the Christian stories made a certain sense) with the notion of a dominantly mechanical world without any secondary qualities—colours, sounds, tastes. The new world needed geometrical expression and seemed to leave little room for the hand of divine providence. The struggle to adapt to this was matched by the struggle to adapt Christianity to the outlook of the native peoples.

Descartes was a champion of the scientific outlook, but his usefulness for the Jesuit missionaries stemmed from his demand for a return to the roots of experience, and his insistence on putting to doubt everything which could be put to doubt. This procedure for clearing the mind had been put to good use just before him in the *Méditations* of Eustachius a Sancto Paulo, a philosopher much admired by Descartes and the first consultant on monastic reform employed by Mère Angélique at Port Royal.

On these views, what was left as certain was the existence of ideas, of whatever it was that was simply presented to the mind. In Quebec, the young Martin Bouvart adapted his notion to Augustine's theory of signs. He proceeded to distinguish natural and artificial signs and then to cast some doubt on the distinction between the two. At bottom, that is, one could get to simple structures which could be shared with anyone in any culture and then built upon. Cleared of the accumulated debris, Christianity might stand out as the rational order which Descartes had thought it was. Bouvart was able to draw upon formulations which could be found in Augustine, who was respectable and admired, not only by Catholics, Jansenist and anti-Jansenist, but also by Calvinists, Lutherans, and others affected by the Reformation.

The Cartesianism which had taken root in Quebec only slowly emerged fully into the light of day. In the next century, Jean Baptiste Labrosse, whose text survives intact, was quite clearly a partisan of Nicolas Malebranche, a Cartesian with a good dose of neo-Platonism in his system. Early in the nineteenth century Jacques Odelin emerged on the front pages of the newspapers declaring himself openly a Cartesian and laying down a clear doctrine which, though it may have seemed a little odd to many European scholars, would I think have been applauded by Descartes himself. Odelin saw in Descartes' notion of innate ideas (ideas which all men and women share and which allow them to share, ultimately, in a public truth) the basis of a genuine community, and he urged that only a Cartesian rationalism based on a return to the sources of all human experience could really establish the Church as the universal authority it claimed to be. The authority of reason, he said, always takes precedence over the reasons of the authorities.

This line of thought had always been mixed with the scholasticism of the sixteenth and seventeenth centuries which meant that the discussions were generally seen against a background which had strong Aristotelian and Thomistic components. The aftermath of 1837—the year of the rebellions against colonial authority in both French and English Canada—prompted many intellectuals in Quebec to seek a common basis—one in which they could carry on their own arguments while maintaining a common front in the face of the English. The disputes of the 1830s were over issues about reason and experience, reason and authority, and science and faith. The revival of Thomism came about largely because the situation demanded the kind of reflection which could only be provided by a systematised philosophy within which the issues could be seen in clear relation to one another. Thomism represented a rich mixture of Aristotelian and Platonic (or neo-Platonic) elements within which a balance might be struck on these issues. But it also enabled each side to pursue its arguments, drawing on a variety of texts and counter-texts.

Eventually, after nearly fifty years, philosophers like Monsignor Louis-Adolphe Paquet made serious attempts to provide a "definitive" Thomism, but, though Paquet's multi-volume study of St. Thomas was recognized as a monumental piece of scholarship and went through three editions, there is little reason to think anyone felt much restricted by it, apart perhaps from those charged with writing the manuals which came to be used in the collèges classiques. Though the manual writers provided a condensed Thomism which gave the Thomistic outlook a rather bad name as a body of dogmatic simplicities, even they tended to go their own ways and often provided interesting (and occasionally surprising) pieces of social analyses.

There remained a Cartesian strand in Quebec thought right up to the end of the nineteenth century and traces of it persisted beyond the middle of the twentieth century. And there remained a Menaisien strand in popular thought (though without much intellectual backing) at least until the years of the Duplessis regime. To a large extent, that is, Thomism served as a common language within which many important debates went on.

The results were not what outsiders seem usually to expect. Not every philosophical issue was widely debated. In a society in which the universities and the classical colleges alike were generally affiliated with the Church and in which the clergy formed the backbone of the teaching staff, there was little lively debate about the existence of God. The "five ways" of St. Thomas, buttressed in the manuals with a moral argument, generally sufficed. There were not many philosophers needing to be convinced. One might have expected philosophical theology to be a dominant topic, but in fact it was not, for it was not over the questions of philosophical theology that the disputes arose. From the period toward the end of the nineteenth century when Paquet became a dominant figure through to the post-1966 decline in the dominance of Thomism, the most pressing questions were those of social theory.

It should be emphasised that it was social rather than political theory which predominated. The questions which agitated thinkers in Quebec had to do with their culture and its language and with the question of how the large social responsibilities which had devolved on the Church as the only major French-language institution to survive the British conquest more or less intact should be discharged.

Into this mixture De Koninck himself brought questions about science. Paquet had early on raised the issues of science and religion (and defended the place of science), but De Koninck opened questions about the nature of science within the Thomistic tradition. The situation in the mid-1930s into which De Koninck arrived had developed its own complexities. Cartesianism was dormant (though not dead), and Menaisianism had disappeared into the popular culture and become a doctrine whose original name and origins had been effectively forgotten.

To an outsider, the intellectual situation may have looked tranquil, but there were important differences of opinion amongst the Quebec philosophers. The other outstanding Thomist philosopher of the period was Louis Lachance who worked in Ottawa and taught for a time in Rome before returning first to Sherbrooke and then to Montreal where he became Dean of Philosophy. Lachance's work on natural law and on the political theory of St. Thomas drew wide attention. Lachance and De Koninck had different basic interests.

Lachance saw political and social problems in terms of law and principle and emphasised the natural law tradition and the notion that Thomism could be understood as providing universal and binding rules of conduct. De Koninck, because of his doctrine of the uniqueness of the concrete, held that, since moral science is a branch of theoretical reason, and since individual actions always require a measure of special judgement, moral practice required an element of practical judgement which he usually identified with the Thomistic notion of "prudence." He tended to emphasise the importance of the individual in decision making and the importance of the individual's role in taking ultimate responsibility for actions. ("Prudentia" did not mean prudence in the Hobbesian sense of an action which minimizes one's risk, but represented a kind of skilled or informed judgement, essentially the *phronesis* of Aristotle.)

De Koninck would not have denied the importance of natural law and moral principle as an element which must go into moral judgement and Lachance would not have denied the need for *phronesis,* but he always feared a kind of mechanical morality and jurisprudence and, in his writings on the common good, he emphasised the fact that each person must make an individual contribution to the common good. Lachance feared the collapse of human rights in the political atmosphere of the 1930s—not only in Europe but in Quebec as well—and emphasised the limits imposed by natural law. Lachance, too, was a strong and convinced nationalist, the source of a reasoned (and moderate) nationalism which opposed the more emotional nationalism of Canon Lionel Groulx.

De Koninck had two concerns about Quebec culture which he constantly tried to balance against one another. One was that the language, culture, and religion of Quebec might be overwhelmed in the North American environment. To avoid this he was a strong supporter of the federal system and a strong opponent of what he termed "le grand État." But the other concern was that Quebec might become isolated and turn inward in undesirable ways. To that end he welcomed graduate students from outside Quebec. Many of those who came were American, but others came from Ontario. He was prepared to work with them in English and to write in English for an audience which would include prospective students. His own natural language was Flemish and he knew exactly what it was to have to work in other people's languages and was concerned to protect French in Quebec. Yet he believed in a kind of balance, while Lachance, in a pioneering work on the philosophy of language, warned that bilingualism might leave the young of Quebec incompetent in both languages.

Finally, the period of De Koninck's life saw the rise of what might be called "mediaevalism." This was the period of the creation of the Institute of Mediaeval Studies at the University of Toronto and of its sister institution at the Université de Montréal. They became bastions of the study of mediaeval philosophy and provided a kind of protected environment in which Thomists (and others, for there was always an Augustinian movement particularly among Franciscans) could be sheltered from the winds of hostile philosophies. Their raison d'être was not, of course, to provide sheltered workshops, but to provide centres for the study of mediaeval texts, but they tended, willy nilly, to do both. De Koninck said privately (in a letter) that he did not care much for what was going on in Montreal. He meant, I think, not the philosophy of Lachance but the "medievalist" tendency to make Thomism a kind of museum piece. Lachance was as much concerned to deal with the issues of the hour as De Koninck.

8. Prolegomena to a Critique

This is not the place in which to mount a critical analysis of De Koninck's philosophy. The purpose of this edition is first to open his philosophy to a wider readership and, second, to stimulate others to carry on his projects.

I have tried to make the first moves in this direction by providing an intelligible framework within which his work can be understood. Whether or not that framework will stand the test of time depends not only on how De Koninck's work is read in the future but also on what is revealed by others who attempt to carry forward his projects. What can be done here, however, is to call attention to the frontiers of his work, to the issues which clearly remain unsettled and to problems which he raised and began to address but which the circumstances of his life did not permit him to examine fully.

Central to all his work is a powerful conviction of the reality and complexity of the objects of ordinary experience—objects on which science can cast light but never wholly describe. There are two sorts of problems about these objects in De Koninck's philosophy: one is a problem about how metaphysics is to understand them simply as ordinary objects revealed by the senses and the intellect. The other is a problem in natural theology. De Koninck tended to deal with these objects by employing the Aristotelian notions of matter and form and by explaining our knowledge of them in terms of what are essentially Aristotelian categories of knowledge. His Aristotelian epistemology tended, however, in some respects, to be overtaken by his philosophy of science.

Science does not merely abstract, science shows us as well the complexity hidden from the untutored eye. In so doing, science does not falsify the objects, but its practitioners may sometimes give a false impression by claiming that the "real" object is the scientific object. In fact, there is a kind of dialectical interplay (in the Hegelian sense) between the givens of the senses and the intellectual creations of science. This dialectic does not overturn the Aristotelian epistemology in De Koninck's view because it is simply an extension of what, anyhow, is latent in that epistemology (certainly in its Thomistic developments).

For in that tradition, the intellect plays a role at every stage of knowing even though all knowledge has its origins in the senses. The question, however, is whether this new and complex notion of real objects can be dealt with satisfactorily by the Aristotelian metaphysics. In De Koninck's view, objects really do, I think, have the properties which common sense ascribes to them. But there is a sense in which they also have the properties which physics ascribes to them. To some extent, as Eddington (to whom De Koninck paid a lot of attention) maintained, these properties conflict with one another. It did not seem to Eddington that the objects could have both their scientific and their commonsense properties. But that led to Eddington's mistaken attempt to replace (in some sense) the commonsense objects with the objects described in physics.

De Koninck would in fact have admitted, though, that the alternative claim, the claim that objects really do not have the properties ascribed to them in physical theories but have all and only their "commonsense" properties, is equally unattractive. Had De Koninck adopted it, he would have had to hold that physics is a kind of fiction of convenience. It is his claim, on the contrary, that physics works by genuine abstraction and that, therefore, the properties are, in some sense, there to be abstracted. True, as physics moves from names to symbols, it moves into a different logical realm and ceases to deal with particulars. But the universals with which it deals are not "unreal." De Koninck insisted on the Aristotelian tradition according to which the universal is real and actually has its being in the object. If we hold this doctrine what kind of object do we have?

De Koninck is certainly right in supposing that the Aristotelian notion is closer to what he has in mind than are other popular and historical notions about matter, certainly it is closer than the view that matter consists of lumps of "hard stuff" "out there," i.e., existing independently of us. People often think they are being very up-to-date when they really hold the views of the Greek atomists. Such a view would surely not describe De Koninck's natural objects.

De Koninck is also clearly not speaking of matter in the Marxist sense. For though, like Engels, he may seem at times to be saying that matter can actually rise above apparent contradictions within it, matter is not, according to him, really self-motivating or self-explanatory. Obviously, the Aristotelian notion of matter as the ability to take on form serves De Koninck much better than either of these notions.

Yet the Aristotelian notion of matter does not encompass the possibility that matter might have seemingly incompatible forms at the same time and that scientific investigation might show that it really does have such forms. The problem is not only that common sense and physics clash in a way which fosters these difficulties. It is also true that, within physics, analogous difficulties arise. Is light corpuscular? Or is its real form that of the wave? The answer, in some sense, is "both."

Perhaps we must turn elsewhere for a model which meets De Koninck's needs. Works of art, for instance, may bear more than one interpretation. And this fact holds of visual objects such as paintings as much as of symbolic objects such as poems and novels. Matter begins to look, on De Koninck's view, more like a work of art than like the humanly unresponsive objects described in physics and in chemistry.

De Koninck never objects, in any case, to the hylozoistic elements in Aristotle. Matter, for him, has more, not less, to it than meets the eye. And, to be sure, in some sense it is De Koninck's view that matter is a work of art. It is the creation of God. And it serves a multitude of divine purposes. Like a work of art, it has an inside as well as an outside—it can be seen from within as the work of its creator and as expressing his intentions just as it can be seen from without as an object of physics.

It is here that De Koninck's incipient natural theology begins to emerge. *The Hollow Universe* has this theology as its central theme. Admittedly, the theme is slightly muted.

For obvious reasons, De Koninck hoped that each of his hearers would take it for his or her own personal discovery. But the implication of the whole series of lectures is, if I understand him rightly, that we can see from the nature of matter that it really does have an inside and that the hand of its maker is to be discerned within it. This, if you like, is the argument for the existence of God which De Koninck never quite sets down in black and white. It is a development of the Thomistic tradition just as his view of objects is a development of an Aristotelian tradition. But these developments, if worked out, seem likely to be so dramatic as to constitute virtually a new philosophy, even if one in every way compatible with the tradition. (It surely belongs, at any rate, to what he thought of as the "perennial philosophy.")

Basically, his argument would go like this: science shows us a world of abstractions which must be dealt with by means of symbols, usually numbers. These symbols relate to universal principles. Experience, however, confirms our view that the objects from which these abstractions proceed—and on which they throw such great light as to give us our modern and massive power over nature—are actually unique particulars. These unique particulars do not, per se, have scientific explanations even though they have properties which do have such explanations. The explanation of a genuine irreducible and unique particular must always be a unique action. Such unique actions encompassing a whole universe and rendering it a single unique particular in and of itself must come from God, the only being who would have such powers.

In this introduction, I have not said anything about De Koninck's view of time, but he was deeply impressed by Augustine's worries and yet impressed, too, by the reality of time in our lives. The suggestion of *The Hollow Universe* is that the temporal meets the eternal through the appearance of consciousness. In an article published in French in 1962, "Le cosmos comme tendance vers la pensée," he insisted that the transcendence of mind over time is an essential ingredient in the understanding of the human situation. Consciousness does not evolve, but more of it appears in our world as the development of the world goes on. Perhaps if the eternal becomes fully aware of itself, the predicted end of time will come to pass.

These are ideas which await development. Sometimes, De Koninck may have given the false impression that he did not really welcome philosophical novelty. For, under attack, he often tended to retreat into defences based on long citations from St. Thomas. Partly, he did so because he felt comfortable with St. Thomas and, when his judgement was questioned, he liked to return to what he thought of as his principal source of inspiration. Partly, he did so because arguments about what St. Thomas said were an accepted mode of philosophical debate amongst the philosophers whom he knew best. They understood, well enough, that one could tell a good deal about a philosopher's own thoughts by seeing which passages from St. Thomas attracted his attention, but again, such tactics were a way of maintaining a common front with those with whom one agreed in general principle while continuing to disagree with them in detail. Finally, of course, De Koninck had a genuine respect for papal encyclicals, though he understood the encyclical of August 1879 in the general sense in which it was surely intended: scholasticism was recommended as a source of enlightenment. Above all, the philosophy of St. Thomas was strongly recommended. He respected, as much, the canons which followed later and which laid down the conditions for Catholic teaching in philosophy.

It should be noticed, perhaps, that De Koninck's position has not been overtaken by time, at least in principle: the new canons continue to require the teaching of St. Thomas in seminaries even though the requirements are now somewhat more general and less readily determined for the whole system of Catholic education.

Sometimes, De Koninck did respond to criticism by digging deeper into his own philosophy, but less often than one might now wish. The result has been that the novelty of the view from the frontier which he had reached has not been very much noticed. The task now, I think, is to chart that frontier.

In social and political theory, the now pressing problems about the environment deserve the help which they could get from weighing De Koninck's arguments about our responsibilities to the universe as a whole. There is great need, after all, for a rational moderate position on these questions—one which insists that we weigh the whole but which does not deny the important place of the human being in the ultimate scale of values and does not simply protect the interests of upper- and middle-class inhabitants of the industrialized world against the encroaching pollution of the developing world. Turning other people's worlds into giant game preserves does not create what De Koninck thought of as an acceptable world community. It seems very likely that De Koninck's philosophy can provide a basis for such a strategy which holds promise of rational solutions.

De Koninck's attack on the various forms of the "cult of personality" and on social irrationalism in general are surely timely. The challenge which his social and political philosophy presents to theoretical understanding and to practical application centres on the questions of theoretical and practical reason. There are two kinds of difficulties here. One has to do with his insistence on the uniqueness of the individual and on the need for individual decision making, and the other—which is related to it—with his relative neglect of the social sciences. Both pose problems about the generation of social policy. But there are, within his philosophy, clear enough indications about where he thought that the solutions lay. Let me say a little about each.

The emphasis of De Koninck's philosophy is always on the concrete particular. His notion of freedom depends, as we have seen, on the fact that the context of action is always unique and that the potentialities of the individual do not simply consist in states of affairs which can be described in terms of universal principles. Morality, equally, is essentially a practical concern because moral theory lays down universal principles which are never rich enough to be sure of grasping the particularities of the situation. There is always a decision to be taken by the individual. The problem here, of course, is that social policy must be determined by universal principles and that, in democratic societies, exceptions made for individuals are usually—quite properly—regarded as signs of corruption.

On De Koninck's thesis, however, it would seem that the individual might always be able to claim exemption from any public policy on the ground that it did not do justice to his own situation. The answer is, I think, that it is not at all De Koninck's claim that just any whim whatsoever by the individual is sufficient to overturn public policy. Rather, the claims of the individual, in fact, derive from the nature of the demands of the common good. The common good, on De Koninck's view, is essentially the good of the universe taken as a whole. But each component has a part to play in it and each individual must make a claim in terms of his or her potentialities seen in relation to the common good. We must, if we resist public policy, be able to show that our potentialities to contribute to the common good would be reduced by compliance with the policy. This is a perfectly sensible account which leaves the primacy of the common good untouched. But it would require a serious rethinking of a great array of legal and political institutions.

This approach provides, in fact, the basis for a critique of legal and political life which, if astutely carried out, has a capacity for profound insight into our lives and public affairs. Needless to say, De Koninck did not have the opportunity to carry it out.

The problem of the social sciences might seem acute within De Koninck's system for the same reasons that make difficulties about morals and politics pressing: How can there be a social science if society is composed of unique concrete individuals whose affairs are never adequately conveyed by universal principles? The answer is partly that social science must proceed like natural science by abstraction and, like natural science, must constantly be wary of confusing the abstractions which it studies with the concrete individuals from whom the abstractions are made.

But there is evidently a special difficulty: the abstractions which form the different sciences seem to proceed on natural principles. I do not think that De Koninck's theory of the differentiation of the sciences was fully developed. But it would seem, for instance, that physics has to do with the movements of objects in space and time and that it creates its mathematical symbolic structures by denumerating spatiotemporal regions and by creating geometries appropriate to this task. Chemistry, by contrast, is concerned with the coming together of qualitatively discrete elements and thus is concerned with some of their qualitative properties—those which distinguish one element from another—and not merely with their spatiotemporal movements. It is thus, by a natural principle, one level closer to the concrete than physics. Special sciences such as geology are distinguished by adding properties from the concrete which separate them out from physics and chemistry.

The social sciences, however, have as their subject matter various human activities. Economics derives from human productive activity (and from the fact that, as Aristotle noticed, men are not like bees: what they produce varies with their interests and their training). Sociology stems from the human tendency to form groups, an activity which, again, like production, is not wholly controlled by fixed instincts and so takes many surprising forms. When elk form herds they are not like the Elks' Clubs which human beings form. Psychology may be midway between the natural and the social sciences, though its concerns with the way in which behaviour is influenced by human thought and feeling, as well as by social conditioning, exposes it to the same problems as the other social sciences. Human beings, in fact, make the subject matter of the social sciences and may do so in ways which are subject to constant change. How do we order these activities so as to create a social science? De Koninck's theory suggests that there are not really "social sciences" which are exactly like the "physical sciences." But there are orderly creations of the human intellect which do provide a kind of knowledge. Part of the test of such intellectual contrivances, however, has to do with their success in fitting together with our practical needs.

And, as I suggested, in De Koninck's view, the ultimate fusion of the practical and the theoretical can only take place in theology. There ought therefore to be a theology of the social sciences and perhaps, indeed, if one looks at some of the work of the sociologists of religion, one might conclude that one is beginning to take shape. But its development will not be a simple matter. It should be clear, at any rate, that, for anyone who wants to develop De Koninck's philosophy, there is no shortage of frontiers to explore.

The Dominican University College, Ottawa
October 2005

Charles De Koninck: A Biographical Sketch

Thomas De Koninck

I

Charles De Koninck was born on 29 July 1906, in Torhout, Belgium—a small town in West Flanders, close to Bruges.[1] Both his mother, Marie Verplancke, and his father, Louis De Koninck, hailed from Torhout as well. They immigrated in 1914 to the United States and lived in Detroit, Michigan, where his father worked as builder and contractor. His grandfather, too, had practised the same craft. Charles had two younger brothers, Andrew and Albert, and one sister, Madeleine, youngest in the family, who survives them. They became orphans very early, when their mother died unexpectedly in November 1917. Charles revered his mother's memory and always spoke of her with deep affection and admiration. He was also especially devoted to his aunts Eliza and Marie, both sisters of his father, who remained in Torhout and took care of him whenever he returned to Belgium, as he did first in 1919 for a short while.

In 1921, his father sent him back to Belgium to complete his education at the Collège Notre Dame in Ostende. In the course of his studies there, Charles first experienced serious health problems, which were to plague him for years. His symptoms were only later diagnosed as due to the relatively uncommon Ménière's disease. The theoretical cause of that disease is an increase in fluid in the labyrinth of the ear, affecting balance and hearing. Its chief manifestations—dramatic and violent attacks of vertigo and nausea, sometimes so severe that the patient cannot stand—exactly describe what Charles suffered. The one reliable treatment appears to be surgery in the ears to restore the balance. Eventually Charles would undergo this surgery with success, but not before erroneous diagnoses had forced on him, at least twice, surgical treatment of the stomach, and much distress. Once cured of the disease, he would still retain an extreme sensitivity of hearing and a lifelong susceptibility to sudden motion, which kept him from practising sports he loved.

Charles showed very early a natural ability and a predilection for the sciences, mathematics to begin with. He would have indeed opted for a scientific course without the humanities had it not been for his tutor in Belgium, A. De Coene, who convinced him otherwise. Having chosen instead the classical formation, he soon developed a special liking for literature.[2] He loved Latin, his favourite authors being, mainly for their style, Julius Caesar and Tacitus (notably the *Germania*), and Greek literature, Homer and Sophocles above all. Among the moderns he was drawn first to the great Flemish poet Guido Gezelle, and then to Gogol, a strong influence along with Tolstoy and Dostoyevsky on another famous Flemish author, Stijn Streuvels. Even though by now his studies were conducted in French, it is not clear whether this involved French literature; there his express tastes were later for François Villon and Rabelais, or else for contemporaries such as Paul Claudel, Paul Valéry, and Antoine de Saint-Exupéry. But his preferences went to English literature, notably to Keats and Milton. His chief enduring passion was, however, for Shakespeare, whom he would ever love to recite from memory and held "the best in all modern literature."[3] He learned to play the cello and evinced talents for sculpture (with among other pieces a bust of Heraclitus that won him a gold medal in a contest of professionals). He would always disapprove of those who, like Shakespeare's Cassius, "hear no music," his tastes extending over the whole wide range of classical music, with a slight early bias in favour of Bach and a late one for Mozart. He was also to remain faithful to sculpture and its tactile values as well as to the architectural talents of his own father and grandfather. Here he felt that the highest point had been reached in the French Romanesque cathedrals, although he almost equally admired Michelangelo. Yet he seemed with the years to grow ever more appreciative of painting as exemplified in the great Flemish and Dutch masters—the Breughels, Memling, Van Eyck, Van der Weyden, Rembrandt, Vermeer, Bosch, and others—cherished in his youth.[4]

This brings out a clearly powerful bent in Charles toward the humanities and the arts,[5] but the scientific bent remained nonetheless paramount. Much spare time was expended in a laboratory at the École Normale in Torhout doing experiments in chemistry and in physics with his best friend of those college years, Jules van Houtte. He liked later to say that he owed in large part his discovery of philosophy to a highly competent physics professor called Dr. De Meester who, though himself wary of philosophy, made him see that his incessant questioning belonged more to philosophy than to physics.

He thereafter spent three years reading philosophy (from 1925 to 1928) with the Belgian Dominicans, where the Reverend M. Matthijs became his tutor and encouraged him to pursue his studies as far as the doctorate. This, of course, is how Charles discovered and came to revere Thomas Aquinas. His wife recalls how thoroughly he would study Saint Thomas, memorizing chunks of the *Summa theologia* as was the custom, marvelling at the Commentaries on Aristotle, and querying the relative neglect they suffered. To her mind he was largely self-taught. For a while, he had considered joining the Dominican priesthood, but his recurring ill health prevented that. After a spell in the United States at the University of Detroit, where he befriended, amongst others, James Belleperche, S.J., he came back to Louvain in 1932 at the repeated urging of many, including Matthijs and another Detroit friend, Father Henry Syoen, to whom he would dedicate his reflections on indeterminism. There he obtained his doctorate in philosophy in 1934, *summa cum laude,* with a thesis under Professor Fernand Renoirte entitled "La philosophie de Sir Arthur Eddington."

He had found a kindred spirit in Sir Arthur Eddington, the English astronomer whose writings and own discoveries contributed so much to the understanding of relativity. A great, civilized intellect with a love of science and a marvellous capacity for wonder at the universe and at the human mind, Eddington was an entertaining, witty writer to boot, endowed with that most indispensable quality to Charles, a genuine sense of humour, and respectful of the common mind. His enthusiasm for Sir Arthur was such that, having named their first son Thomas, after Thomas Aquinas, he and his wife agreed over the name Arthur for their second son. This esteem continued unabated till the end. Though, to be sure, Charles' own opinions as to the value of science and the scientific world-view were to become more refined and nuanced than when first formulated in his thesis, he never failed to defend Eddington's soundness for his time as well as his talent for stimulating questions concerning the philosophical presuppositions and implications of contemporary physics.

While in Louvain Charles had met Abbé Georges Le Maître and had been much impressed by his expanding model of the universe, now known as the Eddington–Le Maître model owing to the support Eddington lent it. This helped stimulate Charles to write his first book, *Le Cosmos*, a few years later (1936). This influence serves at least partly to explain why he felt no less at ease with the scientific view of the universe than with the philosophical and the theological points of view and was able to divide his book according to three corresponding parts. One may note also that the Darwinian theory of evolution is already allowed for in that book. "The plan and execution of the work," wrote Ralph McInerny, "exhibit the author's breadth of interest as well as competence at the very outset of his career."[6] The book was followed in 1937 by two sets of important articles on "Le problème de l'indéterminisme," showing, for the first time, another typical concern: contingency.

He had published in 1933 his first important article, "Natuurwetenschappelijke methodologie en wijsbegeerte," in four installments, dealing with scientific methodology and philosophy and discussing the views of both Einstein and Jacques Maritain. Most of his subsequent publications were written either in French or in English (excluding of course translations into other languages). Those were the languages he spoke fluently, unless one includes Latin, which he wrote easily and in which he would be glad to discuss. Of German, Spanish, and Italian (indeed of Classical Greek), he claimed reading knowledge only, yet he loved to engage in fanciful conversation in them, making up words as he went along if his vocabulary failed him.

Meantime he had married, on 27 April 1933, Zoé Decruydt, a girl from Detroit, born of Flemish parents, whom he had met in his hometown, Torhout; she still survives him. His correspondence at the time makes light of Nietzsche's suspicion of the married life for the philosopher ("The bigot theory of the incompatibility of philosophy and married life is bunk. I do not think Aristotle was of that opinion: he married twice").[7] Twelve children were to result from this union, the first being born in Louvain in 1934 and all the others in Quebec; one girl died at birth, four girls and six of the seven boys (Dominique died in 1995) are to this day alive and thriving. He and Zoé always most dearly loved each other. He kept wondering at the energy she deployed holding together and indeed upholding that huge family, at times almost single-handedly, since his work not infrequently took him abroad. She was, he wrote, "la meilleure moitié de mon âme (the best half of my soul)."

II

No sooner had Charles defended his doctoral thesis than Maurice Roy invited him for a semester of teaching at Laval University in Quebec City. Maurice Roy, the future cardinal, was then Secretary of the "Institut supérieur de philosophie" (to become "Faculté de philosophie" a year later, in 1935).[8] Charles' teaching prowess prompted Laval to renew the invitation for another semester, and the next year to offer him a regular professorship, which was in effect to last the rest of his life. He was made dean of the Faculté de philosophie in 1939 (till 1956, as it turned out). He and his wife quickly found themselves very much at home in Quebec, and Charles, like others, was impressed not only by the generosity of French Canadians (as they were then invariably called) but at least as much by their frequently extraordinary intellectual gifts and by their speculative temperament, making the life of the mind seem to come naturally to a greater percentage of them than is usual. He never ceased to pay witness to this, as his experience of intellectual exchange extended over the globe. This goes a long way toward explaining his lifetime attachment to the Quebec milieu and to Laval University.

A similar invitation had been sent simultaneously to Jacques de Monléon in Paris. The results were analogous, but the latter preferred to retain half a year of teaching at the Institut catholique de Paris. Except for the war years (1939–1945) when he stayed in France and two complete years in Quebec afterward with his wife and children, he would return to Quebec for the autumn semester every year until 1973. Jacques de Monléon had been a pupil of Maurice Blondel and had worked as an assistant to Jacques Maritain. He and Charles became close friends, assiduously sharing topics of interest, such as dialectics, political philosophy, and the study of orthodox Marxism, bandying ideas with gusto and a high humour eloquently attested by a most lively correspondence. They also had in common a profound Christian faith and a concern for theological issues, such as the nature of mercy or the role of Mary in Redemption. Charles often repeated that he unfailingly derived enlightenment and encouragement from a discussion with de Monléon, even when they disagreed, which was seldom. He proved a key source of encouragement for some of the chief debates which engaged Charles' energies, accounting, in part at least, for the dynamism of the Faculté de philosophie between the 1930s and the early 1960s, drawing to it so many outside students (for most of that period, well over half the students earning a doctorate there were Americans or English Canadians). The subjects disputed included existentialism, the origins of Marxism, the primacy of the common good, the respective place of the experimental sciences and of philosophy of nature, the theory of evolution, the nature of logic, the question of analogy. Probably de Monléon's only real difference with Charles was in his staunch defence of the strict Thomist school of Cajetan and John of St. Thomas, whereas Charles, together with many of his Laval colleagues, became increasingly critical of them, not least in the light of Thomas Aquinas' own texts.

The bonds of another close and durable friendship were formed in those years with Alphonse-Marie Parent, successor to Maurice Roy as secretary of the Faculté de philosophie, later to be rector of the university and, later still, to head the famous royal commission on education initiated during the Quiet Revolution of the early 1960s and named after him La Commission Parent. They both had deeply at heart the cause of higher education and of academic excellence, to which Monsignor Parent brought immense practical gifts and boundless energy. If Charles assisted with ideas, Parent helped introduce Charles to colleagues of all disciplines and did much to foster the continuation of interdisciplinary exchanges between them as well as with colleagues abroad.

Incomplete and deficient though the *Annuaire de la Faculté de philosophie* for the 1930s and 1940s may be,[9] a glance at it would nevertheless suffice to suggest that such exchanges soon reached the classroom. In 1938, Charles shared a seminar on philosophy of science with Cyrias Ouellet (another good friend), Adrien Pouliot, and Jean-Louis Tremblay, respectively a chemist, a mathematician, and a biologist, all prominent in their field. Similar attempts were repeated in subsequent years, with the addition of the physicist Franco Rasetti, whom Charles held in high esteem.[10] In 1950, the mathematician René de Vogelaere was a guest teacher of non-Euclidean geometry at the Faculté de philosophie. Nor was this interdisciplinary approach confined to the exact sciences. From 1942 to 1944, for instance, Charles shared a course on Marxism as well as on philosophy and history with Auguste Viatte, the French literary historian (who was to become another lifelong friend). In 1943, he held discussions of themes from logic with Mortimer Adler. In 1945, Félix-Antoine Savard, author of the famed epic novel *Menaud Maître-Draveu,* lectured on poetry. The German economist Goetz Briefs, sometime professor at Georgetown University, was also a guest, and Aurel Kolnai, a Hungarian refugee, was entrusted for a long period with political thought. Charles himself was a frequent guest teacher at the Faculties of Theology, Letters, Medicine, and the Social Sciences. So far as I can remember (if I may be permitted some personal memories), our home seemed always open to students, colleagues, or friends of the most varied sort—be it discipline, conviction, language, country of origin, or social class—and was often the scene of disputation and laughter prolonged into the night.

However, the bulk of Charles' teaching centred chiefly round philosophy of nature, philosophy of science, and mathematics at the Faculté de philosophie, though other recurring topics included contemporary philosophy and especially Marxism. His highly nuanced position on the continuity between philosophy of nature and experimental science, for which apparently he is best known on the North American continent, evolved as a fruit of these lectures and found its first formulation in the review *Culture* in 1941.[11] The received view was to admit a radical separation of science and philosophy; he himself had accepted it in *Le Cosmos* as well as in his papers on indeterminism, but it would not bear greater scrutiny. Here emerges, perhaps for the first time clearly, what we will see occurring again and again to the point of becoming a constant with Charles in the face of a number of difficult contemporary issues: when the standard response fails to do justice to the depth and complexity of the problem and oversimplifies traditional views as well, it must be corrected.

He tried in his teaching to generate wonder and focus on genuine problems, to analyse the evidence and evaluate the arguments and, most of all, to make sure the student would be able to appeal to his own experience. It was no less important to read the primary sources carefully, whoever the authors, whether a Marx or an Aristotle. He liked to provoke in order to awaken and spent a lot of care choosing concrete examples most apt to illuminate. Maurice Dionne (to whom we will return shortly) remarked with his usual acumen that Charles was a "natural dialectician"; a good deal of his teaching method reflected that. He greatly enjoyed argument—provided the issues be real ones. As Ralph McInerny observed: "He loved controversy but not, I think, for its own sake, although he exhibited a zest for intellectual battle; for him, problems were to be solved, and in his lifetime he proposed many solutions to pressing contemporary issues."[12] This did much to enliven his teaching.

Thus decadent scholasticism seemed to him the worst corruption because it evaded the common concerns as well as the common conceptions of human beings. Philosophy teaching would be a failure if it did not favour personal discernment on the part of the student and enable the latter to discover for him or herself. It must therefore not only provide students with good tools but also provoke the proper motivation, and thoroughly familiarize him with difficulties and opposite views on important topics before suggesting solutions: the final judgment must be the student's own. Nothing appeared more deadly to philosophy than its reduction to one system or another.[13]

The emphasis on the primary sources extended to the reading of Aquinas himself (in the Latin text, of course, in those years), which in turn lent further support to such an understanding of philosophical training. Like his own sources, most of all Aristotle, Saint Thomas is constantly raising and facing difficulties, arguing and making distinctions of meaning, considering the views of others as well as expounding his own. To realize this, however, acquaintance with his writings, rather than with those of epigones, was vital. This had been lacking in traditional teaching which would sometimes rely too heavily on authority or else be content with history understood as mere report, neglecting the issues themselves. The admiration Charles professed for the ancient Greek philosophers, principally Aristotle, and his well-known reverence for Thomas Aquinas were due in no uncertain part to their respect for the human mind and its capacity for truth. Their works were models of authentic thought and, while constantly aware of the limitations of the human intellect, they showed how far the latter could go (which was farther certainly than Kant later held, to say nothing of Hume). In a word, to borrow a phrase from Leslie Armour in a different context, his students were taught to think.[14]

Here he derived much support from two colleagues, Fathers Maurice Dionne and Jasmin Boulay, whose brilliant minds he held in high regard. After completing his studies at the Institut catholique in Paris, Dionne began teaching at Laval in the early 1940s. He was a man of great intellectual depth, with a razor-sharp mind of lightning speed and a knack for communicating enthusiasm for the life of the intellect. Although he appeared to favour logic above all, he was scathingly critical of standard scholastic logic as well as of anything text-bookish. Very soon he focused on language. Imperfect notes from a famous course on *le mot* and from an even more celebrated course on analogy were long circulated and exercised much local influence. One of the main themes of Dionne's (by that time a monsignor) later teaching was the importance of fostering culture in the sense of Greek *paideia,* as exemplified more precisely in Aristotle's *pepaideumenos,* a name designating the truly cultured human being who is able to discern justly in all matters of import, well beyond specialization. To expect mathematical evidence for metaphysical issues is as out of place as rhetoric, say, would be in mathematics—clear cases of *apaideusia,* the worst form of ignorance. The best way to ensure culture in that sense was *manuductio* ("leading by the hand"), a term used by Aquinas to describe the spirit in which teaching is to be conducted: respect for the student's mind, for what he already knows or what he does not know. The student must be taught to seek the proper evidence available for each type of discourse or intellectual endeavour, and thus to form his own judgment, instead of being turned into a parrot, as a learner of "systems" or a mere gatherer of information. *Dicunt ore, sed non attingunt mente* was a favourite quote from Thomas Aquinas paraphrasing Aristotle: "they say it with their mouth, but they don't reach it with their mind."

Jasmin Boulay had studied in Rome and Paris; his principal fields in philosophy were aesthetics and ethics. He could, perhaps, be best described as epitomizing that acute mind in philosophy which, to quote Aristotle, "will perceive resemblances even in things far apart." He was a former pupil of Maurice Dionne and they became great friends soon after Boulay came from Sherbrooke to Laval in the early 1950s. They worked closely together and shared that same concern for education and its various tools which had characterized the ancient Greek philosophers. But whereas Dionne's range of reading was somewhat confined, Boulay's was the widest imaginable. Students benefited greatly from this example and were encouraged to plough as far and as deeply as they could the vast field of literature together with that of both traditional and contemporary philosophy. All this delighted Charles. He admired Boulay no less than Dionne and never hid the debt he felt toward them; he would in fact call on Dionne to help him out on his argumentation in the birth control issue and to co-author his final paper. Such feelings were indeed reciprocated by both toward him—even more strongly, if possible, after his death. He only deplored the fact that the two preferred oral teaching and failed to write, despite his pressures to the contrary. This sometimes had the effect of enabling so-called disciples to attribute to them their own inept or simplistic views and to propagate these with impunity. Not every Socrates finds his Plato.[15] It must in fairness be added that Charles also derived from them—as he did from Jacques de Monléon—enlightenment and incentive for his theological work, the importance of which Leslie Armour rightly stresses. They often sought the light of faith and of theology as did Charles; Dionne and Boulay indeed taught theology on occasion and they, too, had students who later professed in the Faculté de théologie.

III

But Charles' teaching activities in the broad sense were far from limited to the Quebec periphery. Laval was then a Catholic university with very little money to pay its professors and Charles had a big family. To make ends meet, he lectured extensively abroad, in colleges and universities principally, most of all throughout the United States, yet also in Latin America (mainly Mexico, Argentina, and Venezuela), Europe, and Canada (chiefly Ontario, Quebec, and the Maritime Provinces). The range of subjects was indeed vast. Some of those lectures found their way into his books and articles, myriad others would fill folders with arrays of notes that might have led to more publications if he had lived longer on such topics as humour, clothing, the hand, the sense of touch and the intellect, the fine arts, etc. The typical lecture tour in the United States would see him leave for several weeks at a time (ten weeks in 1948 was unusually long), hopping by plane from one institution of learning to another, between New York and San Francisco, Boston and Houston. Although the travelling was exhausting to him, he seemed to derive a good deal of stimulus from his lecturing—out of personal conviction, I think, as well as because he enjoyed teaching. He held with Aquinas that a thinking life is life of the highest degree and that nothing was more worthwhile than to share as a cause, however humble, in the transmission of such life. To quote from one of his speeches, "Little wonder that the very first fruit of Charity, the foremost among spiritual works of mercy, should be teaching the ignorant (docere ignorantes)."[16]

Many of those lectures were also about theological subjects. The angels were one favourite, witnessed by an imposing mass of notes on them. But the most favoured was Our Lady, Mother of God. To quote Thomas Heath in a homily at St. Mary's College the day after Charles' death: "of his many books and articles and brochures and lectures no subject was more frequently on his lips and his pen than she. He loved to praise her. The best lecture he ever gave here at St. Mary's was on the role of women in the work of redemption, and those of us who heard it remember how the conclusion nearly took us out of our seats."[17] On woman, theology appeared so much better than philosophy; he would never cease to wonder at the inadequacy of philosophers on the subject and would begin by quoting Schopenhauer and Nietzsche as examples. With sometimes odd results, it must be added, as when statements by Schopenhauer taken down by a distracted student were actually attributed to Charles himself and circulated for a while as his own teaching on the matter.

Besides his own wife, his closest friend in the late 1930s and early 1940s was Father Francis Hammang, who had gone to Louvain in 1933 for a doctorate and had been teaching church history and archaeology in St. Paul, Minnesota since 1938. He had suffered a childhood filled with commotion and had overcome great difficulties with a natural calmness and a fortitude Charles was fond of evoking. He died prematurely in 1945 at the age of forty-three. This was a very heavy loss to Charles, who remained for a long time inconsolable. He shared his distress with another dear friend from St. Paul he had met in Louvain, Father William O'Donnell ("Okie"), historian and administrator at St. Thomas College, but, more importantly for Charles, a master of humour. Thenceforward, several of Charles' friends were among his former students, often those who wrote their doctoral thesis under his personal supervision.[18] Space will not permit mentioning most of them, but one cannot omit the first American student, John Oesterle, with a thesis on meaning; his future wife Jean McCall, a philosopher in her own right; Nathalie Lincoln who would give generous scholarships to enable Americans to study at Laval; Ralph McInerny who wrote his dissertation on Kierkegaard; Sheila O'Flynn whose dissertation on rational process he specially admired; Father Anthony Durand (from London, Ontario), very much a distinguished literary person concerned with Shelley on poetry. These were all subsequently to either work with him or help him out one way or another in turn and to become close friends. The fact that the majority lived at a distance accounts for a rich correspondence, much of which is extant.

In 1941 he invited Antoine de Saint-Exupéry, who was then in New York, to give a public lecture in Quebec City. They quickly experienced a genuine kinship and became friends. This was the time Charles' book, *De la primauté du bien commun* (1943), was gestating; Charles was impressed by the views of Saint-Exupéry on the common good that would be spelled out especially in *Pilote de guerre*, which came out first in English (under the title *Flight to Arras*) in New York in February 1942. *Le Petit Prince* would also first appear in New York, in April 1943. When Saint-Exupéry's plane vanished forever on 31 July 1944, it was felt as a personal loss to all of us in the family old enough to understand.

IV

Charles' first public stand achieving notoriety was probably his attack on anti-Semitism in 1943 in the affair surrounding Jacques Salomon Hadamard, the eminent French mathematician, also invited from New York at Charles' suggestion to lecture at Laval University and at the University of Montreal. Hadamard's adherence to Judaism had provoked censure in some quarters. It may be said at once that few things angered Charles more than bigotry, as would become increasingly evident, most of all in his last years. Was one to emulate those German universities of the day that forbade teaching the theory of relativity because it was the work of a Jew? The search for truth is a common endeavour and truth must be seized wherever available, even from those we may disagree with on other matters, wrote Charles. And there, the weapon of disagreement must invariably again be free argumentation, not censure or force. Even should one's name be Stalin, and the concern his own conception of dialectical materialism, the latter must be made welcome provided he is ready to present it without prior recourse to arms. Insinuations against Jews are wounding to Catholics in their very Lord Jesus Christ and in his Mother, who are Jews too, together with so many saints worshipped by Christians.[19] These positions did not convince then as easily as they presumably might today, so when Jacques Maritain commended him for his lucidity and courage in this dispute, Charles was most grateful.

His reference here to the arch totalitarian, Stalin, was to give rise to a story claiming Charles had boasted to invite Stalin if he came to Quebec to meet with Churchill and Roosevelt at the Château Frontenac![20] The truth is that it was a recurrent theme in his teaching that totalitarianism was indigenous to orthodox Marxist conceptions as well as to Nazism. Lenin complied with basic Marxist tenets when he saw the State as "a special machinery for suppression" or when he wrote that to suppress exploitation "the greatest ferocity and savagery of suppression are required, seas of blood are required, through which mankind is marching in slavery, serfdom, and wage-labour," to quote from his *The State and Revolution.* Charles thought Stalin's little work, *Dialectical and Historical Materialism,* whether he be its true author or not, helped one understand what Marxism-Leninism had come to mean, and he made it a standard text along with others by Marx, Engels, and Lenin for his classes on Marxism. The fundamentally atheistic nature of orthodox Marxism—as of Nazism and similar ideologies—entailed in effect and practice the rejection of human dignity. The twentieth century did not fail to give us repeated proof of this hard consequence. Shocked though he would have been, nothing would have surprised Charles less than the fuller revelations of Stalin's or Mao's systematic atrocities in the name of Communism, nor, for that matter, than the June 1989 killings in Tiananmen Square in Beijing.

In the same year (1943), *De la Primauté du bien commun contre les personnalistes. Le principe de l'ordre nouveau* came out, evincing the same preoccupations over totalitarianism, yet dissatisfaction again with standard reactions, the constant we observed earlier. Totalitarian regimes use the pretext of the common good to enslave people in the most ignoble fashion and perpetrate abominations in its name. Does this mean, as a consequence, that one should side with those who would, instead, put their own personal dignity above the common good as tyrants do? Indeed the paradox is that the philosophies fathering modern totalitarian regimes have in theory exalted man more than ever before, in the case of Marxism, as far as the explicit denial of God. Appeals to human dignity can thus be ambiguous, to say the least. Indeed, *must* the good of the person and the common good be mutually exclusive? There lay the basic fallacy shared by opposite camps. The book is intent on showing that the dignity of the person is in fact inseparable from the common good and ultimately consists in being related to God as common good.

It is not possible to go any further here into the denunciations and the doctrine contained in this short volume. The preface by Cardinal Villeneuve opened with the words: "L'ouvrage que voici n'est pas un livre ordinaire.

Il est de pure sagesse." It sold out in no time. The story of the ensuing controversy has been told many times and need not detain us long. Its high point was a virulent attack by Father I.T. Eschmann from Toronto, *In Defense of Jacques Maritain*; it was the occasion of the lengthy reply entitled *In Defence of Saint Thomas* (1945). Yves Simon, friend alike of Maritain and of Charles, said at the end of his life in 1961 that he thought the reply even better than the book itself, an assessment with which Charles was inclined to concur. Simon's own review in 1944 had high praise for the doctrinal content of the book, while he remained sure that Jacques Maritain would not disagree with any of its fundamental positions. The burden of his criticism was that not all names were given, a prudential decision Charles never disavowed. (This recurs in their correspondence, which is at once very forthright and warm; he was "indeed a friend" not mincing words, as Charles had described him in his reply, to his delight.) As regards this anonymity, one could not put it better than Leslie Armour: "He opposes doctrines, not men."

Charles allowed a translation to be published in Madrid in 1950, under the care of his friend the Spanish philosopher Leopoldo Eulogio Palacios, but as time went on, with positions and problems shifting, he came to adamantly oppose any further reissuing of the book as it stood. He hoped instead to produce a new one without polemics, a project he did not live to complete. I have since found his fame abroad, in South America and Europe, for instance, but also (to my surprise) in Southeast Asia, to rest chiefly, though not solely, on his work concerning the common good.

Last but not least, 1943 also saw the publication of *Ego Sapientia: La Sagesse qui est Marie,* the first of three books of Marian theology. Its style is both philosophical and meditative, in the spirit of the great Christian tradition, which it abundantly quotes—from Scripture to Augustine, to Bernard of Clairvaux, Bonaventure, and Thomas Aquinas, to Grignion de Montfort. Apart from wisdom, the most salient theme is probably mercy, a constant in all his theological work, centred as it is on the Incarnation. "Charles De Koninck aura été le philosophe de l'Incarnation," justly commented Clément Lockquell, extending this to much of his other work as well.[21]

La piété du Fils (1954) is perhaps more strictly philosophical. It is mainly concerned with the doctrine of the Assumption. He himself judged *La piété du Fils* his best book all round, largely owing to a long chapter (VI) on the death of the Blessed Virgin where philosophical argumentation reaches a peak. *Ego Sapientia* was dedicated to his wife and to his daughters Godelieve and Marie-Charlotte; so were the chapters of *La piété du Fils* one by one, adding Maria and Zita, born since. In the latter, an appendix on Saint Joseph bore a dedication to his father, followed by a quote from Paul Claudel: "cette grande et un peu mystérieuse figure de saint Joseph dont le nom seul fait sourire les gens supérieurs." The whole book was dedicated to his sons. *Le scandale de la médiation* (1961), more ecumenical in purport, was published in France and inscribed to General George P. Vanier, an old friend, then Governor General of Canada, whose discreet, devout Christian faith Charles valued. There is, inevitably, a lot of philosophy in it too: failing to understand universal causality and the all important role of intermediate causes leads one to underestimate mediation, Mary's in particular, in the economy of Redemption. At the end of his life, he declared himself particularly glad to have written those three books. In 1962, he obtained a doctorate in theology from Laval University with a thesis on "La mort 'glorieuse' de Marie," a resumption of part of *La piété du Fils.*

V

Leslie Armour tells of how he met Charles at an international student seminar at Pontigny in France in 1950. In point of fact, Charles was for a long time very active in such affairs, founding associations and preparing philosophical meetings himself. The list would be tediously long; significantly, however, the first symposium he organized at Laval, in 1936, was on the theory of evolution; it would be followed by a second one on the same theme in 1952, marked by the presence of Ludwig von Bertalanffy among other guests. In 1945 moreover, he founded together with A.-M. Parent (acting as administrator) the *Laval théologique et philosophique,* a bilingual journal of philosophy and theology. The international *succès d'estime* that review has since come to enjoy was hard won at the beginning, as will be understood by anyone with experience at pioneer tasks. I have already alluded to the fact that Charles had difficulty convincing immediate colleagues to write and the journal was soon years behind schedule as a consequence. Since delayed issues had to be filled to help the journal catch up, he found himself obliged to do so partly with extracts (usually somewhat revised) from deserving dissertations and partly with his own writing; a few issues seem in fact to flow almost entirely from his pen.[22] Rushing to meet constant deadlines meant a lot of stress, and it took a while before a greater number of outside contributions finally began to lessen the burden. To be sure, however, the pressure served to increase his output.

But one of the chief claims on his time must have been the direction of doctoral dissertations. Not all of them, of course, made the same demands, for their authors were often already quite autonomous. Still he took this responsibility more seriously than appears common. It would be both fascinating and revealing to follow the patterns of ideas and preoccupations through that medium on a parallel with his teaching and writing—something we cannot even begin to attempt presently. The clearest example that springs to mind is L.-E. Otis' *La doctrine de l'évolution*, published as a two volume book in 1950. The second volume, presenting the philosophical and theological points of view, with an ironic preface by Charles, created quite a stir in traditional circles because it showed that the Darwinian theory of the evolution of species is quite acceptable provided one makes the proper philosophical and theological distinctions. (This is not to say it is true—that remains for the experts to establish from ever better knowledge of the evidence—nor that it is philosophically faultless: see his paper entitled "Darwin's Dilemma.") The content of that volume furnishes good clues to Charles' own teaching regarding teleology, matter and time, universal causality and contingency, for instance, as well as on the points of view of Saint Augustine or of Holy Scripture relevant to the issue. Again some so-called orthodox reactions against the theory were proving skin-deep and suffering in any case from a lack of critical awareness of the true depths of traditional thought.

Even leaving aside the theological work, the 1940s and 1950s were years of an extremely varied, intense production, which one cannot begin to recount in such a short treatment of his life as this. Only a few emerging pieces can be singled out for their greater significance or because of the personal commitments they illustrate. One major concern was existentialism, its emphasis on contingency and other vital themes he particularly welcomed. His position was once again paradoxical, witness the following sentence from "The Nature of Man and His Historical Being": "The philosophical doctrine that properly concerns the opinions advanced by Existentialism is not the doctrine of being; rather, it is the doctrine of the good." He had matured this view while preparing for the 1949 Mendoza (Argentina) congress, but the basic doctrine had already been outlined in his important acceptance speech to the Royal Society of Canada on 18 November 1945.[23]

By all accounts, one of his most remarkably thorough pieces of writing must be "Introduction à l'étude de l'âme" (1948). A manual of Thomistic psychology for which he was asked by the author, Abbé Stanislas Cantin, to write a preface, provided the occasion. Though this manual was a quite competent composition in the genre, Charles thought it necessary to update it by discussing points of method taking into account contemporary experimental science and emphasizing in contrast the certainty provided by internal experience, but not without warnings of pitfalls. The result was a long, tersely written essay on the study of the soul today, which was out of tune with the rest of the book. Later editions of the textbook were, understandably enough, to omit the preface which in any case stood better on its own. Charles intended a later book incorporating much of it, with the title of *The Anatomy of Mind,* but there is no doubt that even in its present version this "Introduction à l'étude de l'âme" could be of service to many. Nothing like it is available anywhere.[24]

In describing "Concept, Process, and Reality" (1949) as "one of the centrepieces of his thought," Leslie Armour shows uncanny flair, and I see nothing to add to the excellent explanation he provides for this assessment. Moreover, he agrees with Charles himself, who wrote of it: "It's truth I felt in my very bones."[25] It must be read in conjunction with another paper, "La dialectique des limites comme critique de la raison" (1945), and with passages from *Le Cosmos.* If only we could know everything in just one concept, instead of needing a distinct one for each nature, which in turn entails discourse and the fabrication of time in thought—but we cannot. Nevertheless, our minds tend, however inadequately and imperfectly, toward that more perfect type of knowledge, witness the use of the limit in mathematics. This observation and the larger question of "the cognitive means by which we reach what we know," is indeed present under many guises everywhere in his thought; when he took it up in conversation or in his lectures, his face would light up and he became quite voluble. Though frequently critical of Hegel, he perceived now a possible *rapprochement* and later submitted the article to the great Oxford Hegelian, G. R. G. Mure, when the latter expressed his near total agreement with *The Hollow Universe.*

Nor can we omit his work for the Quebec Royal Commission on Canadian Confederation, the so-called Tremblay Commission, in 1954, embedded in "La confédération, rempart contre le grand Etat," followed by several annexes, the main one entitled "Deux tentatives de contourner par l'art les difficultés de l'agir," a penetrating essay on systematic attempts to escape ethical behaviour, including the aesthetic and the Marxist evasions (many key themes of his thought are at work here). The title of the paper on confederation expresses the gist of its thesis: federalism protects us from the Big State. With regard to the political and cultural tensions proper to Canada, the comment has been made that "Charles De Koninck, a Belgian by birth, expressed in his contribution to the Tremblay commission a strong sense of those tensions and a clear response to them." He did seem, in comparison to others, "more closely involved in the deepest concerns which have always tended to unite all Canadians."[26]

With *Un paradoxe du devenir par contradiction* (1954), one enters anew, not so much into the refutation of Marxism (although there is a little of that, too) as into Aristotle's *Physics* in some of its most profound, neglected aspects (at least until the recent work on it by the French mathematician René Thom); the analysis of becoming into its quantitative parts, where different forms of indivisibility play an essential part. This is high-powered philosophy of nature of the most exigent sort, as anyone will realize who has seriously read Book VI of the *Physics*. Charles loved working at such demanding questions and such hard texts; it would doubtless have turned into his main occupation had he not been so solicited elsewhere. By neglecting them, one failed to address problems whose solutions could shed light on much of modern thought and, even more importantly, on the nature of reality. As the German economist Goetz Briefs justly remarked in a personal tribute, "his overriding concern was *Die Warheit der Dinge*, truth about things."

In May 1958, while in Charlottetown, Prince Edward Island, on a lecture tour, Charles suffered his first heart attack (a coronary thrombosis with infarction). He would very soon be fifty-two. It did not slow him down for long. Confined to the hospital there for a few weeks, he kept a cheerful correspondence, developing ideas for future work. He had less than seven years ahead of him, three books, countless lectures and articles and, in addition to family responsibilities, more than one controversial cause to espouse.

VI

For longer than he cared to remember, Charles had a contract with Prentice Hall for a philosophy of nature textbook. It was an important source of stress; his family required the money. Writing was always difficult to him in any language, so he warmly welcomed the slightest possible improvement his friends might suggest for the texts he submitted to them. For English, he relied primarily on the support of his former pupil Anthony Durand. This time, however, the task appeared well nigh insuperable to a man without an inch of the schoolmaster in him, although it did not prevent him from drafting chapters to submit for revision to friends. Yet he could not stomach writing as if in a void, failing to attend to the cultural context in which his student readers would find themselves. Hence a new spate of papers concerned with the contemporary scientific world-view, e.g., "Random Reflections on Science and Calculation" and "Abstraction from Matter," the closest approximation to a final version of parts of the textbook; the latter never saw the light of day.

On the other hand, having been nominated by the University of Notre Dame for their Distinguished Professors' Program, he spent the fall semester there, which again served to make him better aware of English-speaking readers. It also provided another opportunity to delve deeper into analytic philosophy, which was gaining ground on the North American continent. He had long—ever since the Eddington years—been a reader of Bertrand Russell, whose influence prevailed in spite of Wittgenstein and other critics who, for all their worth, owed him their initiation to philosophy. Charles enjoyed Russell's transparent prose and his wit; the pot boiler *History of Western Philosophy* should be read as a comical book, he thought. The "trouble is, people credit him with far more brains than he has";[27] but superficial though it proved, his work on mathematics was useful, and there were fine passages in *My Philosophical Development.* A far more genuine philosopher was Whitehead.

When the invitation came from McMaster University to give in 1959 the Fourth Series of Whidden Lectures, he seized the opportunity to practice the art of dialectics and do some "leg-pulling." The title *The Hollow Universe* is a significant counterpart to *Le Cosmos,* his much earlier book displaying the marvel of the universe and its manifestation of a wondrous intelligence, which fascinated Einstein. The young girl quoted in the preface put the difference well: "Is the hollow in the universe or in our heads?" The target was in no way, of course, science itself, nor the world-view to be gathered from it, but the simplistic reductions contrived by some of its most influential interpreters, Bertrand Russell, A. M. Turing, and others, as well as the effect this had on uncritical minds. Some of the most effective passages of those lectures have to do with symbolization and symbolic construction as opposed to ordinary language, another lifelong preoccupation. The fact that Turing's work on computers has been accorded more prominence today than at the time lends even greater relevance to an Epilogue to these lectures entitled "Reckoning with the Computers," which is directly levelled against Turing's article "Computing Machinery and Intelligence," in *Mind*, 1950.

As is well known, in the Quebec province the early 1960s witnessed stirrings soon to be followed by the Quiet Revolution. There were some in the Church too; John XXIII had become pope in 1958; on 11 October 1962 he opened the Second Vatican Council (it would be closed by Paul VI on 7 December 1965). Charles' two last books, *Le scandale de la médiation* (1961) and *Tout homme est mon prochain* (1964) are in tune with both these lines of events, as were other publications and much of his public activity then, including two causes he adopted that brought him controversy and would stay with him till his dying day: religious freedom and birth control.[28]

"Jean XXIII fait savoir sans équivoque que tout homme est son prochain." This was the original statement that suggested the title *Tout homme est mon prochain*; it occurs in a chapter on John XXIII, originally written while that great pope lay dying in May–June 1963. No sentence could better express what it meant for Charles to be a Christian. It was nothing new, of course, nor was religious freedom, whose basic principles were plain to see in traditional thought as well as in both the Bible and the writings of the Fathers of the Church. But a truth can become more and more distinctly communicated and made more manifest, as Saint Vincent of Lérins, who died before 450, had so aptly urged on the subject of progress in religion. Charles thus welcomed the Council with open arms and was delighted to be asked by Cardinal Roy to work on religious freedom to that end.

On another front, the rights of agnostics to have schools in which to educate their own children in accordance with their personal convictions were being questioned in Quebec. Charles defended those rights, arguing besides that religious freedom, taught by the Church, recognized by the State, is a positive good protecting the freedom of the act of faith. It is the same right one appeals to in support of denominational schools; it respects furthermore the way human beings come to learn fundamental truths in the purely natural sphere.[29] This stand brought him a fair amount of abuse, in the press as well as among his own colleagues. Former students of a traditionalist bent attacked him publicly—in some instances the very same who after his sudden demise would claim him as their master. Eminent authorities declared he would soon retract. Yet Charles was so much at home with those traditional truths—the constant we observed emerges again—that he sailed serenely through the storms, finding new arguments on the way as was his wont. "Jamais De Koninck n'en manifestait la moindre rancune. Bien plus, il répondait à ses contradicteurs par une recrudescence d'amitié à leur égard," wrote one editorialist who had differed sharply with him on the whole issue.[30]

The position Charles took on the issue of birth control raised no less of a storm. In order to understand it, two texts must be considered: his own "Réflexions relatives à la régulation des naissances" and "Le problème de l'infécondité," which he co-authored with Maurice Dionne.[31] It is very nuanced and cannot be adequately summed up in a few lines. One forceful point was that responsible parenthood should take into account the good of the offspring, *bonum prolis,* which, for a human being, is threefold: existence, nutrition, and education. To omit the second two, particularly education, requiring much care and many years, is irresponsible, so there must be some planning. The crucial problem concerns the means. The pill had recently been discovered; arguments against its use, as unnatural, for instance, did not convince him at first, for they usually betrayed confusion over the manifold meanings of "nature," or over the role of medicine. Infertility was often sought by nature, during pregnancy for example, and could be seen to be a good in many instances. Thus the question became: What means to ensure infertility are truly "natural," i.e., would be employed by nature if it could, and is the pill such a means? He had doubts at the end and the pill is not mentioned in the second paper, published after his death.

His friend Gérard Dion, from the Social Sciences Faculty, had asked this philosopher, theologian, husband, and father of so many children to help clarify things in his periodical *Perspectives sociales.* Oversimplifications had seemed rife as much on one side as on the other. One would have to know Charles very little to expect him to believe he could ever nail down the definitive answer on such complex issues, but it was evident he could be of assistance.[32] Cardinal Maurice Roy clearly thought likewise, for he assigned him to a subcommittee on birth control for the Council, in addition to his other duties as a theologian. His last weeks were spent in Rome accordingly. He died there in the Columbus Hotel, on 13 February 1965. He was fifty-eight; the medical verdict was acute coronary thrombosis—the second heart attack, so far as one could tell. It was a Saturday morning; he had just completed his task for the subcommittee, had lectured the night before at the Canadian College in Rome, and was scheduled for a private audience with Paul VI on the Monday. His body was flown to Quebec to be buried there. The family was overwhelmed with tokens of sympathy from everywhere.

VII

He never seemed happier than with his family. His older children recall camping trips with him along the St. Lawrence River toward the Gaspé peninsula, or more often in Charlevoix, at St. Joseph-de-la-Rive or la Baie-des-Rochers. Félix-Antoine Savard tells how he discovered the philosopher on the beach there at five in the morning preparing a breakfast of fresh herring next to the fishing net, happy as a child, or how he would shoot at ducks with no threat to the latter.[33] These were not unfamiliar sights to us. He would love to take us to see the whales at Les Escoumins, long before it became fashionable to do so and before belugas, which were legion then, started dying out from pollution. Since sports were forbidden to him, the best relaxation he knew was to work at home with his hands, to putter in a basement workshop and do repairs, or some carpentry, manufacturing loud-speakers or fabricating a gigantic kitchen table, or to cook, make bread, for instance—mobilizing the whole kitchen, to his wife's despair.

His last years were markedly serene and joyful, despite a host of worries. He watched with pride and delight his children's progress, each in a different sphere, many of them at the same time proficient in sports, especially swimming. He could begin to see the family evolving into a miniature university; as it turned out, educational science, history of art, sociology, and linguistics divided up between his four daughters; philosophy, civil engineering, geography, psychology, mathematics, and twice electronics among his seven sons; the majority with doctorates and in the teaching profession.

Impatient as he was apt to be with stupidity or pretentiousness, he was incapable, as we saw, of rancour; the enemy was crass ignorance, or lies, or intolerance, never any person.[34] He was the most convivial of men, as must be clear by now, too; *bon vivant,* fond of good food and drink no doubt, but much more so of good company. He put to frequent use a gift for onomatopoeia and a knack for inventing playfully pompous names, like Bummelklotz or Scoffobondre. Humour in its various forms, preferably the British sort, was with him the salt of life. He was not above the Rabelaisian or Falstaffian kind either, in his correspondence especially, reverting then to Flemish or something close, or else to a Latin of his own. But his most defining characteristic, said an old friend quite rightly, was that "he loved people."[35] Whenever he returned to his former hometown, Torhout, he would make an effort to visit what looked like nearly everybody; people lifted their spirits by pouring their life stories and their problems to "Sarle." "He was a man of exceptional mental energy," wrote the London *Tablet,* "and intensely sociable, so that international gatherings, not least the Vatican Council, were occasions into which he entered with great enthusiasm."[36]

His lifelong meditation on contingency convinced him that divine Providence is most manifest in chance encounters, where no other *per se* cause is traceable. No one was less of a snob. His life was filled with acquaintances and friends of every condition, with all of whom he felt equally at ease, although he did often show a preference for simple people. When the Habsburg family, the Empress Zita and her numerous children, took refuge in Quebec City during the war, she asked Charles to be a tutor to her sons Charles-Louis and Rudolph, who were for a while students at Laval University. An intimate friendship ensued with the entire family; chiefly, however, with Zita herself whom he admired and with Rudolph, the youngest son whose company and sense of humour he enjoyed. He would keep in close touch with them until his death, visiting them whenever he was in Europe. But he was just as assiduous with Monsieur Miller, a cripple suffering from diabetes whose legs were finally amputated. Charles would regularly visit him after work at the university or take us along to see him in the evening at his home down in the Quebec lower town near the docks. He spent hours listening to him and encouraging him and his family. Though Mr. Miller had not had the benefit of much instruction, he would keep him informed of his books and of his lectures and would ask him to pray. When Mr. Miller died, Charles was deeply moved, beyond expression.

Shakespeare's theology of mercy was impeccable: "'Tis mightiest in the mightiest." Thomas Heath tells of "the last day of his stay here [at Notre Dame, Indiana] that year, a cold January day, when he asked me to take him over to visit with Sister Gretchen in the Infirmary. She had been in charge of him in his early years here and he never forgot her kindness. On that day I met Sister Gretchen for the first time, and saw her hands all crumpled with arthritis. Charles and she visited together and then when it came time to say goodbye Charles went down on one knee and kissed her hands. He never knew how that gesture pierced me with respect and love for him. Sister Gretchen died about a month after that visit."[37] One could cite many similar incidents. He was called more than once by Quebec hospitals, especially l'Hôtel-Dieu, to help the dying. His frequent, sometimes long stays in hospitals had made him familiar with sickness and death, and he seemed particularly happy to be of service to the dying. His most profound personal devotion was for the Eucharist; "many times in giving him Communion," said Father Heath, "I was deeply touched by his child-like reception—it was something on his face."[38]

It is impossible to capture Charles De Koninck in one category or another. "Isms," left and right, will not fit. Perhaps the least inadequate words are Shakespeare's: "His life was gentle, and the elements so mix'd in him that Nature might stand up and say to all the world 'This was a man!'"

NOTES

1. I wish to extend very grateful thanks to Abbé Armand Gagné to whose painstaking research into my father's life this brief sketch owes a good deal. His "Bibliographie de Charles De Koninck" in *Mélanges à la mémoire de Charles De Koninck* (Quebec: Les Presses de l'Université Laval, 1968), 7–22 (hereafter, *Mélanges*) is a model of its kind.

2. Cf. Emile Bégin, "Charles De Koninck," *La Revue de l'Université Laval* 19, no. 8 (April 1965): 699–700: "Il savait toutes les littératures, spirituelle, profane, anglaise,

française, allemande, celle des mystiques et celle des poètes, celle de sa patrie et aussi la nôtre. Même le folklore l'intéressait parce qu'il y voyait l'âme des peuples. Aussi dialoguer avec lui était-il un délice pour l'esprit."

3. Written to the author in 1950. Cf. Félix-Antoine Savard, "A la mémoire de Charles De Koninck," in *Discours* (Fides, 1975), 143–46: "Il m'expliquait aussi Shakespeare qu'il lisait à la perfection. Il aimait mastiquer les mots, faisait sonner les consonnes, y trouvant pulpe, jus et saveur et comme la chair elle-même des idées et de la poésie." According to Clément Lockquell, his knowledge of things English "contribua largement à dilater son humour naturel et cet appétit de vivre intensément qui le caractérisaient"; cf. "In Memoriam Charles De Koninck," *Dialogue* 4, no. 1 (1965): 96–98.

4. The British author and Shakespearian actor Robert Speaight wrote perceptively of "what seemed to me the Flemish cast of De Koninck's mind, temperament, and even physique. . . . For all the power of his intellect and the rigour of his reasoning, he was resistant to the abstractions with which the French try to clarify the *chiaroscuro* of life. He had a naïveté—dare I say a *gaucherie?*—which was ill at ease in a climate of pure cerebration. . . . I remember agreeing with him . . . that the creative genius of the French had touched its highest point in the sculpture and architecture of the Romanesque. . . . When Charles De Koninck died . . . I wondered afresh about De Koninck's Flemish forbears, and although I knew nothing of them, I found it easy to imagine him in the company of those who had given to Europe one of its greatest schools of painting. He would have been as at home, it seemed to me, with the healthy sensuality of Rubens as with the humble piety of van Eyck" ("With the Flemish Masters," in *Mélanges,* 353–61).

5. It may be noted here that one of his first essays was entitled "Thought and Beauty," according to a letter to James Belleperche dated 27 November 1933, but it was not published and the manuscript is no longer extant.

6. See Ralph M. McInerny, "Charles De Koninck: A Philosopher of Order," *The New Scholasticism* 39, no. 4 (October 1965): 491–516 (hereafter McInerny); the quote is on p. 494. This remains one of the best essays on Charles De Koninck the philosopher. Yet see also Richard J. George, "Teacher-Scholar: The Traditional Wisdom of Charles De Koninck," *The American Benedictine Review* (1965): 586–97; Henri-Paul Cunningham, *Coup d'oeil sur l'histoire de la Faculté de philosophie* (Quebec: Université Laval, 1985) (hereafter Cunningham) and "La culture d'expression française en Amérique et la philosophie," in *Urgence de la philosophie,* ed. T. De Koninck and L. Morin (Quebec: Les Presses de l'Université Laval, 1986), 605–28; and Leslie Armour, "Charles De Koninck, the Common Good, and the Human Environment," *Laval théologique et philosophique* (hereafter *LTP*) 43, no. 1 (February 1987): 67–80.

7. Letter to James Belleperche, 27 November 1933.

8. For a well-documented history of this Faculté de philosophie, see Cunningham, and further, "La culture d'expression française en Amérique et la philosophie."

9. The interval between the academic years 1944/45 and 1948/49 is missing from it. The Graduate School *Annuaire* is not much more helpful, for it becomes sporadic in 1947 and fails from then on to list special courses and seminars in different disciplines.

10. The Rasetti Lectures were created in his honour in 1988. Dr. Larkin Kerwin, then president of the National Research Council, delivered the first of these, in which he eloquently describes Rasetti's work. For the text of that remarkable speech, see "Les contributions de la science à la philosophie au 20e siècle," *Philosophiques* 16, no. 1 (Spring 1989): 149–61. Larkin Kerwin there recalls exchanges between Franco Rasetti and "le grand Charles De Koninck" in the following terms: "Rasetti et De Koninck figuraient alors ensemble lors de colloques et de tables rondes, nous émerveillant non seulement par leur érudition et par leur sagesse, mais aussi par les panoramas intellectuels qu'ils nous déployaient—même si c'était avec des points de vue souvent fort dissemblables" (149–50).

11. This position is excellently outlined by McInerny, 494–506.

12. McInerny, 491. Speaking of the French Canadian educational milieu, Gérard Pelletier wrote: "M. De Koninck y a exercé une influence très importante, non seulement auprès de ses confrères qui pensaient comme lui mais également auprès de ceux qui se posaient en adversaires. Ces derniers eux-mêmes reconnaîtront, je crois, que la seule présence de Charles De Koninck a fortement contribué à élever le niveau des études philosophiques dans notre milieu. L'homme avait de la carrure, une étonnante érudition, une rare capacité de travail et le don plus rare encore de captiver un auditoire étudiant par ses exposés, même les plus abstraits" (*La Presse*, Montreal, 16 February 1965).

13. Emmanuel Trépanier summed it up well: "S'il est vrai qu'il n'aimait guère être qualifié de 'thomiste', c'est qu'il abhorrait tout ce qui suggère l'idée de 'système philosophique' avec sa construction factice et l'étroitesse de ses perspectives" ("In Memoriam Charles De Koninck," *LTP* 21, no. 1 [1965]: 11).

14. See Leslie Armour, "The Social and Philosophical Origins of Rational Religion in Quebec and English Canada," in *Friendship and Dialogue between Ontario and Quebec*, ed. H.-P. Cunningham and F.T. Kingston (Windsor: Canterbury College, 1985), 153.

15. Monsignor Maurice Dionne actually published one paper, "La grâce de Marie est d'ordre hypostatique" (*LTP* 10, no. 2 [1954]: 141–45), to which may be added the one he co-authored with Charles in January–February 1965 (see further below); and parts of Jasmin Boulay's doctoral thesis on the moral virtues can be read in *LTP* 16, no. 1 (1960): 20–52; no. 2: 265–77. Though they both survived Charles several years (he died in 1965, Father Boulay in 1974, Monsignor Dionne in 1980), their health had by then begun declining. A few students of that late period, among others Yvan Pelletier and Louis Brunet, have produced transcripts, revised by them for publication, of some of the last courses Dionne gave, thus rendering a signal service to those who will try to reconstruct his teaching. But absent in these transcripts are the enthusiasm, intellectual stamina, and shining wit of the 1940s, 1950s, and early 1960s; one could hardly recapture the high spirits of those earlier years from them. Gérard Dion undertook a similar task for notes from Father Boulay's classes.

16. Quoted from the 1961 commencement address, Mount St. Vincent College, Halifax, Nova Scotia: "Teaching as a Function of Divine Government." Cf. also John Oesterle, "The Nobility of Teaching," in *Mélanges*, 295–300.

17. Thomas R. Heath, O.P., "Homily for Charles De Koninck," Sunday, February 14, 1965, delivered at Saint Mary's College, Notre Dame, Indiana. Charles' main tie to that college was his deep personal friendship to Sister Madeleva, then president of the college and a justly famed poet. He often quoted H. L. Mencken saying that the best contemporary poet was "a little nun from Indiana."

18. The interested reader will find appended to the above-mentioned bibliography by Armand Gagné a very useful list of forty-seven such candidates who completed their doctoral work at Laval under his direction, with the titles of their dissertations (*Mélanges,* 21–22). The number of Americans among them appears to be over thirty.

19. See the "Semaine religieuse de Québec," 3 June 1943; reprinted as the first chapter entitled "Contre l'antisémitisme," of *Tout homme est mon prochain* (Quebec: Les Presses de l'Université Laval, 1964), 13–15.

20. For a repertoire of such ineptitudes, together with an intelligent refutation of them, see Roch-M. Boulanger, "Culture et idéologie," Thèse de maîtrise en philosophie, Université Laval, Quebec, 1985. Cf. also Cunningham, 26–29.

21. Lockquell, "In Memoriam Charles De Koninck."

22. Cf., for example, *LTP* 6, no. 2 (1950); vol. 8, no. 1 (1952); vol. 12, no. 1 (1956). Those delays explain certain discrepancies of dates, as when a reprint appears before the original!

23. Reprinted under the title "Du bien qui divise l'être," in *LTP* 10, no. 1 (1954): 99–103. Cf. "La nature de l'homme et son être historique," in *Actas del Primer Congreso Nacional de Filosofia, Mendoza 1949,* II (Mendoza: Universidad Nacional de Cuyo, [1950]), 1045–49. "The Nature of Man and His Historical Being" (*LTP* 5, no. 2 [1949]: 271–77) is actually an expanded version of the French original; it "has been called by a leading Kierkegaardian one of the best things written on the subject" (McInerny, 514). See also the posthumously published "Tout contingent opposé au nécessaire implique un rapport au bien" (*LTP* 24, no. 2 [1968]: 201–14), which spells out distinctions that often came up in his lectures and explicates a disagreement with Maritain over contingency (cf. "Un paradoxe du devenir par contradiction," *LTP* 12, no. 1 [1956]: 17, note 2 *in fine*).

24. It was reprinted in *LTP* 3, no. 1 (1947): 9–65. As already explained, the discrepancy in the dating (the original publication being 1948!) is due to problems the journal experienced in its first years.

25. Letter to the author, 5 May 1958.

26. Leslie Armour and Elizabeth Trott, *The Faces of Reason: An Essay on Philosophy and Culture in English Canada 1850–1950* (Waterloo, Ontario: Wilfrid Laurier University Press, 1981), 512.

27. Letter to the author, 15 June 1957.

28. "D'aucuns le considéraient comme un incorrigible traditionaliste, voire comme un intégriste. Ils durent déchanter, voici deux ans, à la suite de ses interventions retentissantes, d'abord sur l'importance d'accorder des écoles neutres aux parents qui en réclament, ensuite sur certaines façons par trop simplistes de condamner certaines méthodes de limitation des naissances" (Gérard Pelletier, *La Presse,* Montreal, 16 February 1965).

29. Cf. *Tout homme est mon prochain,* 43–79 and *passim.* The book's dedication reads: "A mon frère dans le Christ, le professeur David Carlton Williams, de l'Université de Toronto." Carl Williams was a psychologist and a Protestant; it was his little daughter who asked the question quoted in the preface to *The Hollow Universe.*

30. Lorenzo Paré, in *L'Action,* 16 February 1965. The context is worth quoting too: "D'ordinaire le public en général connaît peu les philosophes. La passion qui animait Charles De Koninck et le rêve toujours lancinant de passer de la pensée à l'action ont rapproché cet universitaire des auditoires populaires. Et même si le contact avec le public, dans le feu de la controverse, perdait parfois les sérénités académiques, jamais De Koninck n'en manifestait la moindre rancune. Bien plus, il répondait à ses contradicteurs par une recrudescence d'amitié à leur égard. C'est à l'intention de ce public, qui déborde les cadres de l'université, que Charles De Koninck a publié cet admirable petit livre qui porte en titre: '*Tout homme est mon prochain*'. C'est cette maxime qui résume le mieux, aujourd'hui, la vie et l'oeuvre de ce professeur prestigieux. . . ."

31. Respectively in *Perspectives sociales* 19, no. 4 (July–August 1964): 74–94, and vol. 20, no. 1 (January–February 1965): 10–16.

32. Gérard Dion paid this witness afterward: "Quand il s'adonnait à l'étude d'une question, il le faisait avec un enthousiasme et un don total. C'est en s'exprimant verbalement qu'il réussissait le mieux à clarifier et à préciser sa pensée. Essentiellement communicatif, lorsqu'il avait trouvé quelque chose de neuf, il lui fallait immédiatement en faire part, quelle que soit l'heure du jour ou de la nuit. Ardent polémiste, il ne se dérobait pas devant un contradicteur et jamais il ne s'abaissait à faire des personnalités. Il professait toujours un grand respect pour son interlocuteur. Avec simplicité et modestie, il accueillait les observations qu'on pouvait lui faire. Il ne craignait pas de se corriger. A sa façon, il était un peu perfectionniste. Pour lui, un texte n'était jamais complètement achevé. S'il acceptait de le publier, c'est qu'il croyait pouvoir être utile à l'avancement de la science ou servir une cause qu'il avait à cœur" (*Perspectives sociales* 20, no. 1 [January–February 1965]: 3).

33. "J'avais, la veille, tendu un filet, et la marée avait été copieuse. Or, à ma grande surprise, je trouvai mon savant commentateur d'Aristote et de saint Thomas, en petite tenue, sur la grève, et tout simplement en train d'éventrer quelques douzaines de harengs pour son petit déjeuner. Il fallait le voir, notre bon Flamand, en appétit, plongé dans la tripaille et joyeux comme un enfant. Ce spectacle fit tomber tout à coup toutes les préventions que j'avais contre la philosophie . . ." (Savard, "A la mémoire," 144). "Je le vois, encore, torse bombé, fusil à l'épaule et riant un peu de lui-même, partir pour la chasse aux canards. Oh! une chasse bien inoffensive où il ne tuait jamais rien, content de tirer comme cela, en l'air, entre deux gibiers . . ." (145).

34. In his own acceptance speech to the Royal Society, which is about Charles De Koninck, A.-M. Parent sees him as exemplifying magnanimity and humility together; cf. *Société Royale du Canada,* Section française, Année académique 1965–66, pp. 23–27. The same observation is made by Clément Lockquell in his "In Memoriam Charles De Koninck."

35. The friend's name was Louis Dugal, a former student become judge. In Félix-Antoine Savard's words, "Charles De Koninck aimait les êtres tels qu'ils sont," or Emile Bégin's, "Il avait cette simplicité d'enfance dont parle l'Evangile qui faisait disparaître entre son interlocuteur et lui toutes les distances."

36. *The Tablet*, London, 27 February 1965.

37. Heath, "Homily for Charles De Koninck."

38. Ibid.

The Philosophy of Sir Arthur Eddington

Thesis presented to the
Cardinal Mercier Institute of Louvain
for the obtention of
the doctorate in philosophy

Charles De Koninck

1934

PART ONE

Some Theses in the Philosophy of Science

Introduction

Sir Arthur Eddington was born in Kendal, England, on 28 December 1882. His father was the principal of the Quaker School at Stramongate, the school in which John Dalton had been sub-master. Eddington himself is a fervent Quaker and, as we shall see, his religion has had a profound influence on his philosophy. He received his higher education in Manchester first, at Owen College, and then at Trinity College, Cambridge. It was there that he was the "senior wrangler" in 1904, a title given the student who excels in mathematics and literature equally. His writings have an exceptional literary value. His knowledge of classical and modern literature is astonishing. In 1907 he was given the Smith prize from his college and in the following year was elected a Fellow of that celebrated institution.

His first scientific writings were published while he was assistant to the head of the Greenwich Observatory (1906–1913). To that point he seemed destined to have a career as a professional astronomer. But in 1913 he was named Professor of Astronomy in the Plumian Chair at the University of Cambridge, a chair that he still occupies today.

In 1914, he was put in charge of the Cambridge Observatory and in that same year was named a Fellow of the Royal Society. He is a member of many scientific societies, in England and abroad. He has been awarded prizes and medals everywhere, too many to enumerate here. In 1930, he was knighted and acquired the title Sir.[1]

In 1920 another Eddington showed himself with the publication of a work which marked an epoch in the philosophy of science: *Space, Time, and Gravitation.* This work demarked for the first time the domains of science and of philosophy in what concerns the theory of relativity. With this work he became the leader of philosophers of science. And he inspired confidence, because he was himself one of the most celebrated representatives of modern science. With him, there could be no question of preconceived ideas.

It has been said that the work is merely one of popularization. It is much more than that. It is first of all a philosophical contribution to the problem of modern science. His contributions have not been merely negative, as has been the case with many other modern scientists, Einstein included, who are content to chase philosophers from their domain—very rightly, moreover. In the work, *The Analysis of Matter,* Lord Bertrand Russell writes: "(Eddington), better than Einstein or Weyl, has the theory (of relativity) in the form best adapted to the needs of philosophers. . . . In philosophy, I have been guided almost exclusively by Eddington."[2]

The Nature of the Physical World, the Gifford Lectures of 1927, were an even more important revelation than the preceding work. The demands of these lectures in Edinburgh obliged him to deal with transcendental problems, something he did with extraordinary skill. This work assured him of a place among the most distinguished contemporary philosophers. He has been sharply criticized but today everyone must take him into account.

For us, Eddington has a double interest. First, he has carefully delimited the philosophical problem of relativity and quantum indetermination. But he has also given us a rather complete metaphysical system. He calls himself an idealist, an interesting point, because he says that he was carried toward idealism by his scientific work.[3]

The problem of the relation between scientific knowledge (in the restricted sense) and metaphysical knowledge interests us profoundly, especially because this problem is presented in a rather embroiled way by our own philosophers. Perhaps Eddington, who knows the sciences in depth, and who is no less a philosopher, offers us a chance to make the relation precise.

SECTION ONE

Epistemology and Metaphysics

Let us review the chief original contributions of Eddington to science in the experimental domain as well as in the domain of theory. This will enable us better to situate his personality. For it must be acknowledged that Eddington is above all a physicist who does philosophy only on the side—"a little," in his estimation! His competence in the scientific domain make his extra-scientific speculations all the more interesting in that he is capable of envisaging these problems from within physics. His assertion that we must go beyond physics is therefore all the more grounded. We cannot overlook this point. He is, very exceptionally, a great physicist and a great philosopher. These two qualities are inseparably united in his very personality, and we would distort it if we neglected either the one or the other.

I. The Double Stellar Current [*Le double courant stellaire*]

It was in 1906 that he attracted the attention of the astronomical world on the occasion of his first presentation to the Royal Society, entitled "The Systematic Motions of the Stars."[4] In this study he takes up a hypothesis advanced by the celebrated Dutch astronomer Kapteyn in 1904, an hypothesis which held that the movements of the ensemble of stars is not fortuitous, as the current opinion would have it, but that there are two favored movements. Until then, this hypothesis had had no success. Here Eddington already displays "the feeling of being on the right path before any proof," of which he often speaks.[5] He allows himself to be first guided by the aesthetic appearance of a theory.

This is how this problem should be situated. Since the time of Herschel the hypothesis has been suggested that the galactic system has the form of an extra-galactic nebula. This hypothesis extends only to the static form of the system. The known movements were considered to be proper to each star taken individually, whereas the movements of the whole were fortuitous. It was then that Kapteyn showed that the stars seemed to follow two opposed directions in the galactic plan: the movement of stars in the neighborhood of the sun would follow two opposed courses: there are two systems, one in a movement opposed to the other.

Eddington wanted to verify this hypothesis by an independent investigation. The rotary movement of the nebula was known. The demonstration of this hypothesis would show that the galactic system is itself a dynamic system, just like the extra-galactic nebula. This demonstration would provide a point of reference for new studies of the origin of this system and of its situation in the whole universe.

His investigation took from eight to nine years. In 1914, we find these results synthesized in a volume titled *Stellar Movements and the Structure of the Universe.* The conclusion was affirmative. It was based first of all on a minute analysis of the Catalogue of Professor Boss which gave the proper movements of about six thousand stars. Applying the statistical method, Eddington showed that it is necessary to divide them into two systems. He found a second confirmation of the hypothesis of Kapteyn in the spectroscopic speed of stars.

By this quantitative demonstration of the Hollendale hypothesis, the name of Eddington would remain associated with this branch of sidereal astronomy. This work taken in its entirety marked, according to the expression of de Sitter, an advance in the history of astronomy.[6]

II. The Internal Constitution of Stars

The first attempt to classify stars according to their spectra was made by the Italian Jesuit Secchi (1818–1878). He divided the life of a star into four stages which marked a greater and greater decrease of temperature. Then Lane (in 1878) showed that when a gaseous body contracts in losing heat, its temperature increases. It was therefore equally possible that stars having a reddish [*rougentre*] spectrum, and thus belonging to a lower stage, increased in temperature while losing heat. Therefore they could be, contrary to the view of Secchi, in their youth. In 1913 H. N. Russell and E. Hertzsprung showed that it was necessary to place stars in two categories: giants and dwarfs. The first are of great size, but of weak density, whereas the second are shrunk, more dense, and losing temperature. Thus each star passes twice through the same degree of temperature.

Eddington's study, "On the Radiative Equilibrium of the Stars,"[7] gave a theoretical explanation of these observations. The investigations were conducted on the basis of the laws of a perfect gas. They were thus restricted to the study of giant stars, the dwarfs being thought to be too dense to obey these laws.

There are therefore in a star two opposed tendencies: the upper strata cooling by contracting, whereas the lower strata increase in pressure. But, observation shows us that the structure of stars is relatively constant: so two tendencies of equilibrium must be recognized.

The mass and superficial temperature of the sun are two known magnitudes. Eddington asked himself if there were not a way to explain this equilibrium by a theory based on the known laws of the internal structure of stars. Direct calculations made on known magnitudes lead to impossible results.

III. The Theory of Relativity Generalized

Even before taking up the problem of stellar equilibrium, Eddington had been much interested in the theory of relativity. Perhaps it was because of this that he advanced his theory of the pressure of radiation with such confidence.

Already in February 1915, therefore before he knew the developments achieved by Einstein, he had written,

> It is scarcely too much to say that the nature of gravitation remains as much a mystery to-day as when the law was first formulated by Sir Isaac Newton. In the meantime, theories of matter, of aether, and of electricity have arisen, have held their vogue, and have been superseded by others; but gravitation stands apart from these changing views. No experiments have as yet shown any relation between it and the other phenomena of nature; the simple law, unconditional and universal, has been all-sufficient hitherto. We have grown accustomed to regarding gravitation as something outside the scope of ordinary physical theories. If a new model of the atom is put forward, we ask if it accounts for

> the Zeeman effect, for chemical affinity, for the dispersion of light, and a host of incidental phenomena; but it would be considered unfair to suggest that it ought to account for the one fundamental and universal property of matter—gravitation.[8]

Then, after rejecting explanations given up to that time, he suggested: "Does gravitation conform to the Principle of Relativity?"

There is an interesting remark in this same article. The possibility of finding an experimental phenomenon in favor of an application of this principle to gravity catches his attention. "It would be extremely difficult to detect this deflection [of light] even during a total eclipse. . . . But a positive result would mean that gravitation has been pulled down from its pedestal, and ceases to stand aloof from the other interrelated forces of nature."[9]

It was Eddington himself who, on 1 February 1918, drew the attention of the members of the Royal Society to the possibility of exploiting the total eclipse of 29 May 1919. In articles and conferences he spread the idea. And all this during the war, for which, being a Quaker, he had a supreme disdain. It was under his direction that the two expeditions were made, one to Sobral, and the other to the Ile de Prince. The result was positive. This was an experimental proof in favor of the theory of Einstein. The first communication of these results was made to the Royal Society in the *Philosophical Transactions of the Royal Society of London* (220, series A [1920]: 291–333).

It was from the enthusiasm of this success that was born the work *Space, Time, and Gravitation.* He no longer hesitated. The whole basis of physics must be profoundly rethought. The philosophical conceptions of physicists are altered by these demands. There remain only philosophical prejudices and Eddington gave himself the task of reversing them.

Up until now, his part in the development of the theory of relativity was purely experimental. It was Eddington, and Eddington alone, who presented Einstein to the English public. But he also played a role in the theoretical development itself. This contribution appeared in 1921 under the title "A Generalization of Weyl's Theory of the Electro-magnetic and Gravitational Fields,"[10] and was incorporated into the synthesis, *Mathematical Theory of Relativity.*[11] For Einstein, mass and the quantity of motion were equal to certain characteristics of the geometry of space-time. But Eddington had shown that mass and quantity of motion are not the names under which we recognize these geometrical characteristics in physical experiments. Einstein invoked a law of nature which is cause of this equality, whereas Eddington reduces this putative law to a tautology. It is here that he showed his skill in scientific methodology and made a rigorous application of this theory of physical theory, which always contains two aspects.[12] The mathematical theory of relativity is above all an analysis which operates on certain symbols. When we apply this theory to the physical world, we should find the connection by the identification of properly physical entities with the entities of the mathematical analysis. These constitute there two parallel systems which ought to be identified at each point. But there must be also some identities which are fundamental and from which one can deduce the others. Without that, we will have no point of reference. It is on the basis of the identity of the mass and of the quantity of motion that one can identify the other parallel entities.

There are then three domains in which he excelled. It was Eddington who was among the first to be captivated by the theory of quanta, and who made the first applications of it in the domain of astrophysics. It was Eddington who discovered Abbé Lemaitre, who moreover had been one of his students. To trace a precise and adequate portrait of Eddington the physicist is quite outside my competence, but these few remarks perhaps suffice to convince us that we have to do with a flexible spirit, youthful, who has an exceptional flair for the truth, and to introduce the physicist whose philosophy we will study.

SECTION TWO

The Philosophy of Exact Science

In the second and third sections we propose to give as objective as possible an exposition of the doctrine contained in the different philosophical works of our author. Is this possible? Let us from the outset introduce necessary reservations. We have, first of all, our own philosophy, and I think it is difficult to abstract from it. When a non-scholastic author speaks of "reality," "actuality," and of "substance," and so on, and does not give us a sufficiently precise definition of these terms, we are inclined to assimilate the meaning of these expressions to our own. And in the case of Eddington who does not pretend to give us a well-defined and achieved system, the danger is considerable. It is indeed possible that here and there I force the matter. Sometimes he comes remarkably close to a metaphysics akin to ours and then goes in a direction in which he would refuse to follow us. The doctrine treated here was dispersed almost everywhere in a sketchy manner. The very wish to systematize ideas not always firmly delineated runs serious risks, and we will not be able to systematize them without tightening them. All the same, we cannot simply juxtapose his ideas and make a dictionary. But we will refrain from tightening them too much. By seeking to establish an explicit continuity among these elements, we are doing something that Eddington has not done for us. One further remark. We cannot study all the points that Eddington calls "philosophical." The meaning of this term is very ambiguous among the English, as we shall soon see. Even problems to which scholastics have given a philosophical value will not occupy us. Such as the problem of the end of the universe based on the second fundamental law of thermodynamics.[13] This physical law, whatever its real value, cannot be made into a philosophical truth. The philosopher can have his own reasons for predicting the end of the universe, but these will never be assimilable by the physicist. A theory can be scientifically true, but that does not give it a value, or rather a meaning, that is philosophical.

The restriction that we impose on ourselves is not arbitrary. We find its basis in distinctions made by Eddington himself. Thus, the distinction he makes between "the point of view" of relativity and the "principle" of relativity. The first is clearly philosophical. But Eddington does not explicitly characterize it as such. And the same is true for the problem of indeterminism.

Chapter I. The Sources

Space, Time, and Gravitation is the first philosophical work of Eddington. He wrote it as a result of the famous expedition to Sobral and to the Isle of Prince that he himself organized. Einstein's theories had been received with a great deal of skepticism by English physicists and philosophers. Eddington perceived that the prejudices were philosophical and not of the scientific order. And it seems to us that he succeeded wonderfully in dissipating them.

The Nature of the Physical World is the series of Gifford Lectures that he delivered in Edinburgh in 1927. Their subject was dictated by the foundation. It is thanks to these requirements that we have a view of the whole on his philosophy. The conferences that he gave before these appeared contain nothing that is not assimilated in them.

Science and the Unseen World is a lecture as well, one he gave to a religious society, the Society of Friends, better known as the Quakers. They contain important precisions on the problem of God and on the religious problem generally.

Since then we have from him two important philosophical articles. The first, "Physics and Philosophy," appeared in *Philosophy.* This was a lecture given before the British Philosophical Association. The second appeared in the *Collection des Actualités Scientifiques et Industrielles.* Both are above all precisions on the problem of indeterminism. Two other works, less philosophical, but which contain many important precisions, have been used: above all, *Mathematical Theory of Relativity* (1923), an elaboration of the appendix to the French translation of *Space, Time, and Gravitation,* which was exclusively mathematical;[14] second, the little book, *The Expanding Universe* (1933), which contains interesting remarks on physical theory.

I do not think that one can find any evolution in Eddington's ideas. The extensions and clarifications of the more recent contributions are all in direct continuity with the first. I will not hesitate, accordingly, to assemble texts from different works without regard to their dates.

As for the historical and ideological sources of Eddington's philosophy itself, it seems to me that it would be difficult to trace them. He certainly knows Hegel and Berkeley.[15] And yet his idealism (we will soon see how it is with his idealism) has nothing specifically in common with these two philosophers. He even has a rather naive conception of the subjectivism of German idealist philosophers. He also knows Bergson. We find in him distinctions to be found in Bergson as well, such as the distinction between realism and idealism.[16] His terminology and the way he poses transcendental problems recalls the English philosopher Bradley and his disciple Bosanquet. But the indications given will not suffice to establish a true dependence. Moreover, the conclusions differ radically.

The one source we can determine with certitude is his religion. Eddington is above all a religious man, and of the species Quaker. We have a special chapter on this subject in which we will try to determine to what degree it exercised an influence on his philosophy. His colleague, Sir James Jeans, defends ideas very analogous to those of Eddington, but much less precisely. In any case, the philosophical works of Jeans are later than those of Eddington.[17]

Chapter II

Article 1. The Notion of Philosophy

Before raising the special problem of his philosophy of science, it will be interesting to know what Eddington himself means by "philosophy." Unhappily, he does not give us any sufficient indication. Occasionally, he mentions some of its properties or functions.

There is first of all the text in *Space, Time, and Gravitation* which attributes a proper point of departure to philosophy, "physical theory starts with the simplest constituents, philosophical theory with the most familiar constituents" (166 [205]). The distinction is clear enough. But one must read it in its context. It is a question notably of a distinction introduced when speaking of the materialist philosophy of Mach. But the thesis envisaged has absolutely nothing to do with a philosophical problem. At bottom, it is a question of things as being ultimately material in a quite physical sense. But, Eddington says, this theory is in the domain of physics, since it deals with the simplest elements. Philosophy should begin from the familiar world. "Perhaps they will reach the same result, but their methods are often incompatible." What exactly is this philosophical method? He doesn't say. What is its aim? In part it coincides with that of physics. Perhaps they will obtain the same result. If not, what then is the value of the philosophical theory? The sense of this distinction is thus not as clear as it seems when one isolates it from its context. But here is another text which suggests the direction we could go in search of a solution.

> I think it will be agreed that there is a domain of investigation where physics and philosophy overlap. There are branches of philosophy which do not approach the subject-matter of physics, and a great part of the work of practical and theoretical physicists is not aimed at extending our knowledge of the fundamental nature of things; but questions which concern the general interpretation of the physical universe and the significance of physical law are claimed by both parties. I suppose that ideally the physicist should be allowed to elucidate his own universe up to a point, and then hand it over to the philosopher to ascertain its exact status in relation to a wider outlook. But in practice we have not sufficient confidence in one another, and we both make raids over the border to suggest all sorts of ways in which the other fellow may be deceiving himself and us. The fact is that in approaching the more fundamental problems of science the physicist finds it necessary to adopt a more philosophical outlook than is habitual to him; and if the philosopher wishes to handle results ascertained scientifically he must enter to some extent into the scientific outlook.[18]

The first point that interests us in this text is the affirmation that there are domains absolutely proper to philosophy. On the basis of latter developments in *The Nature of the Physical World*, we can even affirm that these domains are absolutely irreducible. In this his view is clearly distinct from that of Bertrand Russell.

The latter writes,

> as soon as definite knowledge concerning any subject becomes possible, that subject ceased to be called philosophy, and becomes a separate science. Every study of the heavens, which today belongs to astronomy, was once included in philosophy; the great work of Newton was called 'the mathematical principles of natural philosophy.' Thus, the study of human intelligence which was until recently a branch of philosophy has now been separated from philosophy and become the science of psychology . . . : questions to which we are already capable of giving a definite answer are included in the sciences, whereas those to which we are still not able to give a definite answer constitute the residue called philosophy. [*The Problems of Philosophy* (Home University Library, 1932), 240]

In Russell's opinion, there is no philosophical problem on which we have absolute certitude. Without any doubt, Eddington does not hold this opinion. But there is this domain in which science and philosophy meet. Moreover, science itself leads to philosophical conclusions. Eddington clearly asserts that his works treat the philosophical consequences of science. And in this sense, there are some philosophical problems intimately linked to science.

Without doubt, Eddington has no intention of giving us a theory of philosophy. He probably accepts the current view of the English according to which the philosophy of nature comprises the ensemble of the sciences of nature, and most especially physics.[19] Here is how it is described by Pringle-Pattison in his article "Philosophy and Philosophical Studies" in the *Encyclopedia Brittanica:*

> Philosophy pretends to be the science of everything . . . the synthesis of the parts comprises something more than the detailed knowledge of the separated parts attained by the man of science. It is in the final synthesis that philosophy occurs; it must show that the subject that we treat in detail is truly an ensemble, composed of articulated members. Evidently, he senses that the relation between philosophy and the sciences will be, up to a point, a relation of reciprocal influence. Of the sciences it can be said that they provide philosophy with its matter, but the philosophical critique reacts on the matter furnished and transforms it.

One can liken this view to that of A. E. Taylor and J. A. Thomson: "one of the aims of science is to distinguish 'that which separates' from that which 'is,' and to do this generally and not in particular is the principal task of metaphysics."[20]

And the mathematician Jeans writes: "before philosophers are allowed to seek, they should first of all ask of science to tell us what it knows of established facts and provisory hypotheses, and only then can the discussion legitimately enter the domains of philosophy."[21] Eddington will make precise that the function of philosophy is to link the scientific world with the familiar world, to identify them.[22] So much so that it certainly possesses an element that it does not borrow from science.

All these views are rather vague and confused, but there is something true in each expression. Bertrand Russell is clearly right when he says that the problems which belonged to philosophy have been passed on to the particular sciences. But that is a historical remark. We will say that, in these evolutions, philosophy is rid of false philosophical problems. There can be no doubt that science has philosophical consequences. That is because it makes precise extrinsically the content of our philosophical concepts. Relativity has shown us that we do not know as much of space as we think in philosophy, and the same is true of the problem of indeterminism.

These considerations, at first sight superfluous, are very important, for when it becomes a question of understanding what Eddington means by idealism and materialism, we will see that these terms must not be assimilated to ours. The matter in question here is not that of our philosophy; it is a question of matter in its purely physical sense. We find these conceptions clearly defined in a little work of Millikan, *Time, Matter, and Values*,[23] "the materialism of the 18th and 19th centuries pretended that the world can be interpreted in terms of a definite number of unchangeable atoms . . . that one could explain the universe in terms of the movements of material particles of a certain species, etc." Then the theory of relativity and of quanta intervened. "As a result, dogmatic materialism in physics is dead . . . experimental physics has banished this philosophy from its house, root and branch."[24] And Millikan uses this thesis to defend religion. Unhappily, that won't work against a materialist metaphysics that one could defend whatever the physical structure of the matter. Thus, for modern physicists, as soon as one no longer holds the thesis of matter in the physical sense, one is no longer a materialist.

Eddington has certainly surpassed this rather naive conception. But, when he uses the term 'philosophy' in relation to these problems he makes it mean what it does for Millikan. Problems of reality as such, the principal problem of philosophy, is not a philosophical problem for Eddington. "In most subjects (perhaps not excluding philosophy) it seems sufficient to agree on the things that we shall call real, and afterwards try to discover what we mean by the word. And so it comes about that religion seems to be the one field of inquiry in which the question of reality and existence is treated as of serious and vital importance."[25] It matters little that he incorporates a specifically metaphysical problem into the domain of religion, provided that it is a problem to which he gives a solution that we could call metaphysical.

These few remarks were necessary for a correct understanding of what follows.

Article 2. The Problem of the Physical World

Eddington insists on the fact that the physical problem cannot pretend to pose and resolve all the problems of our experience. "The problem of the scientific world is part of a broader problem—the problem of all experience" (NPW 328 [325]).[26] The field in which all the problems are posed is called the "familiar world."[27] In this field we will meet the physical problem. And this is the way that particular problem is posed. On the one hand, the universe is given to us as an absolute, characterized by its "reality," by its "actuality,"[28] and as being independent of our contingent observation,[29] as an "in itself."[30] But, on the other hand, the infrastructure of this universe is not made explicit for us in this same experience.[31] And yet we know that "reality" and "structure" are inseparable. There must be absolute entities in the universe.[32] We seek a way of reuniting these two antipodes, we will seek everything that observation can furnish us. We will call the "physical world" the structure that will be uncovered for us in observation. The problem is thus posed in the familiar world, and the physical world will be an attempt at a solution.[33] But the problem of the structure of the universe is not easy to delimit. History shows us that neither the physicist nor the philosopher have succeeded in defining it.

Spontaneously enough, we begin with the idea that things are more or less the elements of our sensible experience without discrimination. More, we think that the whole of reality ought to be translatable in terms of sensible experience. Thus the atoms of the physicist at the time of the reign of Queen Victoria were small grains of dust, that is, grains of dust as we know them in our familiar experience, but much smaller. It is only their smallness that transcended our faculties of representation.[34] But in proportion as our knowledge of the universe increases, we will discover that our whole sensible experience in its totality cannot serve as the basis of work. The entities at which one arrives no longer have this sense translatable into terms of vulgar experience. Thus the world doubles before our regard into a familiar world and a scientific world that one no longer knows how to define in terms of the first. To the first we attribute such attributes as substantiality, solidity, permanence, it is in blossom, beautiful, etc.[35] But the second has become more and more a stranger to all that. Objects we call substantial disintegrate into unrepresentable electric charges, which, afloat in a mysterious void, agitate in a disordered way, and are at enormous distances from one another. The man of science speaks of electrons and quanta, but when he is asked to give us in concrete terms what all that means, he does not know how to answer. The very elements of the physical universe no longer have correspondents in the world of vulgar experience.

This investigation of the universe of observation has not only established a disjunction between the familiar and scientific worlds, it has shown us that the characteristics of the familiar world are subjective and illusory.[36] Thus two men who look at the same object see a different color.[37] The world being given to us independently of an observer, we attribute the color to the observer as being a projection of his mind.[38] Accordingly, we retain only what is the same for both—the length of the wave.

By "concrete" we usually mean to say something tangible. But the physical elements are absolutely untranslatable in terms of tangibility. When one asks the man in the street what he means by "real" he very likely replies "That which is concrete," of which the most critical character is its tangibility. Then, if whatever we call "concrete" is "real," we will be inclined to abandon reality itself as an illusion. And we will ask ourselves if science does not end by replacing the familiar world in its totality. Evidently not. The physicist cannot deny the other elements of our experience which cannot be resolved by the physicist. His very point of departure is scientifically intransposable. He does not explain "that which is," his investigation concerns only the structure of that which is observable.[39] Therefore it is necessary to delimit the field in which objective observation is possible; the properly physical field of investigation. It is a matter of recapitulating by what procedure we have found it, what method we ought to follow so that this world might have a value. No physicist can abstract from the value of his science and his scientific world. But here we face a transphysical problem, that of "values."[40] Eddington resolved the problem by making a minute analysis of the point of departure, and of the object formally envisaged by the physicist. The determination of the object of physics allows him to resolve the problem of the relation of this particular science to other problems posed by our more general experience.

Let us follow him in this delimitation.

Chapter III. Determination of the Object of Exact Science

First of all let us make precise what Eddington means by exact science. Generally, he identifies the domain of physics and the domain of exact science (NPW, 250 [253]). "[T]here is general agreement that physical science approaches closer to a complete system of exact science that all the other sciences take as an ideal" (SUW, 77).

1. The Material Point of Departure

We here introduce a scholastic precision that cannot be found explicitly in Eddington: he makes no mention of the material point of departure of physics. And it is that neglect perhaps which has been responsible for many misunderstandings by his readers. Still, with a little good will, we can find all the elements.

In order to situate the problem clearly, permit me to quote a scholastic author who has defined the point of departure of the physicist precisely.[41] Next, having found the corresponding elements in Eddington, we will try to deduce from them the definition as a conclusion. If I coordinated the elements without mentioning the synthesis that guides me, I could perhaps be accused of going beyond Eddington's intent. I want simply to show that the point of departure defined by Professor Renoirte *seems* to be implied in Eddington's theory.

Quite recently, Renoirte wrote: "To attain truly objective physical knowledge of the world, all I strictly have need of is knowledge of a differentiated spatio-temporal exteriority, whatever be its quality, which is variable and whose differences assure me that I am confronted with an absolutely homogeneous infinite which could teach me nothing."[42] I think this "exteriority" should be taken in the sense of "extraneity," a scholastic expression. This *extraneitas* is given like time and space as the extended that we define by reference to immediate experience. Neither time nor space can be defined, properly.[43] This datum is anterior to the space-time of physics which will give a physical definition of their magnitude. This presupposed datum is not mentioned by Eddington. He seems to refuse to speak of time and space before they have been measured, for him from the outset there are physical magnitudes. "Extension which is not relative to something in the surroundings has no meaning" (NPW, 144 [153]). This expression is clearly ambiguous. Space *is*, for Eddington, the *definite* relation among the given points. But the character of the perceived exteriority is anterior to the definition of the relation physically established in this exteriority. The physicist does not fabricate space, by measurements he fabricates physical magnitudes in that exteriority.

Evidently when he discusses with philosophers the thorny problem of space he will not perhaps be speaking of the same thing. The philosopher must confine himself to the "exteriority," which is already in space, or in time, in order to search for the metaphysical conditions, whereas the physicist should confine himself to that "exteriority" as physically measurable in order to define its physical magnitude. Spatio-temporal exteriority is thus the point of departure, the material object of the two sciences.

Is this merely a question of words? In any case, this ambiguity lends itself to many confusions in the discussion. Eddington, before rejecting prephysical space, should have asked himself if the word 'space' could not have meant something else, and to concede to philosophers, "Yes, you know what space is, as we all do, but you will know nothing of spatial magnitudes and their geometric structure without becoming a physicist." These are not defined in the perception of exteriority.

This is not meant as a criticism of Eddington's ideas (we will reserve that for the end of our study), we make this criticism in order to disengage his ideas. He tells us explicitly that the physicist starts with simple and indefinable data: "The first simple concepts are necessarily indefinable, and their nature is beyond human understanding." But this very clear text is followed immediately by this: "Time and space—the familiar terms—are derived concepts to be introduced much later in our theory."[44] The philosopher has given a name to these first simple concepts, he calls them space and time.

It must also be said that Eddington makes an important distinction between time as an external datum and time as immediately perceived in the consciousness we have of our existence as a becoming. This becoming we attribute to the external world as directly perceived by consciousness. But this is not properly physical time which is a measure-number furnished by a clock.[45] This time of consciousness is precisely the exteriority envisaged, and Eddington will take the trouble to show that it is in this time that the physician makes his temporal measures.[46] Physical time is known mediately, that is, by measurement which defines temporal physical relations.

Clearly Eddington has all these distinctions in his mind. He insists on the fact that we establish relations between *given points.* But he does not give them their conventional name, and that can lead to futile discussions. Reproaching the ancient physicist for being a metaphysician, he writes, "You keep some notion of a space which is superior to measurement," after having conceded, "I have no knowledge of space apart from my measures. . . ."[47] He has no consciousness of the physical structure of space before having measured it. No doubt he would not have gone so far had metaphysicians (I refer to historical personages) been a little more modest as to the content of their own concepts.

All this is therefore only a critique of vocabulary, which was necessary to disengage his ideas in precise and recognized terms.

2. *The Formal Object*

The qualitatively differentiated spatio-temporal exteriority can be considered by the philosopher,[48] the mathematician,[49] and the physicist. The physicist wants to know the real structure of this exteriority insofar as it is physically measurable. As to what is meant by physically measurable, one can only show it. It has an aspect that it is not directly intuited and the means for attaining this knowledge are given. The comparability of quantitatively and qualitatively differentiated data is the only exploitable datum. It is with these comparisons that one is going to reconstruct the world, discover its suspected, but for now physically indefinable structure.

We could first envisage discrete individual data. These are numbers. The numbering is an absolute operation.[50] This activity can be directly effected without intermediate conditions. It is only an accident that we have to use instruments.

He does not insist on this point. Number is an absolute magnitude, but we will see later that the meaning of this absolute is subject to some restrictions. One would have expected to see the notion of "magnitude" introduced with more circumspection. But he abruptly introduces without commentary continuous magnitude. This is a regrettable neglect, for later it will pose problems concerning the transcendental signification (inherent to the external world) of the continuous and discontinuous which are doubly obscure. It will be impossible for us to give his ideas on this point. But let us say that it, too, is an immediate datum, whatever the epistemological implications, and that we know sufficiently with what we have to do.

When Eddington speaks of distance, for example, he always means a definite distance: length, distance between two points—they are the same thing. (Ought we correct ourselves: a length is the *definite* distance between two points?) Length is the response to the question: How much distance is there between two given points?

In order to answer that question, we have to make a comparison. We execute this comparison by a certain practical activity called "a physical experience." This activity defines the magnitude of one given in function of another. Specifically, length will be the result of a comparison established between two given distances, of which one has been defined as standard. The magnitude in function of which we are going to define the other physically is a given continuous material object. The result of this operation is a *physical magnitude.*

There are two things to notice: (a) we come to define the property called magnitude by means of a certain given object, a standard, that *we take* as the sole means of definition; (b) length is the result of a comparison with this given material standard. The standard is not an ideal magnitude, such that if we made appeal to another thing, we would no longer speak of length as we have defined it. "Obviously the adopted standard of length cannot change length, whatever it is made of. If a metre is defined as the length of a certain bar, that bar can never be anything but a metre long; and if we assert that this bar changes length, it is clear that we must have changed our minds as to the definition of length" (STG, 4 [5–6]). At no moment can we abstract from the standard with which we have constructed physical magnitude. The property thus obtained is, so to say, "*a manufactured article*—manufactured by our operations" (MTR, 1). That goes for all other physical properties. They are not the data presupposed: they are results obtained by measurements made on what is given. The whole formal sense of the result resides in the manner in which it was obtained: its process of measurement is its definition. "A physical quantity is defined by the series of operations and calculations of which it is the result—We do not need to ask the physicist what conception he attaches to 'length'; we watch him measuring length, and frame our definition according to the operations he performs" (MTR, 3–4).

We choose arbitrarily a given magnitude as standard of measurement, but we do not fabricate arbitrarily. We are guided by objective conditions. We are confident that our measurements are grafted onto the "world-condition," that they refer to a condition or relation existing in the external world—a condition not fabricated by our operations. But our measurements define this condition only insofar as it is expressed in measurements (MTR, 2).

The operation called 'physical experiment' is accompanied by calculations expressing the number of times the standard is contained in the result (MTR, 1–2). The measure is thus a certain number. But what is the profound significance of this number? Its unit is the standard chosen. Its meaning is therefore purely relative, insofar as it depends on the magnitude of the standard chosen. No objective divisions (*coupures*) in the magnitude obtained respond to this number.

What we use to effect measurements is called an "instrument." A measurement is impossible without an instrument. But the meaning of "instrument" is ambiguous. In fact, we measure lengths without a conventional standard, we measure weights directly by muscular tension, and temperature by the sense of touch. To this Eddington responds: there is no essential difference between such measurings and those effected by means of strictly material instruments. "In either case our acquaintance with the external world comes to us through material channels; the observer's body can be regarded as part of his laboratory equipment, and, so far as we know, it obeys the same laws" (STG, 31 [40]). Except that strictly material instruments have the advantage of giving us magnitudes devoid of what our psychology might introduce.

They exceed our senses in precision and resistance. Everything they give is controllable. The elements due to a projection of mind, such as color, are uncontrollable, subjective, and absolutely useless in physics. We know their measurable homologues, and that suffices. Physics must remain objective, since we seek the structure of the external world as it is in itself.

"The essential point is that, although we seem to have very definite conceptions of objects in the external world, those conceptions do not enter into exact science and are not in any way confirmed by it. Before exact science can begin to handle the problem they must be replaced by quantities representing the results of physical measurement" (NPW, 253 [255]).

We must take account of this thesis which radically modifies our idea of physical knowledge. It is not as intimate as we might think at the outset. It is number-measure itself that is the formal object of physics. The condition of the world is known only insofar as it is translatable into number-measures. Henceforth we have to do only with reading the gradations of given instruments. Physical properties will be differentiated by the nature of the instrument. These instruments do not define the condition of the external world in an absolute fashion, such that they establish objective differentiated cuts (*coupures*), but only a way of defining this underlying condition.

But then, are physical magnitudes real magnitudes? "When defined in this way, there can be no question as to whether the operations give us the real physical. . . . Physical quantity is the measure-number of a world-condition in some code; we cannot assert that a code is right or wrong, or that a measure-number is real or unreal; what we require is that the code should be the accepted code, and the measure-number the number in current use" (MTR, 4). "Measure-numbers may be assigned according to any code, the only requirement being that the same measure-number always indicates the same world-condition and that different world-conditions receive different measure-numbers. Two or more physical quantities may thus be measure-numbers of the same world-condition, *but in different codes,* e.g. parallax and distance; mass and energy; stellar magnitude and luminosity" (MTR, 2).[51] Let us not exaggerate then the meaning of the differentiation of physical magnitude introduced by the qualitative difference of our instruments.

It remains to note that the immediate datum, underlying our measures, does enter into the formal object. Its magnitude is known only by our measurements. Provisorily, it is only the number attained that interests us.

We have nothing to do with unmeasured magnitude. But that remains always the ideal to be approached. It is a matter of making our instruments as precise as possible.

But Eddington does not insist much in an explicit way on this point concerning the always approximative character of our measurements. He does not pursue this idea to the bottom, but constantly presupposes it. This neglect will be a cause of misunderstandings.[52] But what is important is that the magnitudes proper to physics are always real despite their approximative character as to the condition of the universe. And that in two ways. First, they are really approximative of this condition, even though they do not express it with objective precision. But it is not this condition that we directly study in physics. The magnitudes we manipulate are manufactured magnitudes, and whatever their approximative value, they are really what we have made. Whether now the whole superstructure that we base on these measurements be a faithful transfer of the real structure of the condition of the universe is another question. If the physicist had to wait for perfect measurements, physics would be forever impossible.[53] The essential point of this whole thesis is therefore that the object manipulated by the physicist is a magnitude fabricated by a certain procedure of measurement and not its indefinable correspondent—and thus physically unknown—in the absolute universe. Eddington's whole philosophy of science is based on this precision concerning the object of physics. Specifically, that allows him to respond to objections against relativity. Moreover, it was in order to respond to these question that he has made it so precise.

3. *The Content of the Formal Object*

We have said that this definition allows him to respond to objections against relativity. Precisely because this definition implies the point of view of relativity, but such that this whole thesis is perfectly independent of a certain physical theory that one advances after having made properly physical observations. "Perhaps if it had been guided by philosophers, or a certain school of philosophers, physics would have been relativistic long before Einstein" (PP, 30).

Let us then come closer to this object to see how we can extract from it the point of view of relativity, a point of view that ought to be independent of every physical principle of relativity.

What information does this manufactured object give us with respect to its fundamental structure? "The physicist is not generally content to believe that the quantity he arrives at is something whose nature is inseparable from the kind of operations which led to it; he has an idea that if he could become a god contemplating the external world, he would see his manufactured physical quantity forming a distinct feature of the picture" (MTR, 1). The manufactured article is evidently something in the physical world. But how? It is here that the relativist separates himself from the classical physicist. (This is at bottom a philosophical problem that the physicist presupposes.)

The first thesis of the classical physicist to be looked at in relation to this question is that in nature there is an absolute correspondent to length. Eddington rejects this thesis by showing that such length has no sense. In fact, length is, by definition, what we obtain, what we manufacture by a certain procedure of measurement. Such a length would be a length known outside the process of measurement. But the whole signification of length is in this process. ". . . I cannot conceive of any 'length' in nature independent of a definition of the way of measuring length. And, if there is, we may disregard it in physics, because it is beyond the range of experiment" (STG, 8 [10]). Evidently, there must be a correspondent in nature, but what right do we have to call it length?

Length corresponding to a measure-number will be an absolute length. But what does that mean? "There is no such thing as absolute length; we can only express the length of one thing in terms of the length of something else" (NPW, 141 [151]). This standard, the other thing, is defined, and enters with all that it is into the magnitude obtained. Let there be a certain bar defined as "one meter." To say afterward this standard has changed its length, and that it has thus deviated from absolute length, shows that we have surreptitiously changed our idea of length. We are free to speak of an absolute length, if we define it as it ought to be. But it is not of that of which it is a question in physics (STG, 8 [10]).

Let us get closer to this idea of absolute length. What the physicist understands by that is that his measurements give him directly information on the structure of the universe considered in itself independently of his measurements, and that the magnitude obtained ought to have a universal value, however only approximative. And it is this thesis which has put the classical physicist in opposition to the new physical theory.

It is here that Eddington takes stock of the meaning of the Einsteinian criticism. To attribute to our physical magnitudes a directly universal value is to abstract illegitimately from the procedure of measurement, which has been effected in determinate physical circumstances, which enter into the definition. But these circumstances can differ. To measure an object with respect to which we are in motion and to measure an object in respect to which we are immobile is not the same thing. Thus one can measure the distance between two points on a scale whose speed is the same as the two points. These will then be in contact with two determinate divisions of the rule. The magnitude obtained is called "proper length" (STG, 11 [14] & NPW 141 ff. [151]). But to measure the distance between two points in relation to which we are in motion implies an element which was not considered for the object in relation to which we are immobile. We have to introduce the notion of simultaneity, and this in turn must be defined in such a way that it has a physical sense. The length obtained will then be other insofar as it has another definition (STG, 13 [17]). One should not be astonished accordingly if the results differ.

That is what is meant by the relativity of physical magnitudes: the physical circumstances all enter into the definition itself. One should also define the system in which the measurements have been effected.

Evidently, since the universe envelops all systems, the fundamental structure is independent of one or the other particular system. Do not then the magnitudes in question in physics only count for the circumstances in which they have been defined? Isn't all physics thereby necessarily relativist?

Yes, if we cannot find a magnitude which will be equal for no matter what observer[54] in no matter what circumstances.

This is the attitude Eddington calls "the standpoint of relativity" (STG, 28 [36]). This point of view is implied in the very definition of the object of physics. Our measures do not necessarily give us information on the absolute structure of the universe. We cannot confuse this point of view with the physical principle of relativity. That is the translation of an experimental fact that can be true or false.

This point of view in no way implies that physics is relativist by definition, in such a way that it would never tell us anything of the absolute structure of the universe. On the contrary, it allows us to give a definition of the absolute universe. The structure of the absolute universe is that which will be the same for no matter what observer whatever the circumstances in which he measures.

Therefore, if some day we find such a magnitude, the situation will be saved. The physicist has created this magnitude in the isotropy of light (STG, 14 ff. [18]).

But this already belongs to a domain proper to physics, and no longer concerns us in philosophy. We know that there is an absolute structure, we do not know if the physicist has in fact found the means of discovering it.

We think that Eddington has been the first to emphasize the distinction made between the point of view of relativity which is a logical consequence of the definition of physical magnitude, and the principle of relativity which is in the experimental domain, and which must be experimentally verified.

We could call this distinction a distinction between the philosophical point of view of relativity and the physical principle.

Habitually physicists put the problem into relation with ether, thus confounding the physical problem with the physical. Perhaps because philosophers, historical personages, have themselves substantialized their space in ether. Eddington's reasoning abstracts from all that. It is in no way dependent on a purely physical principle or theory. It prevails against the objections of philosophers.

Intimately linked to this last theory is that of the geometric structure of the universe: the classical physicist, quite like the philosopher, was convinced that this structure must necessarily be Euclidean. But this theory again goes beyond physical magnitudes.

It is in making an application of his definition of the object of physics that he refutes this conviction as a pure postulate. Here is how he attacks this thesis.

4. Physical Magnitude and Mathematical Magnitude

Since the measures in question are numbers, since the quantitative aspect or, rather, the metric aspect is the only one utilized in physics, one might ask what difference there is between a physical quantity and a mathematical quantity. The physicist and mathematician both speak of 'length,' 'speed,' 'potential,' etc. Eddington cites the famous text of Bertrand Russell. "One can define pure mathematics as a study that does not know of what it speaks or whether what it says is true." When a mathematician uses expressions like 'length,' 'speed,' etc., it is a question of ideal magnitudes to which he attributes qualities arbitrarily. The only thing he need do is be logical with the axioms that he postulates.

But the physicist knows very well of what he speaks. He is a realist. He seeks the real structure of the universe. Other universes are possible, but that does not concern him. The actual universe has a determinate structure which is not given to us unconditionally. The only way in which it is given to knowledge is by measurement. The magnitudes of which he speaks are real magnitudes, the results of measurement.

The geometry of the physicist is not that of the mathematician. The former must be discovered experimentally. And it alone can be true in a realist sense.

To say that the structure of the universe is constituted according to such and such a geometry before having measured it makes no sense.

But that does not mean that real geometry, or to use Eddington's expression, "natural geometry," is different from no matter what abstract geometry. It is a matter of finding the particular form of geometry to which the universe conforms. It is in this that the practical utility of abstract geometry resides.

But he adds that etymologically and traditionally geometry is the science of the measurement of the space around us. "[H]owever much the mathematical superstructure may now overweigh the observational basis, it is properly speaking an experimental science" (NPW, 161–62, esp. 159 [169–70, esp. 167]). He is of the opinion that in school one should teach students to verify by measurement that certain geometrical propositions are true or close to the truth.

Moreover, he explains how it comes about that we think that the structure of space should necessarily and universally be tridimensionally Euclidean.

> We have two eyes that from our infancy have never ceased crying out to our brain that the world ought to be regarded from more than one point of view. Our brain responds by giving us the notion of relief, which allows us to appreciate in a living manner the world in three dimensions, something that would have been almost impossible for us if we had been habituated to see only tableaux of two dimensions. We do not simply deduce from that the reality of the universe of three dimensions: we see it.

> But we have no similar help for the synthesis corresponding to different motions. If we had been endowed with eyes mobile with different speeds, perhaps our brain would have developed the necessary faculty in us. We would have perceived a sort of relief of the fourth dimension in a manner to combine and group in a single same tableau things seen with different speeds. (STG, 40)

Physical magnitude is therefore essentially distinct from mathematical magnitude by two characteristics: it is a real number, the result of measurement. By real we mean that it is drawn from the world that our consciousness recognizes as real, it is furnished to us by a practical operation and by a material instrument. It has a homologue in the absolute world, but that is absolutely indefinable. We have no intuition of it. Physical magnitude has been manufactured, it is a result. In this sense it is abstract. But it is not a logical abstraction: it is the isolation of a real aspect of a larger reality. Measurement is physically calculated on reality.

No cuts in the world correspond to the number, when it is a matter of the continuum. This parceling is purely formal, due to the way in which we must make our measurements. The unit is arbitrarily chosen from among the objects given. The number of this physical continuum has therefore nothing absolute as has pure number.

Eddington provides us with rather obscure ideas on the physical nature of the continuum. The continuity seems to be a necessity of representation. The nearer we approach the fundamental elements of the universe, we encounter atomicity. "Whence arises this discontinuity? At present, there seems no ground for believing that discontinuity is a law due to the mind; indeed the mind seems rather to take pains to smooth the discontinuities of nature into continuous perception" (STG, 199 [244]). He even cites, with respect to this question, a text of Kronecker: "God made the integers, all else is the work of man" (NPW, 249; STG, 199 ff. [244]).

I will not attempt an interpretation of this idea. Note simply this. It is impossible to represent a purely physical discontinuity. (I am not speaking of a multiplicity of distinct continua.) We have a kind of evidence for the fact that every physical entity must have a certain continuity. But is it truly evidence? Is not our psychology mixed up in that? "The theory of quanta, avoiding fractions and insisting on whole numbers, appears to us strange to every plane our subconscious would have imposed on the framework of natural phenomena" (NPW, 249).

Do our measure numbers truly express the whole of physical reality? "In delving ever more deeply into that which lies at the base of physical phenomena, we ought to expect to find entities which, like many things which exist in our consciousness, are in no way measurable by numbers; this idea suggests to us besides how the exact sciences, that is, sciences of phenomena linked to measure-numbers, can repose on a base of this nature" (NPW, 249).

There is in fact a theory, that of Dirac, which allows us to deduce the number measures obtained in observation. But this does not take us beyond the subject of this section, which was simply to show that we cannot say that it is not possible to go beyond measure-numbers in speaking of physical reality. As long as these transcendent elements are in logical continuity with the measure-numbers, they have a physical sense. We cannot arbitrarily limit the field.

5. Conclusion

We have insisted particularly on this question of measurement because it constitutes the basis of the whole scientific methodology of Eddington. It is in making precise the point of view of physics that we arrive at determining its relation to philosophy. Eddington has well seen that all the objections against relativity arise from a misunderstanding of this quite fundamental principle. He has shown that relativity does not pose, as is often said, an epistemological problem which has to be resolved by the rejection of the value of our objection, or by a relativist metaphysics. He has shown that in our prephysical concepts of space and time, there is nothing to reconcile with what we discover in physics. The physical datum is quite new and has no homologue in pre-physical conceptions. Physics is clearly disjoint with the other domains of our experience, and it has its own criteria. Its system is necessarily a closed system. Having isolated a certain portion of our experience, its entities cannot give information about what they set aside. It has no way of penetrating beyond these entities. From within physics, a beyond physics makes no sense. But Eddington hastens to add that this does not mean that a beyond physical entities makes no sense at all. The physicist himself has his roots in that beyond. At bottom, this beyond has more meaning than no matter what physical entity.

The problem of measurements leads us logically to the problem of laws. Eddington gives us no less profound considerations on these.

Chapter IV. Physical Laws

1. The Law of Identity[55]

Eddington divides physical laws into three categories: the laws of identity, statistical laws, and transcendental laws.

I dare not say that this division is original, but in any case English authors attribute it to Eddington.

According to Eddington, the laws usually called physical laws, such as the law of gravitation, the electromagnetic laws, and all the laws of conservation, are not truly laws but pure truisms. They express identities.

Let us take for example the laws of conservation. We posit conservation necessarily. Its denial entails an epistemological problem. Moreover, Eddington resolves it by his immediate realism. The important point is that this principle is not the result of measurements. We posit apriori (relative to physics which begins with measurement) that "some thing conserves itself." We do not know what this thing is that conserves itself. Is it matter? Is it mass? That has nothing to do with the fundamental law. In making measurements of a determinate object, we suppose that it is always the same object. But what is "the same object?" We need one. Without it, our measurements would make no sense. But before an object can gain entry to physics, it has to present itself through measurements. The conservation of "some thing" must be replaced by a physical magnitude. It is then that the principle enters into experimental physics. If in making measurements of an object, we find a continuous equality between the number-measures defining its mass, we will say that it is the mass of some thing that is conserved.

But what does that explain? Not mass, not conservation. From the identification posited mass cannot be deduced. The identity is a simple truism, posited necessarily, due to the nature of our understanding which requires such points of reference, or to nature itself, but that does not concern the physicist. The important point is that the physicist must identify one magnitude or another as permanent before he can progress.

This law is inviolable, since we posit it necessarily. It is only its identification with one or another magnitude that could be false.

It does not therefore express a relation between measurements, we identify it with them, but always on an experimental basis. Conservation itself is not expressible in measurements, it is not a number.

This whole problem is a bit confused. The texts are rather obscure. He is content to say that such laws are finished business, and it is epistemology that must explain this fact.

We will defer discussion of Eddington's own epistemological considerations until Part Two.

2. *Statistical Laws*[56]

The developments Eddington gives us of the second category of law are of great interest. They are original and touch on the currently very controversial topic of determinism. These considerations are of great philosophical importance. Let us situate the problem.

The ideal law of classical physics was the primary law. It has always seemed enough to say that it is "the law of nature itself" to indicate what it meant. Here is Eddington's definition. "Some things never happen in the physical world because they are *impossible;* others because they are *too improbable.* The laws which forbid the first are the primary laws; the laws which forbid the second are the secondary laws. It has been the conviction of nearly all physicists that at the root of everything there is a complete scheme of primary law governing the career of every particle or constituent of the world with an iron determinism. This primary scheme is all-sufficing, for, since it fixes the history of every constituent of the world, it fixes the whole world-history."[57] The primary law is the law which regulates the behavior of individual entities. It implies that, if you had perfect knowledge of a single phenomenon, you would be able to deduce the others from it, that is, the spatio-temporal structure of the universe, since all phenomena are fundamentally linked. In order for us to be able to apply this law and predict the behavior of a particle, for example, we would have to have a sufficient knowledge. And this knowledge is called "sufficient" insofar as it enables us to predict this behavior.

The law of nature, so defined, is characterized by its necessity; the classical physicist thought he knew several phenomena which obeyed this law.

So one thought he understood why we never encounter equilateral triangles whose angles are unequal, by saying that this is *impossible.* They are not to be found in nature because they are impossible.

At present, physicists do not know any phenomenon that obeys primary laws, but most would say that it is one thing that nature is governed by primary laws and quite another that we do not know them, since our experience is quite limited.

In practice, we must be content to define the behavior of physical entities with a certain probability. Laws describing the probable behavior of a physical entity are called secondary laws because of their imperfection, perfection demanding an absolute definition in terms of "necessary" and "impossible." A typical law of this type is the second law of thermodynamics concerning the irreversible process of degradation of energy. This process introduces more and more of chance into nature. The practical measure of the chance element which can increase in the universe and never decrease is called *entropy.* Why does it never decrease? Because that is impossible? No. Because it is too improbable. Why should we restrict ourselves to predicting the effect with a probability? The answer is twofold.

The classical physicist would reply: because it is a question there of the behavior of a large number of particles that we do not know sufficiently. Entropy increases, necessarily, but because of our imperfect knowledge of the elements considered, we have yet to formulate this necessity in an adequate way.

Up till now, secondary laws concerned exclusively the probable behavior of a large group. The probability of predicting its behavior increased by reason of the greater number of the particles making it up. When the number is very large, the probability is so great that it is equivalent, in practice, to necessity. The point to notice is that the possibility of an exception is never equal to 0. It is always a precise positive number.

With this we come to the crisis of modern physics. The very elements of physics no longer obey primary laws, which have been replaced with laws of probability. The provisory laws have absorbed absolute laws. There are no longer actually formulizable determinist laws. Is this in opposition to the determinate laws of nature itself, independently of us?

That is the problem. There are physicists like Einstein and Planck[58] who say that the indeterminism of the laws of modern physics is a subjective indeterminism due to the insufficiency of our knowledge of the details of phenomena, whereas Eddington declares that the very laws of nature are indeterminist. Indeterminism is objective. Of determinism he says that "there is no such thing in Nature" (NPW, 225 [229]). Already in 1920 he wrote, "the law of nature is that the real state of the universe is that which is statistically the most probable" (STG, 128). He was fully aware of the revolutionary character of this thesis. "It is probable that here we part company from many of the continental relativists, who give prominent place to a principle known as the *law of causality*—that only those things are to be regarded as being in causal connection which are capable of being actually observed. . . . The principle itself is debatable; that which is observable to us is determined by the accident of our own structure, and the law of causality seems to impose our own limitations on the free interplay of entities in the world outside us" (STG, 156 [194]).

This thesis is striking in its audacity. It seems that we have the intuition of the very illogicality of the concept of "indeterminism," that an objective indeterminism cannot make sense. How does Eddington justify his position?

First, he gives a refutation of determinism as a physical thesis.[59] Physical determinism is above all a hypothesis which postulates a superfluous element, because in fact the indeterminist or secondary law can be used to predict the future in a way as satisfying as could the primary law, when it is a matter of great number of particles regarded in the majority of our observations. But when it is a matter of a restricted number, or of a single particle, prediction becomes a pure game of chance. Why not say that their behavior is in itself undetermined? Because this is impossible? What experience has shown us that this is impossible?

One no longer speaks as a physicist then, but appeals to a metaphysical principle. In fact, the determinist always answers that these facts do not prove the gratuitousness of his affirmation. He must indeed have a transphysical reason for maintaining the thesis.

The determinist affirmation is a positive affirmation since it posits something that is not postulated in order to explain known phenomena. The determinist must justify this affirmation and he cannot without leaving the domain of physics.

The most important point is that the determinist hypothesis has no physical meaning, and could never have one, because it is physically unverifiable. Doesn't the determinist always postulate an impossible observer? A perfect knowledge? But physical knowledge is necessarily limited. The determinist may have serious philosophical reasons for holding his thesis, but he must take into account that it can never have a physical meaning.

As opposed to the positive affirmation of determinism which certainly explains nothing, that of indeterminism is negative, that is, it excludes everything that is not strictly necessary. But it has a positive value in that it succeeds in explaining the data of present and future observation. The introduction of anything else is superfluous and serves no purpose. "We recognize that 'impossible' and 'too improbable' can both give adequate explanations of any observed uniformity of experience, and the older theory rather haphazardly explained some uniformities one way and other uniformities the other way" (DD, 68 [8]). We can affirm that the indeterminist hypothesis has a physical meaning, and that is experimentally verified, whereas the determinist hypothesis cannot have a physical meaning in any fashion. As physicists, we have no right to speak of impossibility, since 'too improbable' simply suffices, and is alone suggested by experience.

Now one could say: since practically we arrive at the same results, why hold onto this indeterminism? First of all, because in determinism there is nothing that can be held. Then on this physically impossible hypothesis it is impossible to explain the known phenomena. It would be necessary to give a reason to show that this explanation is not true.

Eddington puts the whole problem on the same footing as the problem of relativity. It seems to me that one could say that he holds to the view of indeterminism just as he does the view of relativity. Indeterminism cannot be contradicted.

But what about the philosophical principle of determinism which holds that the very concept of indeterminism is illogical?

Note that Eddington has not formulated the metaphysical thesis of determinism. He is content to say that it has no physical meaning. But one cannot deduce from all that that he rejects the notion of 'impossible' in its transcendental sense. He is not a relativist metaphysician: 'actuality,' 'possibility,' 'impossibility,' 'true,' and 'false' are absolutes. So much so that one can make him say 'everything that is is determined.' Does that mean that he contradicts himself? Absolutely not.

The spontaneous objection to this indeterminism is certainly based on the evidence of the elementary principle: everything that is is determined. The application is rather simple: an electron is, therefore, it is determined.

In fact, the application is not at all simple. Is it indeed evident that we can apply this principle directly to physical entities? One will object: aren't physical entities things? Surely: the body which weighs two kilos does not weigh three under the same respect. That is all too clear: it necessarily weighs two kilos when it weighs two kilos and that is the case whatever be the meaning of 'body' and of 'two kilos.'

I think that the reason Eddington does not dwell on this point is that he hopes that his readers have respect for his intelligence.

But does this principle entail the impossibility of indeterminism? We are already familiar with this simplism. An analogous application to physical magnitudes has been made: *omne ens est aliquid,* therefore length is absolute. In more intelligent terms that comes down to saying: an object two meters long has two meters of length. That is without the least doubt absolute enough.

We postulate that we know perfectly what it is a question of when we speak of electrons, of quanta, etc. (We might say that these physical entities have been elevated into metaphysically defined entities.)

What is a physical entity? It is a bundle of number measures. Here is how he returns to his fundamental definition of a physical object: "the nature of an object, insofar as it is guaranteed by scientific inquiry, is the abstraction of its relations with all the surrounding objects" (NPW, 260–61). The measurements give us a definite "slice" by the measurements themselves. As soon as we give another meaning to "physical object," we go beyond the data in an arbitrary manner.

The gross error of the protagonists of physical determinism consists in their substantialization of the physical object bundled in measurements. They attribute an ontological meaning to the slices physically effected. But one does not have the right to isolate the bundles of measurements, for the simple reason that the measurements do not define them so. Not because our measurements are imperfect, but because they do not have this meaning at all. (Does one define a man by his quantity of electrical charges?)

We speak of 'one' or 'two' electrons as arithmetical integers, perfectly defined in themselves. "We often think that when we have completed our study of *one* we know all about *two,* because 'two' is 'one and one.' We forget that we have still to make a study of 'and'" (NPW, 104–5 [116]). Observation shows us that the 'ones' always have an appendix 'and.' To abstract from their 'and' comes down to abstracting from their 'one.'

Eddington says that he hesitates as to whether or not he should make the following remark:

> We rather freely displace integers from the familiar world into the physical world. The 'twoness' of two atoms is usually thought of as being like the twoness in our mental picture of two apples. But I doubt whether it really is so. At any rate, it does not apply to electrons, for in the modern theory the twoness of two electrons is not completely like the twoness of two apples. In fact, multiplicity should be regarded as a property (indescribable in familiar terms) which, being by its nature discontinuous, has been correlated to the series of mathematical integers, just as continuous properties are correlated to continuous measure numbers. (PP, 36–37)

Happily, Eddington decided to make that remark. It settles the question in a fundamental manner.

Some authors have tried to satisfy both determinists and indeterminists by introducing a distinction in the domain of our experience. This is double: there is first of all the macrocosmic world having observability as its fundamental character; then there is the unobservable microcosmic world. In the first determinism reigns, in the second indeterminism. Examples of observables are rocks, stars, bars; the electron is among the unobservables.

But Eddington remarks that the electron is no more hypothetical or unobservable than a star. One can count electrons as well as stars. 'Macroscopic' is a purely relative term. A star is no more isolable than an electron. A macroscopic entity is microscopic to a superior entity. In the sequence: electrons, atoms, molecules, rocks, stars, nebulae, each object is microscopic relative to the higher. Indeterminism goes all along the line. Only it diminishes by reason for a growing number of composing elements. This is the true law: the state of each entity is such because it is the most probable. And it behaves in such a way because that is most probable. Let us not exaggerate the meaning of indeterminism: it is not absolute, such that one could say, no matter what comes from no matter what.

Is all this pure chicanery? No. It is a matter of well-defined numbers. The possibility of an exception is never equal to 0.

(I think one could deduce from Eddington's arguments that a true determinism would require an infinite number, therefore the impossible, since, whatever the number in question, the possible but too improbable exception, is always a definite number.)

This indeterminism goes for the universe taken as a whole as well as for its components. The actual state of the universe is that which is statistically more probable. And this remark is logically compatible with everything which precedes. If the whole were determinist, the composing parts would be so as well.

In effect, Eddington rejects the determinist definition of the poet:

> . . . the first Morning of Creation wrote
> What the Last Dawn of Reckoning shall read.
> (DD, 67 [6])

"The question whether from a complete knowledge of the past we can predict the future does not arise because a complete knowledge of the past involves a self-contradiction" (Heisenberg, quoted in NPW, 228–29 [233]).

With that the 'absolutely impossible" and the "absolutely necessary" are banished from the domain of physics. As soon as one uses these expressions one immediately places himself on a terrain alien to physics. The conclusion of all these considerations is, therefore, that the physical laws of nature are in themselves statistical laws, and this necessarily. Determinism is in the metaphysical order and tells us nothing about the structure of physical laws. These must be sought with the means provided by physics if they are to have a physical sense. (We could sum it all up in the expression that nature is determinately indeterminate.)

We reserve for the second part the epistemological speculations that Eddington attaches to this problem because they presuppose his metaphysics of consciousness.

3. *Transcendental Laws*

Eddington has only two short and excessively obscure passages on this subject. We will try to disengage some of the ideas suggested (STG, 198 ff. [244]; NPW, 245–46 [248–49]).

Transcendental laws are distinguished from other laws because they impose themselves—we do not impose them. They concern the discontinuity in nature; they are laws of atomicity.

He seems to imply that these laws are irrational because their terms are irreducible. It is even possible that laws which have not their origin in the mind may be irrational, and we can never succeed in formulating them. This is, however, only a remote possibility; probably if they were really irrational it would not have been possible to make the limited progress that has been achieved. But if the laws of quanta do indeed differentiate the actual world from other worlds possible to the mind, we may expect the task of formulating them to be far harder than anything yet accomplished by physics (STG, 200 [247]).

He does not exclude the possibility that we will come to posit them as identities, "if [our analysis] could be pushed further to reach something still more fundamental" (STG, 199 [244]). The methods of Dirac seem to assume this emancipation.

> If we are to discern controlling laws of Nature not dictated by the mind it would seem necessary to escape as far as possible from the cut-and-dried framework into which the mind is so ready to force everything that it experiences. . . . [Dirac] starts with basal entities inexpressible by numbers or number-systems and his basal laws are symbolic expressions unconnected with arithmetical operations. The fascinating point is that as the development proceeds actual numbers are *exuded* from the symbols. . . . By furnishing numbers, though itself non-numerical, such a theory can well be the basis for the measure-numbers studied in exact science. The measure-numbers, which are all that we glean from a physical survey of the world, cannot be the whole world; they may not even be so much of it as to constitute a self-governing unit. This seems the natural interpretation of Dirac's procedure in seeking the governing laws of exact science in a non-arithmetical calculus. (NPW, 210 [215–16])

We regret that Eddington did not develop the problem of the physical continuum.[60] It seems to us impossible to disengage a coherent ensemble from these few notes. We will return to them in the second part of this study.

Chapter V. Physical Theory

Eddington does not give us a complete theory of the systematic manner of physical theory. But he has clarified some fundamental points.

In the past century, the ideal of the explanation of natural phenomena consisted in the construction of a mechanical model which would show in a representative fashion how it goes with things. This mentality was not yet rid of the prejudice that physical entities are the results of an extended analysis of the elements of the familiar world as familiar (MTR, 104–6). These physicists did not take into account that "the primordial elements of the theory of the universe should be of a nature of which it is impossible to give an intelligible definition."[61]

> [T]he familiar things of experience are very complex; and the scientific method is to analyze them into simpler elements. Theories and laws of behavior of these simpler constituents are studied; and from these it becomes possible to predict and explain phenomena. It seems a natural procedure to explain the complex in terms of the simple, but it carries with it the necessity of explaining the familiar in terms of the unfamiliar. There are thus two reasons why the ultimate constituents of the real world must be of an unfamiliar nature. Firstly, all familiar objects are of a much too complex character. Secondly, familiar objects belong not to the real world of physics, but to a much earlier stage in the synthesis of appearances. (STG, 185 [227])

Whatever the usefulness of a mechanical model, it does not give the last explanation of phenomena (MTR, 106). On the contrary, it is to the mathematician that one must go for the construction of a theory, the elements from which one starts being essentially number-measures. A theory is essentially a system from which one can deduce the laws posed or imposed by way of conclusions. One posits some equations from which one can logically deduce what has been suggested by observation.

The theory thus has a double aspect: first, its logically deductive coherence, and then its value for a real explanation of phenomena. Thus, one ought first show how one can put to the proof the truth of the postulates, and also show how the laws they express relate to the structure of the universe, and on the other hand one descends from this determination to deduce from it the phenomena of observation. In the theory, there is therefore a reciprocal current. All that one can ask of the theory itself is that it be coherent and logical, and in this sense one can say that it is true. Whereas from experiments one asks in crescendo whether they verify the theory, how they suggest it, and finally whether they require laws that we can posit (MTR, 105).

And then? One can show that a certain structure posited in the theory will explain the known phenomena, but one cannot show that any other would not do as well.

Thus every theory is provisory as to its real value. In this sense no theory is true *tout court.* Theories advance by changing, by being replaced. "A feature of science is its *progressive* approach to truth. The kernel of the advances achieved by one theory is preserved in its successor, although the outward shape is often radically different" (PP, 30).

It is this that is so disconcerting for philosophers. If by truth we mean the logical value of the theory, one ought to say: "Physics demands of its scheme of nature something else besides truth, namely a certain quality that we may call convergence. . . . Physics is an exact science because the chief essentials of a problem are limited to a few conditions; and it draws near to the truth with ever-increasing approximation as it widens its purview. The approximations of physics form a convergent series" (STG, 154 [191–92]).

Physics is so to say a movement toward a real term forever inaccessible in its entirety. Eddington is radically opposed to the conception which attributes only a utilitarian and conventional value to theory (STG, 182–83 [224–25]; NPW, 346–47 [342–43]). Neither are physics and reality two parallel systems: physics *converges* on reality.

Eddington also underlines the importance of theory in the development of the sciences. In fact, the majority of theories pride themselves on basing their ideas uniquely on observation. But in that case, Eddington says, there is no astronomical science for example. "There are no purely observational facts about the heavenly bodies."[62] Without exception, astronomical measurements are phenomena which take place in a terrestrial observatory. It is only by the theory that one translates them into a knowledge of the external world. The observer who supposes that the rectilinear propagation of light posited in astronomy has been verified by a terrestrial experience is mistaken.

Chapter VI. Physical Synthesis

The complete synthesis of physics will be essentially a metric and cyclic system, constituting a closed domain. It will be a metric system because we can only dispose of number-measures for objects. "If then only pointer readings or their equivalents are put into the machine of scientific calculation, how can we grind out anything but pointer readings?" (NPW, 252 [255]).

> It will be a cyclic system because no element is definable in an absolute fashion but always by another. And if we wish to know what are the "potentials" of the theory of relativity, one would be obliged to resort to 'intervals.' The intervals are relations among events. These relations have been deduced by us from measurements by means of graduated scales and clocks. What are they? They are made of matter. What is matter? It is what we define by 'mass,' 'momentum' and 'force.' And what are they? "They are rather formidable looking expressions containing *potentials* and their first and second derivatives with respect to the coordinates. What are potentials? Why, that is just what I have been explaining to you!" (NPW, 260–62 [262–64])

Does all that make a vicious circle? Not at all. We have defined the point of departure of physics in which we have an immediate experience of a real exteriority. It is that substrate, undifferenciable, that we define all along. At the beginning these are of Mr. X who knows "some thing." This some thing he is going to define with the means at his disposal. He does not work in a void. It is at this point that we observe that physics is not fundamentally independent. Mr. X cannot exclude Mr. X.

But the domain proper to physics constitutes a closed cycle, because in this domain we cannot introduce any element which has no physical meaning. The physical synthesis, insofar as it encloses all theories, obeys the law of theories. It is provisory, approaching nearer and nearer to reality.

Here we have to introduce a corollary of indeterminism that we discussed earlier. On the supposition that our experience will be complete, will there be a means of making a perfectly adequate image of the universe?

This supposition contains two ambiguous terms: 'complete experience' and 'image of the universe.' Evidently, if by complete experience we mean an experience such that it embraces the universal in its spatio-temporal ensemble, and not simply the universe at a certain limited time, we would say that only God knows the universe in this way. But if we understand by complete experience an experience which would embrace the universe at a certain definite time, it would be impossible to make an image of it. In fact, that would suppose that the universe was ruled by determinist laws. A perfect image of the universe can only be the universe itself, and that is an image being constantly made. An experience of the present does not suffice to deduce the past rigorously, but only with probability. The universe does not follow a rigorous theory.

Our theories are thus doubly deficient. First because they are only approximative of a given state, and then, being mathematical (and inevitably mathematical), they tend to a rigor that nature itself ignores.

Chapter VII. The Limitations of Exact Science

The greatest limitation is that it has no sense unless it is attached to the ensemble of our experience. The physicist does not treat the 'true,' and 'false,' the 'real,' the 'actual,' 'consciousness,' etc. He supposes all that. Eddington insists on this point because most physicists think that their science suffices for everything and that it is only in science that one touches the real.

Physics is only an abstraction for a certain aspect from a certain field of reality, the metric aspect. It gives us only a world of shadows against a background inexpressible in physics (NPW, xiv [16], 109 [121]).

Eddington indicates some limitations in the very field of physics. The physicist has need of mathematics. But he has made some suggestions which have been misinterpreted, such as that apropos of the need to have recourse to the time of consciousness in order to give a meaning to physical time, such that physics has need of this element proper to consciousness for the elaboration of its own structure.

But it is necessary to understand Eddington's procedure. In fact, in the two chapters of *The Nature of the Physical World* (IV–V) in which he treats of our double experience of time, he means to introduce gradually his theory of indeterminism. This is how one should order his argumentation, it seems to me. First of all, the time of primary physics (primary laws) has no direction. The time of secondary physics which treats of organization has a direction. In this that time agrees with the time of consciousness which advances in a determinate direction that we call the future. But the lovers of primary physics do not love consciousness or secondary laws. They hope one day to convert all secondary laws into primary laws, and one of the first consequences of this will be the disappearance of the arrow of time.

Eddington rejects the fundamental postulate of the determinism of primary physics, that the time of entropy (the second law of thermodynamics) has a physical meaning. As we have seen, the secondary laws are laws of nature. The time of secondary physics is a truly physical time.

He finds interesting the fact that this time has some characteristics of the time of consciousness, but he in no wise bases its physical value on this agreement, as some have thought. He shows that here physics and consciousness join one another without at the same time fusing. We see that fundamentally it is a question of the same thing differently expressed. It is one of the points where we can identify a familiar entity with a scientific entity.

Therefore, Eddington does not contradict himself with this thesis. In short, physical science is materially dependent, formally independent. "It is true that the whole scientific inquiry starts from the familiar world and in the end it must return to the familiar world; but the part of the journey over which the physicist has charge is in foreign territory" (NPW, xiii [14]). Even mathematical expressions have to be translated before they can be useful in physics. The physicist looks on them rather as instruments. This dependence is real but needs to be understood by its signification.

We have come close to the great problem of integral experience which will allow us to situate physics in a more precise fashion. What is the background of measure-numbers? Before we take up this question, let us first introduce some considerations critical for the philosophy of science. What do they mean for us scholastics?

SECTION THREE

Critical Considerations

It seems to us that there is nothing in these fundamental theses of Eddington's critique of science that we could contest. On the contrary. The fundamental points of this new philosophy of science have already been explained by a scholastic author.[63] Others have wanted to incorporate them in scholastic philosophy, but the incorporation has resulted in a transformation such that they can no longer be recognized. The philosophy of science of M. Maritain is no longer at all that of Eddington or of Renoirte.[64] Renoirte has been contradicted and Eddington sifted. But Eddington cannot be sifted. Renoirte has formulated these theses in precise terms for scholastic readers. The terminology of Eddington is less familiar, and sometimes vague, he is not a professional philosopher. It is that which allows M. Maritain to disengage the points which appear most interesting to him and to neglect or simply contradict the rest. What is important is not that M. Maritain does not accept the fundamental definitions. He assimilates only the superstructure, but this no longer has the meaning attributed to it by Eddington.

We are convinced that the theses of Eddington with all their consequences must be accepted. There is no choice to make. We hope to justify this position. We will study the problem of the object of physical science and its immediate consequences. Then the problem of indeterminism. This is rather new and has not been criticized in scholastic circles, save in book reviews which do not justify the criticism. As to what concerns physical theory, the doctrine of Eddington is commonly accepted and one even finds some texts in St. Thomas suggestive of it. We will be concerned with the first two problems.

First of all, is there a philosophy of science and what does it include? What is the meaning of these "philosophical consequences" of science?

The philosophy of science is that branch of general philosophy which especially studies the situation and significance of the mathematical and experimental sciences in the ensemble of our knowledge. In that which concerns physics in particular, it studies what constitutes this science formally, delimits its proper field, and determines the general significance of its object. All that precedes the work of the physicist himself. Some theses, like that of the point of view of relativity and the point of view of indeterminism, are theses in the philosophy of science which have nothing to do with properly physical principles. But there is a very important distinction to be made between the ideal philosophy and ours, which progresses in a human fashion. From time to time physicists remind us that professional philosophers have forgotten to treat one or another problem, and even that they are mistaken. Physicists defend unmistakably philosophical theses which were attacked by professional philosophers. But none of that has to do with the philosophy of science.

The relativity of Einstein has drawn the attention of philosophers to the philosophical problem of relativity and Eddington does the same thing for indeterminism. Are these problems consequences of scientific theses? Historically, yes,

But even this concession is too broad. For Einstein and Eddington have first posited these philosophical principles before being able to construct their properly physical theory in a logical way.

It is only in this sense that we can speak of philosophical consequences. The properly scientific conclusions never acquire a philosophical sense. There is no continuity here. The certitude of no matter what physical thesis does not make it a philosophical truth, and it is not necessarily less true for that. It belongs to another domain of knowledge. But all that shows the importance of the development itself of the sciences. They constitute with regard to their formal aspects isolated compartments, but in practice we are interdependent with regard to the signification of certain problems raised. "Philosopher" and "physicist" are not abstract beings. It is man who must disentangle the problems. A philosopher who ignores the sciences does himself a wrong, he will not even succeed in posing properly philosophical problems. The physicist cannot ignore all philosophical problems, he necessarily presupposes them.

The problem of the possibility of a science of the physical world, and its necessary conditions, is a properly philosophical problem.

Chapter I. On the Object of Physics

1. The Thesis

Since it has been said that the developments of Eddington on this subject do not suffice, let us try to see what they lack by following the criticism of M. Maritain.

Let us begin at the end. M. Maritain affirms that real space is necessarily tridimensionally Euclidean.[65] This implies either that he has a species of intuition of the metric structure of space, or he does not accept the definition of the object of physics.

In fact, he affirms that he has this intuition, and on the other hand gives no fundamental definition of the object of physics.

As for this intuition, we can say that we do not have it. But we can also explain why M. Maritain thinks he has one.

Whatever the meaning of 'imagination' implied by his expression "constructability in the imaginative intuition," it is certainly not a matter of pure intelligibility. With respect to that, no matter what abstract geometrical structure is equally intelligible. We must then make a descent. Either there is a domain intermediate between intelligibility and the possibility of representing to oneself spatial dimensions in sensible imagination, or there is not. To affirm an intermediate domain is a pure postulate.[66] The fact that we cannot represent to ourselves imaginatively a geometric structure other than the three dimensional is an inevitable consequence of our physical situation and of our psychology which is grafted on it. The verification of a geometrical proposition is not done in intuition, but in a purely rational fashion. We cannot abstract from our physical situation and its psychological consequences for what concerns imaginative representation, but can for what concerns intelligibility.

It is just this point that M. Maritain has neglected. In fact, he writes, "in truth, the non-Euclidean geometries presuppose notions of Euclidean geometry, not indeed in their own structure and their own logical development, but as the foundation of the logical coherence of the entities they may construct and as *the psychological basis of conceptualization*."[67] That is to give a very important role to imagination and its reach.

What criterion have we then which allows us to distinguish real space from an unreal space (physical or mathematically real)?

> In our search for a criterion two ways, and two ways only, lie open. We may either analyze the genesis of the notions in order to see if the entity in question, without involving any internal contradiction or incompossibility in its constitutive notes (in which case it would have no mathematical existence), does not imply a condition incompossible with existence outside the mind. (Thus a logical entity, such as Predicate or copula, is certainly not intrinsically contradictory, but it would be a contradiction to suppose it existing outside the mind.) Or we may consider a condition to which the philosopher knows that the reality of mathematical entities is subject. (He knows that for these entities to exist outside the mind means to exist with sensible existence, and that whatever cannot be constructed in imaginative intuition, which represents freely and in a pure fashion whatever belongs to quantity, has *a fortiori* no possibility of being posited in sensible existence.) This condition is direct constructibility in intuition.[68]

It seems to me that this text refutes itself. Everything we know of the necessary conditions for a material being to be possible is that it be spatiotemporal, and as such composed of prime matter and form. Its sensibility is purely relative. He should have said "material existence" instead of "sensible existence." Not everything that is material is sensible. To elevate sensibility into a criterion of material reality is a restriction of it to what can be imaginatively represented. A quantum is a phenomenon which absolutely surpasses our representative capacities and which has no representative sense. Yet it is quite real. It is not in any way reducible to a representation, and that by definition.

We say that the philosopher knows absolutely nothing of the structure of space or of quanta. The physicist would have to transform them into physical entities for that. And that makes no sense.

All that the philosopher knows of space is that it is an exteriority, that being an immediate given. Point A is not point B, they are each outside the other. What does it mean for the one to be outside the other? This is inexplicable, it is intuited. He can make analyses of the conditions underlying this exteriority, but that is all. The mathematician also begins with this exteriority to construct a geometry. With only two points he can perform a tour de force that surpasses the imagination. But when he is asked: What is the distance between *this* point *here* and that point *there*, he does not know how to answer. It is the physicist who gives us the response. The domain of real distances, of real geometry, is his domain. To be able to speak of those things one must be a physicist.

No doubt the real space of M. Maritain is metric. How has he measured it? That is the whole problem. In measuring according to the only effective method, he will see that space is not necessarily three-dimensionally Euclidean. Why should one hesitate to accept it as real?

As a philosopher he can say nothing of the metric structure of space. That is for the physicist. And he replies that there is curved space. M. Maritain answers: that is impossible. The physicist asks why. M. Maritain: because it does not agree with the metrics of my space. The physicist: and which is that?

M. Maritain does not take into account the importance of the definition and meaning of physical magnitude. And, it seems to me, that is how he goes wrong.

There is a little story behind this. We will tell it to situate the problem. In 1924, Renoirte wrote,

> Is there in things an absolute corresponding to length? The enumeration that enables us to attain a pure number is an absolute operation. Length is not a pure number, it is a physical magnitude. Its definition resides in the description of the process of measurement which includes an instrument one can only show.
>
> Since an affirmation of physics signifies that such a procedure applied to such an object has furnished such a measurement, can one suppose correctly that this affirmation gives us information about the object independent of the procedure of measurement? Could one say that length *tout court* is an absolute?
>
> Laying side by side a meter and an object of experience we will say that we measure the 'proper length' of an object, but we exceed our rights in affirming that such 'length' is in itself a property of the body.[69]

In 1925, Roland Dalbiez, warning Renoirte of metaphysical relativism, wrote:

> Is there in things an absolute corresponding to length? A philosopher professing a frank realism would answer that all existent magnitudes have to be determinate, it is the principle of identity itself that demands

> it, *omne ens est aliquid,* but one must carefully distinguish the affirmation of the existence of an absolute magnitude and the possibility for us to make precise *in concreto* what is that absolute magnitude, to affirm for example that such a material object conserves the same absolute magnitude. The answer to the first question is a very firm "Yes," the answer to the second is an eternal *ignorabimus.*[70]

The case is therefore very serious, since the position of Renoirte seems to compromise the evidence of evidences themselves. But what do we get in applying the principle in question that makes us formulate the proposition: "Every existing magnitude must be determinate?" This: a length of two meters is a length of two meters; the length of an object is the length of that object. That is all. That is all the absolute there is in length, that it is what it is, whatever it is. No doubt, Roland Dalbiez has extended this further, so much so that he does not speak of the same thing that Renoirte does. He speaks in effect of magnitudes that we can make precise *in concreto.* Here the problem changes aspect. It is no longer a question of a length of two meters which is necessarily two meters since it is two meters. (Pardon the proof.) It is a question of something else.

What is that something else? Absolute length. What can that still signify? The length of things in themselves. What is that? We can never know.

This pessimism is not encouraging for the physicist. Happily, he spoke of something else. The length in question for him is an article fabricated by a certain procedure of measurement. He knows no other. Certainly, there is a state of the world corresponding to the length obtained, but that is not known except insofar as it is expressed in the physical magnitude obtained. Is it that state that is absolute? Certainly, since being what it is, it is what it is.

That is absolutely all that a metaphysician can say, that is, absolutely nothing. All the dimensions of nature are absolute, since they are. But how are they? It is that that we cannot know before having measured. "Absolute" tells us absolutely nothing.

The point that scandalizes these philosophers is that the relativists speak of magnitudes which differ according to the system of reference. One cannot conceive how it is possible that an object have different lengths according to the systems of reference. But for the physicist, a length is by definition a length obtained in a *certain system of references.* He does not know how to speak of length outside of a certain system of reference. The definition of the property he handles differs, since this property is defined by the description of its procedure of measurement. But procedures of measurement differ. The definition differs too. Where is the difficulty? It is imaginary. We give to length a meaning it does not have. A physical magnitude is relative by definition: the definition is an expression of a relativity.

How would one define absolute magnitudes in physics? A magnitude which would have the same metric value for no matter what system of reference? But for the metaphysician this one is no more or less relative than the others. In *The Degrees of Knowledge*, M. Maritain takes up the ideas of Dalbiez, but without mentioning Renoirte. Here is a significant passage:

> The philosopher knows that bodies have absolute dimensions, that there are absolute movements in the world, an absolute time, absolute simultaneities for events as far apart as you wish in space. Here *absolute* signifies entirely determined in itself independently of any observer. The philosopher does not try to know what they are, i.e. to discern these dimensions, these movements, these times, these absolute simultaneities (at a distance), with the aid of our means of observation and measurement. He willingly concedes that that is not possible. It is sufficient for him that they be discernible by pure spirits, who know, without observing from a point of space or at a moment of time. The physicist makes a like renunciation, and with good reason.[71]

The philosopher of whom M. Maritain speaks is an ambiguous personage. There are philosophers who know nothing of all that: 'dimensions,' 'movements,' 'time' are pure identities. But simultaneity is another story. And what is an observer?

Is he speaking of physical magnitudes? Certainly not, since these are magnitudes indefinable by definition. It is for that that M. Maritain knows them: because they have no need of being defined since he knows what they are.

Thus we are no longer speaking of the same thing. If M. Maritain wants to call these dimensions of length, of time, he does so arbitrarily. In any case it is not what Eddington and Renoirte understand by these expressions. There remains for him only to give definitions of these things and to show how he derives consequences.

We would say that the pure spirits know an absolute time if time is absolute, and a relative time if it is relative, and all that absolutely. Relative time is no less "entirely determinate in itself" than absolute time.

It seems to me that this is a question of words. In applying "absolute" to physical magnitude, he gives to the word a physical sense, and this he cannot do. The disagreement therefore is at the point of departure. Either Eddington's definition is true, and then one must accept all the consequences, which imply the point of view of relativity, as has been sufficiently demonstrated above; or M. Maritain must give us another. But he does not.

That does not seem to interest him. Why not? Because he thinks he knows too much as philosopher. He thinks that it is as a philosopher that he knows the metric structure of space. He confuses the extended with physical magnitude; extension and quantity are the same thing for him.

This neglect has a profound effect on his whole philosophy of science. Only the philosopher knows the real world, real magnitudes. None of that interests the physicist. It does not concern him, he says, because "he is only concerned with what he can measure."[72] In place of the absolutes known by the philosopher he is content to deal only with relative entities reconstructed by means of measurable determinations: *entia rationis cum fundamento in re.*[73]

All that is very vague. If only M. Maritain would tell us what he means by "measurable determinations." A length is something measurable. That is what the physicist measures. It is only as such that he knows it. But in what is it less absolute than the absolute dimension of M. Maritain? Is it not what it is, is it not intrinsically determined in itself?

The physicist seeks absolute magnitudes in nature, directly or indirectly measurable. As for non-measurable magnitudes, he does not conceive them, and neither do philosophers. Whatever absolute magnitudes are, they ought at least imply measurability. That supposes a definition, which implies a process of measuring at least abstractly definable. We would say that a magnitude is physically absolute when it would have the same value for no matter what observer. And by observer we do not necessarily mean "some one"—"some thing" would suffice. The physicist rejects the magnitudes of M. Maritain, because they are inconceivable.

That is why Eddington does not talk about them. He attributes the value of reality to the magnitudes of physics, and the negation of this fact would entail an epistemological problem. M. Maritain seems to have forgotten that Eddington speaks of the reality of the physical world and of the real value of physical entities. In fact, he writes, apropos of a text of Eddington, "the world of physics has become a world of shadows": "Mr. Eddington seems to forget here that the measurements gathered from nature by our apparatus deliver to us something of the real."[74] But M. Maritain, too, seems to forget here that the number-measures of Eddington are real, that the number-measure is the isolating of an aspect of reality, and not a logical abstraction, that "the cleavage between the scientific and the extra-scientific domain of experience is, I believe, not a cleavage between the concrete and the transcendental but between the metrical and the non-metrical" (NPW, 275 [276]). Real space is not universally Euclidean because we have found the contrary parting from real number-measures. These number-measures are shadows because they do not express the whole of our experience, which cannot be assimilated in its entirety by physics. Eddington leaves room for the metaphysician.

On the contrary, it is M. Maritain who seems to forget that measurements give us something of the real when he assimilates physics *à l'excès* with pure mathematics.[75] Physical magnitudes are not "cuts mathematically effected," but physically effected, which is quite another thing. Physical magnitudes are not merely beings of reason *cum fundamento in re*. Insofar as knowledge of them is solidly established, they express reality. They do not express the whole of reality. Insofar as a theory is experimentally verified, it is *really* true.

All along he seems to ignore the last metaphysical chapters of *The Nature of the Physical World*. There he would see what Eddington understands by actuality and reality.

It seems to us that the error of Dalbiez and Maritain is due to the fact that they have not been concerned to give a definition of physical magnitude, or even to give a definition of absolute dimension which is not the expression of an identity. These are chimerical absolutes which would make it naive to attribute a real value (in the ontological sense) to relativity. The point of view of relativity is a philosophical principle expressing the real relativity of our measurements. That is what is implied in the definition of physical magnitude. The principle of indeterminism is equally implied.

Still, M. Maritain admits the theory of relativity as a physical theory, after having tried to find technical errors in it. This is an interesting point.

Didn't he look for a technical error because he has a certain metaphysical conviction that this theory was really impossible? This attempt failed.[76] What did he do? He changed his theory of physical theory. He thought it preferable to abandon that rather than abandon his conviction of the absolute of movement, as if the theory of relativity implied that relative movement was not absolute.[77] These few remarks suffice. M. Maritain has not addressed the basic problem. His whole philosophy of science is thereby vitiated.

It remains to be seen if the fundamental definition of the formal object of physics given by Eddington is critically verifiable.

2. *Critical Justification of the Definition of the Formal Object of Physics*

We are doing philosophy of science and we cannot formulate definitions arbitrarily in order to find out later if they work. In fact, many philosophers of science say that a definition is good because in applying it and the consequent method science has in fact succeeded. Evidently that is insufficient. We must be able to demonstrate that this object alone is necessarily the object of physics, and that it could not be otherwise.[78]

Eddington seems to restrict the affirmation of a fact when he writes, "The essential point is that, although we seem to have very definite conceptions of objects in the external world, those conceptions do not enter into exact science and are not in any way confirmed by it. Before exact science can begin to handle the problem they must be replaced by quantities representing the results of physical measurement" (NPW, 253 [255]). And a little later he writes, "I should like to make it clear that the limitation of the scope of physics to pointer readings and the like is not a philosophical craze of my own but is essentially the current scientific doctrine. It is the outcome of a tendency discernible far back in the last century but only formulated comprehensively with the advent of the relativity theory" (NPW, 254 [257]).

Sir James Jeans also writes, "The essential point is not that science has tried this method. It is that it has been constrained to apply it by the brute facts of nature. One physical concept after another has been abandoned, not willy-nilly but of necessity. . . ."[79]

Is there a way to demonstrate this thesis that would satisfy the demands of the philosopher? He is not content with a fact which could be simply contingent. It seems to me this can be done and that we find the necessary elements already in Aristotle and St. Thomas, notably in their doctrine concerning proper and common sensibles. Proper sensibles are indefinable, they are the proper object of sense and intuitive. It is impossible to define sensed heat. This knowledge is incommunicable. One must have the sensation even to know what it is. And this knowledge cannot analyze the datum or define it. Proper sensibles are as facts irreducible, the one cannot be used to explain the other. They are only reducible as "proper sensibles"; and this has no abstract definition: it is defined by reference to sensation.

It is in this sense that sensible qualities are subjective (which does not mean that they have no objective foundation). If our knowledge of the world were limited to this, there would indeed be a metaphysics and an arithmetic, but a discursive knowledge of the objective structure of the world would be impossible. But there is more. In the sensible there is not only this aspect.

> Sic autem se habent sensus ad cognoscendum res, in quantum similitudo rerum est in sensu. Similitudo autem rerum est in sensu . . . uno modo, primo et per se; sicut in visu est similitudo colorum, et aliorum propriorum sensibilium. Alio modo, per se, sed non primo; sicut in visu est similitudo figurae, vel magnitudinis, et aliorum communium sensibilium.[80]

> [S]ensibilia primo et per se immutant sensum, cum sint qualitates alterantes; sensibilia vero communia omnia reducuntur ad quantitatem. Et de magnitudine quidem et numero patet quod sunt species quantitatis . . . sentire motum et quietem est quodammodo unum et multa. Quantitas autem est proximum subjectum qualitatis alternitivae, ut superficies est subjectum coloris. Et ideo sensibilia communia non movent sensum primo et per se sed ratione sensibilis qualitatis, ut superficies ratione coloris. Nec tamen sunt sensibilia per accidens, quia hujusmodi sensibilia aliquam diversitatem faciunt in immutatione sensus. Alio enim modo immutatur sensu a magna superificie et a parva; quia etiam ipsa albedo dicitur magna vel parva; et ideo dividitur secundum proprium subjectum.[81]

> [The senses relate to knowledge of things insofar as there is a likeness of things in sense. The likeness of things is in sense, first, primarily and

per se, as there is a likeness of colors in sight, and so it is with the other proper sensibles. Second, per se but not primarily, as the likeness of shape or magnitude or other common sensibles are in sight.

(S)ensibles affect sense first and per se, since they are altering qualities; all the common sensibles are reduced to quantity. Magnitude and number are obviously species of quantity . . . to sense motion and rest is in a way one and many. Quantity is the proximate subject of altering quality, as surface is the subject of color. Thus common sensibles do not affect sense primarily and per se but by reason of sensible quality, as surface by reason of color. But they are not sensibles per accidens, because such sensibles cause diversity in the immutation of sense. The sense is affected differently by a large and small surface, because whiteness itself is said to be large or small, and thus are distinguished according to their proper subject.]

Notice that it is a question here of the quantitative aspect properly speaking, as response to the question "how much?" and not to the exteriority underlying all quantity of which we will speak in a digression on the transcendental laws. (The exteriority and quantity both imply a comparison, but the one tells us "how" and the other tells us "how much.")

The interesting point in this problem is that this quantitative aspect is a common sensible independently of proper sensibles in their distinctive note. Not only could we make comparisons which would allow us to define the objects (homogeneity gives us a genus, and quantity the distinctive note), but this knowledge will be objective since we attain an aspect of material reality independent of the quality and number of our senses.[82] In this domain a veritable science of nature becomes possible. Quantity is defined by measurement (*quantitas est id quod mensura cognoscitur*). A quantity or physical magnitude will be defined by the way in which we have measured it. And that gives us a certain number specified by a certain procedure by which it has been obtained. The different procedures of measurement will establish a qualitative distinction between physical magnitudes.

What gives a critical value to this distinction is that another knowledge of nature in an experimental way is impossible. Our sensation of heat simply tells us that there is heat, and the repetition of this sensation, in hearing, for example, allows us simply to affirm that the sensation of heat and the hearing of sound differ. Outside of that, their domain cannot be explored, and that is explained by the fact that they are "proper" sensibles by definition. But the moment we ask "how much heat?" a fertile investigation becomes possible by comparison which will give us information about heat insofar as it is a magnitude. And what is remarkable is that a measure of this aspect is executable independently of the proper sensation itself and that this procedure allows us to define temperatures which are above or below our sensibility with a precision which far surpasses that of the senses.

Quantity being a universal property of the world of our experience, the science which concerns the quantitative aspect will be able to attain the world in its general structure. We will not be limited by the number of our senses, nor to those aspects which react on our senses. We will attain realities which have no sensible meaning.

It seems to us that it is in this sense that a critical study of the object of physics should be made. It is not because of the imperfection of our qualitative sensation that we can utilize it, but by reason of its very nature. This is the central point. If therefore the formal object of physics is number-measure, it is mathematical-physics by definition. We cannot therefore say that physics has in the past felt the attraction of ontology and that recently we have observed that a physics informed by mathematics and not ontology was possible, in short, a physics under the attraction of mathematics, of a mathematical physics.[83] So long as physics was not mathematical it was not physics. There is no question of an attraction, but of a mathematical constitution, or rather mathematical-physics. And that is not the same thing. Pure mathematics is indispensable for the physicist but it does not enter into the definition of his object and is in fact useful only insofar as it is translatable into terms which refer to the number-measures of the physicist.

It seems to us that Eddington understands his definition to have a critical, and philosophical, value and that it is in this sense that one can make its value explicit. As a corollary we could also say that the expression "For the empirical science of nature, on the contrary, in saying *ens sensibile,* sensible being, it is not on the *ens* but on the *sensibile* that one should put the accent" is a very ambiguous one. That certainly does not give us a proper definition of the object of physics, sensation is implied in the point of departure, and in physics one stays closer to that than in metaphysics or mathematics, but *sensibile* does not give us the formal note of the object of physics. The proper sensible is not formally envisaged. Nor is the metric aspect of the common sensible envisaged as formally sensible but as metric; sensation was only the prior necessary condition. Physics leads us to entities which have no sensible meaning and whose metric aspect cannot be resolved into the sensible, unless very indifferently. Thus a quantum is not representable even though a large quantity of quanta become sensible. It is not because they are thus reducible to the 'sensible' that they are real, because taken formally they have properties which would be contradictory for properly sensible objects. They are not a parceling of the gross objects of our sensation. But they are not unreal because they are by definition insensible. A thing is not real because it is sensible. The material real is offered us in sensation, but it is not by sense that we recognize it as real, nor formally as material. From the moment a physical entity is in logical continuity with the measure-numbers of most advanced observation it has a real value. Understanding requires no more than that. To demand more is to restrict material reality to our measure, to our psychological complex. When one deduces from a mathematical formula the wave-particle character of a photon, this is because this character is a real property of the photon, though we do not find similar properties in our more immediate observation, and it is imaginative not representable, or non-familiar.[84]

The definition that Eddington gives us is therefore sufficient enough. To add the term 'sensible' would be to vitiate it.

It is not because Aristotle or St. Thomas have not pressed their critique far enough that it cannot be incorporated into our philosophy.

Chapter II. The Problem of Indeterminism

The statistical law could be defined as follows: *A law of nature which determines a phenomenon with a probability which grows by reason of the number of elements composing the phenomenon.* ("Elements" imply time as well.)

The sticky point is that we call that a "law of nature." Apropos of that objectification of probability, or of indeterminism, Einstein has said:

> That is not only nonsense, it is reprehensible nonsense. So say it! Indeterminism is a completely illogical concept. . . . This is because one confuses

> the subjective world with the objective world. The indeterminism of quantum physics is a subjective indeterminism. This must be related to something, without which indeterminism would make no sense, and in this case it is related to our incapacity to follow the course of individual atoms and predict their activities. . . . Here our concept is limited to an event contained in a section of time. It is cut off from the whole process. Our present way of applying the causal principle is very superficial. . . . I am in entire agreement with our friend Planck in the position he takes with regard to this principle. . . . He admits the impossibility of applying the causal principle to the inner processes of atomic physics in the present state of things; but he is definitely opposed to the thesis that states that from this *Unbrauchbarkeit* or inapplicability we should conclude that the process of causation does not exist in external reality.[85]

And when Einstein is told that it is the Englishmen Eddington and Jeans who hold the thesis of objective indeterminism, the following distinction must be made. "It is necessary to distinguish the physicist from the literary man when the two professions are combined in the same man. In England we have a great literature and a great discipline of style. . . . What I want to say is that there are scientific authors in England who are illogical and romantic in their books of popularization, but in their scientific work are subtle and logical thinkers."[86]

On the one hand Einstein is in agreement with Planck and on the other hand Planck declares himself in agreement with Einstein.[87] At bottom, he bases himself on the same principle, metaphysical moreover, that whatever is has been necessarily determined.

Surely there is no exception to that, as length does not make an exception to the absolute in being relative. All that is a truism, which tells us absolutely nothing of the structure of the physical world. Physical indeterminism is no more incompatible with metaphysical determinism than relative is with the absolute.

The physicist does not cut the world into ontologically defined entities, and he does not envisage his entities as being. The entities dealt with in physics are cuts physically effected. These cuts are not made arbitrarily. There are cuts in the world external to us independent of us. The discontinuity of matter imposes itself. Substances and accidents do not correspond to these discontinuous entities defined by the physical limits of these entities, and this, not because we do not have sufficient means to know them, but because it makes absolutely no sense.[88]

The universe of physics is a universe constituted by objects which we define by a bundle of number-measures obtained by a certain procedure of measurement, and that we link in a bundle by positing, on the basis of observations, provisorily sufficient for the needs of the physicist, an identity. When we speak of physical laws it is a question of laws which govern the behavior of these bundles, and not of laws which govern material beings as material, which is the business of the metaphysician. It is a question of laws which govern atoms, stars, electrons, not as being, or material, but as physical entities, bundles of number-measures. To study a fly as a being is to say nothing of the fly save as being, and for such purposes it might just as well be a shoe. Of course physical entities are determined, and everything that is is being, whatever it is. But what light can that shed for us? We can only utter truisms. An electron is necessarily an electron, and, having such mass, it has such mass, and choosing such an orbit in an atom it chooses that orbit, and being in the one it cannot be in another. It is all that insofar as it is all that. It changes necessarily when it changes.

Are not all these words? Precisely. We express quite simply in a more comprehensible fashion what they say who think they have to oppose physical indeterminism "because whatever is is determined."[89]

This metaphysical determinism is extended, not precisely where one cannot because whatever is is determined, but one gives the principle a physical sense. Thus, it will be said that the electron is necessarily in such an orbit, because it could not be in another, and there are physical reasons why it is necessarily there.

But the physical reason for which it is there is precisely that it was too improbable that it should be elsewhere. This reason is expressed in well-defined numbers, and what is remarkable is that the counter-chance is always a positive number, and never 0.

We can then choose: either this probability is purely objective, or it is of the nature of physical entities. For the first thesis, there must be physical reasons. But there aren't any. Determinism makes no physical sense. Therefore the thesis is entirely gratuitous.

Einstein wants to change the point by saying that our physical entity is severed from its environment. That is true, but in saying that this is the reason we do not succeed in finding the determining element we always postulate that there has to be an element that determines in an absolute fashion. But that is what must be shown physically, and it cannot be.[90]

Einstein and Planck do not take into account that the principle they invoke is of the metaphysical order. The principle of causality of Aristotle and the scholastics was incomplete, according to Einstein, and it was Newton who completed it.[91]

But in fact in Aristotle and the scholastics it was a question of something else. Moreover, Einstein gives Newton's principle of causality a metaphysical value. And he does not see the difference. Planck does the same thing. Both are doing metaphysics in physics.[92]

Some scholastics have allied themselves with Einstein and Planck because they think that Eddington's opinion calls into question the metaphysical principle of causality. There is no question of the latter in physics.[93] Once more, this causality is not envisaged in physics, not because our knowledge of phenomena is incomplete, but because it makes no sense there. This is not to say that there is not causality in the world but only that the physicist does not look at it from that point of view. And because this world of the physicist does not furnish entities that the metaphysician can handle, the latter does not find there matter which would allow him to find in it the relation of causality.

The causality of which the physicist speaks is an expression which does not at bottom designate only determinability. The determination it envisages is not necessarily absolute. It is what he finds there.

With the exception of Einstein and Planck, most modern physicists are in agreement on this last point. It is a question of hypothesis. That which succeeds will be the true theory. Thus Hermann Weyl writes,

> Natural science is too easily condemned as a brute materialism because of its adherence, down the centuries, to a strictly determinist position. One who takes into account the extended applicability and precision of the mathematical laws of nature, as these are revealed principally in astronomy and physics, must admit that this position was the only fruitful one; the limits of determination by law will be discovered when one follows the law to the end, and not by evasion, compromise, indolence or sentimentality. We think we have firmly touched these limits in quantum mechanics. . . . Classical physics, after decades of invasion by statistical

> theories, has actually been at last superseded by quantum theory, and a new situation has presented itself.[94]

For Weyl, determinism was therefore a legitimate hypothesis. Millikan goes a little farther.

> The hypothesis of determinism in the domain of macroscopic physical phenomena has succeeded up until now, and has furnished us much knowledge. In some microscopic or elementary processes, its exactitude has been put in question by physicists. I refer obviously to Heisenberg's uncertainty principle, but this raises no question for macroscopic phenomena and for applications, that is, these phenomena are in conformity with the working hypothesis of scientific determinism as the physicist has always used it. I am in no way interested in metaphysical or philosophical determinism because this represents precipitous generalizations or assertions of universal value, one even trespasses on domains which lie outside those in which, by a long process of prediction and experimental verification, the principle in question has been found to be a useful and dependable working hypothesis. . . . For me, philosophical determinism is a pure dogma without interest for the physicist. . . .[95]

The text is ambiguous. Eddington goes farther and states that determinism cannot even be considered a working hypothesis, precisely for methodological reasons. The physicist ought to take into account that such a hypothesis surpasses any need and is absolutely unverifiable.

The determinism of macroscopic phenomena is only apparent, just as the absolute of length was only apparent. Only, in length, there was something true, whereas determinism is fundamentally false. It is a postulate that makes no sense. The physicist who gives an absolute value to length sins by generalization; in macroscopic phenomena there is not even a point of reference.

In the world of the physicist "impossible" has no meaning. Everything is possible but many things are too improbable to be realized. Observed uniformity is an average uniformity. In this thesis chance becomes normal, an element of which one takes account along with regularity; it becomes a numerical function every bit as determinate as average uniformity, it becomes a rule, an element of uniformity. In classical physics, chance was a strange intruder that one indeed interpreted as due to the imperfection of our knowledge, or as due to a defect in the universal machine. But in statistical laws, "the exception becomes the rule," as Eddington wrote. The theory of indeterminism is a physical explanation, whereas the other theory has recourse to an impossible metaphysics. And one posits it to explain the givens of observation which seem incoherent precisely because one has posited the determinist requirement.

The classical affirmation that in identical circumstances, a certain phenomenon will present itself in an identical fashion, is an ambiguous claim. In a sense it is true, insofar as it is only the expression of a truism: one defines the circumstances as identical. But in physics, the definition of this identity must be physical, and that in no way requires determinism: circumstances will be the same only if one falls into the metaphysical truism.

What relation could there be between this physical determinism and a cosmological determinism? That is a question that can be asked, the material object of natural philosophy and of physics being the same in what concerns the inorganic. Cosmology, applying the principle of causality, will say that the effect is predetermined in its cause, which is its measure. The free agent is an auto-determiner. The non-free agent acts in a determinate way to the exclusion of every other possibility. He acts thus because he could not act otherwise. The free agent could act otherwise on condition of another determinate agent. The non-free agent has no choice, it does not dispose its own activity. And in this sense it is determinist.

But, again, this term 'determinist' is ambiguous. As opposed to 'free,' it is legitimate. But indeterminism is not equivalent to freedom. Scholastic cosmology is used to dealing with realities such as prime matter which is the determinably undetermined by definition. Obviously it does not exist, but it co-exists. Even so it is a principle of material being which is determinable in any way it is. Is there determinism in the being and activity of individual material beings? (We speak of a determinism that is not the expression of a pure truism.) In such a way that such a material being (whatever it is) is necessarily, and necessarily as it is? Another ambiguity. Obviously there is nothing that does not have a cause, but the problem is to know how it was in the cause. What is the element that made it be and to be thus? Of course, some determinate reason. And this, could it not be "because that is the most probable"? Because that suffices for this thing to be and to be as it is.

We cannot contradict this except by giving the truism "whatever is is determined" a meaning it does not have. Such an application would even lead to the negation of the possibility of freedom. The difference between freedom and indeterminism is that freedom is auto-determinist, whereas indeterminism in non-free nature acquires its determination according to a law of nature, and that is statistical.

Note that we have already slid into a domain foreign to cosmology. The "such a material being" of cosmology is a vague being. "I am a material being," without any doubt. But don't ask me to define my physical homologue. That would not work at all. The only way in which we make cuts in the world of observation is physical, and ontologically defined entities do not correspond to these cuts.

Unless we can prove that this statiticity does not suffice for material beings to be (whatever they are) and that they are such. The philosopher could not deny that. In fact, the physicist tells us why his entities have for him such determinations, notably, because they are probable. That is the only determinism we need.

When we speak of contingency in nature, we speak of a phenomenon of observation. Is there really contingency in nature? Determinism answers that this contingency is only apparent and that if there are exceptions to laws that is because there is a certain disequilibrium in nature. But this disequilibrium does not provoke contingency in the strict sense of the term, for the very exceptions are strictly determined by fundamental laws, as the working of a defective machine. There is at the bottom of nature a necessity which governs the behavior of all material beings with mathematical rigor.

But all that is a pure postulate. Because a certain determinism permits us to predict phenomena, must we deduce that this determinism is rigorous? The contingency observed in current life, isn't it only apparent, in such a way that it is due to the imperfection of our knowledge of the fundamental laws that govern phenomena that leads us to speak of contingency? Let us take a shorter route and say that the exception is a rule implied in the very definition of laws. Why not? The only reason that we could not bring in is that there is a "premeditated" determinism, which does not explain the fact we are confronting.

For a Thomist, the objective indeterminism of Eddington ought to be the most natural thing in the world. And it is not without emotion that we have read the two paragraphs that Father Sertillanges devotes to this subject in his magisterial *Saint Thomas d'Aquin* (book II, chapter iii). Since the statement of the principle of Cournot, he has given an objective value to it.

We retract what we said earlier in this study. Here is an eminent Thomist author who has treated the problem in a fundamental manner.

Indeterminism is in nature and not only in our way of conceiving events.

> Those who have believed it possible for an intelligence which proceeds as ours does, that is, by abstraction from matter, to establish a general formula of the world such that every single event would be covered by it, do not understand what matter is. They imagine that the singular is one with the universal, and that this is entirely penetrated and exhausted, whereas the universal abstracting always from some thing, and that every idea, even the most precise, being inevitably a schema, it is forever impossible, by human means, to get into laws everything that nature realizes.[96]

"We do not know the whole of anything." That is more than an observation; there is an arrest because the whole one would penetrate envelops the infinity of potency, because this whole is not even a whole, being undetermined with regard to every power of acting and of knowing.

> Moreover, that which we say escapes laws, that is, the cadres of abstract thought, is no less contained under the law, being posited and ineluctably posited by the ensemble of conditions of the real. What comes from matter, as opposed to form, proceeds no less from nature. Matter too is nature. He who would master it by a knowledge which would hold all the contingent within it, for he would know all by this activity, the impediments and the rest. But it is not in laws that he would know all, it would be by a total intuition. . . . So one sees that what is repudiated here is an outrageous intellectualism or notionalism; it is the prejudice according to which the real is only an agglomeration of abstractions, which enumerated, would enable us to hold the other. It is only the creative idea that we admit as an idea exhausting the whole of reality, and when it pleases God, that he communicates to spirits. (68–69)

Father Sertillanges deduces all that from the fundamental principles of our philosophy and not from the applications made by Aristotle and St. Thomas. Not having the idea of progress, they considered the world as always being what it is. They have cut the world into changeless species, and the universal cortege marches in a circle. Contingency in nature was due to accidents. In the indeterminist thesis, the 'accident' enters into the law. It is part of the immanent order. As Eddington said, "The exception becomes the rule."[97]

Therefore everything that takes place in nature has its reason in the absolute of being, without becoming necessary. "[T]he principle of sufficient reason has lost nothing here that belongs to it as it expresses the law of being, that is, insofar as derived from the principle of contradiction. One only says that being, in its amplitude, comprises the undetermined, and therefore reasons which are not the reasons of the rationalists" (69).

The limits imposed by indeterminism then are not due exclusively to our way of conceiving the real but are limits of the things themselves. It would be impossible for us to foresee the whole "because these causes contain a dose of irremediable indetermination" (70).

"It obviously follows that the contingent as such is inaccessible to understanding. Probabilities are tailored to mind, but the contingent under this respect is no longer contingent. For if it is contingent that it rains in summer it is not contingent that it rains more in summer than in the spring or autumn. The frequent, as frequent, constitutes in its manner a law; the accidental as such does not, because the pretended *ensemble* of its conditions cannot be integrated, the undetermined introducing itself there as an irreducible element" (67). "[N]o certitude immanent in the world englobes all the effects produced there; no prognosis is sure, even when proceeding from an achieved science, if it has a relation to the flow and counterflow which have their seat in nature" (74). The future is not rigorously predeterminable because this future is not rigorously predetermined by the present. As Heisenberg says, "a complete knowledge of the past implies a contradiction," in this sense that the present is not the only possible result of the past.

What Sertillanges says is a strong argument against those who have seen in the indeterminist thesis a reflection of the idealism of Eddington. Evidently, this thesis has an idealist air for those who say apriori that the indeterminism of our laws is subjective. The achievement of the things themselves (whatever they be) follows an indeterminist path. This is not to say a purely indeterminist path! It is the things themselves that lead us from that angelic knowledge which should envelop the material universe in what it will be, because it knows what is at present. For a spirit that contemplates the universe in its present entirety, the future would be in large part a matter of conjecture, insofar as the real itself is an affair of conjecture in that which concerns the future. Here is a fundamental development of Sertillanges with respect to this:

> Truth comes to intelligence from its conformity with things. Conformity, that is to say, in Thomist language, participation in the *form,* reception in us of the intelligibility diffused in the world and by which it is; for nothing is that does not have its intelligible reason (*propria ratio*), that is not defined by mind and for mind: I say *by,* thinking of creative thought; *for* because of the reflection of it that the object of human intelligence communicates to us after having been realized in matter. It follows from this that it is true at a given moment that is, for that moment, defined intelligibly in itself or in its causes. Therefore, if a source of indetermination is found in nature, a background that universal intelligibility does not envelop, there would be a black hole there, a limit to the truth immanent in the world. One would therefore surpass the true in saying of a future contingent: That will be, because 'that will be' would have truth only if it is referred to an *act,* that is, to a really given intelligibility; but the future contingent arises by definition from potency, from the obscure depth that the soul of the world does not penetrate: it cannot be called true, and what it will have later, if it comes to be, cannot make a return to the past to sanction an affirmation without a foundation of actual intelligibility.
>
> It has been said that the contingent as such has no generation; that is because it has no being. And how will it be since nothing is ordered to it in nature; since it has no proper form; that is, one which represents an idea of nature, that sees its elements contained in this frame at once ideal and real that we call form. I understand form in its most general sense, be it only a form of order, based on real relations. But that which is pure encounter arising from the indeterminable depth of things, that is not a natural reality, for first of all, it is not a work of nature, being sought by nothing, and second, it is not *one* save in the mind that joins the terms. It is a linking one can form afterward by calling it true, for the reality obtained repeats itself there, but this only furnishes the elements taken separately, and the linking is as such our work. It follows that the intelligibility that it contains does not come from the depth of nature, it is born from the relation of the facts obtained, not from the intelligible

> relation of causes. There is then no regression of truth and that it may be true that it rains today does not prove that yesterday it was true to say, tomorrow it will rain. (71–73)

Sertillanges is here closely following St. Thomas[98] who gives us the means to solve the question. From the side of cosmology there is no objection to Eddington's thesis. There is indeterminism in nature and the physicist will find this indeterminism in his laws. What could be more natural? The thesis of indeterminism, postulated as a methodological principle, is therefore not a pure working hypothesis. It is philosophically justifiable whereas that of determinism is not.

The determination of the world is therefore that of statistics. And this is contradictory only by falsifying the meaning of the truism "determination." "God, in creating the contingent, determined it to be, but precisely because it is contingent we must say it is that God determined it. It does not thereby become necessary. If one could put it so: God determined it to be indeterminate" (77).

We think that these few reflections will suffice to show that the thesis of Eddington is not as illogical as has been thought, and that it was already, with respect to its fundamental principles, incorporated in Thomism in all its range.

M. Maritain is not at all in agreement with this way of seeing things. In a paragraph on *liaisons dangereuses,* he tells us, just as he had done on relativity, that "To give a philosophical value to this abandonment [of determinism] which makes sense only in the empiriological domain would be a grave mistake."[99] He does not see that it is precisely the point of view of indeterminism which is in the philosophical order, just as he had not seen the point of relativity which has nothing to do with the physical principle.

Again he brings in pure spirits which would see the absolute dimensions, absolute time, absolute simultaneity, in order to see strict causality in the phenomena of nature.

> It is impossible for human science to know determinately the behavior of a corpuscle at each instant. For it observes and measures things with the aid of material instruments and in virtue of physical activities, and can only see an electron by jogging it with light. But suppose a pure spirit, who knows *without material means* (and so, no longer by means

> of empiriological concepts) the behavior of this corpuscle at each instant, it would see that the principle of causality applies strictly and in its full ontological sense. The hypothesis of a pure spirit has no meaning for physics. But if it had no meaning for a metaphysician, there would be no metaphysics.[100]

He explicitly rejects Eddington's way of seeing. For M. Maritain if there were no *free* agent in the universe, "it is clear that a certain event which has occurred here below (for example, the fact that a certain squirrel is climbing up a certain tree at a certain moment) was infallibly predetermined in the configuration of *all* the factors in the universe posited at the beginning. But in that case, there is only a necessity *of fact,* no necessity *of right.*"[101]

Nowhere does he make explicit the basis for this clarity. It seems to me that after examining the doctrine of Sertillanges, this clarity has been sufficiently dissipated. Without doubt, M. Maritian closely followed the developments of St. Thomas who was content with interpreting in an orthodox way current doctrines without however granting them philosophical value.[102] Moreover, we will see in the second part of this study, that the distinction between necessity *of right* and necessity *of fact* introduced to save the situation is rather superficial and that, contrary to the ideas of Maritain, Eddington was right to put indeterminism in relation to freedom and even to require physical indeterminism for the exercise of freedom. His doctrine is more profound than has been thought. The liaison is a happy one.

One further remark. Indeterminism introduces a certain spontaneity into inorganic nature. The term 'spontaneity' that once was applied exclusively to organic phenomena has become ambiguous. Is this to say that there is no longer a distinction between these two? Not at all. The term has become generic. It is a question of finding the specific difference, and that has to be worked out by physicists and biologists.[103]

Chapter III. The Problem of the Physical Continuum

In our discussion of the transcendental laws we said that Eddington makes no effort to clarify the underlying problem concerning the nature of the continuous and discontinuous in physics. The continuous seems to be introduced into nature by the knowing subject, but he makes no definitive pronouncement.

This is not a very easy problem. Continuous and discontinuous seem to be immediate data. But it is difficult to disengage the subjective element from the objective element in perception. We observe what we sense as continuous is not, that sensation is crude and gives us a twisted image of reality. And then it can be legitimately asked what is objective in perception.

It seems that the physically discontinuous itself is inconceivable without a certain continuity. The property of spatial exteriority, of having notably parts outside of parts *quoad se*, seems to imply the continuous itself when it is a matter of actually distinct parts. Without that, the homogeneity[104] of the parts is inconceivable. They can only be outside one another spatially, that is, in an extended fashion. The continuous thus seems to be a prior condition of the discontinuous. But, on the other hand, the discontinuous is a condition of the perception of the continuous. An infinite continuous homogeneity is inconceivable. We even define the continuous by divisibility, by its potential parts, but the continuous as such is not divided.

How does it imply exteriority while being one and having parts only in potency? Note that the fundamental problem is to find why it implies physical exteriority, and not simply to take the datum of perception to dogmatize about it. It is not an analysis of this perception that will provide us light. Such an analysis makes absolutely no sense.

Mathematical analysis will not tell us why the physical continuum is spatially extended. Notice that the physicist seeks, in part, to find how things are extended. But if he wants to go farther this procedure will lead to contradiction. What does that signify but that the quantum of action is indivisible? One might reply that it is indivisible in fact, but not of right. It is at this point that an ingenious escape toward mathematics is made, or toward metaphysics. That explains absolutely nothing about what we are looking for. It is useless to compound the difficulty with foreign complications. What this signifies is that every continuum, applied to physics, is divisible by right. That has no meaning in physics and it is precisely that which we seek.

The continuum is a necessity of representation to the degree that the atomicity which is a fact of experience is a mystery to us, and in fact our mind makes an effort to level the discontinuities of nature in a continuous perfection.[105] Thus we bend nature to the needs of our representation. Our imagination bumps up against things. The continuous such as we represent it is in some way an obstacle. It has been remarked of Eddington that he makes the continuous subjective and that it is evident that is a mistake and that every physical entity has to have a certain extension, which, at the end of the day, is only "smaller" than what we imaginatively represent. Eddington's difficulty is not grasped. But Eddington is exceptionally a man who knows more than he grasps and more than he can express. If one requires that we speak only of things we can formulate, everyone must close his mouth, for we do not know the whole of anything. The things that we do not know how to express are the most interesting. What then of the metaphysical definition, so clear, so evident? It is too clear to be false. But it is not clear how it applies to the physical continuum, and it is not at all clear that it has a representative sense. It is not clear that the fundamental elements of nature are extended like the objects of our crude and not too clear perception.

Eddington indeed recognizes the difficulty. What does it mean that every physical element is divisible by right, that a quantum of action is divisible by right? How is it continuous? We must find the answer.

PART TWO

Beyond Number Measures

SECTION ONE

Epistemology and Metaphysics

We have already said that Eddington has no intention of giving us a coherent and achieved system of philosophy. His intention is rather to make some suggestions. Above all, he addresses his colleagues who deny too easily that which is not transposable into differential equations, who envisage the physical world as the only realm of reality, the only field of valuable experience. In fact, his suggestions are very profound, and one does not know how this genius has been pigeon-holed as an intelligent man, very capable in scientific matters, but who is certainly not at home in philosophical matters. These judgments are superficial and ridiculous. I do not hesitate to call him one of the greatest philosophers of our time.

Notice that all the criticisms without exception have condemned him as an idealist in the classical sense of the term, a subjectivist idealist. I do not understand how this has been possible. He calls himself an idealist, but that is only a question of words. But the critics have taken him at his word. We will take these criticisms into account as we lay out his doctrine, and if we insist too much on points that seem evident, it is to reply in advance to objections that have been raised.

The exposition of this second part will be less systematic than the first, because what he gives us does not lend itself to that. We will begin with a simple exegesis of certain texts. In the critical part we will try to coordinate the underlying ideas.

Terms like "metaphysics" and "epistemology" do not have the same sense for Eddington as they do for us. We are going to use these terms in their scholastic sense.

Chapter I: Some Fundamental Notions

Here is a text that created a scandal: "no one can deny that mind is the first and most direct thing in our experience, and all else is remote inference—inference either intuitive or deliberate" (NPW, 281 [281]).

This text in isolation is absolutely ambiguous. One has sought to make Eddington say that thought itself is the first and formal object of thought, and that he deduces from this that reality itself is pure thought. But there is nothing to this.

Let us first of all analyze some fundamental notions and afterward situate this famous text in the ensemble of these notions.

1. Knowability, the Fundamental Attribute of What Is[106]

One can answer the question "What is matter?" in two ways. Either by the physical properties defined by their procedures of measurement or indeed that which is the object of knowledge: "Something Mr. X knows."

The fact that matter is knowable as some thing raises this attribute to a fundamental property of matter (NPW, 264 [266]). What is meant by "knowable"? To be knowable is to be actual. Actuality distinguishes that which is from that which is merely possible and does not in fact exist. It is actuality that distinguishes the world of our experience from other conceivable worlds but to which our consciousness does not react (264 [265]). The actual world is the one to which our consciousness reacts (265 [266]). The knowability of that which is is described as the capacity to awake consciousness in us. "That which is," as such, and consciousness of "that which is" require neither definition nor justification. They are immediate data.

My individual consciousness of that which is does not imply that it is just because I know it. Its actuality is given as independent of my contingent consideration. What is is not given as knowable because *I* know it, rather actuality itself is given as knowable.

"If actuality means 'known to mind' then it is a purely subjective character of the world; to make it objective we must substitute 'knowable to mind'. The less stress we lay on the accident of parts of the world being known at the present era to particular minds, the more stress we must lay on the *potentiality* of being known to mind as a fundamental objective property of matter, giving it the status of actuality whether individual consciousness is taking note of it or not" (NPW, 267 [268–69]).

I see an object, say carbon. Does this immediately mean that I have an intuition of carbon? Not at all. "*Immediate* knowledge [is] of something (not carbon) in my own mind." The point of contact between my mind and carbon is not in carbon. "Light waves are propagated from the table to the eye;

chemical changes occur in the retina; propagation of some kind occurs in the optic nerves; atomic changes follow in the brain. Just where the final leap into consciousness occurs is not clear. We do not know the last stage of the message in the physical world before it became a sensation in consciousness" (NPW, 267–68, 269 [269, 270]).

So there is no question of a simplistic immediacy. We cannot identify the voice that comes to us over the telephone with everything at the other end. But it is precisely the search for what is at the other end that Eddington calls "inference."

It will have been noticed that "mind" is a rather broad notion implying whatever is related to consciousness and not exclusively the intellectual faculty. Moreover he does not give it any further precision elsewhere.

Before elaborating this theory of inference, let us examine another fundamental notion.

2. *The Concrete and the Real*[107]

Eddington has a holy horror of these two terms. When the man in the street is asked to point to something real, he will choose something concrete, and will reject as unreal whatever does not strike him within a bold imaginative representation.

This conception is foreign to physics; what is more typically real for the physicist is matter (in the sense of physics) because it is less charged with ambiguous attributions stemming from our psychological makeup.

What does the physicist mean by reality? "Physical reality is the synthesis of all possible physical aspects of nature. . . . Reality is only obtained when all conceivable points of view have been combined" (STG, 182 [223–24]). By these points of view Eddington does not mean to say only the different physical situations, but also the agreement among physicists concerning the value of exteriority of a certain entity.

"The only subject presented to me for study is the content of my consciousness." (Recall that this content of consciousness includes the object immediately perceived by consciousness insofar as it is immediately perceived.)

> You are able to communicate to me part of the content of your consciousness which thereby becomes accessible in my own. For reasons which are generally admitted, though I should not like to have to prove

> that they are conclusive, I grant your consciousness equal status with my own; and I use this second-hand part of my consciousness to "put myself in your place." Accordingly my subject of study becomes differentiated into the contents of many consciousnesses, each content constituting a *view-point.* There then arises the problem of combining the view-points, and it is through this that the external world of physics arises. Much that is in any one consciousness is individual, much is apparently alterable by volition; but there is a stable element which is common to other consciousnesses. That common element we desire to study, to describe as fully and accurately as possible, and to discover the laws by which it combines now with one view-point, now with another. This common element cannot be placed in one man's consciousness rather than in another's; it must be in neutral ground—an external world. (NPW, 283–84 [283–84])

That is a text that has troubled many critics. Is it truly in contradiction with what was said in the preceding paragraph? Not at all. Precisely because this aspect of the world is inferred. We seek that which is truly external to us and how it is independently of us. This is not to say that agreement among different consciousnesses is the sole guarantee of exteriority, since, if that were true, we would not even know what exteriority meant. But we do not fabricate it. What we wish to know is the truly external and to distinguish it from what we project into the external world.

Does that mean that realities like color are purely subjective? No, color has a homologue in the external world on which all are in agreement. But color as a sensible quality is something outside our control. It is linked to our psychological complex that we do not know how to exteriorize. We do not know how to locate these qualities physically. "I can understand that a philosopher may wish to assert that when we experience the taste-of-an-apple there must be something in the external world that may appropriately be called taste for us to experience; but wherever the taste in the external world may reside, it certainly does not reside in the apple. When I am asked to believe in an actual apple with an actual taste in it—or an actual dentist's drill with an actual pain in it—I can only answer that science made up its mind long ago that the relation of the actual objects to our sensations was not of that simple kind" (PP 33).

The assertion of the subjectivity of color does not come down to a simple negation of its reality, but its physical reality, which is a conventional reality.

Reality obviously has a more profound sense than the conventional reality of the physicist. In fact, the latter must derive his sense from a more profound reality he in some way presupposes. "When we (scientists) assert of anything in the external world that it is real and that it exists, we are expressing our belief that the rules of the symposium have been correctly applied. . . . We refuse to contemplate the awful contingency that the external world, after all our care in arriving at it, might be disqualified by failing to exist . . ." (NPW, 285 [285–86]).

What at bottom is it to exist, to be real? Eddington here leads us back to the first paragraph. The physicist gives a definition of reality. But reality taken formally is not defined. It is "that to which consciousness reacts. This immediate consciousness is the point of departure of every inference. Physical entities are real insofar as they are in continuity with this fundamental consciousness. If we are to find for the atoms and electrons of the external world not merely a conventional reality but 'reality (loud cheers)' we must look not to the end but to the beginning of the quest. It is at the beginning that we must find that sanction which raises these entities above the mere products of an arbitrary mental exercise" (NPW, 287 [287]).

So let us say that implicitly reality is such that it is able to act on a consciousness. There is then a certain homogeneity between what is and consciousness. We could put this another way, namely, that what is is the *stuff of mind.*

3. *The Nature of Reality*

The expression "mind-stuff" has also caused scandal. Yet it is only the expression of the homogeniety between the knower and the known. (We would say that being is intelligible.) The consciousness that we have of ourselves does not differ essentially from the consciousness we have of the other. "The mind-stuff of the world is, of course, something more general than our individual conscious minds; but we may think of its nature as not altogether foreign to the feelings in our consciousness" (NPW, 276 [277]). This does not mean that this mind-stuff is conscious by definition. It is only here and there that this stuff comes into consciousness.

This homogeneity should not be confused with an identity. Mind-stuff, a general attribute, is not incompatible with distinct parts (NPW, 277 [278]).

> It is sometimes urged that the basal stuff of the world should be called 'neutral stuff' rather than 'mind-stuff,' since it is to be such that both mind and matter originate from it. If this is intended to emphasize that only limited islands of it constitute actual minds, and that even in these islands that which is known mentally is not equivalent to a complete inventory of all that may be there, I agree. In fact I should suppose that the self-knowledge of consciousness is mainly or wholly a knowledge which eludes the inventory method of description. The term 'mind-stuff' might well be amended; but neutral stuff seems to be the wrong kind of amendment. It implies that we have two avenues of approach to an understanding of its nature. We have only one approach, namely, through our direct knowledge of mind. The supposed approach through the physical world leads only into the cycle of physics, where we run round and round like a kitten chasing its tail and never reach the world-stuff at all. (NPW, 280 [281–82])

We have dwelt on this text because it has been generally criticized, and misinterpreted. Eddington opposes himself here to the irrational of positivism which would have it that reality and thought are heterogeneous. But he insists that what we do not know, individually and collectively, is still real, knowable. In this sense the stuff of the world is, independently of our contingent consciousness, mind-stuff.

If this is idealism, what would we mean by realism? Let us cite here a relevant text of Monsignor Noël: "the whole ontological theory of knowledge according to the scholastics rests on assimilation and on the union which definitively supposes a relationship between the knower and the known, a homogeneity of nature. If that is idealism, there remains to represent realism only an irrational materialism of which there are rather obvious instances in the course of history."[108]

4. The World of Inference

Let us look more closely at the problem. Whatever is not in our mind is a remote inference, that is, all that of which we do not have immediate experience, and not, as it has been interpreted, all that which is itself mind. "We are acquainted with an external world because its fibers run into our consciousness; it is only our own ends of the fibers that we actually know; from those ends we more or less successfully reconstruct the rest, as a palaeontologist reconstructs an extinct monster from its footprint" (NPW, 278 [279]).

Therefore we begin with the sensible data in our mind. We do not know what they are. Matter, electricity, potential? It matters little, they refer to external objects. Still, let us note that perception in our mind is something quite different from the physical object, although our knowledge of physical objects is finally derived from such perceptions. To confuse the mental object with the physical object,[109] is to confuse the clues with the criminal.

In sensible data we notice certain regularities, recurrences that the physicist enumerates. Regularities are analyzed into laws, and thus give us the rules of inference (PP, 33), which allow us to find the underlying scheme of these regularities. Regularities have the guarantee of their exteriority in the agreement of different minds, and what is furnished us by instruments. Such are the requirements of the physicist.

Note that the inferential procedure of the man in the street does not differ essentially from this. The inferences differ in degree, not in nature. The familiar objects that we handle are also inferred; like a remote star that we infer from a feeble image on photographic film, or an undiscovered planet inferred by the gravitational influences manifest by the movement of Uranus. Only the physicist confines himself to what is controllable.

Thus the law of the rectilinear propagation of light enables us to locate the object which has produced the visual sensation. Light and the object that emits it are expressed in number-measures, symbols. The steps of the inference are thus exactly the inverse of those of the physical transmission which bears the information. "Commonly we think of it only in its second aspect as a physical transmission; but because it is also a line of inference it is subject to limitations which we should not necessarily expect a physical transmission to conform to" (NPW, 270 [272–73]).

All this inferential knowledge is symbolic insofar as it is physics. Insofar as we have strictly applied the rules of the symposium, it can be attached to the fundamental property of that which we immediately perceive, that is, what is real knowledge, that the symbols are the physical structure of the stuff of the world, of mind-stuff.

Again, note the distinction that Eddington establishes between intuitive and willed inference. It is spontaneous inference that we make in opening our eyes and which is the precursor of scientific inference. Willed inference is that we make in scientific research with the intention of expressing as objectively as possible the external world.

This immediate realism is therefore not so simple a thing. It does not imply that we have an intuition of physical objects which would define the objects physically, but simply that we have the perception of a sensible datum as real object in consciousness. What in fact might be the perception of a cerebral entity, or even the object to which this is referred by way of spontaneous inference, that for the moment is not of importance.

5. *The Critical Value of Consciousness*

"Thought is one of the indisputable facts of the world. I know that I think, with a certainty which I cannot attribute to any of my physical knowledge of the world" (NPW, 258 [260]). "There is no question about consciousness being real or not; consciousness is self-knowing and the epithet real adds nothing to that" (NPW, 265 [267]).

This consciousness is formally the consciousness of the actuality of consciousness. It reacts to what is actual and in this reaction it perceives itself as actual. And Eddington quotes Clifford: "The succession of feelings which constitutes a man's consciousness is the reality which produces in our minds the perception of the motions of his brain" (NPW, 278 [279]; STG, 191–92 [235–36]). It is a question therefore of a consciousness conditioned by a sensible object. Thus the perception of becoming is a condition of consciousness. This consciousness of becoming is immediate and becomes an attribute of the subject. "If I grasp the notion of existence because I myself exist, I grasp the notion of becoming because I myself become" (NPW, 97 [110]).

In no way is it a question for Eddington of a pure consciousness, but always of consciousness of some thing. In the consciousness of himself, the 'himself' is always envisaged as a real, an existent, an actual consciousness which is awakened by the perception of the sensible.

But his expressions are often ambiguous. Thus, the object immediately perceived is interior to mind. But it is not mind. He calls this object the "mental image, which is in our minds and not in the external world" (NPW, 254 [256]).

But it must be understood. We must extend the notion of mind. Thus, sensation is in the mind, and in this, what sensation as sensation is is interior to mind. This object is not inferred, and in this sense it does not belong to the inferred world that one calls external insofar as it is established according to the laws of the symposium of physicists. It is not accordingly a matter of exteriority as such[110] which is the foundation presupposed by number-measures. It is the real object with which consciousness is in immediate contact (whatever be the meaning of this contact). It is an image, not in the sense that it is a mental image in which we perceive a reflection of a real object. This image is of the real, but of the real per se which comes by way of spontaneous inference to another real that we call external insofar as it is inferred by the rules of the symposium. In this sense it is an image.

It seems to me that all this is the purest immediate realism. (Beware of confusing this 'image' with the scholastic 'species.' Eddington does not press his analysis of the ontological conditions of knowledge that far.) Its critical value resides in the fact that the object is fundamentally given as real, as actuality, as mind-stuff, and not as pure consciousness or thought. There is no question then of a *cogito ergo sum,* but of a 'I think the real' and 'I think myself as real.' This reality is not a term of reasoning judgment, but it is given in the act of thinking itself.

That is the point of departure of all true science. "We can only reason from data and the ultimate data must be given to us by a non-reasoning process—a self-knowledge of that which is in our consciousness" (NPW, 333–34 [330]). ('By itself' means 'without intermediary' or immediate.)

6. The Objectivity of the External World

We bring up this point because strange things have been said of Eddington concerning the objectivity of the external world. One reads the following in the epilogue of Planck's *Where Is Science Going?*:

MURPHY: If you say that the man of science is content to be assured of the mathematical logic of his mental construction, you will soon be cited as confirming the subjective idealism promulgated by modern men of science like Sir Arthur Eddington.

EINSTEIN: That would be ridiculous.

MURPHY: Evidently that would be an unjustifiable conclusion but you have been widely cited in the British press as subscribing to the theory that the external world is derived from consciousness. . . . M. Joad has written an excellent book on this entitled *Philosophical Aspects of Science.* This book is a contradiction of the attitude taken by Sir Arthur Eddington and Sir James Jeans and your name is mentioned as confirming their theories.

EINSTEIN: No physicist could believe that for he would no longer be a physicist, anymore than the physicists that you have mentioned. It is necessary to make a distinction between a literary mode and a scientific statement. Why would one take the trouble to look at the stars unless he thought the stars were really there? On this I am in total agreement with Planck. We cannot logically prove the existence of the external world, anymore than you could logically prove that I am speaking to you now and that I am here. But you know that I am here and no subjective idealist could persuade you to the contrary. (212–13)

Long before this Eddington had written: "There is a doctrine well known to philosophers that the moon ceases to exist when no one is looking at it. I will not discuss the doctrine since I have not the least idea what is the meaning of the word existence when used in this connection. At any rate the science of astronomy has not been based on this spasmodic kind of moon. In the scientific world (which has to fulfill functions less vague than merely existing) there is a moon which appeared on the scene before the astronomer; it reflects sunlight when no one sees it; it has mass when no one is measuring the mass; it is distant 240,000 miles from the earth when no one is surveying the distance; and it will eclipse the sun in 1999 even if the human race has succeeded in killing itself off before that date."[111]

Speaking elsewhere of this same doctrine he adds that it has absolutely nothing to do with the fundamental problem of reality.[112] Moreover, it is not by kicking the stone that one refutes even the idealism of Berkeley. "When Dr. Johnson felt himself getting tied up in argument over 'Bishop Berkeley's ingenious sophistry to prove the non-existence of matter, and that everything in the universe is merely ideal,' he answered, 'striking his foot with mighty force against a large stone, till he rebounded from it,—"I refute it *thus.*'" Just what that action assured him of is not very obvious; but apparently he found it comforting. And to-day the matter-of-fact scientist feels the same impulse to recoil from these flights of thought back to something kickable, although he ought to be aware by this time that what Rutherford has left us of the large stone is scarcely worth kicking."[113]

For Eddington, the question of proving the existence of the external world does not arise. It is thus that it is given to consciousness.

Let us keep these speculations on the conditions of consciousness, such as unity and permanence, and its objects like the beautiful and the good, for a later chapter, and take up next what Eddington calls "the problem of the meaning of values," a metaphysical problem.

Chapter II. The Problem of Meaning and Value

1. The Transcendental Point of View

"The interaction of ourselves with our environment is what makes up experience."[114] The exploration of the domain of the senses conducts us into the physical world. But the problem of experience is not limited to an interpretation of sensible impressions. There is a more fundamental problem. We have already seen that the problem of reality taken as such surpasses the strict limits of exact science. In physics, and likely in all the other sciences, it is sufficient to know how a definition "domesticates" and conventionalizes reality.[115] But there is the problem of reality itself which precedes every scientific problem and which embraces the scientific world, a problem which is raised by the immediate experience of reality.[116]

We have in us the innate conviction that the real given in immediate experience should have a more profound signification which must be sought by ways other than those of physics. The solution of this problem requires that we place ourselves in a more transcendental point of view.[117] We are led by an inner necessity to pose this problem, by a light that precedes us. Reality haunts us.[118] We have within us a desire for pure truth, a desire to know the fundamental why of things.[119]

> We have learnt that the exploration of the external world by the methods of physical science leads not to a concrete reality but to a shadow world of symbols, beneath which those methods are unadapted for penetrating. Feeling that there must be more behind, we return to our starting point in human consciousness—the one centre where more might become known. There we find other stirrings, other revelations (true or false) than those conditioned by the world of symbols. Are not these too of significance? We can only answer according to our conviction, for here reasoning fails altogether. Reasoning leads us from premises to conclusion; it cannot start without premises. The premises for our reasoning about the visible universe, as well as for our reasoning about the unseen world, are in the self-knowledge of mind. . . . Consciousness alone can determine the validity of its convictions. (SUW, 73–74)

That is a passage that requires exegesis. We have deliberately dissociated these passages and expressions from their context. For Eddington, this experience is essentially mystical, by it we share in the divine order, and the problem in question is essentially religious.[120] Critics have classified all this as the pious reveries of Eddington. But they have been misled by the words 'mystical' and 'religious' which are in fact ambiguous. But there is not the least doubt that what Eddington is looking for are the metaphysical conditions of the real, present to consciousness. Moreover, we will see how he resolves the problem.

But the problem appears to depend on our individual sense, on our personal conviction of that which needs a solution. We have no way of proving that the problem is a problem. "We cannot pretend to offer proofs. . . . Religious conviction is often described in somewhat analogous terms as a surrender; it is not to be enforced by argument on those who do not feel its claim in their own nature" (NPW, 337 [333]). "The starting-point of belief in mystical religion is a conviction of significance or, as I have called it, the sanction of a striving in the consciousness" (NPW, 333 [329]). "The conviction is scarcely a matter to be argued about, it is dependent on the forcefulness of the feeling of awareness" (NPW, 334 [330]).

The conviction thus seems to be a personal affair and to depend on our mystical sense. (So you will tell me that I am wrong to wish to interpret all that as metaphysics.) By that, Eddington wishes simply to insinuate that if a man hasn't this sense, he is not a metaphysician. And who could contradict that? Not all men are metaphysicians, they do not have this sense, this conviction that what reality offers to our consciousness poses a transcendental problem. If this consciousness is not in them, how could we prove that they do not have it?

Furthermore, he seems to pose this problem as posterior to the physical problem, but in other passages he assures us that the problem comes before any other problem and embraces them. No one thinks that physics is going to answer all possible questions. (And in fact, philosophy was at bottom physics, historically). In this sense, we return to the point of departure and we realize that the problem posed there is immediate and does not depend on others; on the contrary, the sense of the others depends on it.

If the physicist wants his world to make sense, to be real, to be true, he must at least recognize the problem of the real and the true. But the real and the true belong to a domain that transcends physics. To be logical, it is necessary to admit the simple fact of this problem which conditions his. "Is it merely a well-meaning kind of nonsense for a physicist to affirm this necessity for an outlook beyond physics? It is worse nonsense to deny it. . . . For if those who hold that there must be a physical basis for everything hold that these mystical views are nonsense, we may ask—What then is the physical basis of nonsense? . . . [The physicist] may regard the distinction of good and evil as too remote to bother about; but the distinction of sense and nonsense, of valid and invalid reasoning, must be accepted at the beginning of every scientific inquiry."[121]

Notice as well that the problem of values in question is not the epistemological problem that we have already resolved. Value is the real absolutely given that he wishes to justify, to which he wants to give a meaning. He has emphasized the absolute fashion in which the real is given and now he underlines the no less absolute problem that it raises. Let us not be afraid of his vocabulary. Moreover, we will see in his solution what he means by meaning and value.

2. *The Absolute Evaluator* (Appreciateur)

The statement of the solution is rather brief: the real of consciousness is possible, has a sense, if it is a participation in a transcendental absolute. We will look in vain for any explicitation of the argument underlying this statement. For Eddington, the existence of God seems evident. Not that we have an intuition of God, but rather evidence of the necessity of the transcendental Absolute in order to be able to account for the real, both absolute and relative, offers to our consciousness.

No doubt, this Absolute is at the term of an argument, but what Eddington emphasizes is that this reasoning makes sense only for those who take account of the requirements posed by the real of consciousness. In this he is quite right. When on the other hand he insists that the existence of God cannot be proved he would have better said that the necessity implied in the real of consciousness cannot be proved. This is quite simply and absolutely true. As soon as one is fully conscious of this fact, one is led to God. The God of Eddington is a lived God. Individuals who do not have this lived sense of the real do not understand the implications of this real, and neither will the Absolute have a lived sense for them. He who truly knows that God exists by this enters into an intimate relation with this transcendental personality.[122]

Does he indeed give us a proof of the Absolute? The only passage that has the air of an argument is unfortunately quite embroiled and very ambiguous. We are going to quote it, but we have to say that we lift it from a context which does not allow us to see it as an intended proof. There is no question of a metaphysical argument; rather it is addressed to the agnostic physicist by posing a dilemma for him. He does something he does not like to do, he makes a concession to his interlocutor about the point of departure. But from this fact his argument slips into an epistemological terrain.

> In viewing the world in a practical way values for normal human consciousness may be taken as standard. But the evident possibility of arbitrariness in this valuation sets us hankering after a standard that could be considered final and absolute. We have two alternatives. Either there are no absolute values, so that the sanctions of the inward monitor in our consciousness are the final court of appeal beyond which it is idle to inquire. OR there are absolute values; then we can only trust optimistically that our values are some pale reflection of those of the Absolute Value, or that we have insight into the mind of the Absolute from whence come those strivings and sanctions whose authority we usually forbear to question. (NPW, 331 [327–28])

This passage has the air of being a mixture of epistemology and of metaphysics: it seems to require a metaphysical solution of an epistemological problem. Indeed, it makes a concession after having resolved the epistemological problem by an immediate realism. His Absolute seems to be introduced only to eliminate the evident possibility of the arbitrary. If we were to put the basis of his thought in continuity with the premises of the first paragraphs, this search for an absolute standard would have a metaphysical sense, and could be likened to the *quarta via* of St. Thomas.[123]

But it is a matter here of an appreciation of consciousness, of the value of this appreciation. And what does "the world from a practical point of view" mean? We do not formulate metaphysical propositions in ordinary life, in our appreciation of a physical theory, in our ordinary judgments. The values which come from human moral consciousness suffice for that. We make good judgments and appreciations of value without metaphysical reflection. But when he glides into "the evident possibilities of the arbitrary in this evaluation" he immediately puts himself in another point of view that he does not justify. It is implied that it is now a question of human evaluation as such and of its epistemological value.

But it is not so evident that this was Eddington's intention. We could circumscribe that evaluation as follows: our evaluation of the real is authorized at least to find an absolute standard, and without it we cannot account for the real. But then this standard is a requirement of the real of consciousness as such. Our appreciation of the real does not immediately seize the underlying conditions of this real, it must be sought. But it is not the possibility of the arbitrary which leads us to look for a metaphysical solution. And what moreover is the evidence for this possibility? Is it not the existence of God thus postulated that will assure us that we are not mistaken.

The second part of the reasoning is better, but one again encounters there this concession in the dilemma: either there are absolute values or there are not. But this dilemma is superfluous, the premises of the first paragraph do not give us this choice. His epistemology assures that we attain the real in an absolute and non-discussable way. There is then an absolute value immediately given in consciousness which is beyond question. So much so that the reasoning reconstructed and adapted to the requirements of the premises would rather be expressed as follows: on the one hand there are absolute values given to human consciousness but which, on the other hand, posit a requirement for they do not account for themselves and are in that sense relative. But such values are impossible except as participations in a value absolute as such which gives an entire account of itself. Therefore, there is an absolutely Absolute Value.

This statement goes beyond the formulas of Eddington. But if we look at the passages in which he affirms the necessity of God if sense is to be made of the real offered to our consciousness and if we transpose the argument given in this direction, it seems to me that we can then account for the thought of Eddington.

It is in any case false to say that he pretends to have an immediate evidence of God, an immediate experience. The domain he calls "mystical" is at bottom the domain of metaphysics. It is his concern to find the Living God, the Supreme Personality with which ours is in intimate and friendly relation that explains that he gives short shrift to the logical formalities that lead us there.

What is important is that he has a horror of so-called "scientific" arguments for the existence of God that are found in manuals of apologetics.[124]

They could not give us the assurance that one finds in immediate experience, an assurance so overwhelming that "the soul and God laugh together over so odd a conclusion" (SUW, 70). Atheists are like people who would try to prove that our best friend does not exist. Scientific arguments for the existence of God are futile proofs which alter with the changes in physical theory and are not at bottom proofs and which do not give us the God of the real of our consciousness which is out of the reach of all that. Thus he holds, as physical theory, that the universe should have a beginning in the not infinitely remote past, but he keeps himself from deriving from that an argument for the Creator God.[125]

All these superficial speculations do not give us, moreover, anything but a certain intelligence inherent in nature and not a Personal God. "The idea of a universal Mind or Logos would be, I think, a fairly plausible inference from the present state of scientific theory; at least it is in harmony with it. But if so, all that our inquiry justifies us in asserting is a purely colourless pantheism. Science cannot tell whether the world-spirit is good or evil, and its halting argument for the existence of a God might equally well be turned into an argument for the existence of a Devil" (NPW, 338 [334]).

But by "the actual state of scientific theories" Eddington alludes to quantum indeterminist theory which belongs to the mathematical order rather than to the mechanical order, and by which mechanists want to dispense with a true intelligence working in nature and replace it with a machine. "[A]t that time it was the general assumption that the Creation was the work of an engineer (not of a mathematician, as is the fashion nowadays)" (NPW, 104 [117]). But elsewhere he remarks: "Nowadays we do not encourage the engineer to build the world for us out of his material, but we turn to the mathematician to build it out of his material. Doubtless the mathematician is a loftier being than the engineer, but perhaps even he ought not to be entrusted with the Creation unreservedly" (NPW, 209 [DeKoninck used the English edition here, again criticizing the French translation]).

In this Eddington reveals himself to be more profound than Jeans and Weyl who speak of the Creator as a Pure Mathematician. Eddington wants his God to be above all a metaphysician.[126] God is the Creator of the real, and the mathematical harmony of the world is only one aspect of the real.

But how prove the Personality of God? The indications are slim. Here is the principal one:

> It seems right at this point to say a few words in relation to the question of a Personal God. I suppose every serious thinker is rather afraid of this term which might seem to imply that he pictures the deity on a throne in the sky after the manner of medieval painters. There is a tendency to substitute such terms as 'omnipresent force' or even a 'fourth dimension.' If the idea is merely to find a wording which shall be sufficiently vague, it is somewhat unsuitable for the scientist to whom the words 'force' and 'dimension' convey something entirely precise and defined. On the other hand, my impression of psychology suggests that the word 'person' might be considered vague enough as it stands. But leaving aside verbal questions, I believe that the thought that lies behind this reaction is unsound. It is, I think, of the very essence of the unseen world that the conception of personality should dominate it. Force, energy, dimensions belong to the world of symbols; it is out of such conceptions that we have built up the external world of physics. What other conceptions have we? After exhausting physical methods we returned to the inmost recesses of consciousness, to the voice that proclaims our personality; and from there we entered on a new outlook. We have to build the spiritual world out of symbols taken from our own personality, as we build the scientific world out of the symbols of the mathematician. I think therefore we are not wrong in embodying the significance of the

> spiritual world to ourselves in the feeling of a personal relationship, for our whole approach to it is bound up with those aspects of consciousness in which personality is centred. (SUW, 81–83)

These indications are too vague for us to analyze them. But they amply suffice to enable us to affirm that the God of Eddington is a Personal God, and that he is not a monist, as is often said.

Let us add another consideration which can perhaps advance that of personality, that notably of the unity of consciousness. Unity is a condition of consciousness and we grasp a certain necessity of unity in mind-stuff. Some unities of this stuff are from consciousness, others are inorganic. Obviously this unity should be transposed to God (NPW, 315 [312]). If we had more precise and more developed indications perhaps we would find a certain relation between his notion of personality and that of unity, which being a condition of mind-stuff, is a condition of being, a characteristic of the personality of conscious beings implying a certain lived unity.

But that is all Eddington has told us. These are simply metaphysical suggestions which are not pressed very far. We do not have the right, it seems to me, to infer more, for his intention in these lectures is not to give us a coherent metaphysical system.

But it is still certain that he makes an annoying confusion between metaphysics and religion, and it is indeed because of this that he refuses to engage in dialectic.

> We may try to analyse the experience as we analyse humour, and construct a theology, or it may be an atheistic philosophy, which shall put into scientific form what is to be inferred about it. But let us not forget that the theology is symbolic knowledge whereas the experience is intimate knowledge. And as laughter cannot be compelled by the scientific exposition of the structure of a joke, so a philosophic discussion of the attributes of God (or an impersonal substitute) is likely to miss the intimate response of the spirit which is the central point of religious experience. (NPW, 322–23 [320])

There is truth in that, but it is no less true that his knowledge of God is based on an at least implicit reasoning.

Chapter III. Reality and Illusion

1. Illusion

To understand what Eddington means by "illusion" we must adopt the point of view of the physicist who calls anything not transposable into equations an illusion, such as consciousness, humor, beauty, even reality itself, whose formal aspect is not analyzable. The scientific analysis of a joke is not comic, but the joke itself is. This is because we have eliminated its reaction on consciousness.

It is the same with permanence which seems equally to be an illusion. But here one touches the physicist to the quick, for if he rejects permanence, he will not even be able to do physics even though permanence is not objectively formulable. He posits it in his law of conservation but he does not explain it. The whole of physics is based on permanence which is essentially an object of consciousness.

> When the eye surveys the tossing waters of the ocean, the eddying particles of water leave little impression; it is the waves that strike the attention, because they have a certain degree of permanence. The motion particularly noticed is the motion of the wave-form, which is not a motion of the water at all. So the mind surveying the world of point-events looks for the permanent things. The simpler relations, the intervals and potentials, are transient, and are not the stuff out of which mind can build a habitation for itself. But the thing that has been identified with matter is permanent, and because of its permanence it must be for mind the substance of the world. Practically no other choice was possible. . . . It is the mind which by insisting on regarding only the things that are permanent, has actually imposed these laws on an indifferent world. (STG, 196–97 [240–41])

It is the selectivity of our mind which imposes the laws of nature (NPW, 239 ff. [243]).

Subjectivism? Not at all. Permanence is indeed there, for consciousness, not for the physicist. It belongs beyond the number-measures, to their background. What is in appearance the most subjective is at bottom the most objective. "[E]ntropy which is frankly of a much more subjective nature than most of the ordinary physical qualitites. Entropy is an appreciation of arrangement and organization; it is subjective in the same sense that the constellation Orion is subjective. That which is arranged is objective, so too are the stars composing the constellation; but the association is the contribution of the mind which surveys. . . . This exceptional appearance of subjective and objective apparently in their wrong worlds gives food for thought. It may prepare us for a view of the scientific world adopted in the later chapters which is much more subjective than that usually held by science" (NPW, 95–96 [108–9]).

Therefore permanence is a property of mind-stuff, immediately by consciousness. It is a condition of being. "We see in Nature what we look for or are equipped to look for. Of course, I do not mean that we can arrange the details of the scene; but by the light and shade of our values we can bring out things that shall have the broad characteristics we esteem. In this sense the value placed on permanence creates the world of apparent substance . . ." (NPW, 330 [326]).

So it is with actuality, with beauty. These are properties of the mind-stuff, independently of our individual consideration, but they can only be defined with reference to a mind; it is by consciousness that we are able to give them their meaning. But the basis for the reference is in things (NPW, 266–68 [268–69]).

In all this mind is constantly found and it can be seen that the physicist constructs his world in an intermediate domain that he explores. It is the intermediate world that is unknown. The more consciousness succeeds in imposing its views, the more the world approaches us, the more penetrable it becomes. Probability is a striking example of this. Ordinarily we have to do with probabilities which arise from our ignorance, and we would think that with more perfect knowledge we would have less recourse to probability and would substitute for it exact facts. In fact, all the probabilities reside on a basis of probability apriori and one could not say whether they are great or small without having admitted that basis. But it is then that we discover that the basis adopted is an element constituting the structure of the world (NPW, 305 [303]). "We have found a strange foot-print on the shores of the unknown. We have devised profound theories, one after another, to account for its origin. At last, we have succeeded in reconstructing the creature that made the foot-print. And Lo! it is our own" (STG, 201 [247]).

To be faithful to the profound thought of Eddington, we would have to add that this 'ourselves' is our self before an understood real.

The notion of substance that reduces to the domain of illusions to reintegrate it into the objective world as the result of permanence, clearly has nothing to do with the scholastic notion of substance, for he considers only the durable aspect of nature and its 'in-itself.' Far from rejecting the idea of substance, a consciousness is essentially an 'in itself,' a unit distinct from all others (NPW, 241–42 [245]).

Before looking more closely at consciousness, a few words on a passage that has provoked severe criticism.

2. *Illusion in Reality*

"Perhaps, indeed, reality is a child which cannot survive without its nurse illusion" (NPW, xiv [16]). This does not mean that the real is illusion but that we always accompany the real with some illusion, inevitably we place there familiar images, there where they make no sense. We can find an example in the law of conservation. We know that something is conserved. We have first of all identified this something with matter. That was an illusion for afterward we discovered that it is not matter that is conserved but energy. Is this final? If we say yes we will be victims of a veritable illusion. But there is no longer a veritable illusion if we proceed all along "as if" energy is conserved, knowing well this is not the final step. Must we forego making necessarily provisory identifications because they cannot be definitive and never will be, and must we always make some illusion for ourselves? There is always some part of truth in these illusions. There is truth in all our familiar images, but it is difficult not to give them a sense and reach that they do not have, and it must be asked whether illusion is quite inevitable. It is wisdom and truth to take account of all that.

If we adopt the point of view of the physicist and call whatever is not transposable into number-measures an illusion, the physical world is suspended in air for it is only with reference to a consciousness that perceives it as real that it is real. In fact, it is inferred, and ought finally to be identified in some fashion with something that consciousness recognizes as real in an immediate way. But these immediacies do not concern the physicist, they are out of his reach. His world is doubly an illusion unless it has some real value (NPW, 287 [287]).

Chapter IV. The Mind-Matter Relation

1. The Attempt to Reach Mind by Way of Number-Measures

It is by demonstrating the abyss that separates these two aspects of the real that we can reveal their profound relation.

Let us then perform a physical operation on Mr. X to see what we can find there of consciousness and other illusions we cannot rid ourselves of. What do we find? An inferred series of symbols: atoms, electrons, etc. Is that all? Whatever be the ultimate physical elements we can assure ourselves in advance that we will find nothing but symbols, we will never find consciousness, a thought, because they are not reducible to symbols.

Would we be justified in denying them because they are not reducible to symbols? "But what knowledge have we of the nature of atoms which renders it at all incongruous that they should constitute a thinking object? . . . science has nothing to say as to the intrinsic nature of the atom. The physical atom is, like everything else in physics, a schedule of pointer readings. The schedule is, we agree, attached to some unknown background. Why not then attach it to something of spiritual nature of which a prominent characteristic is *thought.* It seems rather silly to prefer to attach it to something of a so-called 'concrete' nature inconsistent with thought, and then to wonder where the thought comes from" (NPW, 259 [261]).

So Eddington does not say, as his eminent critics think, that atoms are thought, but that they are the metric aspects of an object that thinks. Not only is there no contradiction in this identification, we have consciousness of this unity. We have consciousness that our body is ours in our immediate consciousness of exteriority. It is the only case where the identification is immediate (NPW, 259–60 [261–62]). Does that mean that we have knowledge of physical nature in this same experience? Not at all. Immediate knowledge is not a physical knowledge. *All* physical knowledge is, for Eddington, inferred. (The material object should not be confused with the formal object.) This consciousness does not extend to having consciousness that there is carbon in our brain, though this carbon is closer to our consciousness (if that makes sense) than any other represented object. The carbon is found in the inferential way and we need an even more indirect procedure to conclude that there is some in our brain after having discovered it in Mr. X.

The most important point is that we can never say what carbon is. It never becomes a thing but will always be the metric aspect of some thing which is not carbon, for if this something were carbon, it would be a symbol of something else. This is evidently what we usually do. Carbon is something in the brain, but the whole brain as we describe it experimentally is a series of symbols. Let us not say that the brain is a symbol. "To be a symbol" makes no sense. And indeed this series of symbols is precisely the metric aspect of some thing which is not symbols. And what is it of which the symbols are the metric aspect? Mind-stuff (NPW, 269–70 [270–71]).

The materialist identifies the symbols with the something of which they are the metric aspect. He does not know that he passes over the "something" and surreptitiously identifies it with a symbol. His brain is an absurd entity. Usually one imagines thought to be something which acts on atom "things." And a point of contact between the physical entity and mind is sought. But that makes no sense. The symbol is not something which is in contact with something. It is not something corresponding with something. The symbol corresponds with something, it is an aspect of something. The background of the symbol is not another "thing." The background is the stuff of mind which has a metric aspect that we represent with a symbol.

That is why Eddington does not like the term "concrete," for it usually leads to a substantialization of an exclusive symbol. If one wants atoms to be concrete appendices to something that thinks, atoms no less than thought would become more mysterious than ever.

We do not carve out a mental state according to the cuts (*coupures*) in our symbols. "The brain-matter is a partial aspect of the whole mental state; but the analysis of the brain-matter by physical investigation does not run at all parallel with the analysis of the mental state by psychological investigation" (NPW, 279 [280]).

Let us stop speaking of the interaction of mind and body as an interaction of two things. "I do not believe that the activity of matter at a certain point of the brain stimulates an activity of mind; my view is that in the activity of matter there is a metrical description of certain aspects of the activity of mind. The activity of the matter is our way of recognizing a combination of the measures of structure; the activity of the mind is our insight into the complex of relations whose comparability gives the foundation of those measures" (NPW, 268 [269–70]).

Without the shadow of a doubt this passage is shocking. But is it anything other than a simple conclusion from what we would say of the object of physics? Must we cede to imagination which concretizes all objects?

Since the atoms of Mr. X are a metric aspect of his "mind-stuff," must we conclude that every mind-stuff is conscious?

> This might give rise to some difficulty if we were postulating complete identity of mind-stuff with consciousness. But we know that in the mind there are memories not in consciousness at the moment but capable of being summoned into consciousness. We are vaguely aware that things we cannot recall are lying somewhere about and may come into the mind at any moment. Consciousness is not sharply defined, but fades into subconsciousness; and beyond that we must postulate something indefinite but yet continuous with our mental nature. This I take to be the world-stuff. We liken it to our conscious feelings because, now that we are convinced of the formal and symbolic character of the entities of physics, there is nothing else to liken it to. (NPW, 279–80 [DeKoninck used the English edition here])

Let us not call Eddington a monist in the current sense of the word. Everything that is is the stuff of mind or, in other words, intelligible. But the unity of this stuff is not monist, indistinct. Each being is an individual wave. But there is a certain homogeneity among all beings, man is not a body (some thing) *and* a mind (another thing).

Eddington never speaks of the body, probably because "body" is too concrete a term, and too easily one thinks he knows what it means. A physical body is not an ontological entity, it is purely symbolic of some thing.

Nor is it a question of a simplistic and imaginary parallelism. Symbolic knowledge never becomes intimate knowledge. Intimate knowledge is a fact of consciousness and intransposable. Symbols do not express thought. The immediate knowledge that we have our own exteriority is not symbolic. The metric aspect of my subject is known in an inferential way, and no more directly for me than for another. What is important is that this knowledge of the symbolic aspect tells us nothing of the intrinsic nature of things. It is only of ourselves that we have some intimate knowledge and of that which is given to us as having homogeneity with our consciousness, that is, as mind-stuff. But that does not mean that what we attain in these two ways (consciousness and inference) are of other things, nor does that lead to the identification of the two aspects, that is, that one is at the basis of the other.

Thus we are far from the naive idea which holds body and mind to be two concrete systems which act on one another and whose point of contact we must seek some place in the body. Let us not conclude that the localization of the psychologist has no sense and that he should abandon his efforts. It is simply that account must be taken of the fact that symbols that are manipulated in objective psychology are not things to which things correspond.

Eddington makes no distinction between the different degrees of knowledge, or between the different faculties—or rather he does not mention them. Moreover, he had no occasion to do so. So let us say that he simply doesn't. He does not offer us an achieved philosophy. The only distinction that he mentions is that between intimate, intuitive knowledge and inferred or symbolic knowledge. He posits a distinction between the inorganic and organic worlds. But let us follow him closely in this evolutionist theory to see how consciousness is born.

2. *Evolution toward Consciousness*

Eddington adopts Jeans' conceptions with respect to the evolutionary process of the cosmos.[127] The coagulation of the matter of the stars takes its origin from the gravitational disequilibrium of the primitive chaos. A second cosmic accident provokes the birth of our earth. Two stars came too close in their courses, the one provoked tides in the other, a great protuberance condensed into planets. A third accident gave birth to the organism. Carbon produced more and more elaborate structures which ended by becoming living organisms (SUW, 11–20).

How are living beings distinct from the inorganic? It may be that the observational difference between the organic and inorganic is in the configuration of the physical molecules of an individual and the living corresponds literally to a chemical compound. But biological laws could just as well designate something superadded which is special to living matter and which is not yet included in the series of physical entities. "But that is an escape" (SUW, 11–20).

The fundamental point is that one cannot say that a living being is made from atoms. That makes no sense. The physical elements are ontologically defined *things*. Eddington's evolutionism does not say that atoms have evolved into a living being, for that implies a contradiction. The living is defined in opposition to atoms, as a thing of a species, opposed to others, of another species, which would mean one is deriving life from symbols. Thus all that implicitly supposes that we know what an atom ontologically is.

One sees again here how profound are the consequences of the definition of the object of physics. Once admit that the object of physics is *things* and it will become difficult to consider vital phenomena as anything other than epiphenomena. But it is not a matter of admitting or not admitting, it is a question of truth or illusion.

Evolutionism is abominable only in appearance. One usually gives it a meaning it does not have. Expressions such as "accidents" do not encroach on the ordering thought of the Creator (SUW, 23). Let us not attempt to replace the religious idea of creation with scientific evolution, or mix science and religion. "I think it is not irreligion but a tidiness of mind, which rebels against the idea of permeating scientific research with a religious implication" (ibid., 25).

It is not irreverence to say that the course of events has produced a certain organ called the brain and that thus we come to man. And Eddington seems to insinuate that man is the term aimed at by organic evolution. ". . . Nature made nearly every possible mistake before she reached her greatest achievement Man—or perhaps some would say her worst mistake of all" (ibid., 21). And not only organic evolution, but the entire universe. In terms that remind us of Laplace, he writes, "We know the prodigality of Nature. How many acorns are scattered for one that grows to an oak? And need she be more careful of her stars than of her acorns? If indeed she has no grander aim than to provide a home for her greatest experiment, Man, it would be just like her methods to scatter a million stars whereof one might haply achieve her purpose" (NPW, 177–78 [185]).

This is not to say that terrestrial man is this unique term and that there are no other inhabited planets. Eddington is of the opinion that *actually* our race is the only one endowed with consciousness, but it is even very probable that others have preceded us in other places (ibid.).

Isn't there a contradiction in this conception? On the one hand man is seen as the aim of the whole evolution of the universe, whereas on the other hand he was possible only thanks to catastrophes, to exceptions to the rule. Indeed this conception would be bizarre for a determinist, for whom man would thus be produced because of a defect in the universal machine. But for an indeterminist, the exception enters into the rule, and nothing prevents us from considering the exception as the term aimed at by the rule.

Chapter V. The Problem of Indeterminism and Free Will

Most critics have remarked to Eddington that free will has nothing to do with either physical determinism or indeterminism.[128] To which Eddington responded: "I do not see how (the physical world and the human mind) can be kept separate, since human movements are phenomena of the physical world. . . . Mental indeterminism is conditioned on physical indeterminism" (PP, 41).

The critics all seem to me to have erred in taking only isolated passages from Eddington without taking his whole philosophy into account. Thus when one has studied in depth his doctrine on the relation between spirit and matter, the conclusion concerning the relation between free will and indeterminism follows quite logically, so much so that it must be said that if there truly was determinism in nature, the exercise of free will would be impossible.

We can approach this problem from two sides. First of all, by affirming that determinism makes no sense, so that the problem as it is usually framed does not arise. There is no conciliation to be made. This negation settles the question in a fundamental way, since the problem "if there were determinism, would the exercise of freedom be possible?" is inconceivable. Even the difficulty makes no sense.

Attacked from the other side, Eddington's solution is found in his doctrine of the relation between body and mind. Physical elements are not "bodies" in a philosophical sense. They are bundles of measure-numbers which represent the metric aspect of the mind-stuff that is the world. It makes no sense to speak of the will as a power which seizes a certain atom and sends it in a direction contrary to its natural tendency. In this case, man's every spontaneous movement would constitute a rupture of the "natural" course of physical elements. But precisely, nature is not just atoms and man is not composed of atoms and nothing else.

In order to grasp Eddington's thought, one must adhere strictly to the meaning that he gives to the word 'physics.' The physical world is not the world of bodies of which the scholastic cosmologists speak, and who call entities such as atoms and molecules bodies. They are not bodies but the metric aspect of something corporeal which is not marked off by physical cuts (*coupures*).

Determinists fall into this confusion (and one finds scholastics among them). They speak of the world of atoms and molecules as of an inorganic world. And they pose this dilemma: a being is either free or it is not. If it is not, it is determined. But atoms are physical, inorganic, non-free, that is, determinist.

In fact, atoms are not inorganic beings, nor organic. They represent a metric aspect of an organic or inorganic being. The atoms of a living being are no less atoms than those of an inorganic being, and they obey the same laws as the atoms of an inorganic being. It is not atoms as such which differentiate beings, but the structure of units of mind-stuff of which the atoms represent only the metric aspect. It makes no sense to speak of an organic or of an inorganic atom according as the atom belongs to a certain gentleman or to a stone, as if an atom were a certain entity which is in the temporary possession of a certain gentleman which we can exchange like pieces of money. The putative problem of conciliation as it is usually stated thus arises from a misunderstanding concerning the meaning of physical entities. We have submerged them in "things" and now face the difficulty of extracting them again.

We are again struck by the logical manner in which Eddington applies his definition of the object of physics. He resolves the problem by denying it, in showing it to be nonsense.

It is false to consider the free man as a foreign intruder in the physical world who provokes preternatural perturbations. Man is no less physical than an inorganic being. The metric ensemble of a man does not define an independent entity which governs its will to a certain degree. This structure is that of the free man, it is his metric aspect which is no less physical for being that of a gentleman. The gentleman is distinguished as the organic from the inorganic, and not from the inorganic of physics.

How does all that relate to the problem of statistical laws? How does statistics allow for liberty, whereas determinism does not? "[W]hatever supplementary considerations may be needed to explain human actions, they are not in conflict with the laws of physics" (PP, 41). Precisely, if the behavior of matter is dictated by determinist laws, there is no room for these supplementary considerations.

A determinist ought to find it very strange that man is in a way an ensemble of atoms, because he is constantly steering them off course. From his point of view, he is indeed right to seek the physical element which would have determined this extraordinary behavior. And if he is not afraid of materialism (and to be logical he should be a materialist; moreover he is already one at the point of departure) he ought indeed to conclude that the will is something physical that one should find in the configuration of the elements. (Not that he gives "physical" an ontological sense.) On the contrary, for the indeterminist, the behavior of a given atom is never strange, precisely because it does not have an absolutely defined behavior. Its behavior depends on the ensemble of which it is a certain metric aspect, which cannot be isolated, and which should be defined as much as possible in function of the whole ensemble.

The behavior of an atom of Mr. X will differ from the behavior of an atom of a typewriter, but these behaviors are both perfectly physical. Neither the one nor the other would be if the atom had an inherent and perfectly defined behavior by itself which must be troubled by the impertinent will of a certain gentleman. The atoms of Mister Eddington do absolutely nothing that would be contrary to their inherent law, for their truly inherent law has a kind of contempt for the strict law, and they permit the atoms of a gentleman as well as those of a stone. They are properly his own; there is nothing in the atoms of Eddington which would prevent them being properly his.

We would not be able to understand Eddington's thesis if we thought it a simple preamble to the explanations of determinists who respect equally free will, because it is simpler. Eddington is convinced that any other explanation is absurd, and that if we adopt the determinist thesis in any fashion, the possibility of the exercise of freedom is implicitly denied. The determinist error is above all a metaphysical error concerning nature itself, due to a confusion between the physical object and the ontological object. Having identified these two, one must appeal to ridiculous structures to explain how will can succeed in disturbing the famous laws of physical nature. The laws of physical nature are not the laws of inorganic nature. This is the confusion Eddington discloses. And that is how he shows the nonsense in the problem of conciliation.

There is one more point to clarify. How does the behavior *in fact* of an atom of a gentleman differ from the behavior *in fact* of an atom of a non-gentleman? The behavior of an atom of a gentleman is determined by his mental decision, "or, one may say, the scientific description of that behavior is the metrical aspect of the decision" (NPW, 312 [310]). In this case, the decision between possible behaviors is what we call volition. The important point is that the different behaviors were possible, the one as well as the other, and that by reason of the physical nature of the atom itself, and not by reason of the greater power of the will which is more than the atom would have of itself. The atom does nothing "of itself." It is the imagination of those who do not understand what an atom is.

If the behavior of an atom is not the metric aspect of a decision of a will, what then is it? When the decision of an atom is made between its possible quantum jumps, is that also 'volition'?[129] This indeterminism that implies will and the indeterminism of the laws governing the atom make decision possible. A determined decision is *a fact* in the physical world which carries consequences for the future, but which is not tied to the past by causal relations. When it is our decision, we know the Why, we have made our choice. The fact was not necessary before the decision, it is only in the decision that it has come to be. It is only of this fact, a physical phenomenon, that it is a question, and obviously that it was decided, because it is. But it was not necessarily what it is now. Autodetermination is a cause of the decision, but this autodetermination to such a choice was not necessary—that would be a contradiction in terms. That is what Eddington means by calling the decision "something outside causality."[130]

As for the atom of a non-human, its behavior is not necessarily decided by a necessitating will, but by statistics, which amply explain why it *in fact* acts as it does. This is only the extension of a truism into a domain where he who obliges us to demand more, to demand that at bottom this atom behave either freely or determinately. In fact it behaves itself determinately in both cases, and that suffices.

We have isolated an atom in a somewhat schematic way, but that has nothing to do with the basis of the problem. To find if we ought to attribute to mind the power to decide the behavior of individual atoms, but also to affect systematically numerous groups, is a psychological problem (NPW, 312–13 [310]). In fact one could always say nothing of a single observed atom, for it is not decided in the atom why it behaves rather in this way than in that. One must observe it in an ensemble. "There can be no unique probability attached to any event or behavior; we can only speak of 'probability in the light of certain given information,' and the probability alters according to the extent of the information" (NPW, 314–45 [312]).

We must suppose that the physical aspect of the human brain immediately implied by the mental decision presents a reciprocal dependence in the behavior of atoms which is not present in inorganic matter, a special unity of the ensemble, which has for foundation the background of number-measures, and of which it is the metric manifestation. The characteristic unity of this background is manifested to us in our consciousness. "There must be some corresponding unity in the relations of the mind-stuff which is behind the pointer readings. . . . The atoms will individually be in no way different from those which are without this unity in the background. But it seems plausible that when we consider their collective behavior we shall have to take account of the broader unifying trends in the mind-stuff, and not expect the statistical results to agree with those appropriate to structures of haphazard origin" (NPW, 315 [312]).

Notice as well that determinism is for Eddington synonymous with modern materialism (SUW, 50). That is because he has seen the necessary consequences of determinism which takes its point of departure in materialism. One elevates physics into ontology. Our intuition of liberty does not count, only the pretended intuition of the necessity of determinism in the physical world, with which everything must be reconciled. In fact, the domain of our experience is larger than that. The intuition we have of our freedom is a fact of immediate experience, the physical world is an inferred system. It is absurd to want to deny the facts of immediate experience in order to accommodate our imagination which has projected determinism into a world which does not know it. The problem of experience is that of all our experience.

Free beings constitute for Eddington the world of minds. These consciousnesses are indeed at home in the physical world. Freedom is exercised there freely, thanks to the basic indeterminism of the physical world.

Indeterminism therefore is in a way a transcendental notion, enveloping mind-stuff, be it organic or inorganic. And if we understood, the philosopher would say that the indeterminism of the physical world emanates, or rather that it is the metric aspect of the indeterminism of mind-stuff.

Chapter VI. The Religion of Eddington

Eddington is a Quaker. It would be interesting to trace the influence of his religion on his whole philosophy. He is a profoundly religious man, a man with an infinite respect for mystery. A Quaker is a Christian; he believes in revelation, the Trinity, the divinity of Christ. But he does not like to formulate these truths in dogmas. By "creed" he understands a dogma; but that does not mean that he is an unbeliever. Faith should be simple, we should kneel before the uncomprehended. But, always a Quaker, he does not want the objects of faith to be formulated with too much precision, for great precision tends to use concepts and terms that are too concrete and encroach upon the transcendence of these truths, transforming them into inert dogmas. "Quakerism in dispensing with creeds holds out a hand to the scientist."[131]

It must be noted that the religious problems he treats are purely philosophical, with which he mingles his sentimental and aesthetic reaction. His metaphysics is sincere. He takes perfectly into account its vital consequences. This metaphysics is transcendent and absolutely independent of the development of the sciences with respect to its basis. We should not then expect the advancement of science to become religious. Religion was as true ages ago as it is today. Those who desire the truth are by that very fact religious (NPW, 353 [349] & 346 [342]).

SECTION TWO

Critical Considerations

One might expect that I would launch a rather severe criticism of these considerations risked by Eddington. And one might perhaps expect an apology for taking it all so seriously and even for seeking links with our metaphysics, which indeed goes beyond all that. Why waste time trying to bring Eddington onto the side of the angels? Even if one succeeded, what would have been gained by all that save that Mr. Eddington would be, after all, a good metaphysician and, having discovered so much himself, he is indeed a very intelligent man, but that is a personal matter, of little interest to the philosopher.

But it is philosophers who have criticized Eddington severely and I am convinced that they are wrong *on all the points they have criticized.* The only criticism one could make is that his system is incomplete and sometimes rather vague. But even this won't hold for one who reads his works and takes into account the intention of the author as well as the limits he has placed on himself. The books are, for the most part, lectures. The methodological problems of relativity and of indeterminism are the only ones he has studied in depth, insofar as they are methodological problems. For the rest, he wishes only to make suggestions. He must be studied with all that in mind.

But there is more. I am convinced that we find new things in those suggestions, new ways of looking at old problems, above all that of the relation between body and mind, and the relation of physical indeterminism and freedom. These are two points on which he has been sharply criticized. But let us pass in review the few theses in which Eddington would have sinned.

1. *Knowability, the Fundamental Attribute of That Which Is*

Put like that, it is hard to see what could be brought against this thesis. It is rather the expression "mind-stuff" which has led critics to think him an idealist. But isn't being intelligible? And isn't this intelligibility a transcendental property of being, and identical with being? And if he makes precise that it is actual being to which our consciousness reacts, what is ambiguous about that? It is above all existential being that we know; the possible is known insofar as it can possibly be and we do not react to it as we do to actual being, but as the possibility of being. But at bottom it is always actual being that is the aim.

The whole abstract order that is discovered as the metaphysical conditions of the sensible being offered to our experience makes sense only in the total reality of this sensible. It is material reality which is immediately offered to consciousness. In this material reality Eddington seizes on actuality as the transcendental character, and in this same grasp is given the transcendental intelligibility of that which is. Starting from sensible reality as he does, it is surprising he hasn't been accused of materialism rather than idealism.

What seems to have been lost from sight is that he defines being as knowable and not as known by a particular consciousness. How can he possibly be called a subjectivist idealist for whom reality is derived from consciousness? Unless one can call idealist one who establishes the homogeneity of the real and the knower.

Evidently, being *is known* by the Absolute. Eddington defines intelligibility by reference to a transcendental consciousness, but being is intelligible even when we don't know it, and on the other hand this intelligibility would make no sense if it had no fundamental relation to some consciousness.

Since when has immediate realism implied any other immediacy than that described by Eddington? Since when must our consciousness be in immediate contact with all that we see and sense? The photons that bombard the retina are not the sun, and the nerve currents which propagate shock are not necessarily channels that carry bombarding elements. Do the chemical transformations in my brain mutilate reality and deceive me into thinking I am confronted with the thing I profess to know? The star I see is in reality not there where I see it and perhaps it was extinguished millions of years ago. The man I see and speak with is not completely the same as he was when I saw and spoke to him before. Are we deceived by all that? Must we reject experimental facts in order to safeguard appearances? If that knowledge is to be truly objective we must critically follow the path of inference. We follow it in a rough way in familiar experience. That is imperfect and must be corrected.

Fortunately the fundamental problem of epistemology has nothing to do with all this. All that is necessary is that I know a sensible object in an immediate fashion. Whether it is the carbon in my brain or a remote star has no importance. I am conscious of something sensible, of a color, of a sound. Whatever the physical implications of this sensation are has nothing to do with the problem. We are like radio receivers. Whence come the sounds, and in what way, the only fact that interests us is that we hear something. And that cannot be put into question, even if I hear in a dream.

All this is not all that original. If we have understood correctly the epistemology of Monsignor Noël, this is how immediate realism is to be understood.

One usually forgets that Eddington insists on the immediate consciousness of the real, conditioned by the immediate presence of something sensible. It is this sensible that puts us in relation with the external world. It is of the external world but it is not properly physical. Whatever is physical is symbolic. The immediate object is not given as a symbol of the real. It is indefinable. It is sensible.

Therefore, a distinction must be made between the immediately present object and that with which it also puts us in contact in some fashion with the inferred world, spontaneously. It is this last aspect that would have to be subjected to a critical investigation. When I say that the object is there, I suppose the rectilinear propagation of light. Perhaps experimentation will show me that this attribution was precipitous, but it will never lead to showing that I see nothing. When I regard my environment with green glasses, I could attribute the obscuring to the things I see. In fact, transformations take place in my brain. Does that diminish the objectivity of my sense knowledge? In some way, of course, but not in such a way that the epistemologist has need of it. All he needs is the fact of the sensible, whatever be the physical implications which in some way accompany perception. Having eliminated all these implications, there remains for us the fact that we sense something whose physical structure we do not know, and we may never know the physical structure of this object. It will be found by the inferential path, but the hiatus would not have been made precise.

M. Maritain does not accept the inferential construction of the physical world according to Eddington as the only way of attaining the real structure of the universe. According to Maritain, the reality of this inferential world is not real in the philosophical sense. He has a certain intuition of the real structure of the universe, real in the proper sense of the world. He also wants to go beyond the sensibly real and takes his point of critical departure in a kind of transcendental intuition of being as such.[132] But is it really necessary to have recourse to all these chimerical intuitions?

Apart from Eddington's sometimes imprecise vocabulary, it seems to us that at bottom his thought should be accepted.

2. *The Concrete and the Real*

Given the meaning he gives to the term "concrete," he must reject it. And the same for what he calls the physically real. He is not a metaphysician when he does physics. To call this real conventional is a manner of speaking. At bottom, it is real in the proper sense as well. The symbols of physics are not pure symbols but always symbols of something, provided that the rules of the symposium are observed. And this real is the only one that represents to us the real (in the proper sense) physical structure of the universe. Therefore, it is more profound than the physical real of M. Maritain. Eddington, contrary to what Maritain thinks, knows quite well that his number-measures are a real aspect of a real more profound but not as such made explicit by these numbers. The symbols are perfectly known as symbols, as being only the metric aspect of some thing.

3. *The Nature of Reality*

The expression Eddington has given this problem has disconcerted his critics. But one must adopt Eddington's point of view which is here envisaging directly the irrational of the materialists. Even matter is mind-stuff. Moreover, it is his point of departure. The fundamental intelligibility includes matter since it includes all that is. The expression "mind-stuff" is very happy, and P. Sertillanges seems to have used the same expression. It expresses well the homogeneity between being and intelligence. Eddington is no more of an idealist here than Aristotle or St. Thomas. The only point on which one might reproach him is that he calls himself an idealist, and his critics have seized upon the word.

If matter is in some fashion irrational for us, that is, if we have no adequate knowledge of its complete structure, this is due to our way of knowing. It is absolutely rational insofar as it is being.

Even M. Maritain speaks of the idealism of Eddington.[133] Is it possible that one could read Eddington and say such things? Is mind-stuff quite symbolic? It is everything that is most real in the metaphysical sense. And if Eddington stresses its intelligible character as the nature of reality, that is because at the end of the day it is by this character that it is manifested to us, that it is cognitively accessible by us. Evidently, what we first of all grasp is the real, and because we know the real as the real we conclude to its intelligibility as real. Put in scholastic terms, this problem seems sufficiently acceptable that we need not dwell on it further.

4. *The World of Inference*

We have already stressed this point. What is there that is really unlikely in this thesis? In a recent article Eddington repeats,

> A few years ago I had occasion to write: 'Mind is the first and most direct thing in our experience and all else is remote inference.' Judging from the criticisms, this seems to have horrified the philosophers—even those who on the whole dealt very kindly with my views. The condemnation seemed unanimous, and my remark was evidently looked upon as a well-known elementary blunder. On the other hand, I have never heard it questioned by a physicist. Many would at once recognize it as the proper scientific view; those who had not previously reflected on the position would, I believe, concede it after a few moments' thought. It would almost seem that this is a fundamental cleavage between physicists and philosophers (or a prominent school of philosophers). (PP, 32)

M. Maritain, who seems to have synthesized all the criticisms of Eddington, says that "he seems to incline towards a sort of idealism or pure symbolism when he reflects on physics (since for him, as it would seem, sensorial perception is already symbolic—that involves a whole metaphysics). . . ."[134]

That is a facile, even superficial, interpretation. Where does one find this? The immediately perceived is in the real, and the only real, immediately accessible to us and with which we begin every metaphysical or physical construction. But the physical object to which this sensible is referred by the inferential path is not immediately sensed. My consciousness does not touch the sun that is there. Whether it be the sun or an object that I touch, it is not distance that differentiates the case. My electrons do not touch one another. Still it is the mass of electrons which constitute a body that I sense and which gives the solid character (if that makes sense here) to the object that does not touch my organs. Let us not look for concrete liaisons in this domain, that is, let us not speak of things that we don't know. On the other hand, physical symbols move against an obscure backdrop which is the order of non-intuited yet quite real essences: even more real than the metric aspect that "we" know, and it is indeed this background that gives a meaning to symbols. They are not pure symbols. They are not abstract mathematical magnitudes. But it is precisely M. Maritain, who has so assimilated physics to mathematics, who now wishes to lay on Eddington's shoulders these symbols become too abstract. The symbols of Eddington are not cuts mathematically effected, but physically. They are the isolation of a real aspect of a larger reality. They are the metric aspect of reality. But this does not mean that they make explicit to us that reality in its ontological cuts (*coupures*), in its essences. As Professor Renoirte wrote long ago, "the instrument does not know the substance." But Maritain wants the physicist to give us the means of cutting (*decouper*) the world into substances, and he takes the trouble to ask whether or not an atom is a substance. It is just that that Eddington will not allow us to do. And one is astonished to see Maritain make this effort after having chased physics into pure mathematics and having given the physicist a reality quite different from the reality of the philosopher, he now wants to make use of physical entities and make substances of them.

Another critic, also an eminent philosopher, does not understand why Eddington wants to hide the intrinsic nature of the atom from us, and in fact he finds Eddington in contradiction with himself. "After having claimed that 'Science has nothing to say of the intrinsic nature of the atom' Professor Eddington writes, 'We have at our disposal; two principal ways of grasping what goes on inside the atom; we can observe electrons going in and coming out, and we can observe the light which enters and exits.'"[135] Such a criticism is truly disconcerting. Since when is the intrinsic nature of a thing the physical interior of an entity? That has a rather naive air. Yet it is not only G. D. Hicks who seems to make this confusion. There must be a similar idea in the heads of Gredt and Maritain, who try to do what this English philosopher does here. Maritain quoted Eddington where he tells us that we know nothing of the intrinsic nature of the atom to show how the physicist is obliged to avow his ignorance in the matter of essences, which are the matter of philosophy.[136] But by what right does M. Maritain do just what he forbade the physicist? The philosopher becomes a rather schematic and superfluous a personage. If that is philosophy, the physicist would have been able to do as much without quitting his domain, for such an essence or substance would be a pure truism. For it must indeed be a question of pure truisms that M. Maritain can do what he does with the 92 chemical elements. Why take the trouble?[137]

The illustrious American Neo-scholastic Fulton Sheen also takes a position against Eddington with a truly crushing certitude.[138] Eddington seems to him to perform a superficial trick. Modern physicists do not comprehend the profound theses of scholasticism concerning the nature of the physical world. In that, they are not very intelligent. He comments ironically on the fashion in which the physicist resolves the notorious problem of the elephant. He does not wish to understand it with mathematical physics. The ancient scholastic incorporated physics into philosophy and there is no reason the moderns should not do the same. With respect to what Eddington says of the intrinsic nature of the atom as unknown by the physicist, Sheen writes: "Thus modern science has nothing to say about the intrinsic nature of any atom; whether or not there is a determinable element called matter and a determining element called form does not concern him. . . . Here it is not a question of knowing whether science is or is not justified in misunderstanding natures, whether or not mathematicians can interpret reality; it is quite simply a question of fact: mathematical physics misunderstands natures, substances, essences."

Of course if it does not know them it does not misunderstand them by disdain, as Sheen would have it, but quite simply because they do not concern it, because it does not know how to know them. One could ask how Sheen arrived at his very suspect hylomorphism, and what he understands by matter and form, since he seems to want the physicist to dissect physical elements in an experimental fashion. No doubt he has in mind one of the examples usually brought forth, such as combustion, in which the physicist should see evidence of a substantial transformation.

It is of course that atoms suppose in some way a substrate composed of matter and of form. But how to find that in a series of symbols? It is on the side of the material real formerly taken that one must find this composition. And even if an "atom substance" made sense, what particular profit would the physicist gain from knowing it? What would that teach us about the physical nature of an atom?

He seems not to know what physics is. One might at least expect him to make a generous effort to understand Eddington, but what is worse is that he seems not to know what philosophy is.

May we be excused this severity. But it is insupportable to see these people attack the great Eddington whom they have completely misunderstood, probably because they are convinced that there is no light save in our camp, and they haven't taken the trouble. That they should attack him with such assurance, and a bitter irony, with so much superiority, with a dogmatism that they do not even attempt to justify, all that is evident for them. And they exhibit disdain for all those who do not wear the sign "scholastic" on their breast. It seems to me that if they had had a more profound comprehension of their own system, they would have been better disposed and prepared to understand intelligible things even when they are not expressed in their grammar. For it seems that for them philosophy is only an arid grammar.

It is they who judge who must be judged.

They speak too easily as if they were certified corporations of the very soul of scholasticism. They have constantly on their lips that "the philosopher knows," "the philosopher should," "the philosopher can," "moderns are not intelligent enough to understand us," "Eddington speaks of things which surpass his competence." But we seek in vain the Why of all these dogmas.

But let us move on. It was only necessary to mention them because they are men of reputation, because they are thought to be important representatives of modern scholastic thought, because they are considered the heralds of orthodoxy. Whatever their great merits, these do not excuse their levity which has such great consequences for our reputation among non-scholastics, who are often not far from us save in language. It is not a matter of benevolent charity, but of the truth, from wherever it may come.

But this has become a sermon.

The Mind-Matter Relation

1. Symbols and Mind-stuff

We see no difficulty in admitting the fundamental thesis of Eddington. We often say that the soul is the form of body, and that the body is prime matter.

But the body is already something composed, not an essential element, a principle. It is prime matter that is informed by the soul. Physical entities are the metric aspect of that which is composed of prime matter and an intellectual substantial form. Eddington does not speak to us of different virtual degrees of the powers of the human being, but this in no way weakens the fundamental thesis. He leaves all the free play one could desire. Let the philosopher make his analyses beyond the symbols with a method of his own, only he must not take the symbols for concrete things to be ontologically explained. Certainly, there are aspects of man which are closer than metric symbols, and other aspects. But the fundamental unity of human nature is not cut into distinct supposits.

It is our imagination which constantly imposes on us and which causes us to confuse such relativities as solidity, the spatio-temporal decoupage, as if they were true ontological units, 'hard' realities, with purely metaphysical notions. It is these concretized entities that we unconsciously try to study in their respect to thought. Imagination thinks badly of science when it is assured that man is above all a void, and the distance between his particles is equal, proportionally, to that which separates the stars. Then, like Gredt, one seeks continuity in the ether. And it all ends by being a very complicated salad which not only explains nothing but makes absolutely no sense. Why thus fear a void which has no metaphysical meaning? The void doesn't separate things. And one does not ask in philosophy if the void exists, is not in one way or another a thing. It is idle to ask, one has defined void as a nothing, if a thing can or cannot act on another by means of nothing. What then is it except nothing? Is this a well-formed question? Is not the formulation quite absurd?[139]

Is it not because one has made a purely imaginative representation of body that he says: "anima humana in toto corpore praesens est"? And then this formulation which constantly recurs: "anima humana est forma corporis."[140] There are parts virtually distinct in the human being, but none is before being the result of the union of substantial form and prime matter. It is therefore inexact to say that a virtual part is informed precisely by that which constitutes it as part, and which is *natura prius.*

If one pressed these formulations far enough we would arrive at a veritable psycho-physical parallelism. It is very ambiguous to say that the soul acts on the body. "The idea that the soul lifts the arms and agitates the legs for a proper action is an idea of a savage. . . ."[141] And further on Sertillanges adds, "In truth, this question so often posed and more often badly resolved: how is the soul united to the body in order to move it, has not been resolved and is badly posed because at bottom it poses nothing."[142]

What is there shocking in the formulation that declares that the physical entities resulting from measurements made on a certain gentleman are a metric description of an aspect of a subject which thinks? There is difficulty only if we give these physical entities a sense they do not have.

2. *Evolutionism*

Such as it is presented by Eddington, it presents no difficulty for it does not touch the background of physical entities. The problem of depth, which is that of the evolution of species, has been resolved, in my opinion, by Sertillanges.[143] These two aspects will thus be in perfect agreement.

The expressions "accidents" and "catastrophes" are in no way in disagreement with a perfectly ordered finality, as Eddington himself says, and that thanks to his indeterminist thesis.

Eddington is opposed to special interventions of the Creator insofar as one wishes to introduce in that way discontinuity in the creative activity of God. It is not our opinion that this intervention seems discontinuous and in some way strange. The formulation of Eddington is very prudent. We will not try to disengage in more detail his thought, for the indications are absolutely insufficient, and are found in a context in which he does not formally address this problem.

There remains for us to make several remarks on our Chapter V on the problem of indeterminism and free will.

The problem of determinism and of freedom is a false problem, since it presupposes nonsense. This has been sufficiently shown in the paragraphs devoted specially to the subject of indeterminism.

To the remark of M. Maritain concerning *les liaisons dangereuses,* it must be responded that there is no other liaison possible than that made by Eddington.[144] A freedom that has to vanquish a fundamental determinism in things is inconceivable. A thing is determined by its very nature, or it is so conditionally. If it is only conditionally, it is not absolutely. Not to be absolutely determined is in some fashion to be undetermined. It is indeed insofar as there is indeterminism that an act commanded by will is possible. And if determinism is such that only a destruction of the entity renders this exercise possible, that also implies a background of indeterminism, a background relatively determinable. But that would entail that every movement commanded by will would imply a continual destruction of the physical entities in question, in our body and in the environment.

But we have already conceded too much. The physical entities of M. Maritain are "things" *sui juris,* at least atoms are. (We do not see why all the others are not equally so.) They are from the outset entirely determined in themselves. It is this imagination that is at the basis of the reproaches against Eddington. He understands this entirely determined in a domain where it no longer makes sense. It is by liberating himself from these images that one can pose this problem to himself.

In a paragraph on natural contingency and human freedom, Father Sertillanges writes: "It arises, finally, from the comparison of our case with that of soul and body, of form and matter, that the roots of freedom and those of contingency correspond with one another. The products of contingency arise from the unsoundable depths of matter; those of free will from the unsoundable depths of the rational will, which is infinite of power. Just as, in order to exclude natural contingency, it would be necessary to suppose a first activity whose effort would be equal to the potentiality of pure matter, so, to exclude freedom, there must be a good equal in amplitude to vacuity of the soul."[145]

This fundamental character of prime matter which takes account of contingency explains how free activity can be exercised in nature. Evidently there are limits to that. And Eddington gives us a valuable precision: "It is one thing to allow the mind to direct an atom between two courses neither of which would be improbable for an inorganic atom; it is another thing to allow it to direct a crowd of atoms into a configuration which the secondary laws of physics would set aside as 'too improbable.' Here the improbability is that a large number of entities each acting independently should conspire to produce the result; it is like the improbability of the atoms finding themselves by chance all in one half of a vessel" (NPW, 314 [311]).

The determinism of this fact is not a true one, for it implies simply a necessity of fact and not of right, that is, that the contrary is too improbable. To this passage we can juxtapose the following of Sertillanges: "What must be conceded to the arguments of materialism is that this will which, speaking absolutely, we declare is free, is no less conditioned from within and without by material activities. All the weight of the world weighs on us, sometimes inclining us in the direction of our law, sometimes inclining us in the contrary direction" (ibid., 276).

The distinction we have established between 'of right' and 'of fact' has a quite different sense than that of M. Maritain. It is precisely by reason of fundamental indeterminism that it makes sense. These few remarks seem sufficient to show that this thesis of Eddington ought not frighten us so. As we have seen, it is not as novel as it appears.

General Conclusion

So we come quite abruptly to the end of our study. Eddington very likely would not enjoy seeing his ideas cut up as we have done. But others have done it to criticize him, and we have followed an analogous procedure to justify him. This study has perhaps too much the air of being an Apologia for Eddington. And we do not wish to dissimulate. We have as it were forced ourselves to comprehend it. But it would take us yet more time to give a just appreciation of the whole of his philosophy, insofar as it is possible to systematize the occasional lectures he has given.

We have no fundamental criticism to make. No doubt there are some points on which one could dwell more, such as that of intensive qualities, that of the approximative character of our measurements which dominate the whole of physics, a point on which Professor Renoirte has much insisted. Moreover, it is by following Renoirte's systematic expositions that we have been able to systematize the scattered ideas of Eddington.

It is Professor Renoirte who introduced me to Eddington. There is nothing original in this study. Anything of value it may contain was suggested by him. It is by applying his critical principles that I have tried to disengage a little the implications of indeterminism. We acknowledge with a full heart the extraordinary generosity he has shown in sacrificing weeks of his time to direct this study. It will show that we have not been able to profit in an adequate way from his direction. But I hope that there will be found in it at least something that will be a remote suggestion of recompense for his benevolence.

NOTES

1. *Encyclopedia Britannica,* entry "Eddington."

2. Bertrand Russell, *The Analysis of Matter* (London, 1927), 395–96.

3. "I would like to recall that the idealistic tinge in my conception of the physical world arose out of mathematical researches on the relativity theory. In so far as I had any earlier philosophical views, they were of an entirely different complexion" (Eddington, *The Nature of the Physical World* [Cros Tr.], p. vi [8]).

4. Eddington, "The Systematic Motions of the Stars," appeared in the *Monthly Notices* of the Royal Astronomical Society in December 1906. The articles of Kapteyn are also of 1904 and 1905.

5. "In science we sometimes have convictions as to the right solution of a problem which we cherish but cannot justify; we are influenced by some innate sense of the fitness of things" (*The Nature of the Physical World,* 337 [333]).

6. Cf. W. de Sitter, *Kosmos,* 3.

7. Eddington, "On the Relative Equilibrium of the Stars," *Monthly Notices* (November 1916 and June 1917). See, too, *Nature* 106 (1920) and his article in the *Encyclopedia Britannica,* "Stars." All this theory is synthesized in *The Internal Constitution of the Stars* (Cambridge, 1926), and in a popular work, *Stars and Atoms* (Oxford, 1927). There is a French translation by Rossignol, *Etoiles et Atomes* (Paris, 1930).

8. Eddington, "Some Problems of Astronomy, XIX Gravity," *Observatory* 38 (Feb. 1915): 93.

9. It has been said that Eddington only knew Einstein after 1916 (see, for example, Presidential Address of Drey, *Monthly Notices* 84 [1924]: 535). Since he constantly refers to articles of Einstein in the *Annales der Physik,* we have evidence that he followed the developments of theory from its first appearance.

10. Eddington, "A Generalization of Weyl's Theory of the Electro-magnetic and Gravitational Fields," *Proceedings of the Royal Society,* series A (1921): 104.

11. Eddington, *Mathematical Theory of Relativity* (Cambridge, 1923).

12. Ibid., 105.

13. Cf., for example, Jos. Gredt, *Elementa Philosophiae,* vol. 1, 4th ed., Theses XVII & XX, pp. 281 & 291.

14. The translation of this work, appearing under the title *Espace, Temps, et Gravitation,* is from Rossignol (Paris, 1921). Our references are to the pages of this translation.

15. Cf. the English text of *The Nature of the Physical World,* p. xiv and especially 328. The [French] translator has omitted these allusions to the philosopher Berkeley. For Bergson, see the [French] translation, p. 53 [p. 36 of English edition]; for Hegel, p. 136 [p. 125–26 of English edition].

16. See Henri Bergson, *Matière et Mémoire,* Avant-Propos, "idéalisme et réalisme sont deux thèses également excessives . . . il est faux de réduire la matière à la représentation que nous en avons, faux aussi d'en faire une chose qui produirait en nous des représentations mais qui serait d'une autre nature qu'elles." In J. Jeans we find the same distinction: "the two conjectures are those of the idealist and the realist—or, if you

prefer, of the mentalist and the materialist" (*The New Background of Science* [Cambridge, 1933], 299).

17. The first work of Jeans containing philosophical speculation is *The Universe around Us,* which appeared in 1929.

18. Eddington, "Physics and Philosophy," *Philosophy* (Jan. 1933): 30.

19. Cf. André Lalande, *Vocabulaire de la Philosophie,* at the word 'philosophy.' The members of the British Philosophical Association are all physicists, mathematicians, biologists, etc. and their proceedings contain only strictly scientific articles.

20. J.A. Thomson, *Introduction to Science* (Home University Library, 1927), 196–97. We will find this idea in Eddington. "From the beginning I have been doubtful whether it was desirable for a scientist to venture so far into extra-scientific territory. The primary justification for such an expedition is that it may afford a better view of his own scientific domain" (*The Nature of the Physical World,* p. vi [8]). In Jeans we find a no less interesting text: "I have sketched a portrait on a background rudely drawn from rudimentary philosophy—the philosophy of a man of science, and not that of a metaphysician—because I believe as does the majority of scientists that without a background of this kind it is impossible for us to see our new knowledge as making up an ensemble nor wholly to understand its significance" (*The New Background of Science,* p. vii). And here is an interesting remark by Max Planck: "There were times when philosophy and science were strangers, if not antagonists. Those times are past. Philosophers have taught themselves that they have no right to dictate to men of science as to goals and the means of achieving them. And men of science have also learned that the point of departure of their investigations is not found solely in the perceptions of the senses, and that science is impossible without at least a little bit of metaphysics. Modern physics impresses on us the truth of the ancient doctrine that teaches us that there are some realities existing apart from our sense perceptions, and that there are problems and conflicts in which such realities are of greater value for us than the richest treasures of the world of experience" (*The Universe in the Light of Modern Physics* [London, 1931], 106–7).

21. Jeans, *The Mysterious Universe,* preface.

22. "[The scientist] has good and sufficient reasons for pursuing his investigations in the world of shadows and is content to leave to the philosopher the determination of its exact status in regard to reality" (*The Nature of the Physical World,* p. xiv [16]).

23. Robert A. Millikan, *Time, Matter, and Values* (University of North Carolina Press, 1932), p. x.

24. Ibid., 94–96. This argument has been exploited by some apologists.

25. *The Nature of the Physical World,* 326 [323].

26. From now on we will use the following abbreviations:

NPW = *The Nature of the Physical World*
STG = *Space, Time, and Gravitation*
MTR = *Mathematical Theory of Relativity*
SUW = *Science and the Unseen World*
PP = "Physics and Philosophy"
DD = "The Decline of Determinism"

27. This doctrine of the familiar word is set forth in the introduction to NPW. As for its more profound meaning, we refer to the second part of this book.

28. Cf. NPW, 265 [266]. The French translator has used "réalité" for "actuality," but for Eddington "reality" and "actuality" are two perfectly distinct notions, as we will see later.

29. NPW, 225 [230]. This affirmation is moreover justified by his immediate realism that we discuss in what follows.

30. This expression is not found in Eddington, but the idea is implied by his metaphysics.

31. Eddington explains that we have an immediate awareness of actuality, but the infrastructure of this actuality, reality, has to be discovered.

32. STG, 42 [53], 155 [193]; NPW, 335 [331].

33. PP, 31.

34. NPW, chaps. XII & XIII.

35. Evidently, Eddington does not use the terms "substance" and "permanence" in their scholastic sense. As a mark of this substantiality he gives: occupying a space to the exclusion of any other substance. In metaphysics he will come back to make this notion precise, by giving it a metaphysical sense quite remote from the vulgar notion. So, too, of color, which he calls subjective. He has his own notion of subjectivity. Evidently the physical world is beautiful, but it is not the physicist as physicist who perceives it so.

36. These terms have a purely relative sense. Several characteristics of the familiar world are illusory insofar as they are not translatable into physics in a formal fashion. Thus he calls even reality an illusion. But there are illusions to which ontological actualities correspond. The procedure that he employs here is purely didactic. He means to show that many of our true illusions are illusions apropos of illusions, which are transphysical realities.

37. Cf. SUW, 79; MTR, 107–8. The center of this problem does not reside in the subjectivity of colors, demonstrated by Daltonism, for in this case one could say that the two are mistaken with respect to the true color. It is rather the fact that we are unable to compare our impressions themselves when the experiences reveal that we see the same color. "The same color" poses an insoluble problem; it is that which cannot become the object of a scientific investigation.

38. NPW, 94 [108]. Note that for Eddington "mind-spinning" is not synonymous with intentional, in such wise that everything that the mind projects into nature is subjective in the proper sense of the word. We will return to this below.

39. Cf. the interesting developments in MTR, 41 & 224 ff.

40. "Truth and untruth belong to the realm of significance and values" (SUW, 61). "*[V]alues* are created by the mind. All the 'light and shade' in our conception of the world of physics comes in this way from the mind, and cannot be explained without reference to the characteristics of consciousness" (NPW, 243 [246]).

41. Cf. F. Renoirte, "La philosophie des sciences selon M. Maritain," *Revue Néo-scolastique* (1933): 96–106. We have used the three works of Renoirte listed in our bibliography as background for this study. It has enabled us to present Eddington's philosophy of science in a schematic way.

42. Ibid., 104. For what follows, see especially the dialogue of STG, 1–16 [1–21]; NPW, chaps. I–III and pp. 141 ff. [151 ff.]; MTR, 1–7.

43. "Exteriority" does not mean "external to the knowing subject" but rather what scholastics mean by the "partes extra partes quoad se" of the object. Time and space are immediate data which can only be described with reference to experience. It would be impossible to explain to someone what space is if he had never had immediate experience of it.

44. STG, 186 [228]. "The space which you are speaking of [i.e., the space of the physicist] must be a sort of abstraction of the extensional relations of matter" (ibid., 8 [11]).

45. NPW, 99 [112] & 51 [67]; MTR, 23 ff.

46. NPW, 100 [114].

47. STG, 6 [8]. "[P]erceptual space and time is the same as the measured space and time, which is the subject-matter of natural geometry" (ibid., 15 [19]).

48. Eddington would say that it is perceived by consciousness, a remark that presupposes what is developed in the second part of this thesis.

49. This is not said explicitly by Eddington, but he refers to Bertrand Russell. See G. Lemaitre, "Le grandeur de l'espace," *Revue des Questions Scientifiques* (1929): 208–9.

50. "Counting appears to be an absolute operation. But it seems to me that the other physical measures are on a different footing" (STG, 8 [10]; NPW, 23 [41]).

51. "All the knowledge [of the physical world] is derived from measurements made with various instruments. The instruments used in the different fields of inquiry are not fundamentally unlike. There is no reason to regard the partitions of the sciences made in the early stages of human thought as irremovable" (NPW, 136–37 [146]).

52. Cf. NPW, 154–55 [162–63].

53. MTR, 4, and PP, 30–31.

54. The famous observer of relativity has caused much confusion. "Ceterum studium et ardor quo multi ardent pro theoria relativitatis non tam ex rationibus e scientiis naturalibus deductis quam ex rationibus philosophicis provenire videtur. Ideo amore moventur pro theoria relativitatis, quia haec doctrina respondet idealismo et positivismo quo mentes eorum imbutae sunt" (J. Gredt, "Theoria relativitas einsteniana excussa secundum principia aristotelico-thomistica," *Congressus thomisticus* [1925]: 105–13). Thus he thinks that Einstein makes physical magnitudes dependent on the observer as a psychological individual. But "the observer can be regarded as a mechanical automaton, and can be replaced by scientific measuring-appliances" (STG, 183 [225]). Bertrand Russell makes an interesting remark in his article on the "Philosophical Consequences of Relativity," *Encyclopedia Britannica*: "Realism and Relativity. It is an error to suppose that relativity adopts an idealist portrait of the world—taking 'idealism' in its technical sense as implying that there is nothing independent of experience. The 'observer' so often mentioned in expositions of relativity need not be a mind; it could be a photographic plate or no matter what other recording instrument. The fundamental supposition of relativity is realist, notably that the aspects on which all observers concur when they register a given phenomenon can be taken for objective, and not something furnished by the observers."

55. NPW, 244 ff. [247], 156; STG, 40 ff. [50]; MTR, 115, 119, 222.

56. STG, 156 [194], 173 [213]; NPW, chaps. IV, V, & XIV; FD, II.

57. NPW, 75-6 [90]. "[I]t is supposed that the primary laws constitute the complete scheme of prediction. In general, only the primary laws have been regarded as fundamental; the other laws being only stop-gaps representing the progress of knowledge in regions which are not yet sufficiently hooked up with the scheme of primary laws."

58. Max Planck, *Where Is Science Going?* Preface by Albert Einstein, tr. James Murphy (London, 1933). This translation is followed by a Socratic dialogue between Einstein and Murphy, and Planck and Murphy. See, too, N. J. Dingle who attacked Eddington's views in two articles that appeared in *The Month,* "What of the New Physics?" (Jan., 1931) and "Science and Causality" (Sept., 1933); and in the same publication, the article by H.V. Gill, "Whither Science?" (Feb., 1934) which appeared as well in *The Catholic Mind* (April, 1934).

59. Cf. the different definition of "determinism" in Lalande's *Vocabulaire technique et critique de philosophie.* To be found there is an interesting remark of Claude Bernard (*Introduction à la médicine expérimentale,* 303): "The experimental critique puts everything in doubt except the principle of scientific determinism." In philosophy, determinism is the doctrine "according to which all the events of the universe, and in particular human actions, are linked in such a way that things being what they are at any given moment whatever of time, there is for each of previous or later moments, but one state and one alone which is compatible with it." See, too, "chance."

60. Cf. Guérard des Lauriers, "Analyse de l'être mathématique," *Revue des Questions Philosophique et Théologique,* nos. 3 & 4 (1933), which contain very profound suggestions on the origin of our idea of the physical continuum.

61. "The ultimate elements in a theory of the world must be of a nature impossible to define in terms recognizable to the mind" (STG, 185 [English edition]). "Recognizable to our mind" is quite different from "intelligible." In the present case, the terms are sufficiently intelligible, but one finds no homologue of them in the familiar world. "Mind" cannot always be translated as *esprit* or intelligence, but usually embraces sensation as well. Thus, colors are products of "mind-spinning."

62. Eddington, *The Expanding Universe,* 17.

63. I allude to the three contributions of Professor Renoirte which appeared in *La Revue Néoscolastique,* already cited.

64. J. Maritain, *The Degrees of Knowledge,* chaps. II & IV.

65. Ibid., 331.

66. Here are the characteristics of this intuition of M. Maritain. "The intuition of which we are speaking here is not an intelligible intuition (nor a pure intuition in the Kantian sense), as the geometricians believed for a long time when they thought that their proper object was a world of Platonic models delineated in an amorphous milieu which pre-existed the figures that specified it (an eternal container conditioning the universe) and which would be 'space.' Nor is it an experimental intuition belonging to external perception, with the observations and measurements we effect by means of our senses and our instruments. It is an imaginative intuition, an intuition of the 'in-

ternal sense' which depends on external perception only as a presupposition, as does the imagination itself. We can clearly grasp this role of the imagination from the fact that quantity, which is the first accident of corporeal substance, precedes (by a priority of nature) the whole qualitative (energetic and physical) order and therefore the whole sensible order, and yet is itself known to the senses by means of sensible qualities, though not without the whole synergic elaboration of perception (for it is a 'common sensible'). Thus the imagination at the service of the intellect can penetrate into the world of pure quantity, detached by abstraction from sensible matter. It can do this, moreover, precisely insofar as the imagination, though it presupposes the external sense, is free from it (by which I mean its objects are not subject to the conditions of relativity which affect *hic et nunc* those of perception and which derive from actual dependence on external physical circumstances). And so it is that the intuitive schemes of the imagination—which are not at all the object itself of mathematics but only the sensible symbol or illustration of that object—manifest to us in a sensible way, though independent of every experimental condition, essences and properties which of themselves precede the sensible order and are independent of it" (ibid., 153).

In relation to this, it should be added that M. Maritain identifies "extension" and "quantity": "When we consider things from the point of view of the philosopher and not of the physicist, and speak the former's language, then quantity, that is to say the extension of substance and of its metaphysical unity into diverse parts according to position, is a real property of bodies. There are in nature real dimensions, numbers and measurements, a real space, a real time. It is precisely under the conditions and modalities of this real quantity, or, to put it in another way, it is as quantitatively measured and regulated, that the interacting causes in nature develop their qualitative activities" (ibid., 151–52).

Let us add the following text: "Under the pretext that space is a network of distances (but which the geometrician 'measures' ideally and deductively), one will pretend to give geometry (as a 'natural-science') as object of a network of distances materially and empirically measured with the aid of physical apparatus" (ibid., 182).

M. Maritain therefore knows some ideal measures which have the characteristic of furnishing real ontological magnitudes. How they effect them, he does not say. This real space is according to him evacuated of everything physical. "[T]he geometric properties of existing bodies, the properties that the mind recognizes in them when everything physical is voided, are those which characterize Euclidean space. It is Euclidean space which appears to the philosopher to be *ens geometricum reale.*" See, too, p. 184.

We think that these two confusions have led M. Maritain to elaborate this chimerical theory. First, his confusion of extension and quantity, which is grave. Then, the fact that he does not grasp the import of relativity founded on the relativity of measurements.

By quantity, scholastics understand "that which is known through measurement." The extended is the property of having parts outside of parts "quoad se." Evacuated space has absolutely no real sense. The extended as such is not measured. Evidently, identifying the extended with quantity, M. Maritain surreptitiously introduces measurability.

67. Ibid., 179. My emphasis.

68. Ibid., 178–79.

69. Renoirte, *La critique einsteinienne.*

70. Roland Dalbiez, "Dimensions absolues et mesures absolus," *Revue thomiste* (1925): 153–54. It is indeed Dalbiez who lacks frank realism: the length of Renoirte is indeed real whereas that of Dalbiez is unreal, only its correspondent being absolute, but still unknowable *in concreto.*

71. Maritain, *The Degrees of Knowledge,* 167–68.

72. Ibid., 168.

73. Ibid.

74. Ibid., 170.

75. Cf. the criticism of Renoirte, "La philosophie des sciences selon M. Maritain," 103.

76. See the articles of Maritain that appeared in *La Revue Universelle,* "La métaphysique des physiciens" (15 August 1922) and "Nouveaux débats einsteiniens" (1 April 1924). See, too, the refutation of these objections in *La relativité* of André Metz, 158–87.

77. One can even define the absolute of relativity "as a relative which is always the same no matter what it is relative to" (STG, 82 [102]). This absolute has nothing to do with that of M. Maritain, which is a pure truism applied to no matter what.

78. We have developed this point in *Kulturleven,* "Natuurwetenschappelijke methodologie en wijsbegeerte II" (Jan. 1934) in an extended fashion (pp. 51–70).

79. Jeans, "The Mathematical Aspect of the Universe," *Philosophy* (Jan. 1932): 13.

80. *Summa theologiae,* Ia, q. 17, a. 2, c.

81. Ibid., q. 78, a. 3, ad 2; see also John of St. Thomas, *Cursus philosophicus,* t. 3, p. 281.

82. Cf. Renoirte, *La théorie physique,* 334, and "La philosophie des sciences salon de M. Maritain," 104. See, too, the interesting developments of Max Planck in a 1909 work published only in 1915, *Eight Lectures on Theoretical Physics,* 4–7.

83. Maritain, *The Degrees of Knowledge,* 29. In his critique, M. Renoirte recalls how it comes about that physics is mathematical (103).

84. Compare with *The Degrees of Knowledge,* 184: "The same considerations hold, *mutatis mutandis,* for the mathematization that the Quantum Theory accomplishes on the physical real in other ways than that of Relativity. They hold particularly for the structure that the New Physics attributes to the atom, or better, the continuously varying structure of the atom demanded by it for some years now. It seems that science tends to form a pure abstract mathematical equivalent of this structure—which thereby becomes unrepresentable to the imagination, and at the same time divested of any ontological meaning. This equivalent tends to become a more and more fictitious and more and more perfect symbol of the real nature, unknown in itself, of that existing something or other to which determinatively corresponds the name atom. Thus it knows this nature more and more profoundly, yet more and more enigmatically, and metaphorically, to put it bluntly, in the measure that it constructs the myth—a being of reason found in re—which takes its place." And also, p. 193: "Still, according to our

principles, the Einsteinian universe of four dimensions and its curvature, as well as the electron or proton of today, must be regarded as pure physico-mathematical beings of reason founded on the real. The question then arises as to what relation the Philosophy of Nature can have, not now with the facts or the *entia realia* more-or-less completed by reason, but with the pure *entia rationis* and the well-founded myths of science."

Emile Meyerson takes an analogous position (or is it Maritain who follows him?) when he says to Eddington that when he pretends "that the physicist 'who had the habit of borrowing his materials from the familiar universe, has it no more,' that 'his brute materials are ether, electrons, quanta, the potentials, the Hamiltonian functions, etc." and that at the present time he 'takes scrupulous care to keep his notions from any contamination by conceptions taken from that other universe' he is certainly the plaything of an illusion. It is *necessary* that, on the one hand, the concept of scientific theory recalls that of common sense, without which the physicist would not know how to proceed" ("Realism and Determinism in Quantum Physics," 19). But Eddington does not deny that. It is a matter of understanding what one means by 'on the one hand.'

In fact, the physicist takes his point of departure in the familiar world, but he isolates its metric aspect. As long as his entities have a metric aspect, they have all that can be expected of them, and that suffices for them to be real.

Meyerson moreover feels himself to be encumbered by quanta which put us in the presence of *two* perfectly contradictory images, "irreconciliable in the imagination." Bohm, Born, and Heisenberg want, according to Meyerson, to escape this dilemma by idealism. They "have been able to affirm that the difficulties of the theory do not have their source in the duality of corpuscle and undulations, a duality they judge, on the contrary, perfectly comprehensible. That is because these scientists are quite accustomed to be moved, in this order of ideas, into abstract mathematics and then the contradiction of the concrete physical image appears negligible to them" (ibid., 40). Since Meyerson seems to identify the physically real and the imaginable, the error of quantum physicists is evident to him: they absolutely want the basis of physical realities to be irrational. Why? Because the rational is imaginable?

85. In Max Planck, *Where Is Science Going?* epilogue, 201, 210.

86. Ibid., 211.

87. Ibid., 220. Also, the little work published under the title *The Universe in the Light of Modern Physics* in which he seems to be less categorical than before. Thus he writes: "If one were really obliged to grant the step [to indeterminism], the goal of physicists would become more and more remote, and this would be a disadvantage of which it would be impossible to overstate the importance. In my opinion, as long as there remains a choice to make, determinism will always be preferable to indeterminism, quite simply because a definite answer is always preferable to an indefinite answer" (48).

88. This remark may appear completely superfluous. But here is what one reads in a recent manual of scholastic philosophy said to be "up to date" with respect to modern science. "De atomismo autem dynamico spectatim de doctrina electronum dicimus, non apparere rationem philosophicam, ut rejiciantur, sed esse admittenda,

in quantum probantur aut probabiliter suadentur, et explicanda. Quapro dicimus a) electrones et ea, quae nucleum componunt, esse composita ex materia et forma tanquam ex principiis substantialibus. Idem dicendum de aethere qui admittitur tanquam medium in quo moventur electrones. b) Quia ex nucleo et electronibus oriuntur elementa chimica derivata, et ex elementis caetera corpora chimice composita tanquam typi stabiles, abrupto inter se distincti notis stabilibus et determinatis, etiam haec elementa ex electronibus exorta et caetera corpora chimice composita novas species substantialibus constituunt. Cum igitur determinatus numerus electronum secundum determinatam strusturam conjunguntur cum nucleo aut efformandum elementum, in tota hac mole, quae atomum elementi constituit, nova oritur forma substantialis, forma substantialis elementi. Quare atomus elementi est una substantia. Singuli electrones et nucleus desinunt esse per se, et inter se continuuntur aut immediate aut potius mediate, mediante aethere in quo moventur, qui profunde etiam ipse ad substantiam atomi pertinet. Aether enim ille intermedius secundum typum suum externum apparet mutatus et in tensione electrica totius compositi est electronibus involutus. Tota igitur moles constitua ex nucleo et electronibus et aethere intermedio una forma substantialis informatur, quae est forma elementi. Similiter fit, cum ex elementis oritur corpus aliquod chimice compositum. Etiam tunc oritur nova substantia specifica diversa et nova forma substantialis. Molecula corporis compositi est una substantia. Element desinunt esse per se et constituunt unam molem continuum. C) Sed etiam corporea major ex multis moleculis constituta, una est substantia continua. Hoc certe obtinet in corpore vivente. At vero non tantum in corpore vivente moleculae inter se continuantur, sed etiam moles corporum non-viventium ex moleculis inter se continuis conflantur. Nam nulla est ratio, ut dicantur hae moles conflatae ex moleculis inter se discretis; microstructura enim corporis ex nucleo et electronibus aethere inter se conjunctis quoscumque permittit motus mechanicos, qui secundum physicos intra molem corpoream contingere dicuntur. Immo est valida ratio ut dicatur, moleculas ejusdem speciei, cum perfecte inter se conjunguntur (mechanice, sole contactu, si sunt in statu liquido aut seriformi, calore seu confistura, si sunt in statu solido), etiam inter se continuari (mediante aethere qui ad earum constitutionem pertinet) et effermare unam substantiam. Tunc singulae moleculae amittunt suum esse per se et singulae earum formae substantiales in una conjunguntur forma substantialis quae extenditur per totum molem. Est enim haec forma extensa.

"The hylomorphic doctrine, for example, is as true today as it was in the time of Aristotle. Its vocabulary and exemplifications have grown old, but not its substance. The four elements of former times are replaced by the ninety-two elements of Mendelejeff's Table. They correspond to a very different scientific notion. We have a much more rigorous knowledge of this family of elements than did the chemists of a hundred years ago. We hold as probable that they all derive from the atom of hydrogen by a series of changes which a philosopher must needs regard as substantial mutations. The phenomena of radioactivity offer the spectacle of such changes of *nature* in the world of bodies. This is not a pure and simple scientific verification. (It belongs to philosophy, not to science, to establish a fact, whose formulation implies notions of substance, nature, species, etc., metaphysically understood.) But it is a remarkable empiriological indication or 'sign' which the philosopher can prudently point to as such" (Maritain, *The Degrees of Knowledge,* 191–92; see as well 191, note 72).

Expressions like "the philosopher ought" and "can" are gratuitous affirmations. He should show us with exactly what right the philosopher does all that. The question arises only for someone who has not understood the meaning of physical properties. The attribution of substance, or of nature, to some physical entities is only a gamble, and absolutely unjustified.

89. "If by retrospective inference we infer characters at an earlier date and then say that those characters invariably produce at a future date the manifestation from which we inferred them, we are working in a circle. The connection is not causation but definition, and we are not prophets but tautologists. We must not mix up the genuine achievements of scientific prediction with this kind of charlatanry, nor the observed uniformities of nature with those so easily invented. . . . To avoid vicious circles, we must abolish purely retrospective characteristics—those which are never found as existing, but always as having existed. If they do not manifest themselves until the moment that they cease to exist, they can never be used for prediction except by those who prophesy after the event" (DD, 72–73 [14–15]).

If this had not been written in 1932, we could take it as a direct response to the objection of Einstein, published only in 1933 (*Where Is Science Going?* 202).

90. "If no reason for asserting [the determinist claim] can be given, it collapses as an idle speculation. It is astonishing that even scientific writers on determinism advocate it without thinking it necessary to say anything in its favor, merely pointing out that the new physical theories do not actually disprove determinism" (DD, 76 [18]).

91. Planck, *Where Is Science Going?* 203.

92. See the long discussion of Planck on causality in ibid., 107–69, where he constantly confuses metaphysics and scientific methodology. This same confusion will recur in Eddington, but much less gravely, when he studies the relation between physical indeterminism and freedom. We will discuss such matters in the second part.

93. Cf. Renoirte, *La théorie physique,* 360: "To express the law in a causal form is to make a metaphor or to interpret it by means of a principle alien to physics."

94. Hermann Weyl, *The Open World* (1932), 35 and 47. Bertrand Russell seems to find nothing inconvenient in objective indeterminism. In *The Analysis of Matter* (1927) he writes: "So far as quantum theory can say today, atoms could indeed be endowed with free will, not limited to one of several choices. . . . In macroscopic phenomena, there is nothing that suggests the quantum, and it could be that other traits of such phenomena result quite simply from a statistical mean." But in a note he adds: "This is probably a temporary state of affairs" (38). Elsewhere he seems to insinuate that determinism would be indemonstrable (214). It always postulates a practically unveriable, even superfluous, ideal element. Still he remarks that physical determinism does not necessarily entail psychological determinism (390), which suggests that physical determinism is at least possible. But it should be said that at that time the problem of indeterminism was not as pressing as now. Eddington had such convictions from 1920.

95. Millikan, *Time, Matter and Values*, 97–98.

96. Cf. St. Thomas, *Q.D. De anima*, a. 20.

97. Here is another interesting passage, but one presupposing as well a certain confusion of physics and philosophy, borrowed from the *Mécanique ondulatoire* of Louis de Broglie: "Constantly, where it is a question of the macroscopic or the microscopic order, do we not seem necessarily to have to make appeal to an indispensable principle, by itself undetermined, undefined, unqualified, unquantified . . . [d]eterminable by another element of our sense knowledge which is capable of giving it its value, its own permanent and persistent constitution—at least in its requirements—giving a proper character to manifestations of the ensemble and making the structure of the given material complete? The incomplete, passive, potential principle, persistent under all accidental and substantial modifications, that is what Aristotle called prime matter. The principle giving to the finite being its perfection and surely deriving from the prototype, recognizable, moreover, with respect to what there is being is due to its characteristic unity of existence, action, movement, constitution, stability, is form" (cited by P. Tiberghien in *La science mene-t-elle a Dieu?* [Paris: Blond & Gay, 1933], 89–90). If we only knew what he means here by accidental and substantial modifications.

98. St. Thomas, *In I Perihermeneias*, lectio 14; *Q.D. de malo*, q. 6, art. Un., ad 21; q. 16, a. 7, ad 24 & 25.

99. Maritain, *The Degrees of Knowledge*, 203.

100. Ibid.

101. Ibid., 31.

102. See, for example, questions 95 and 96 of the first part of the *Summa theologiae*. A celebrated American astronomer, H. N. Russell, attempted an analogous conciliation of determinism and freedom in a series of conferences on *Fate and Freedom*, delivered in 1925 and published in 1927. In physics he holds a rigorous determinism. Whether or not he still does, I do not know. He was a great admirer of Eddington and it is possible that he changed his mind.

103. On this subject, see the suggestive article of P. Jordan, "Die Quantenmechanik und die Grundprobleme der Biologie und Psychologie," *Naturwissenschaften* (Nov., 1932). But it should be said that if one wants to define living things as indeterminist macroscopic phenomena one has to make precise that this indeterminism approximates that of the fundamental elements, as opposed to the macroscopic phenomena which are also undetermined although to a lesser degree, insofar as they include a greater number of composing elements. But that only gives us degrees of indeterminism.

104. It is homogeneity which distinguishes the parts of external from other realities which we call parts, and which are also in some way excluded. Thus, intelligence is outside will insofar as they are distinct faculties in finite beings, But they are not homogeneous parts. They share of course in the notions of 'being' and 'faculty,' which are analogues. So much so that the homogeneity of the parts of spatio-temporal exteriority is a distinctive note of material beings.

105. "[T]he mind seems rather to take pains to smooth the discontinuities of nature into continuous perception" (STG, 199).

106. NPW, 260–66 [262–68].

107. Ibid., 282–89 [282–89].

108. L. Noël, "La méthode du réalisme," *Revue Néoscolastique* (1931): 445.

109. We should remember that the mental object in question is not the mind of the subject, but the object immediately present to mind. But 'mental' is sometimes taken as synonymous with 'mind-stuff,' and then the word has another more transcendental meaning. Thus Jeans takes 'mentalism' as the synonym of 'idealism,' and 'materialism' as the synonym of 'realism' (*The New Background of Science*, 298). Yet Jeans is not an idealist in the traditional sense, although we find in him rather ambiguous expressions on the mathematical nature of reality taken as such. The Creator is for him a Pure Mathematician. But he also fears the word 'real' that is so often used as synonym of the irrational.

110. Exteriority can be taken in the sense of *extraneitas, partes extra partes,* but also in the sense of 'external to the knowing subject.' And it is that latter that Eddington means by externality. In this externality it is necessary to distinguish the object in consciousness and all the same external to consciousness, from the external to the object immediately present to consciousness, the inferred object.

111. NPW, 226 [230].

112. "The physicist, so long as he thinks as a physicist, has a definite belief in a real world outside him. For instance, he believes that atoms and molecules really exist; they are not mere inventions that enable him to grasp certain laws of chemical combination. That suggestion might have sufficed in the early days of the atomic theory; but now the existence of atoms as entities in the real world of physics is fully demonstrated. This confident assertion is not inconsistent with philosophic doubts as to the meaning of ultimate reality" (STG, 180–81 [222]).

113. This passage, NPW, 326–27 of the English edition, is missing from the French edition.

114. SUW, 39. "Experience may be regarded as a combination of self and environment, it being part of the problem to disentangle these two interacting components. Life, religion, knowledge, truth are all involved in this problem, some relating to the finding of ourselves, some to the finding of our environment from the experience confronting us" (NPW, 328 [325]).

115. "In most subjects (perhaps not excluding philosophy) it seems sufficient to agree on the things that we shall call real, and afterwards try to discover what we mean by the word. And so it comes about that religion seems to be the one field of inquiry in which the question of reality and existence is treated as of serious and vital importance" (NPW, 326 [323]). This passage would shock philosophers who are not generally content to see their real treated as a convention, but Eddington's domain of religion is precisely the domain of metaphysics. It is merely a question of words. He does not like the term "metaphysics," for the metaphysicians have had intuitions and certitudes which have been found to be pure dogmas. For Eddington, a metaphysician is above all a good fellow who dogmatizes about notions like space and time (STG, prologue). (Thus Eddington would call M. Maritain a metaphysician when he speaks of imaginative intuitions, and this would not be a compliment.)

116. SUW, 41.

117. Ibid., 44.

118. NPW, 326 [323].

119. SUW, 41.

120. The way in which we have experience of the real is for Eddington a divine revelation insofar as this experience raises a problem which will reveal our divine destiny. It is a problem which poses moral problems. But he distinguishes this revelation from Revelation properly so called. Cf. SUW, 72.

121. NPW, 344–45 [340–41]. He gives there a long dialectic development of the problem. See, too, SUW, 61.

122. SUW, 82–83.

123. *Summa theologiae,* Ia, q. 2, a. 3. We also are reminded of q. 44, a. 1: "Necesse est igitur omnia quae diversificantur secundum diversam participationem essendi, ut sint perfectius, vel minus perfecte, causari ab uno primo ente, quod perfectissime est. Inde et Plato dixit quod 'necesse est antem omnem multitudinem ponere unitatem.' Et Aristoteles dicit quod 'id quod est maxime ens, et maxime verum, est causa omnis entis et omnis veri: sicut id quod maxime calidum est, est causa omnis caliditatis.'" For Eddington, all that is evident, so evident he doesn't want to insist on it.

124. NPW, 351 [347]; SUW, 72–73.

125. "For a long time this has served to combat a too enterprising materialism; a scientific proof has been fashioned for the intervention of the Creator at a not infinitely distant epoch. But let us not draw hasty conclusions from that. Scientists, like theologians, are obliged to consider how very rough is the naive theological doctrine that one now finds (suitably travestied) in the smallest traits of thermodynamics, namely that it is billions of years since God organized the material universe and has since abandoned it to probability. One would have to consider this a working hypothesis of thermodynamics rather than a declaration of faith. There is one of those conclusions one cannot escape: but it suffers from the fact that it is not believable. As scientist, I do not believe, purely and simply, that the actual order of things was put in play with a single act; nor beyond every scientific question do I willingly accept the implied discontinuity in the divine nature. But I can make no suggestion that would get us out of the impasse" (NPW, 989–99). [DeKoninck objects here to the French translation of "implied discontinuity" as "la discontinuité qu'implique la nature divine," because it makes Eddington say exactly the opposite of what he does say. He does not want to put discontinuity in God.]

126. See Jeans, *The Mysterious Universe,* chap. 5, and Weyl, *The Open World,* 28.

127. Cf. A. C. Gifford, "The Origin of the Solar System, Part II, From Jeans to the Present Day," *Scientia* (1932): 203–18, and the exposition of Jeans himself in *The Universe around Us,* 194, and in *The Mysterious Universe,* chap. 1. Eddington's only assents seem to be in *The Nature of the Physical World,* 184, and *Science and the Unseen World,* chap. 1.

128. Cf. for example R. E. Hobart, "Free Will as Implying Determination," *Mind* (Jan., 1934); Maritain, *The Degrees of Knowledge,* 198 ff.

129. NPW, 311 [309]. Compare with the passage from Bertrand Russell, *The Analysis of Matter,* 11.

130. NPW, 311–12 [309–10]. "Causality" here means entirely physically determined.

131. Cf. SUW, 87 ff. See as well the interesting article by Castle, "Quakerism as Adventure," in *The Hibbert Journal* (March, 1934); and the articles in the *Encyclopedia Britannica* and the *Encyclopedia of Religion and Ethics,* under the entry "Friends." They contribute to an understanding of Eddington's personality.

132. Maritain, *The Degrees of Knowledge,* 174–75.

133. Ibid., 175.

134. Ibid.

135. G. Dawes Hicks, "Professor Eddington's Philosophy of Nature," *Proceedings of the Aristotelian Society* 29 (1928–29): 296.

136. Maritain, *The Degrees of Knowledge,* 169 ff.

137. Ibid., 191.

138. Fulton Sheen, "Philosophy and Science," *The New Scholasticism* (April, 1933).

139. Gredt, *Elementa Philosophiae,* vol. 1, n. 346.

140. Ibid., nn. 531 & 526.

141. A. G. Sertillanges, *Saint Thomas d'Aquin,* 83.

142. Ibid., 91. But immediately after he, too, employs the phrase "the soul form of the body."

143. Ibid., vol. 2, 24 ff.

144. We have already alluded to this expression.

145. Sertillanges, *Saint Thomas d'Aquin,* vol. 2, 269.

The Cosmos

1936

ONE

From a Scientific Point of View

Aestimabat abyssum quasi senescentem.
—Job 42:21

1. The Universe in Expansion

Einstein, in his celebrated theory of relativity, shows an entire universe in profile: a universe closed on itself, its total volume finite, but without limits like the surface of an egg. We thus rid our minds of the vague diffused infinite that obsessed the imagination of our fathers, and which has exercised such a profound influence on romantic literature. In the new physical theory of Einstein, we make a tour of space.

The genial theory of the expansion of the universe of the young abbé Georges Lemaître, a theory explanatory of the constant evolution of the astronomical world, not only describes for us a universe bent into itself in space and time, it leads us to the beginning of time.

The principal experimental basis for this theory is given us by the recession of nebulous spirals, some of which move away from us with a speed many thousands of miles per second.[1] This flight of the nebulae will be an indication of an evolution of the universe by expansion. They will depart proportionally from one another like points on the surface of an inflated rubber balloon. Lemaître estimates at only a dozen billion years the entire duration of this evolution of the universe such as we know it today.

The traditional cosmogonies of Laplace and Kant posed, as point of departure for this evolution, a diffuse nebula filling space and progressively condensing into partial nebula, then into stars. To this evolution of the diffuse to the condensed, Lemaître opposes an inverse evolution of the diffuse by brusque and prodigious explosions.

At the beginning, the entire universe finds itself condensed into a sort of giant primitive atom, containing in a state of extreme concentration all the matter now diffused. The primitive nebula would be formed from fragments of that primitive atom which exploded. "The rapid expansion of the primitive nebula resembles rather the smoke produced by some colossal explosion, by a sort of gigantic artificial firework having dispersed, at the same time as space, the matter primitively condensed."[2]

Two forces[3] rule the evolution of the universe: the gravity by which bodies attract one another and the cosmic repulsion (its measure is designated by the symbol λ, and is called a cosmological constant), which tends to distance bodies proportionally from one another. Gravity tends to maintain or diminish the radius of the universe; cosmic repulsion tends to increase it. When the two forces are neutralized, the universe is in a state of equilibrium.[4]

The phenomenon of the recessions of nebulae allows us to affirm that cosmic repulsion has gained the upper hand. But once it has taken the upper hand it will maintain it, since the attraction of gravity lessens by reason of the growing distance which separates the bodies dispersed by repulsion.

> We can conceive that space began with the primitive atom and the beginning of space marked the beginning of time. The radius of space began from zero; the first stages of expansion consisted in a rapid expansion determined by the mass of the initial atom, equal to just about the actual mass of the universe. If this mass is sufficient, and the estimate that we have been able to make suggests that it is indeed such, the initial expansion was sufficient to permit the radius to surpass the value of the radius of the equiliberate.[5]

Nonetheless, it is the braking exercised by the force of gravity that explains the formation of nebulae from the matter left in a homogenous fashion by a first explosion.

> But this homogeneity can only be global. Indeed, both the density and the speed of expansion will vary a little from one region to another. It is easy to take into account that these local fluctuations will have little importance as long as the speed of expansion is great.

It will not be the same during a period of slowing. If in a particular region matter is a little more dense than usual, the attraction of gravity will be greater and it could happen that the expansion would be arrested a little sooner or that attraction again takes the upper hand from cosmic repulsion.

During the second period of expansion, matter will be agglomerated in places; it is the system of conglomerations that will stretch itself out; the conglomerations will separate themselves from one another. We will obtain a state of things that very much resembles the real universe where matter is agglomerated into dispersing nebulae.

We are thus led to identify these agglomerations with the nebulae. Hubble has been able to estimate that the mass of the average nebula is in the neighborhood of a billion suns.[6]

These agglomerations, increasing their relative distances by their concentration, at the same time create conditions advantageous for the cosmic repulsion which speeds it up, thus giving birth to the third stage of the evolution of the universe which has so accelerated as to attain its actual value—the first stage being constituted by the rapid expansion from the primitive atom, and separated from the third by a period of slowing down during which the nebulae are formed.

A word more on the formation of suns in the interior of the nebula. Suppose that the matter of the nebula existed

under the form of meteorites of dust, or gas in free circulation of sufficiently small average, one can see that shocks will be inevitable. These things would have absorbed the kinetic energy and progressively impede the nebulae from rebounding.

At the same time these shocks will have agglomerated matter into considerable and warm masses, that is, the stars.

The nebula will be the crucible in which the stars are agglomerated.[7]

2. The Formation of Planetary Systems[8]

The existence of double stars is a perfectly normal phenomenon. A star gives birth to a double star when, by its rotation or by the exaggerated pressure of its heat, it breaks into two spheres which remain coupled.

The distances that separate the two million suns circulating in our galaxy are so vast that one can compare them to the dimensions of our terrestrial globe inside which fly about four tennis balls. The risk of a collision is so low that normally a star can count on traveling without danger throughout its whole existence. However, if the risk of an accident is negligible for any given star individually, it is far from being nil.

Our sun must have been victim of one of those rare celestial catastrophes: it is to such a collision that we owe the formation of the little planet we inhabit. A more massive star came too close to our sun, bringing to its surface an enormous flood of matter. (Think of the tides caused by the moon.) This shaft of matter extracted from the sun circled around it and as it cooled it was cut into small globes, one of them ours.

It is thanks to such accidents that life is possible in the universe. As long as matter remained agglomerated in enormous masses, as in the stars, it is maintained at a temperature of ten million degrees and more. The lower temperature and the atmosphere which are the conditions of life exist only on a few rare planets. The existence of life on other planets actually has no scientific proof in its favor.[9]

3. Chemical Elements and Preparation for Life

Lately come in the universe, we find the 92 chemical elements already constructed. But no doubt they resulted from an evolution whose history remains almost unknown. We know that their differences are pronounced in the relatively cooled regions of the universe, and in this regard we on earth are especially privileged.

All are constructed on the basis of simpler elements forming structures which from the point of view of the elements differ only numerically. Thus, the chemical properties of the 79th body (gold) arise from its capacity to group around itself 79 negative electrons, whereas the 82nd (lead) has 82.

From a biological point of view, it is the number 6 that is the privileged number: carbon, which gathers around its nucleus 6 negative electrons. While the other atoms form small chains of 2 to 10 members, the carbon atoms assemble by the millions. It is these complex edifices which furnish us the matter necessary for life.

4. The Degradation of the Physical Universe[10]

The pre-astronomic state of the universe can be considered a state of extreme concentration and physical organization. When it is said that no energy in the universe can be lost, a most important distinction must be made. A liter of water at 0 degrees and a liter of water of 100 degrees when mixed will level to a temperature of 50 degrees. However, although the sum of the calories of the mixture is preserved (first law of thermodynamics: the conservation of energy), it is impossible to reestablish the initial disymmetry of 0 degrees and 100 degrees by means of the calories of the mixture. (Second principle of thermodynamics: the irreversibility of utilized energy). As Eddington says, "When Humpty Dumpty had a great fall 'All the king's horses and all the king's men / Cannot put Humpty Dumpty together again.' "

Without the numerical value of the total energy of the universe being lessened, its utilization changes in an irreparable fashion. Whatever happens in the universe is done at the expense of energy: the fall of a stone, the flight of a fly, the flow of rivers, the movement of the stars. Energy is not annihilated, it is disorganized. This degradation of energy introduces into the physical world a growing disorder which at the same time is an impoverishing equilibrium.

It is the irreversible direction taken by this progressive denouement which gives time its arrow, its unique direction. The measure of the disorder of the growing chance which leads to the utilization of energy is called *entropy.* It is entropy that allows us to discern the flow of the universe.

Time bears the universe toward a state of complete exhaustion: thermodynamic equilibrium whose image resembles that provided by the partisans of the primitive nebula, diffused, homogeneous, and uniformly distributed in space.

5. The Degradation of Energy and the Expansion of the Universe

A constant relation exists between the law of degradation and the expansion of the universe: the entropy of the universe is proportional to its volume. The scattering of energy permits the growth of the universe: more and more space is needed for the increasing disorder. A building toy cannot be put into its box unless all its parts have been put in order. "The increase of entropy which characterizes the direction of evolution is the progressive fragmentation of the energy which existed at the beginning in a single package."[11]

While the expansion of a given gentleman can only come about thanks to borrowing from his milieu, the expansion of the universe, since it is not in a milieu—it is its own place—cannot come about at the expense of a milieu. There are for it no reserves of space and time: it cannot borrow volume from some volume. It cannot make a snowball. It must inflate from its own substance like a soap bubble.

The tumbling down of the universe ought to bring something *new,* but a 'new' that must be drawn from the interior of the universe. (Still, the idea of the future is not only a logical dilution of the present.) This 'new' cannot be spatio-temporally determined in the present world unless the new were always present and time did not advance. The new of the future can only be true in the present possibility of a future disorder. The denouement of the present order is a condition of the new. But all that involves a certain dose of indetermination in the present with respect to the future. It is this indetermination that makes the physical world malleable to life.[12]

6. Physical Disorganization and Biological Organization

Just as a building toy is not made in order to remain in a box, but to make little houses, the physical universe, too, serves for a higher end that it approaches by losing its initial state of organization. (See 3 above.) The universe unpacks its matter with a view to a higher construction.

While the physicist observes in the physical world a greater and greater disorganization and diffusion, the biologist encounters living islands heading toward a more and more elevated organization, toward a more intense concentration. Life seems to progress against the grain and at the expense of the current of degradation that carries the physical world toward extinction, like trout or salmon which climb the current of the rapids.

Its ascending impulse vegetates on the physical universe and consumes it. Nutrition, assimilative and enriching from the biological point of view, is combustion from the physical point of view. One might say that the inorganic universe is assumed into life by sacrificing itself to it. It disappears before life.

In a general fashion, these two opposed currents can serve as an experimental basis for distinguishing biology from experimental physics.

The vegetal borrows directly from air, water, and earth the elements necessary for its maintenance under their mineral form. The animal, on the contrary, can nourish itself from these elements only if they have been fixed for it in organic substances by plants or animals.[13] The forms of higher lives vegetate on the lower forms. Lower living things feed the higher. Life is organized by disorganizing that which is lower than the level attained.

7. The Physical World and the Biological World

All the beings we encounter on earth are composed of atoms: rocks, potatoes, dogs, prime ministers, etc. But atoms are physical entities. Therefore all living beings are composed of purely physical elements.

Yes. But, while covering all the beings of our universe from the physical point of view, that does not mean to say that the physical point of view covers the *whole* of beings—that it is an exclusive and exhaustive point of view.

Nothing of the living goes counter to the principle of the conservation of energy. The atoms of a gentleman are as truly physical atoms as those of a rock. But the atoms are not parts of beings as bricks are of a house. The physical world is a *metric* and extrinsic aspect of the world. Atoms exist in the way a smile does.[14]

How to distinguish the biological world from the physical world? Life is not inserted into the physical world like a wedge. They are not distinct like two juxtaposed or superposed things. A living being is not opposed to a physical being, but to a non-living being. A physical being can be either living or non-living.

Most authors always confuse the physical world with the inorganic world. But this confusion can be explained. Although from the experimental point of view physical laws sufficiently explain inorganic phenomena, these same laws, while being verified in the living being, do not suffice to explain the whole from the metrical and experimental aspect of the living things. There are phenomena which, without being against physics, oblige us to formulate laws proper to living beings: the formally biological laws.

This distinction should have an ontological foundation, but that foundation cannot interest the experimental sciences as such. We will come back to this.

Moreover, one can already say that the whole of the physical word is carried along by the ascending movement of life, that it is the same impulse that passes through the living and which prepares the inorganic for life.

8. The Spontaneity of Living Things

The physical world, even among living things, tends to disorder: the nutrition-combustion from the physical point of view is a disintegration. There is also from the physical point of view more and more chance in the universe, for example, the ensemble making up a cigarette in its integral condition is more determined than the smoke it disperses. The primitive atom was more determined, more ordered than are its dispersed fragments. The more this universe is released and scattered, the more difficult it becomes to predict the behavior of physical entities. Let us say that this scale of unforeseeability is proportional to the degree of entropy, entropy being a measure of disorder. At a given moment *t*, there is less chance in the universe that at any later moment *t'*. There is today more disorder and chance in the universe than there was yesterday.

The biologist observes an analogous phenomenon. But for him *unforeseeability is proportional to the degree of organization.* The behavior of infusoria is more difficult to follow than that of a plant. And the behavior of a dog is more difficult to predict than that of infusoria which are still very mechanical. The more organization, the more spontaneity, which, like chance, escapes the grasp of metrical rigor. When we come to man, who presents a maximum of biological organization, his characteristic behavior becomes undetermined: his liberty gives him a degree of spontaneity that entirely escapes the grasp of the metric.[15] One might object that the behavior of a colony of insects is even more, and better, organized that are human societies. But this organization is due rather to a departure from spontaneity and thus resembles the sterile organization of the physical. In physics, disorganization is a condition of progress. There must be distinguished in the living, accordingly, the amount of physical organization retained, conserved, from the measure of biological organization, growing as opposed to the former.

It is thus possible to say that there runs through the scale of cosmic living things a tendency toward the liberty realized in man.

Not that there exists already in an inchoate state a true liberty in infrahumans. Freedom is a species of the genus of spontaneity, and the spontaneity of plants and animals differs. And the latter non-free spontaneity admits of degrees. Lower animals are less spontaneous than higher. There is in vegetable and animal realms ascending gradations of spontaneity, which, if it could be pushed high enough would become freedom. But freedom is proper to spiritual beings. We will come back to this. Between the perfection of living things, that is to say, their degree of organization, and their degree of spontaneity, there exists a constant relation. In living things spontaneity emanates from the subject, resulting from an interior integration: spontaneity is the measure of the degree of interiority. Take the species of spontaneity of which we have the most adequate idea, freedom. I say the most adequate idea, for people generally think that the activity of a non-free being must be like that of a machine. That shows that we can more easily form an idea of freedom than of a spontaneity without freedom. Take the most manifest case, our own freedom. I said that spontaneity emanates from the subject, and I do not mean anything mysterious by that. I can move my arm when I wish. That means that the determination of what I am going to do depends entirely on me. The movement you observe takes its origin from a free decision of which I am the author. The motion of the piston in a motor does not emanate from the piston. Its movement back and forth is due to explosions which drive it from outside. The piston has no interiority: it does not have the biological organization permitting it to execute motions which take their origin from it. It is not alive; it has no self. All living things have a certain self at an inchoate state. They affirm themselves, as is evident in their instinct for self-preservation.

9. Life and Time

The universe in scattering itself enlarges from the point of view of space and diffuses itself from the point of view of time. Time is a separator, a divider, distancing things from themselves, it parcels out and disperses. Time separates us from ourselves. We are separated from the past by an uncrossable abyss. Time divides our existence into distinct and perishing moments.

Physical time is a sign of the impoverishment and aging of the universe. The direction in which it advances leads to growing disorder in the physical world. It is centrifugal.

On the other hand, the biological world shows us an always growing concentration. Its movement is centripetal, arriving at a state of high organization and immanence. Life goes against time's dispersion. Time disperses, life gathers, tending toward structures that are more and more tight. It is a kind of triumph over the scattering of physical time. It is in the awareness of animals and men that we find the most obvious sign, and most specially in memory, the condition of awareness. That is not to say that awareness is memory or that consciousness is impossible without memory. But memory is a condition of consciousness for beings who live in time. Consciousness raises up, concentrating the past and the present above time. Thanks to memory, we conserve that which has been lost in time, which to the degree that it escapes life is the cause of forgetfulness. Memory is a remedy against time. Memory is obviously meta-temporal since it contains that which is no longer in time. Our memory does not merely preserve the past like a phonograph record; by memory we know in the present the past as past, and the past as past is in neither the past nor the present. Thus man not only lifts himself above time like other animals with memory, but he can lift himself above memory. He knows that in a sufficiently perfect being it is possible to know the past without having been caught in it; that there can be a being who sees directly and simultaneously in an immobile and indivisible instant the past, the present, and the future. This shows what a triumph spirit is over the dissipation of time.

Already in man the world is bent in on itself, and in God its extremes touch.

Even while touching it only from without, man, living on earth, already conceives this eternity.

10. Biology and Exact Science

Experimental biology is an exact science. Experimental sciences can be called exact to the degree that they allow us to make predictions. It is in this sense that physics can be called the most exact of the experimental sciences. In astronomy we can predict eclipses which will not occur for centuries within a fraction of a second. Experimental science is essentially metric. It can only define properties by a description of the process of measuring them. No experimental law—an algebraic relation between two number-measures—is absolutely rigorous. However, as a group, strictly physical laws are more rigorous than biological laws.

This is no surprise. We have just noted that there is in living things an always growing spontaneity which in man arrives at true freedom. It is absolutely impossible for the physicist to predict in advance what arm movements I will make in the next five minutes, *if* I pay attention. He can measure the movement I make when I make it. But he cannot from this measurement deduce the next movement. Every moment I use my freedom is something absolutely new in the universe. Thus one can say that the more a living being is free, the more he escapes the reach of experimental science. Thus, of all the experimental sciences, experimental biology is the most inadequate and imperfect, even though it studies the highest form of natural organization.[16]

In philosophy, it is the opposite that is true. The more we move away from man and descend the scale of living things, the more their life becomes obscure. Thus, the life of plants is more obscure for us than animal life. We will come back to this. It is enough to say for the moment that there will be a certain compensatory complementarity between the two orders of knowledge linking them to one another. They are never so distant from one another than at the point where they touch: like points on a non-Euclidean line which are infinitely close but also infinitely distant.

11. The Scientific Problem of Evolution

We constantly use the expressions 'movement' or 'the rising elan of life.' Must we thereby understand a purely static scale of hierarchized beings? A series of beings of different species which would have been given at once as they are without the existence of any dynamic link among them, in such wise that the forms with more complex and elevated organization would have appeared last?

It is not to the philosopher that we put the question. Experimental science must answer it. Since it is a matter of responding to a question of fact, it is experimental science that undertakes the research. Even if the philosopher had already established what he has to establish, he would not for that reason be able to prevent the scientist from finding out what he finds out. And we should be disposed to believe every explicative theory of observed phenomena, insofar as they are within the bounds of experience and logic. But, since we are concerned with experimental phenomena, the theory itself must be formulated in experimental terms. Under these conditions, one finds it difficult to imagine a clash between philosopher and scientist. And when we say 'a theory explicative of observed phenomena' that does not mean that the scientist cannot introduce into his theory undemonstrated postulates which alone permit the theory to direct experimental research. The only thing required is what the scientific method itself requires, which is that the theory be formulated in terms which are strictly of the experimental order.

It would be equally absurd to want to consider an experimental theory only at the time when it is absolutely demonstrated. None of these theories is absolutely true. Like measurements and the relations between measurements from which they take off, the theories themselves are only approximative—but they are truly approximative. The disdain of certain philosophers for scientific hypotheses is an absolutely incontestable criterion not only of their ignorance of scientific matters, but above all of their intellectual incompetence, and competence ought to be greater in philosophy than in any other degree of knowledge. There are some who have furtively taken refuge in a domain where it is easy to speak without knowing of what one speaks and without others being able to perceive it.

12. The Facts to Explain

Let us listen to the word of a specialist in these matters, Brother Marie-Victorin of the University of Montreal.

> Paleontology . . . teaches us in an undeniable fashion that there has been, in organic types, a succession in time of such a kind that the more complex and elevated forms of organization have appeared last. To the testimony of paleontology, absolutely invulnerable, comes to be added

the experience we have of the continuity of life: we know that the simplest organisms did not appear spontaneously. No biologist today would want to deny the following proposition: 'No living being can be born outside of continuity with the plasm of his ancestors.' If we add to this the equally undeniable testimony of paleontology, the conviction that the different living types ought to develop not only the one and the others, but the one from the others, it takes on the dimension of a positive logical postulate. The certitude of the reality of organic evolution would only be upset if experience taught us in the future that an individual organism could arise otherwise than by plasmic continuity, or that all the vital types, the living and the disappeared, existed at the same time at the beginning. No other argument could weaken the logic of the idea of organic evolution.[17]

13. The Evolutionist Theory

It is now a matter of constructing a theory from which one can deduce these established phenomena by way of conclusion.

Example of an experimental theory, the kinetic theory of gases. $_{P}\overset{V}{\triangle}_{T}$ constant relations.

Explanation: We imagine that the inner sides of the recipient which encloses the gas undergo on the part of the gas a pressure proportional to its temperature. But temperature is nothing but the disordered movement of molecules, the kinetic energy of molecules. If one lowers by half the volume occupied by a determined mass of gas, the pressure is doubled as well as the temperature, as one can observe in a simple tire pump.

The Vpt diminishes by half, that is, the number of shocks of the molecules among themselves is doubled, in other terms, the temperature is doubled.

The P is doubled, that is the number of shocks given by the molecules to the inner sides of the recipient is doubled.

This image allows us to *deduce one relation from the other.*

It will not suffice to deduce simply a statistical hierarchy, and I ask myself how such a deduction could deserve the name scientific: it is necessary that the theory allows us to explain the temporal and hierarchical succession of these types of organization. It is necessary to find the laws which govern this ascendant movement: laws which should be formulated in experimental terms, whatever be the ontological demands conditioning these laws. At no time can one have recourse to physical knowledge.

The explanation, or if you will the deduction, can be scientific only on condition of being evolutionist. No other theory could be scientific and explanatory. Since deduction is prohibited in advance, the deduction supposes, in effect, functional links. Either we must abstain from all explanation, from all science in the proper sense, stopping passively before the facts, confining ourselves to a quite material description and classification which make up precisely the givens to be explained, or one must try to deduce the succession. To speak rigorously, every classification is already made in function of a theory however elementary. One must accordingly forbid classification as well.

And if one succeeds in making a deduction sufficiently logical and confirmed by the facts which impose themselves, is it for the philosopher to tell us that it is not true? In doing so, he would thereby enter the scientific terrain: he would have to remove the base of the observed facts and at least suggest the possibility of another theory, which itself would have to explain the facts in experimental terms, not in philosophical terms. Even still he would have to demonstrate on the basis of experimental facts and not on the basis of any philosophical principle whatever that a theory is impossible. That is, he would have to demonstrate that the relations that exist do not exist. Thus, in doing so, he would not speak as philosopher any more than the scientist who appeals to philosophical principles speaks as a scientist. But this is just what has come about with many scientists. And from that arises the conflict between philosophers, scientists, and theologians which is still far from settled.

14. Lamarckism and Darwinism

Lamarck and Darwin tried to explain the ascendant movement of organized types by a process slow and continuous, analogous to the apparently continuous variation in height and color. Partisans of their theories are so convinced of the principle *natura non facit saltus* that they apply it in advance of the very classification of types, attaching by way of hypothetical filiation the forms which depart the least strongly from one another, forcing themselves thus to obtain, as much as possible, a continuous series.[18]

But the theories differ in the laws which govern this continuous ascension.

Lamarck formulated the four following laws which concern organization and which govern all the acts operated in it by the *forces of life.*

FIRST LAW: Life, by its own powers, tends continually to increase the volume of all bodies that possess it, and to extend the dimension of its parts, to the term to which it leads itself.

SECOND LAW: The production of a new organ in an animal body results from a new need which continues to make itself felt and of a new movement which this need gives birth to and maintains.

THIRD LAW: The development of organs and their power of action are constantly by reason of the use of these organs.

FOURTH LAW: Whatever has been acquired, laid out, or changed in the organization of individuals during the course of their life is conserved by generation and transmitted to new individuals which come from those who have undergone these changes.

It is by these principles that Larmarck explained the long neck of the giraffe. His short-necked ancestors no longer finding food on the ground were obliged to turn to trees. The character partially acquired during the existence of giraffe A was transmitted to giraffe B, the lengthening acquired by B was passed on to C, and so on. One has done experiments with rats, cutting their tail, etc. Baby rats are born with full tails.

These formulations have had the advantage of directing research. But such research has given only a negative result. Thus the children of the Chinese who bound their feet for thousands of years persist in being born with normal feet. Guyénot asserts that we still await a correct proof of the inheritance of acquired characteristics, and that it is infinitely likely that it will never be forthcoming.[19]

Darwin proposed two principles which govern the slow and continuous evolution of forms:

A *struggle for existence* inevitably follows from the high rate at which all organic bodies tend to increase. Every being, which during its natural lifetime produces several eggs or seeds, must suffer destruction during some period of its life, and during some season or occasional year,

> otherwise, on the principle of geometrical increase, its numbers would quickly become so inordinately great that no country could support the product. Hence, as more individuals are produced than can possibly survive, there must be in every case a struggle for existence, either one individual with another of the same species, or with the individuals of a distinct species, or with the physical conditions of life.
>
> Again, it may be asked, how is it that variations, which I have called incipient species, become ultimately converted into good and distinct species, which in most cases obviously differ from each other far more than do the varieties of the same species? How do those groups of species, which constitute what are called distinct genera, and which differ from each other more than do the species of the same genus, arise? All these results follow from the struggle for life. Owing to this struggle, variations, however slight and from whatever cause proceeding, if they be in any degree profitable to the individuals of a species, in their infinitely complex relations to other organic beings and to their physical conditions of life, will tend to the preservation of such individuals *and will generally be inherited by the offspring.* The offspring also will thus have a better chance of surviving, for, of the many individuals of any species which are periodically born, but a small number can survive. I have called this principle, by which each slight variation, if useful, is preserved, by the term *Natural Selection,* in order to mark its relation to man's power of selection.[20]

The gigantic combat which troubles the living world is a fact of observation which struck Darwin during his long voyage of exploration in South America and the islands of the Pacific Ocean. And it was necessary to have recourse to a fantastic principle of elimination to explain the relatively restricted number of survivors, for a simple Bacterium would give, by successive partitions, a mass of protoplasm much greater than the earth in less than a month.

But Cuénot has shown that the principle of elimination seems rather calculated on the law of large numbers, and that, far from assuring necessarily the survival of the fittest, would spare only the average type.

As for hereditary variations, they would undergo the sort of transmission of acquired characteristics of Lamarck.

15. Mutationism

Darwin felt the great difficulties that a slow and continuous evolution entail.[21] But the youth of paleontology allowed him free rein to his imagination. The research pursued is far from having encouraged this hope. The links that permit us to range types in a continuous series are defective in too systematic a manner. A regular irregularity calls for an explanation. Do you not seek links that *often* never existed? Has not a methodological error—a *petitio principii*—been committed in the classifications made on the basis of the principle of continuity, to which one appeals to confirm the same principle?

Guyénot cites a passage in the writings of Charles Naudin, founder of *Genetics,* dating 1867: "What the experience of observation teaches us is that the actual epoch of slight or profound anomalies, the alterations that we call, arbitrarily perhaps, specific types . . . are produced brusquely and without there ever having been transitory forms between them and the normal form."[22]

Almost half a century ago the Dutch biologist Hugo de Vries cultivated an enormous number of plants of a new species of Onagre discovered in 1875 and called *Oenothera Lamarckiana.* Among the thousands of these plants he observed that certain types present *new characteristics which are fixed and transmissible.* In other terms: he *observed* an evolution by bounds, sudden leaps, to which he gave the name 'mutation.'

For thirty years one has found mutations in great number and with an unexpected frequency in the animal kingdom as well as in the vegetable kingdom. Totals right off, immediately hereditary, and of whatever amplitude, they are produced by change, that is to say no individual is privileged, no individual of a group is specially disposed to produce a mutation. Moreover, their culture has allowed the drawing of statistical tables which allow us to foresee their approximate number. There is no doubt that we are confronted by a law.

Having no adaptive character, some are favorable, some indifferent, and when they are of great amplitude they realize truly hereditary monstrosities. Overflowing and prodigal nature is subject to a law which makes it deflect these too violent explosions. Evolution reminds us of the trials and errors of the learner. Life in expansion always puts itself on the edge of a precipice. It must go on by trying diverse formulas. The world is littered with the debris lost in the course of the journey. The conditions of survival are so rarely realized that they explain perfectly the elimination necessary if vital species are to be limited to a relatively restricted number over the course of history.[23]

Mutationism makes a blank slate of the active adaptation of organisms to the conditions of their milieu. No doubt the milieu works a selection in suffocating the most unfavorable mutations, it acts as a brake, but it does not form "the new entities by shaping them to its contours. It seems rather that the species, in virtue of a dynamism the essence of which still escapes us completely, and under the stimulus of the environment, produces by chance, in all directions, mutations which themselves have no relation at all to the milieu, and utility." What Brother Marie-Victorin says here of a particular case can be applied to every mutation.[24]

I cite a passage from the *Flore Laurentienne*: "The study of flora fossils, as well as of living flora generally, shows that the development of species does not proceed simultaneously in all points, nor at the same rate, like a wave approaching the shore, but development rather suggests the progression, apparently disordered, of troops over a long line of battle. There are explosions, sudden breakthroughs of some few: genera, families, orders, classes, which explore as it were all the possibilities of a certain formula of organization then return to relative or absolute immobility, and sometimes disappear entirely."[25]

I will not attempt to show how recent research on genes or factors, objects of mutations, let us foresee a general theory of evolution with the range of the most solid physical theories. I have neither the time nor competence for that.[26]

But already the simple *observed* facts sketch an image of a nature which advances by successive explosions in the manner of a rocket, rising to the sky and asking directly from the hands of its Creator the spiritual form of man to which nature has been destined and in which she is liberated.

In this new order, evolution is pursued always in the very interior of humanity. Men are also drawn by the current of degradation whereas the world will continue to fashion itself until the day it is assumed into eternity and we go to rejoin it.

Moreover, evolution which continues in humanity has taken on a different color. It no longer proceeds by essential jumps. We find ourselves from now on on a spiritual plane where plasticity is infinitely greater within the same essential degree. There rises now a quite new type of hierarchization, more profound, more essential. At a subhuman level the world could only enrich and hierarchize itself thanks to essential ruptures of equilibrium, thanks to violent changes, like those of an apprentice swimmer who has to make a noisy display of effort barely to keep afloat, whereas the expert swimmer advances rapidly by executing graceful movements.

Moreover, man seems to have rejected what should be his privilege: his equiliberating domination of nature. He seems to be subject, by the dissociation of his passions from reason, to the law of the corruption of the irrational creature which during millions of years groaned toward the liberation of spirits. He has re-engaged himself in that mortal struggle for life. The same law which is quite natural for subhuman beings—it is good that the lion devour the gazelle—is transformed into a law of hatred in spirits. Men destroy one another. Combat is all the more terrible because it is spirits who are engaged in it. And man, too, must groan for the liberation of his fallen nature.

16. Man and the Scientific Problem of Evolution

The last few paragraphs are of a kind to scandalize both the scientist and the philosopher. Have I not extended evolution to man himself? I remind you that in this part I am speaking from the scientific point of view. The philosopher can only reproach me if he confuses science and philosophy, a worse error, it seems to me, than that for which he reproaches me. The profound distinction between these two domains will appear more clearly when we will have studied the same problem from a strictly philosophical point of view.

Take any electron. What prevents me from following its trail[27] from the water of a spring through the grass eaten by a cow and the cow eaten in its turn by this gentleman? Will the electric charge of the electron undergo transformations as it passed from water to the tip of this gentleman's nose? Let the philosopher introduce as many transformations as he wants, the electron has not undergone any changes that could have an *experimental signification.* I wonder how one could introduce ontological transformations into a differential equation. And I even wonder what the phrase 'an ontological change of an electron' could mean. But what is true of the electron is true of the whole metric aspect of any cosmic being whatsoever.

Scientists and philosophers do not speak the same language. 'Matter,' 'force,' 'nature,' 'life,' 'transformation,' 'species,' etc. are so many absolutely equivocal terms. There is nothing sadder than the conflicts raised by scientists, philosophers, and theologians by assuming a univocal meaning of these expressions. Not that this would have been able to defeat the first evolutionist scientists, for it must be admitted, they gave to experimental science an exhaustive coverage of reality: science was their philosophy. The confusion of philosophers and theologians is more regrettable for they have not always been able to discern what is true in the pseudo-scientific generalizations of a Lamarck or Darwin.

St. Thomas, in the very place where he treats this question, cautions us against a blind zeal that invites the derision of non-believers: "ne quidquid verum aliquis esse crediderit, statim velit asserere, hoc ad veritatem fidei pertinere . . . quia ab infidelibus veritas fidei irridetur, cum ab aliquo simplici et fideli tamquam ad fidem pertinens proponitur quid certissimis documentis falsum esse ostenditur."[28]

The very progress of science involves a precision and purification of its vocabulary in a way that inspires hope. Soon all will see what is and what is not at issue.

Conclusion

Science, while being only a flat projection of what has relief and depth, enables us to foresee the immense effort and the prodigious cost nature invests in the preparation for the coming of man. And whether he knows it or not, everything that happens in the world is done for him. The scale of natural species is only a scale of assault. If man is the *ultimum in executione,* he is nonetheless the *primum in intentione.* The all too poor account that we have given enables us to suspect the richness of the human being who contains virtually all the degrees of perfection of that which is below him. And it is not only in the formidable display of power that we should look for this richness: the reaches of space, the unimaginable masses, the vertiginous speeds of astronomy are not worth a lily. But we have also seen that we have need of the stars to understand the lily. We will only be able to understand ourselves when we understand the universe. Our present is filled with the past.

The more profoundly we understand the world, the better we comprehend that we touch it only with the feet, and that with our head we touch the bottom rungs of another hierarchy of which nature is only a fleeting shadow.

TWO

The Philosophical Point of View

1. Preliminary Notions

a. Becoming

By the term 'nature,' taken in a general sense, we mean the coordinated ensemble of spatio-temporal things which surround us and of which we are a part. Becoming is the common and specific character of each thing in this ensemble. The universality of becoming is most obvious in temporal duration. The natural being which seems not to change or be changed in any other way can only continue its existence on condition that it be constantly renewed. Existence is received by it only in a successive and continuous manner. Successive and continuous duration is the definition of *time.* If this successive duration were not continuous the natural being could only exist by always becoming other. In this regard the whole of nature is in a state of constant flow.

Natural being changes in many other respects. But the other changes, whatever they be, always involve time. Moreover, these other ways of changing are not particular or special cases of temporal duration. It cannot therefore be time which expresses this general mobility of the natural being, a mobility of which time is only a particular case, for even though it is implicated in the other cases, it is distinct from them. Let us say then that a natural being is a *mobile being.* And that nature is an ensemble of *fluxibilia.*

Manifestly we are dupes of a verbal trick when we say that a mobile being is a natural being. 'Natural' is after all a vague term. And to take 'nature' in a strict sense, as we will see in what follows, we must define it in terms of mobility.

It is *mobile being,* not as being, but under the precise angle of mobility, *ens mobile in quantum mobile,* mobile being precisely as mobile, that is the formal object of the Philosophy of Nature.

Note that we have not yet mentioned 'matter' and 'body.'

b. Generation and Corruption

Mobile being only becomes by receiving existence successively. The plant grows, the animal learns, the man becomes ill. Beings are enriched and impoverished. Perfections are incessantly engendered and corrupted.

The cow is nourished by grass. She is enriched. But the grass in becoming cow is decomposed. The capital of nature is limited. When one being is enriched, another is impoverished. So, too, a corruption accompanies every generation.

There are not only accidental generations and corruptions in nature, like the accidental generation in the cow that feeds: this generation entailed the corruption of the grass. And the cow engenders a calf: substantial generation.

c. Natural Species

The ensemble of beings constituting nature is divided into four species: men, animals, plants, and the inorganic. One can know without understanding: animal; live without knowing: plant; be without living: inorganic. These four species are the only ones philosophically definable. The canine species is not a species in the philosophical sense.

Natural species thus constitute a hierarchy. The plant is manifestly more perfect than the rock or a nebula (abstracting from the life it may contain), being at once corporeal and vegetative. The animal is at once sensitive, vegetative, and corporeal; to which man adds rationality. We say that these species are essentially different. One lives or one does not, one can know or one cannot. There is no intermediary.

However, despite the essential difference between the four species, they always have something in common. Man and the dog are truly animals, and like the plant they are truly vegetative, and like the inorganic they are truly corporeal. They have a *common genus.* With respect to man, the genus animal is called the *proximate genus* (*genus proximum*), whereas the vegetative genus is only a *remote genus* (*genus remotum*). The definition of a being should include both the proximate genus and the *specific difference.* We define man as *rational animal.* The inorganic species has only a negative definition: non-living being.

The fact that the animal is sensitive, vegetative, and corporeal does not mean that it is composed of four superimposed beings constituting an ensemble we call animal. It must be *one*: its essence must be one. The essence makes a being what it is. It is the same essence that is at once animal, vegetative, and corporeal. Thus we say that between the different degrees constitutive of an essence there exists only a *virtual* distinction.

d. Individual and Species

Not all natural beings differ essentially. Two men are essentially equal, as are two animals and two plants. They are however profoundly different. We say that they are *individually* distinct, being opposed only in a *homogeneous* fashion, whereas the plant and the animal are opposed in a heterogeneous way.

We call space the homogeneous exteriority constituted by homogenous opposition. Homogeneous opposition exists only between two individuals in the sense defined above. Any homogeneous opposition whatever constitutes spatial exteriority. There exists between the animal and man insofar as he is animal a homogeneous opposition: all beings which have a *common natural genus* are opposed in this manner. And the opposition between any two accidental entities, from the moment that it is real and homogeneous, is spatial. Beings are not only *in* space: space arises from their opposition. In a universe where there is only pure heterogeneity there is no space. These beings would be specifically opposed outside of any *natural* common genus.

2. A Precise Example of a Problem in Philosophy of Nature

The few notions that we have just summarily defined already raise a host of problems, of which the most general is that of becoming, that of mobile being. I say that the problems are raised for mobile being is given in advance. It is *mobile being as given* which raises a problem in our minds. Apparently, a mobile being is a contradictory being. In order to be, it must be successively other. But if it is always other, how can it be what it is? And if it is not always the same across the succession, how can it succeed itself continuously? Mobile being must be a being which changes and which does not change.

Are we going to say that mobile being is composed of two parts, one of which changes and the other of which is immobile? This solution is too easy. And yet it is necessary to arrive at a distinction. What will be the terms of the distinction?

Metaphysics demonstrates that in every finite being, essence and existence are really distinct. Essence and existence are not beings, but simply the principles of being. But mobile being is a finite being. Is this the distinction that will afford us a solution?

Would I say that existence changes constantly while the essence remains immobile, and that it is by its immobility that the identity of the being is safeguarded? That won't work: for such an essence would both *simultaneously* and *successively* have existence. Mobility penetrates to the very essence of a being which exists successively.

But how can mobility penetrate into my essence, if my essence is that which makes me what I am? If, by enduring, I change essentially, I am always essentially other, and my identity vanishes. I could not say that yesterday I gave a lecture, for I would no longer be 'I.'

The problem becomes more and more difficult. It is necessary that my essence be capable of receiving existence successively without losing its identity. We are indeed forced to see in the essence a *multiple.* A multiple not of things, for the same problem would be posed with respect to them (and moreover that would come down to saying that a mobile being is possible only on condition of being some non-mobile beings), but a multiple of elements of another order: an order to which we are led by logic. The multiple in question should enable us to comprehend by what condition a being which endures successively and continuously is possible. The elements in question will therefore be by definition the *conditions of being of the mobile,* and not of beings: principles of the essence of the mobile, one of which permits that essence to receive existence successively, the other to safeguard the identity of the essence.

But on what condition can a multiplicity of principles make an essence *one?* They must be such that the unity of the essence is saved. If the two principles were each an essence, that is, a determination, they could only make an essence double; and there would be only an accidental link between them, as between the essence and existence of the finite being as such.

Thus we are *constrained* to say that one of the two principles is determination and the other indetermination. The first expresses the identity of the mobile being, the second its receptivity vis-à-vis successive existence. This principle of indetermination must be *pure* indetermination, since any limit would make it determinate. In other words, its proper determination consists of not having one: it is pure potency.

These are difficult words, but unless we halt midway we must arrive at these conclusions. We call the principle of determination *form (morphe)*, and the pure potency has the name *prime matter (prote hyle):* two terms which do not have much in common with their current meanings. Let us not be victims of this equivocation. We must be careful not to reify beneath each movement a substrate of immobility by taking refuge, not in the order of things where nothing is explained, but in the order of the *conditions* of the real.

One can arrive at exactly the same conclusion by beginning with the problem posed by any real homogeneity whatever. Wherever one encounters a multiplicity of equal determinations from the point of view of determination one must necessarily have recourse to a principle of opposition in the essential order, a principle distinct from that which renders essences real from the point of view of determination.[29]

Considered in relation to us, mobile being involves a complex essence, because it endures successively and continuously. But to speak absolutely, it endures successively and continuously because its essence is composed. The mobile, essentially unachieved, must pursue its existence and it is, in this perspective, indefinitely separated from itself.

The way in which we have just established the central thesis of hylomorphism is a little forced, despite its appearance of rigor. An argument of the amplitude of its subject—mobile being as such—must arrive at the conclusion *in omni eo quod movetur necesse est intelligere materiam* as soon as it is a question of movement in the proper sense.[30] But, it seems to me, that when one seeks to provide a summary exposition, with duration being so imposing a case, this method is permitted and very economical.[31]

It is understood that in the eyes of the scientist who adopts a formal resolution to refuse all truly philosophical reflection, these principles as well as the problems they seek to resolve have only a barbarous and unaccustomed allure. But it is with the philosophical sense as it is with the sense of humor. All the arguments in the world aiming at showing the humor of a farce cannot make one without a sense of humor laugh. A farce has lost its savor when one has demonstrated its risible qualities. The man without humor will follow our dialectic, but he will not laugh. And already you will no longer have an urge to laugh. Or we will laugh the more at the spectacle infinitely more comic of the man without a sense of humor's grotesque disdain for that which he cannot appreciate.

3. Form and Matter

We have made the foregoing exposition with the exclusive point of showing how different are the notions of matter and form of which we speak in philosophy from the scientific notions bearing the same names.

I will now simply mention several theses which attach themselves immediately to the foregoing.

Prime matter *insofar as it is pure indetermination* unites all material beings in the same matrix which is common to them. It is impossible that there should be several pure potencies. They could only be opposed by some determination. Matter, having no proper determination, cannot subsist alone: it is always associated with a form. It is only given at the outset in a composed thing.

It is again by matter and form that we explain generation and corruption. The cosmic beings which appear and disappear, one after the other and the one from the other, are drawn from the potency of matter by beings already existent, and they are reduced to it by corruption. Prime matter is not a kind of reservoir containing in a latent state determined forms which only await a chance to be released. Prime matter is pure indetermination. Forms can only be contained in it in the manner of possible cuts in an indefinitely divisible line. For natural beings, then, there do not exist forms of structure determined apriori, with the exception no doubt of the form or forms given at the outset, and of the form which will realize the finality of nature as a whole. Moreover, existing forms are by definition determined. Yes, but in the manner of the cuts when a line is actually divided. These forms of existent beings are fixed like whole numbers. Between any two existing forms there is more than an infinity of others possible.

Generation is not therefore in any way a creation, but the act by which a given compound educes another from the potency of prime matter. It is understood that prime matter is created, or rather co-created (since it cannot subsist outside a composite), and that any composite whatever insofar as it is a finite being is a created being. In this respect, the entire universe opens directly on God. But this does not prevent the composite from being generated, and that a created being is its generator.

An important point for the form under which we treat this question is that from the existence of the first composite (supposing that the world had a beginning in time) all possible natural[32] forms were *given* in the potency of prime matter. Hence, no special creative act is necessary to educe them from this potency, provided that there exists some sufficient created cause. And if that created and sufficient cause exists, it is to it that generating causality must be attributed, by virtue of the principle of divine governance by secondary causes.

The principle of sufficient causality requires that the cause in question be at least at the level of the effect to be produced. That is understood. No natural being would have been able to educe from the potency of matter a composite superior to it, unless it is not the principal cause.

Therefore, it is absolutely impossible that any plant should engender any animal whatever, *as principal cause.* Some scholastic authors have held that biological species at the interior of the same philosophical species, defined according to their degree of organization, differ only accidentally. And that within one philosophical species inferior biological species produce higher species.

This accidental difference is an extremely ambiguous thing. Must not the gradualities of the accidental order be reduced to the substance of which the accidents are a function? Let us not be misled by a confusion of the scientific point of view with the ontological, with which we are now dealing. The generator must be the principal cause of the *whole* effect with all its determinate powers.

Form is matter's reason for being: potency is essentially ordered to act. Matter is thus a *need for form.* If it were indifferent to its reason for being, that would be contradictory. We say that matter is a desire for form, not a desire in the order of exercise, but a desire that is matter itself.[33]

This desire attains its goal in the eduction of forms, in the generation and achievement of the composite.

4. The Raison d'être of the Cosmos

Mobile being pursues its existence, but it cannot continue to exist in order to have had a history. Its end cannot consist in the pursuit of an existence always infinitely removed, that is unrealizable. If mobile beings existed in order to exist, their reason for being would be impossible: their existence would even be contradictory.[34] Therefore the terminal point of every mobile being must be in itself immobile, a being which, as terminal point, does not have to pursue its existence. It would have a successive existence insofar as it is composite, but it would be outside time because of its spiritual form. And this is the raison d'être of the whole of nature.

But a being which does not have existence in a successive manner is a being with a simple essence: its existence will be equally simple. Such a being is not, therefore, educed from the potency of matter, it is given from the outset by a creative act. But if it is entirely given from the outset, natural beings would be superfluous. Such a being would be essentially trans-cosmic, a pure spirit. But the particular end of the cosmos ought to be interior to the cosmos. If mobile being as such cannot be that end since it is only a means, its reason for being is essentially utilitarian. But its existence cannot be useful for a pure spirit. That is why a pure spirit cannot be the raison d'être of the cosmos.[35]

The being in which resides the end of the cosmos must be both immobile and cosmic; both spirit and matter must be found in it, its essence must be composed of a spiritual principle which integrates the cosmos. The essence of the being that is the terminal point of the whole of nature will be composed of a spiritual form and prime matter.

Man is manifestly the raison d'être of the whole of nature. Moreover, nature could not be ordered to God except through man. God being the end of the universe, it is necessary that the universe be capable of a return to its Universal Principle—of a *reditio ad principium.* But only an intellectual creature is capable of such a return.

Among beings of this nature, "only rational created nature is immediately ordered to God; other creatures, in fact, do not attain the universal but only the particular; they participate in the goodness of God with respect to existence only, like inanimate beings, or with respect to life and knowledge, like plants and animals. Rational nature, on the contrary, because it knows the universal formality of the good and of being is thereby ordered immediately to the universal principle of being."[36]

In other words, only a creature capable of making a tour of being can rejoin the source of being. At this precise point we can identify the terminal point thus *deduced* as the final condition of the mobile as such—with ourselves. We know that our ideas are universal and that this universality implies, from this point of view, a complete independence of the restrictions of matter.

Man is in the last instance the raison d'être of matter. If it were essentially ordered to mobile being as mobile, and if the mobile as mobile tends to the indefinite, matter would be contradictory. It is by definition ordered to an immobile form, which alone can be a definite term.

> Every creature existing in potency can have no other tendency than to arrive at act by way of motion. So matter, in following its natural appetite, by preference tends toward such an act, if it is the most remote and perfect. Consequently, this natural appetite in virtue of which matter seeks form, should tend, as to the last end of generation, to the most remote and perfect act to which matter can attain.
>
> There are several degrees in the acts of forms. Prime matter is right off in potency to elementary form; reduced to elementary form, it is in potency to the mixed form, because the elements are the matter resulting from a mixture, and are in potency to the vegetative form: for this soul is the form of a body of that nature; likewise, the vegetative soul is sensitive in potency, and the sensitive soul is intellectual in the same way. This is proved by the process of generation: its product begins by being a fetus, which lives in the manner of plants; to this life succeeds that of the animal, and in the third place life proper to man. In the order of beings produced by way of generation and subject to corruption, there is no more remote or perfect form than this last. The human soul is thus the term of completed generation, and matter tends to arrive at this term which is its final form. Thus the elements exist for mixed bodies, and the latter for living bodies: among these, plants exist for animals, animals for man, and man is the end of generation in its entirety. . . .
>
> . . . If then it is true that the motion of the sky is ordered to the generation of beings, and that man is the term of this generation in its entirety, and as the final end of this genus, it is evident that in the order of beings produced by generation and susceptible to being moved, the [proximate] end of the motion of the sky is attached to the existence of man as to its final end.[37]

Man, because he is the raison d'être of matter, is as well the end of all possible natural forms.

Every natural form tends toward man. The idea of man bursts forth from no matter what form, even from a material point of view. The essential desire of prime matter, which always indefinitely exceeds any form received, is to be actuated by the immobile form of man. And in this perspective, subhuman forms are much less states than tendencies.

Let us consider first of all the scale of natural forms according to the *order of nature,* making abstraction from the order of time.

If one can say in advance and with certitude that matter will receive the human form—without this the existence of no matter what mobile being would be in advance contradictory—one can say as much of the deletion of the scale of forms which rises toward man. The multitude of possible forms is indefinite. In other words, possible natural forms are incompossible, like the infinity of possible cuts in a continuum. If one wants to progress, one would have to span the intermediate forms, each bound constituting a clean rupture without any intermediary *in act.* The scale cannot be given in advance like a determinate geometrical figure, to be disengaged from the outline of the lines given. Doubtless the configuration of the scale will be in a certain measure determined by the material given at the origin (there, or the initial forms), but the number and distances of degree cannot be given in advance. The number of steps which cover a journey depends on the length of one's legs, and on the quality of the road.

If each individual form is necessarily determined, the composite also necessarily involves haziness. To say that matter is pure potency is to say that, as such, it always exceeds the form—because the form, itself determinate, does not entirely determine the matter, it cannot be entirely determined *ad unum.* A form entirely determined *ad unum* is by definition a subsistent spiritual form. Moreover, a natural form will be determined *ad unum* in the measure of its perfection, in the measure that it responds more and more to the desire inscribed in matter.

But the margin of indetermination exceeding the form is the root of the contingency in nature. *Causa per accidens est infinita et indeterminata.* The causation of a composite can fail and ought in fact to fail in the measure that its form is not determined *ad unum.* The path leading to man is bordered by the ditch of matter—a ditch more dangerous because the path is, in its beginnings, straighter—but the more one advances, the more forms tighten up and free themselves from the shackles of matter.

Therefore, whatever the initial form given, one will be unable to find in it a rigorous plan. It can show us only a preview of the forms on the scale arising from it. One can say in advance that it must arrive at life, at knowledge, at intelligence, but it is for experimental science to say *how* this world has been molded from the *fluxibilia et non semper eodem modo se habentia propter materiam.* And this role devolves on experimental science precisely because one is unable to make in this domain rigorous deductions in function of the necessary. Science, first of all by its research, tries to reconstitute the path, or the paths, followed *in fact* by nature. But it is also forced—and here is its principal aim—to find essential limits, not doubtless of the plan followed, but of the preview given in advance.

The fixity of subhuman forms is therefore a counterfeit fixity. We are naturally metaphysicians and from that arises the need for the necessary, and in this case, to likening the cosmic hierarchy to the series of whole numbers and to an immobile hierarchy of pure spirits, but these are only analogies. If we are manifestly metaphysicians in our search for the necessary and the purely intelligible, we would delude ourselves in thinking that the necessary should be everywhere realized, and we will show ourselves to be undemanding and poor metaphysicians if we think we see it everywhere realized. And I think I can say that he who wishes to find in this world of fleeting forms absolute immobility does not seem to have a very high opinion of the celestial hierarchy.

Our world is far from being a pure system like crystal and achieved in all its parts like a billiard ball. But if it is opaque, loose and shaky in its first steps, this does not prevent its essential tendency toward the necessity which blossoms forth in freedom—for the necessity of spiritual structures is the root of liberty. The absolute freedom of God flows from His necessity, from His pure actuality, from His absolute determination.

We have said that man is the raison d'être of the entire cosmos, and that in him the desire of matter is assuaged. But a man is only an individual of the human species which succeeds by scattering itself in a multitude of individuals (and we will see later the profound reason for this). To speak absolutely, it is humanity in its entirety that is the raison d'être of nature. Individual humans are indefinitely multipliable. Nevertheless, an indefinite multitude cannot be an end, *quia non habet certum terminum.* The indefinite is by definition unrealizable. We must therefore say that a multitude of human individuals, numerically definite, is the final end of the cosmic universe.

Was the cosmic hierarchy given in advance, once and for all, or must it wait on time, such that the imperfect preceded the more perfect? And if that is so, where do the most perfect forms come from?

5. Nature

The mobile as mobile tends toward the spiritual form of man. Movement in the world has no raison d'être apart from this perspective.

The movement by which each being tends toward its end is proportional to its degree of perfection. But the degree of perfection is determined by form. Under this aspect every form is invariable and immobile, for by definition a form makes a being what it is. If the form changed, and if the form were as such mobile, a being would never be what it is and movement itself would be contradictory. Form is thus *the principle of the diversity* of movements, without itself being a movement.

The desire of matter, while being fulfilled according to the measure of perfection of its actuating form—and in this measure the composite enjoys a certain fulfillment and rest—its essential desire persists unassuaged until it attains the spiritual form of man—let us rather say, of humanity. Matter remains tending, under no matter what natural form, under forms increasingly more perfect. Thus matter is in its turn a principle of movement.

But to be a principle of movement belongs neither to it alone, since it is necessarily associated with a form, nor to form alone, since it is in itself invariable. In order for there to be a *determinate* principle of *movement,* it must be at once matter and form. But matter and form considered thus as the intrinsic principle of movement are called 'nature' in the strict sense. We say 'intrinsic' to distinguish nature from art and chance, the principles of which are extrinsic.

If the perfection of movement is determined by the degree of perfection of the form, this is because form plays the preponderant role in the principle of movement—it is form that is the measure of the perfection of nature.

But no nature remains closed on itself. It is to make this precise that we insist on the notion of nature. "Id enim per se videtur esse de intentione naturae quod est semper et perpetuum."[38] Mobile things do not run along parallel lines to fall like a stone at the end of their journey. That would mean that form is their principal end and that their essential orientation to spiritual form is accidental, whereas it is their raison d'être. A nature is essentially a principle of ascending movement, it is profoundly impulse (*élan*).

But isn't nature a principle of motion, and the activity or passivity of the mobile things, aren't they of the accidental order? Furthermore, isn't the perfection demanded by nature simply of the accidental order? And hasn't any natural being attained its end when it is thus fulfilled?

Let us say that the particular end of natural beings consists in their individual and specific fulfillment in the accidental order. But this particular end is not their principal end. It is true that the more perfect the being, the more its particular end coincides with the principal end. But mobility is essentially function.

Matter and form are essential, not accidental, principles. But it is these essential principals which tend toward spirituality, and accidents are only instruments of substance. Should one say that the composite finds its raison d'être in the actuation of accidental powers, that would say implicitly that substance is for the accidents, and that a subhuman being is principally loved for itself.

But let us not conceal our unease that we have closed our eyes to these logical consequences. We are reluctant to see nature as an ascendance toward more and more perfect form from imperfect forms, to see it proceed temporally from the less to the more perfect. We remember a principle that St. Thomas applied to the whole of nature.[39] If we cannot follow Thomas, isn't this because we have excluded from the universe the efficient and sufficient cause to start the cosmos and push it to the height? Our frightened attitude can be easily explained. Suarez has resolutely shut off the world at the top: we want to explain everything in nature by intracosmic causes. Suarez, in denying the apodictic force of the arguments presented by St. Thomas to show in a strictly rational way the existence of pure spirits, cuts every essential link between the cosmos and the created spiritual universe. Add to that his hybrid notion of prime matter and we come logically to the barbarous creationism of our manuals of philosophy. It is understood that if we sterilize the world at its beginning, nothing further can result. Creationism, which opens the world directly to God, bypassing the universal hierarchy, implicitly rejects what is essential to the universe: the unity of order.

Since Suarez, scholastics have abandoned more and more resolutely the ontological point of view in the explanation of nature. One imagines that scientific explanations replace the philosophy of nature and one retains only what is directly useful for theology. But, if in astronomy cosmic repulsion sufficiently explained the expansion of the universe, and the theory of genes puts us on the way to explain mutations—and it would be ridiculous to call them insufficient from a scientific point of view, which in its fashion constitutes a closed domain—none of that could explain the simple displacement of a material point from an ontological point of view. For that, one cannot have recourse directly to the general notions of metaphysics, we must find the proper causes. If I have a headache because God wishes it, that does not prevent me from attributing it to a too long night and accepting that an aspirin might relieve it.

I say that no intra-cosmic cause can give me an ontological explanation of the movement of the moon, not because the movement of the moon particularly interests me in philosophy of nature, but it is the movement of an inorganic phenomenon and it is as such that I consider it.

6. The Inorganic World

In opposition to what materialists think, speaking *formally,* we know life better and more immediately than non-life.

When St. Thomas wants to show the foundation of the certitude of philosophical biology, he is precise: "Certa est, hoc enim quilibet *experitur in seipso,* quod scilicet habeat animam et quod anima vivificet."[40] This science is certain because everyone experiences in himself that he is living and thus he knows soul as that which makes us living. But this experience is the point of departure proper to the science of life. St. Thomas does not speak there of the life we observe in others, for if the life of another were as such immediately grasped, it would suffice to say *hoc quilibet experitur.* But since the life of another is not immediately known to us, he adds *in seipso.* If it were that of others, one could be mistaken, and it often happens that we are mistaken, as in the many cases we cannot decide whether we are dealing with a living or a non-living thing, with a vegetable or an animal, or as sometimes happens when a work of art gives us the illusion of life. We can only grasp the life of another by means of the *signs of life.*

I am conscious of my vital activities: I think, I will, I sense, I raise my arm, I speak, I walk, etc. These activities are *mine,* I am their principles. But these activities involve objectively observable signs that I connect directly with the activities. But when I find elsewhere similar signs quite independent of the observable signs of my own activities, I attribute them—for they are signs—to a life other than mine, to another subject.[41]

If we have a positive knowledge of life, we do not have that kind of knowledge of non-life—such knowledge would be for us manifestly contradictory. When, while remaining within the pre-scientific point of view where we have placed ourselves, we have to do with something real which gives no sign of life, it would be manifestly absurd to attribute life to it. Such an attribution would be entirely gratuitous and void of sense. Such an affirmation could not arise from experience. It *postulates* that life is coextensive with being, a postulate forever unjustifiable.

But if the principle of hylozoism is in advance indemonstrable in an order where the necessity of demonstration is at issue, it is not a matter of an affirmation which gratuitously postulates more than is necessary to explain the negative phenomenon in question; and even if we know only phenomena which presented signs of life everywhere, would we be able to prove from that that non-life is impossible? Hylozoism always has in its favor manifest vital facts, whereas the materialist who sees in life only a pure epiphenomenon right off puts himself in a point of view that we only attain in a negative manner, that we define by exclusion of that which is attained first off and by experience. How else could we define *non*-life?

And once the materialist principle of the priority of non-life in our knowledge is conceded, it will be forever impossible to arrive at anything but the non-living. The living will only be constructed from the non-living.

Of all the vicious circles one could imagine, that in which the materialist encloses himself is the most primitive, restrictive, and binding.

If non-life is essentially obscure, vegetative life is also for the most part obscure. In it we do not touch ourselves as in conscious life. Although life, which we know immediately in our activities, involves as an *essential attribute* a certain interiority—we know these activities both as *emanating* from the subject and as interior to him—the *signs of interiority* manifest in ourselves, although unconscious, and equally manifest in what we call plants, oblige us to attribute to them some degree of interiority by vital definition.[42]

If on all these points we are in complete agreement with many modern philosophers, we resolutely separate ourselves from them when it is a matter of the formal object of philosophical biology. For if it is in myself that I touch life the closest, and if that more or less intimate knowledge of my own life—knowledge which is moreover conditioned by an *object* of sensation, of thought, of will—permits me to recognize life elsewhere, it is not this life that I make the formal object of the philosophical study of life, no more than I take the paper on which I am now writing, as this paper, as the point of departure of metaphysics, but simply this paper as being. My life as *mine* cannot be the object of a science, even though it conditions in an extrinsic manner my science. The role of my life is thus analogous to the role of my thought in my philosophy.

If interiority, self-movement,[43] is the essential character of life, we ought to define the non-living by denying of it all interiority. It does not move itself. All movement comes to it from without; it is moved and can only move insofar as it is moved.

But before discussing the consequences that this definition has for our subject, I would like to make clear a point which seems to me too often neglected. If we know how—at least in very many cases—to identify a living thing and to say that it is a substantial whole, ontologically distinct from its surroundings, one cannot say as much of the non-living. Is a rock a substantial being because it is in a certain way distinct from its surroundings? Is it spatial separation that provides the criterion? But what then of atoms? Is not man from the point of view of the physicist above all a void in which are scattered rare particles? Can I not sit down on two rocks at the same time and cannot two men ride one horse?

I know of no criterion that would show the ontological cuts of the inorganic world. I do not say either that such cuts do not exist: that would be an equally gratuitous assertion. I only say that I have no criterion to discern them. And I add that I see nothing more unfitting in an inorganic world, substantially one in which innumerable living things vegetate, than in one tree on which insects munch the same leaves.

The inorganic world is essentially moved. Whatever be the exchange of movement which takes place in it, the movement cannot have its active principle in it. Not that the inorganic world is not one, or some natures, in the strict sense—for our definition of nature was large enough to accommodate a being that is natural even if it only has in itself a passive principle of movement. One cannot say otherwise without falling into hylozoism.

These considerations are completely deprived of sense from the point of view of physics, but we speak here of movement from an ontological point of view, which we define as a passage from potency to act. But the inorganic world has in it no active principle which would enable it to move itself, to reduce itself from potency to act. Potential energy which releases itself, or the spontaneous disintegration of radioactive bodies, which are sufficiently defined and explained by the experimental method, make no philosophical sense.

It is granted that no movement whatever can have as ultimate efficient cause anything other than an unmoved mover. But when it is a matter of a particular species of motion, the proper cause must be sought. But, the motion in question—that of an inorganic being—is motion in the strict sense, and implies as potential substrate matter.

The act of inorganic being cannot be cause of its motion—that would make it living. Therefore, it is necessary to look beyond it, not only because the inorganic is in fact in motion, but above all because to the passive potency of matter—essentially ordered to a form—there must correspond an active power sufficient to realize its reason for being.

This active power is necessarily the power of a living thing. But this living thing cannot be intracosmic for two reasons: first, because the motion of the inorganic world is necessarily presupposed for intracosmic life, and, in the second place, because it is prime matter, the potency of every natural being which as such and in advance calls for this corresponding active power.

> Every passive potency has a corresponding active potency; for [passive] potency exists for the sake of act, just as matter exists for form. But, a being in potency can never arrive at act save in virtue of another which actually exists. Therefore, [passive] potency would be useless if there were not an agent endowed with an active power which can bring it to actuality. But there is nothing useless in nature, and consequently, everything which, like matter, is in potency relative to generation and corruption, can only arrive at act by means of the active power which resides in the heavenly body which is the first active principle of nature. But, just as the celestial body is the first agent with respect to inferior bodies, so God is the first agent for every created being.[44]

We know moreover that the celestial body was in its turn moved by a separate substance, by a pure spirit. If we have, centuries since, abandoned the surpassed astronomy implied by this text of St. Thomas, we have wrongly rejected the philosophical idea beneath the argument. If we cannot point to the intracosmic instrument which serves as the being endowed with the active power necessary to the cosmos, we are no less obliged to affirm its existence.

By that argument we do not mean to establish the identity of this cause—is it God or a created transcosmic being, a species of demiurge? But it does show that the cosmos is open to another world which acts on it. And this cause can only be a living being; it is necessarily a pure spirit, a transcosmic being. For if we placed it within the cosmos, the same problem would arise again.[45]

And if the pressure exercised on the cosmos is spiritual, from whatever being it come, it sufficiently explains the ascendant movement demanded by nature.

If the cosmos is thus essentially suspended from the spiritual universe, this does not prevent the tides that rise in it from being natural. It is natural for the world to receive its impetus from above. A nature that has in itself only a passive principle of motion is nonetheless nature.[46]

The spiritual impulse exercised on the cosmos cannot bear directly on prime matter, since it does not have in itself any consistency, and is by definition associated with a form, but on a composite being. Moreover, the pure spirit cannot be the form of a matter. Acting on the cosmos, he unfolds it according to laws inherent in the cosmos, just as the sculptor submits to the exigencies of stone in order to extract his work. But the pure spirit acting on the world does not make a work of art. His influence brings forth natures.

It is hard to keep one's mind on this level and not give free rein to imagination which could falsify the idea. I can imagine nothing more grotesque than the image one would come up with by confusing with the experimental point of view this strictly ontological point of view to which nothing answers on the side of science. The universe of the sciences, if science there is, is necessarily closed on all sides. Equations must find equilibrium within themselves. But already the image of the entire cosmos as essentially ordered to man would appear grotesque from the perspective of the astronomy which provides him a poor little planet born of a catastrophe. It is not yet the moment to take the measure of man.

If in philosophy of nature we close the world at its summit, we will be spontaneously led to explain everything from below. The first evolutionists had the world begin from chance, the imperfect was the unique and principal cause of the more perfect. And Haeckel derived a diabolical pleasure from seeing the world emerge from nothing.[47]

7. The Definition of Soul

The vital activities of which I am conscious flow from my substance.[48]

Every substantial form immediately actuates matter. Thus the form of a living thing is the act of a matter. But the form of the non-living is also the act of a matter. How then can we differentiate between these two species of form?

Let us call *soul* the principle of life that we seek to define. We will say that we are dealing with the corporeal in the narrow sense when we encounter no sign of life in a being. Still, the definition of soul cannot be "form of a body."

We have just made use of a singularly ambiguous term, 'body.' The chemist speaks of simple bodies, of heavy bodies, rocks and stars are called bodies; the physiologist speaks of the body of a cell, of the human body, etc. How to understand this in philosophical terms?

Spatio-temporal beings, such as a dog, a cabbage, a man, are exterior to one another in a homogeneous manner: there exists between them a spatial opposition. But they are not only exterior to one another, they are in a certain way exterior to themselves. The tail of the dog is exterior to its head, one vertebrae in his tail is exterior to another, etc. However, all these parts exterior to one another belong to the same subject and are integrated in it. It is the whole thus distributed that we call a body, and a substance is called corporeal in the measure that it is the root of such dispersion. Moreover, each constitutive part of this whole can be called a body by extension and in an improper sense, in the measure that it is in its turn further divided or divisible.

A homogeneous exteriority is quantitatively measurable. The parts compared among themselves define a magnitude. The body of which the philosopher speaks must be rigorously distinguished from the body as one can speak of it in experimental science. If any exteriority is as such measurable, it is only experimentally defined when it is measured. The physical body is only defined by the description of its process of measurement. A physical body defined as "a cube with four sides" is a bundle of number-measures translating different comparisons which have been made on a given object. The dimensions in question are the result of measures of which three were established by a standard of length arbitrarily chosen, and the fourth, time, by a watch, for example.

The point of view of the philosopher is prior to all that. Not that it is in practice possible to perceive an object without spontaneously making comparisons vaguely defining the sizes, but this formality is not the aim here: it is not a matter of body either as *measurable* (the material subject of experimental science) or as *measured* (the formal subject of experimental science).[49] In the philosophical sense, it is a substantial whole which involves parts external to one another in a homogenous fashion.

Having thus defined body, it is understood that the dog, cabbage, and man are so many bodies. However, since life is essentially an interiority, a living being cannot be just a body.

What in fact does differentiate the body called inorganic from the living body? We have just said that we will base ourselves on *signs* to discern the one or the other. Let us dwell for a moment on a manifestation of life such as it is attained by the philosopher. I see yellow, I feel warm. These sensations are as such incommunicable. It is impossible to make one born blind understand what yellow is, of what is sight. Moreover, I cannot myself define them. But if I cannot communicate to another this intimate experience, nor receive that of another, I can place myself in a point of view where everything becomes perfectly communicable. A blind man can understand optics perfectly and understand the mechanism of sight, and a hypothetical subject anaesthetized to the sense of temperature, could still understand as well as another what is physical heat. However, when we have defined heat as the kinetic energy of molecules, we have from that no knowledge in any way of what it is like to feel warm. It is at this precise point that one notices the inconvertibility of the two points of view. If I know perfectly that a sensation of heat corresponds from the physicist's point of view to a molecular bombardment, and if I know perfectly the physiology of the sense which is its object, I would never know *why* such a physical phenomenon provokes in me such a feeling. I would never be able to derive the inside from the outside.[50] But it is to the point of view of that physically untranslatable intimate experience that philosophy must hold itself,[51] and it is from this same point of view that one must explore the external world. But my sight is manifestly associated with some observable object—the eye. I know, nothing seems vaguer than the organs of which the philosopher speaks. The physiologist could very easily provoke a visual sensation in an individual deprived of eyes in the anatomical sense. However, from the philosophical point of view, the point excited, whatever it is, would still be the *organ* of sight.

So it is with all the organs of the living thing. Clearly, the philosopher is indeed obliged to place himself outside, but this outside has no sense for him save in the measure that it is seen from within. And if this method is perfectly sterile from the scientific point of view, it is the only fecund one in philosophy.[52]

The organs and their function thus recognized as observable manifestations of life enable us to differentiate the living body from the inorganic. The living body is an *organized body,* and is that much more alive when it has a more differentiated organization. The vital functions seem to demand from the side of organization an always increasing complexity, a more and more pronounced heterogeneity.

The body as body requires no heterogeneity—on the contrary: it is a body only insofar as it involves homogeneity.[53] The more life is intense and compact, the more it requires organs differentiated from one another and in themselves, and the more the body is removed from pure corporeity.

These few considerations enable us to define the principle of life. Soul—the substantial form of the living things—is *the act of an organized body.*[54] Not that the substantial form informs an organized body. Form can only actuate prime matter. The organized body is rather the result of the informing. But then, why not say that the soul is a form such that when it actuates matter an organized body results? A definition need not necessarily trace the order of discovery that justifies it.

The reason for defining the soul by organized body is more profound.

Corporeal organization is only a sign that permits us to recognize life: this organization conditions life ontologically. In fact, if the organization of the body is constituted by the actuating form, the composite of matter and form has been engendered—it is the composite and not the form alone which is the term of generation: *generatio non est formae sed compositi*—a composite which involves *actuated* matter, that is, determined by its form.

For the matter of the composite is not pure potency with respect to the form that actuates it, but with respect to the possible forms of which it is deprived. And if the form is the act of matter, it is not the actuated matter. Let us say that every form is proportioned to its matter: *omnis forma est proportionata suae materiae.*

If the actuated matter (and in another respect further determinable by other forms) and its actuating form are the intrinsic and constitutive causes of the engendered composite, their composition is produced by an extrinsic agent. Generation consists in the production both of a determined matter and of a determining form—the two constituting the composite.[55]

These are two perspectives all too easily confused. The generation that is cause of the composite is implicitly cause both of the actuating form and of the matter, and of the determined matter, although in the engendered composite form is the cause of the determination of the matter—matter having *of itself* no proper act. If in the perspective of the generating act the agent were cause only of the form, the composite would be its own efficient cause: matter and form would be generative the one of the other, the form would be the act of a pure potency. Thus, from the perspective of efficiency, the *disposition* of the matter conditions the form—the form can be act only of a matter disposed by the generator, a disposition of which, however, it is the cause in the order of formal causality.[56]

8. Disposition, Alteration, Generation

How is the disposition conditioning the form realized? Does it precede form in the order of time? "In the way of generation," St. Thomas says, "disposition precedes the perfection to which it disposes, in beings which are perfected successively."[57] "A perfectible is united to its form only after a disposition exists in it which makes the perfectible receptive of such a form, for an appropriate act comes to be only in an appropriate potency: thus the body is united to the soul as to its form only after having been organized and disposed."[58]

How can the body precede the form which actuates it? The human body is only a human body by the form which actuates it. And, on the other hand, how can one distribute this disposition in time when the generation of a composite is necessarily instantaneous? In fact, substance, being that which makes a being what it is, is indivisible, invariable. *Substantia non suscipit magis vel minus.*[59]

Every generation presupposes a given matter. It is in this that it differs from creation. Prime matter is given only in a composite. Therefore, every generation presupposes as point of departure—*terminus a quo*—a given composite. The generator cannot act directly on prime matter, this does not exist as something separate. Generation consists in transforming a composite into another. Not that the form of composite *A* is changed to the form of composite *B*, since every substantial form is by definition invariable; but from the potency of the matter of composite *A* the form of composite *B* is extracted.

If matter is *of itself* potency to any form, the composite which is *terminus a quo* of a generation cannot be just anything—which would be to say that it is prime matter, pure potency. In the present case, matter is the potency of *this* composite, and in this respect, this composite measures its potency for the composite to be engendered. If from no matter what no matter what could come to be, every generation would be a purely chance phenomenon, which is contradictory. Just as the matter the sculptor uses cannot be just anything, so it is necessary that the composite be disposed in a determined manner which renders it capable of being the point of departure of the generation of a new determinate composite. And just as the matter that the sculptor uses must be determinate in the measure that the work he conceives is more perfect—such an idea should be executed in granite, not in marble—it is necessary that the composite which is *terminus a quo* be that much better disposed insofar as the *terminus ad quem* is more perfect.[60] The composite which is *terminus a quo* should cede to, should disappear before, the composite which is the *terminus ad quem*, by being, not annihilated, but reduced to the potency of matter. That is what corruption is. When the chromosomes of a spermatazoid (envisaged here as signs) are united to those of the ovulum and a new being is born, the spermatazoid and the ovulum are corrupted—even if the chromosomes of the new being are the same from the experimental point of view, and one has followed them on the track to their new ensemble.[61] And when a dog dies, thus giving birth to other composites, it is reduced to the potency of matter. The form of the dog being indivisible, it either is or is not. It is not its form that can be almost a canine form. From this corruption results necessarily a generation, since matter cannot for even an instant be deprived of a form, being by definition the potency of a composite: to be corrupted is to be reduced to the potency of another composite. Otherwise corruption—which is not an annihilation[62]—would be the generation of prime matter, which is by definition ingenerable.[63] Since on the one hand substance is the root of the accidents of the composite and on the other its substantial form can only immediately actuate prime matter: *quod fiat resolutio usque ad materiam primam.* And yet, if this resolution is integral, it is necessary that there exist between the composites a relation of mutual dependence, since the engendered comes from a composite, which cannot corrupt without engendering it. The generation of the one and the corruption of the other are so intimately linked that they must take place *simultaneously.* In fact, generation and corruption are necessarily instantaneous, since the substance engendered or corrupted is indivisible. Hence, corruption and generation, even while being essentially and formally distinct, cannot be separated by an instant in which the subject of the transformation would be neither the composite *A* nor the composite *B*—which comes down to saying that there would be an intermediate instant during which only the pure potentiality of prime matter would exist, which is impossible. Generation and corruption are therefore simultaneously realized. And still in this respect, the generation of the one is the corruption of the other, depending on the direction one looks. *Idem est in quod terminatur corruptio, et ex quo est generatio.*[64] If in this perspective generation and corruption are instantaneous, we must nevertheless find in the composite *A* and prior to its corruption, a reason for that corruption. Otherwise, its very being would be by definition a disposition to corruption. If every being composed of matter and form is as such corruptible, corruption cannot be its raison d'être. And the corruptible substance cannot be *in itself* successively more or less disposed to corruption, since its form is invariable. When a composite is said to be disposed to corruption or to generation, this disposition taken formally can only be of the accidental order, even though it involves the corruption of the whole. The animal dies from old age, from sickness, of some accident which, wherever it comes from, intrinsically affects the whole. These accidental affections dispose the whole to corruption, and implicitly to the generation of one or more composites. And that a disposition of the accidental order can have substance as its term should not astonish, since accidents are a function of substance. They are its instruments. The active preparation for generation and corruption which involves enrichment or regression is in the accidental order, an order whose term is however substance: it disposes the subject.[65]

If the substance of any being whatever is indivisible, the dispositive qualities are present in a same subject according to different measures: *suscipiunt magis vel minus.* These accidental changes which affect the whole, which have a repercussion on other accidents and which touch the substance, are called *alterations.*[66] It is in alterations that a composite is disposed, or disposes another, either to generation or to corruption, according to the direction in which one regards it.

Alteration is therefore a progressive movement in the perspective of generation, regressive in that of corruption. And if the disposition that brings it on is itself of the accidental order, its ultimate end is in the substantial order. Entailing fatally a corruption, its ultimate end is nonetheless always a generation. In this order, alteration has a double term *ad quem:* one is the disposition which will necessitate the generation, and the other the substantial form of what is generated.[67]

Alteration, St. Thomas tells us, is a continuous motion. But the *whole* of alteration is not. The whole contained between its proper substantial subject and the ultimate disposition toward which it tends is constituted of discontinuous moments which are nonetheless continuously linked among themselves like the actual cuts in a continuum. Moreover, what St. Thomas calls the *tota alteratio*[68] takes place by jumps, by a series of ruptures of the same species which come about in the same subject.

The disposition of which we speak is of the accidental order, however the whole of the composite, including substance, has to be disposed with respect to the composite to be generated. We say that in the dog there is a disposition to engender or to die, and that in a plant there is a disposition to be assimilated whereas there is nothing of the sort in a brick.

And if we understand in generation not only the instantaneous act in which a new composite is generated, but also the dispositive preparation by way of alteration, we must see in it a veritable *factio* in which the generated is modeled,[69] a formation parceled out in time. A living being is under construction before it exists.

When the composite *A* is disposed, and when from this composite is generated a composite *B*, is there a transmission of the disposition, is it the same in the two? Let us take the classic example of the cadaver which has all the signs characterizing the individual who just died. Are we confronted with the same signs? Do we not say that this is the cadaver of such an individual? Would there be perfect discontinuity between the nose of Mr. X and the nose of the cadaver to the point of not being able even to say that nose *was* the nose of Mr. X?

From an experimental point of view, the configuration of the nose has not changed, but from an ontological point of view it is absurd to say that the nose of the cadaver was the nose of Mr. X, since there exists between composite Mr. X and the composite cadaver, a substantial opposition, a perfect ontological discontinuity. But the substance is the root of the accidents of the subject. Therefore, if the composite *B* is absolutely other than the composite *A*, to the point of not even being able to say that *B* was *A* (which would pose the impossible case of two substances being one), a fortiori, the nose of the cadaver cannot be that of Mr. X.

But let us not exaggerate this discontinuity to the point of forgetting the profound relation that links the two composites even from the ontological point of view (and which moreover shows us the foundation of what one observes from the experimental point of view). The generator is truly an efficient cause of the engendered, he models it in advance, and gives it independent existence. What the generated possesses, and which is in no way the generator, nonetheless comes from the latter. Everything is in this formula. And in this respect, the characteristics of the composite *A* are the same; and yet they are numerically different since they belong to substantially diverse subjects.[70] In this quite fundamental perspective, we must say that the cadaver is that of Mr. X. All beings thus bear the traces of one another.[71] Every composite of matter and form is essentially corruptible.[72] No individual form could assuage the desire of matter. Under every actuating form matter remains open to other forms which it cannot take on without losing that which actuates it. But corruption is not the end. Every corruptible is a function of something else: non-being cannot be the end. Corruptibles are naturally sacrificed to future generation. Thus it is necessary to say that every apparent regression is a function of a new generation. And by new generation we do not mean a renewed generation. For if natures tended only to perpetuate indefinitely by pure multiplication, they would pursue a contradictory end, since the indefinite is unrealizable.[73] Therefore, perpetuation cannot be the end. It is necessary that the whole process come to rest at beings at once engendered and corruptible in one sense, created and immortal in another—humanity.[74]

From the corruption of a being there often result composites of a lower level. Must we conclude from that that in this respect nature tends to annihilate itself, and that corruption outweighs generation? This is an artificial perspective. It isolates natures whereas they are profoundly coherent, and if it is an evil for a specific and individual nature to corrupt, being given that it is a function of the ensemble, that it is essentially at the service of *natura universalis,* its corruption can be a good for the ensemble.[75]

9. In Perfectible Things, the Imperfect Is Temporally Prior

How far does this principle extend?

A being whose essence is composed of matter and form can only have a complex existence successively realized. The unachieved character essential to every hylomorphic substance is the cause of time. Moreover, no cosmic being could pursue its own existence as an end, since it would then pursue an unrealizable indefinite.

The hylomorphic substance is perfectible from the point of view of essence, since no form can assuage the tendency of matter to other forms, a tendency which is the very nature of every cosmic substance, even of that which does involve an active principle of movement—the inorganic. If a nature were achieved from the point of view of essence, it would not be hylomorphic, and from that it would follow that it would not be nature in the strict sense.[76] A simple essence, it would have simultaneously its existence, its duration would not be continuous nor successive, it would be above time, it would be a perpetual thing—*in perpetuis non differt esse et posse.*[77] Thus the successive and continuous duration is above all a sign of the qualitative enrichment of universal nature. To speak absolutely, it is this very enrichment that 'takes time.'[78] Every nature tends to surpass itself, since of its very essence it is ordered to ever higher forms, until attaining an essentially immobile term. The very essence of the inorganic is ordered to this dilation. Aren't all possible natural forms contained in the potency of matter?

The higher composite extracted from the potency of matter will be new, not only from the point of view of existence, but above all from the point of view of essence, from the quidditative point of view, the point of view of intelligibility. We have already said that natural forms are contained in the potency of matter only in the manner of possible cuts in a continuum.[79] These forms are not quiddities: it is matter and form which constitute the quiddity of the composite.[80] And such a determinate essence is ipso facto existent. If possible natural forms were quiddities, matter would be act from the point of view of essence; and if forms were quidditatively achieved in the potency of matter—which is manifestly contradictory—they would be at once in act since matter is *real* potency, as opposed to pure possibles. And again this existence would be as simple as that of pure spirits. Their duration would be neither successive nor continuous. Such forms would constitute perpetual things: *in sempiternis non differt esse et posse*—an adage whose consequences Bergson seems to have grasped better than we. Natural essence ought to be *made,* not doubtless in the manner of a work of art, since we are talking of natures, of beings which advance by an inner impulse.

The ascendant movement of natures constitutes nonetheless a tendency toward more and more compact essences, more achieved, more and more simple, necessary and intelligible: a tendency toward simple existence. In fact, man is the term of this pursuit, man who in his spirituality is already above time, man whose simple spiritual form already involves a simple existence.[81]

The higher composite is not absolutely new with respect to the composite from which it was extracted—it was given in the potency of matter, which excludes both univocity and equivocity: two extreme determinations which destroy the very notion of pure potency. If there were univocity, matter would be in potency to only one species of composites; if there were equivocity, the composites of different species would have nothing naturally in common. Matter links all the composites in the same material genus. The new composite always contains virtually the perfections of the preceding one that it goes beyond.

Novelty is realized moreover in well-defined extreme limits: the initial composite, given at the beginning of the cosmos, and man. All intermediary forms bear profound traces of these extremes, as the arms of a statue bear the trace of the chisel, and of the ensemble of which it is part. Nature advances with spontaneity, like the unrolling of a fugue, which is that much more free because it is more determined.

No doubt, the individual form of a composite is invariable, an evolution of substance is impossible. But it is not only the form which is nature, for a form, considered outside its relation to matter, is no longer nature in the proper sense. And yet, there must be an ascendancy in the substantial order. We know in advance that this ascendancy could only realize itself in a discontinuous succession of ever richer substances, by essential and profound ruptures (*usque ad materiam primam*).

But how to establish between them this profound link that permits us to say that higher substances are drawn from lower? The dynamic ascendancy of natural beings is formally realized in the dispositive alterations. If an evolution of one substance ordered to another is impossible, the composite whole is capable of enrichment which disposes it to a higher whole.

Without doubt, an ascendance is already realized in the most elementary of vital functions, nutrition. Grass assimilates air and water, the cow assimilates the grass, and man the cow. (The most hardened fixists will not carry resistance to the point of saying that cows must eat cows in order to generate cows.) But this cycle remains closed on itself if there has only been the inorganic, plants, animals: the world would be open only to individual multiplication. Such an ascendancy is not realized by the internal drive of lower natures ordered to higher, but by an attraction from on high to which they passively submit. In other words, in this hypothesis of a cycle closed on itself in time, the perfect must precede the imperfect, not only in the order of nature (an incontestable necessity), but also in the order of time—they must at least coexist. The idea of progress is thus reduced to purely quantitative increase. But that is a type of evolution which is at bottom only a dispersion, a regression.

It is understood that an individual composite cannot of itself produce alterations which end in a composite of a higher order. Accidental capacities are measured by their determinate and invariable substance. And yet, nature demands an ascendancy by way of alteration. How can this be realized without an already existing higher natural substance?

We have come again to this conception of a spatio-temporal universe closed on itself, and having *as cosmos* no extra-cosmic cause. Already the inorganic world requires us to appeal to a spiritual pressure which causes unfolding without itself being an active principle of motion: not a univocal cause, on the level of the effect, but at least an equivocal cause,[82] a higher substance which contains virtually the perfections of the whole inferior to itself, which is more potent and efficacious than all subordinated causes.

> No being which acts in conformity with its proper species seeks to realize a form higher than its own, for every agent tends to produce a being that resembles it. But the heavenly body, insofar as it acts by the movement proper to it, tends to realize the ultimate form, that is, human intelligence, which is of all forms the most noble, as we have shown. Therefore the celestial body does not act in conformity with its proper species and in the role of principal agent to produce the generation of beings, but its action is determined by the species of a higher intellectual agent, who is the principal agent and of which the celestial body is only the instrument. But, the action of heaven by which it produces the generation of beings consists in the motion it receives. Thus the mover of the celestial body is an intellectual substance.[83]

This same pressure *naturally* exerted on the cosmos—since natures themselves demand it and a nature is not only a form—suffices to extract from the potency of a composite given at the origin all the forms necessary to achieve the goal. And since this pressure is natural, it must act on natures according to the laws inscribed in them. In this ascendant movement, by which more perfect beings are drawn from imperfect composites,[84] the given and intracosmic composite is only an instrument, the spiritual agent being the principal cause. Spiritual pressure would not extract any nature whatever from no matter what composite. The instrument, even while producing under the influx of the principal cause and effect superior to itself, entails however essential limits. The more perfect the engendered substance, the more perfect instruments will they be in their turn.[85]

This eduction of forms would not come about with regularity and economy, whatever the perfection of the principal agent, being given that the impulse is given according to the natures. But a nature is never entirely determined to the point of excluding chance and deviations, which are, paradoxically, natural consequents of the nature.[86] The ascendance cannot describe a single trajectory. It entails deviant ramifications and failures.

What paths have been followed in the execution of this work? What were the steps? What species have arisen in this journey of the whole of nature to man? Without doubt, one cannot deduce them in a philosophical manner, since the ways of nature lack rigor. It is for experimental science to find the traces, to reconstitute the ways which have in fact been followed, and to deduce from them those which ought to have been followed to attain the end actually realized. If we cannot predict on the basis of the initial composite all the species that emerged from it in order for it to attain its goal, the indetermination inherent in nature cannot impede our predicting with certitude that evolution *ought* to arrive at man. For if there is only probability in the intermediate ways, the term is certain and defined: it is the raison d'être of all that has been made; that is, if evolution, despite the deviations and lost efforts along the way, did not arrive necessarily at man, prime matter, nature, all the work that was done, would be in advance contradictory, impossible. It is nature that tends toward man, not chance.[87]

We ought not however seek the intention of nature exclusively in the limits of the torturous road which leads to man, nor to consider all the branches which left the road (and sometimes rejoined it later on) as pure failures. If the fundamental idea of nature was a parsimonious and determinist idea, it would certainly be so. But it is essentially liberal and magnificent, it has a horror of calculation.—We will come back to that.

If we reintegrate into the cosmos spiritual activity which works it in its rising movement, we do not follow the ancients who saw only spontaneous generations (already an improper term) popping up everywhere. It is for experimental science to find where and in what conditions life appeared. Let us add nonetheless that the passage from the inorganic to the organic would probably never be definable from the scientific point of view, the two are as irreducible as physics and biology.

Is there any need to say that this conception does not question the adage "omne vivens ex vivo," a principle necessary in philosophy? What we do reject here is that the living terminus *a quo* must be a univocal cause. The principal cause of cosmic life and of its rising line is neither of the same species nor of the same natural genus, but it is nevertheless a living being.

10. Soul, the End of the Body

What is the proximate end of this rising movement? What is it destined to realize, to extract from the potency of matter? The human spiritual form to which every body is ordered, either mediately or immediately, as such demands the body which responds to a need inherent in the imperfection of this spirit. If spirit is of its essence tending toward body, this is because it cannot exercise the activities essential to it save as a spirit in a body—

because its intelligence and will cannot be actuated by themselves, because they do not have their act naturally, because they have to be stirred up from without. Such a spirit is *naturally* ordered to a body: it is naturally a form of a matter with which it constitutes one substance. Human intelligence, the lowest of created intelligences, considered in itself and in its origin, is empty of all content—a *tabula rasa;* it is so to say totally turned outside itself, it has no innate knowledge like the pure spirits; it is the natural weakness of our spirit which is the reason for our body. Empty of every object, even empty of itself since it cannot not know itself save in knowing an object distinct from itself, it must seek gropingly its object outside; which supposes both homogeneous exteriority (that is, corporeity) and passive experience in the knowing subject (since intelligence is impassible, that is, no lower thing can act on it). In other words, matter and sensation are necessary for it, not in the exercise of its proper activities, but as extrinsic and essential conditions of thought. Human intelligence cannot confront things which are light, which are intelligible in act; spiritual things are that much more hidden in its regard insofar as they are more pure and present. The Being that is closest to it, even infinitely closer than it is to itself, and which is Light per se, is also the most hidden because of the weakness of our sight. Aristotle compared our spirit to a bat. The day of discursive intelligence needs the night of the "outside" and of animality; the shadows of corporeity are born from a need for light. As the astronomer must await the dark to see the stars, although they are equally there in the daytime: it is at night that we see the sky.[88] To speak absolutely, prime matter in its very essence answers to the need of spirit; the body is implicated in the idea of soul, it is in the soul rather than the soul in it.[89]

The body is like an instrument that enables the spirit to exercise its proper activities.[90] But the human soul cannot be the form of matter formed just any way. It presupposes on the side of matter a given disposition which necessitates informing. No doubt this disposition given in advance is not that of a human body, since the body is human only because of the spiritual form which actuates it,[91] but it is immediate disposition *to* the human body. It is this immediate disposition that the whole of nature brings about under the spiritual pressure exercised on it according to the laws of nature.

The soul can be the form only of a particularly disposed matter. This disposition is realized in an inchoative fashion to the degree that one goes up the scale of plants and animals. The soul does not inform a matter disposed only to vegetative life, the matter must be disposed to the life of knowledge, to be subject of an intellectual form. If matter were itself immediately disposed, all human forms would be realized right away since the ultimate disposition is *necessitating*.[92] It is moreover contradictory, and on the side of matter pure potency, and from the side of "all the possible human forms" that are compossible.

It must indeed be granted that evolution follows the general lines sketched by St. Thomas in his doctrine on the evolution of the human embryo—the particular application of the doctrine we have abandoned, but it incontestably holds for the entire cosmic evolution.

> We see no difficulty in the fact that intermediary forms are produced to disappear so soon after, because, not belonging to any complete species, they are simple transitions which lead to the determinate species; consequently they do not receive existence in order to keep it, but only in order that by them the being which is the ultimate end of generation be realized. One should not wonder at seeing that the same transformation does not continue during the time of the generation, but that there is a certain number of intermediate generations; for that is equally the case with alteration and growth, and Aristotle shows us that the only motion that is really continuous is local motion. Therefore the number of intermediate forms which gradually prepare for the ultimate form, and consequently the number of intermediary generations, is in proportion to the nobility of this form and of the distance that separates it from elementary form. That is why, when generation has for term animal and man, whose form is more perfect, there are many intermediate forms and generations and, consequently, corruptions, since the actual form is produced only by the destruction of the preceding one. Therefore the vegetative soul, which first gives the embryo the life of a plant, is destroyed after a period of time and gives place to a more perfect form, which is both nutritive and sensitive. The embryo lives then with animal life, and when the latter is in its turn destroyed, it is replaced by a rational soul which comes from without, although the two others have existed in virtue of an active principle inherent in the sperm.[93]

We say only that in the case of man there exists a man before, a generating cause sufficient to dispose the matter. This cause is univocal, but cannot an equivocal cause realize the same effect? And is it natural to invoke it for the disposition of the body of the first man?

I say "the first man." But one might indeed object that, if the spiritual pressure is sufficient to raise natures to the disposition for the human body, and if this equivocal causality is even more perfect than univocal causes, the latter would have no reason for being. Why don't human beings show up everywhere without human generators?

Such reasoning is that of a delirious mind. We have recourse to equivocal causality only when a univocal cause is insufficient to explain the effect. Thus from the moment there exists a sufficient univocal cause, equivocal causality becomes, in this precise respect and in virtue of ontological economy, superfluous. In other words, *if all humanity could have its origin in a unique first individual, the contrary hypothesis is entirely gratuitous.* The constitution of this univocal cause is precisely the end of this impulse. Just as God manifests His power by creating effects which are causes in their turn, which spreading themselves out, thus imitating on another level, diffusive and creative goodness, so this equivocal causality attains its maximum when it succeeds in producing an effect which from then on is an independent cause.

It can be seen that creationism is a disguised revival of the ancient doctrine of those who rob natures of their proper actions, a doctrine vigorously opposed by St. Thomas, and which suppresses the divine governance by way of secondary causes.[94] God can make the works of nature better than nature herself. The activity of pure spirits is already infinitely more efficacious than that of natural beings. Should one conclude from that that it is worthier of these causes to remove from their effects all activity of their own?

If by the human body we understand a subject disposed *ultima dispositione,* we should then indeed say with St. Augustine and St. Thomas that this body was in the potency of matter from the very origin *secundum rationes causales.*[95] And by these *causal reasons* we understand the initial composite (matter and form) of the cosmos, its ultimate end (man), the efficient cause (the spiritual agent and the composite).[96] But it is understood that if one understands the human body in the strict sense, as that which is formally constituted by the spiritual form immediately created by God which responds to the ultimate necessitating disposition, *it is absolutely impossible that the body was produced by evolution:* since God alone can create the human soul, He alone can make the human body. But if by "to make a human body" we mean all the preparatory and dispositive work preceding in time its formal constitution, one must indeed say that evolution fashioned it, and that it is in this very formation that evolution consists.

Although the formation of man's body preceded the creation of his soul, or reciprocally, it does not follow that the same man is prior to himself; for man does not consist only of his body or only of his soul. True, one of these parts has priority over the other, but there is no difficulty in that, for, in time matter is before form. Here we mean matter insofar as it is in potency to form and not as actually perfected. Therefore, from the point of view of time, the human body precedes the soul when it is in potency to it, that is, so long as it does not yet possess it; but then it does not actually have human nature, which belongs to it only potentially. When it has actually become something human, and that takes place at the moment when it receives its perfection from the human soul, it is neither before or after the soul, but the two exist simultaneously.

From the fact that the active principle in the sperm produces only the body and not the soul it does not follow that that operation of God and nature remain uncompleted, for it is the divine power that gives existence to the body and to the soul, although it forms the body by means of a natural agent, which is the power inherent in the sperm, and that it produces the soul immediately. Nor can one say that the action of the sperm's power is imperfectly exercised, since it makes its proper object perfect.

It is wrong to think that the soul exists for the body because the body is formed before the soul.

> A being can exist for another in two ways: first, because its end is the activity or the preservation of that other, everything that is a natural consequence of existence, and in this sense the being which exists for another is posterior to it; such as clothing with respect to man and his tools to the worker; second, a thing exists for another when it exists that the other may exist, and in this case what exists for another has priority in time, but is posterior in the order of nature. It is in this second way that the body exists for the soul, as every matter does for its form. It would be otherwise if the body and soul did not unite in one common being, as say those who refuse to admit that the soul is the form of the body.[97]

In other words, the whole travail of nature terminates in the rational soul immediately created by God, but *ad cujus causalitatem concurrit caelum per motum suum materiam disponendo: with whose causality concurs that of the heaven and its motion disposing matter.*[98] Not that evolution produces the human body (no more than the parents the body of their child), and God the soul. The two causal lines meet in a being essentially one.[99] But in producing the ultimate necessitating disposition, the equivocal spiritual agent, or the parent, are causes of the union of soul and body, which enables us to say that man is *generated.*[100] What now was this animal whose elevation to the necessitating disposition by way of alteration calls *naturally* for the creation of the soul? It is for experimental science to tell us. And if man and the ape have, in this respect, a common ancestor, how would that detract from human dignity? Why prefer that he came from the mud? A preference somewhat lugubrious from an ontological point of view, a perverse manner of falling back into nonsense, for is it not a sin of angelism for man to deny his humble origins and to wish to have been given right off like a pure spirit? Is it not rather his glory to be the goal of these immense efforts of the world, prodigious and concentrated with an eye to his arrival?

11. Controversies over Evolution

Some scholastic philosophers and theologians seem to think that it is of the very essence of evolutionism to wish to pass over the Creator as much as possible, if not altogether. That is true of some evolutionists, but theories should not be judged by the abuses that can be made of them.

Let us say that there are two ways in which scholastics have sought to honor the Creator. The one consists in diminishing as much as possible the causality of the creature. That is the "idea in the back of the mind" of those authors who are called creationists. They want us to think that it takes a special creative act for the production of each natural and biological species as is the case with the angelic species and human forms. They deny the scientist the right to derive biological species the one from the other.

At the other extreme is found the Thomistic tendency, inspired by St. Augustine, which enriches as much as possible the causality of the creature, not with the goal of eliminating creative intervention, but in order to increase it:

for the creative power, envisaged from the side of its effect is most profoundly at work where created causes are most causes. The more a creature is capable of acting, the more it manifests the power of its ultimate cause, for God is the cause of all causality. From this point of view, He is much more profoundly cause of our free acts than we are ourselves. If we have a dread of the spirit which animates creationism this is because it is not creationist enough: in the final instance, it is a form of occasionalism.

With respect to those Thomists who have thought it necessary to adhere to creationism, their difficulty is based on a methodological error. As we said earlier, in Chapter One, one does not sufficiently distinguish the different points of view one adopts to study this problem. After these lengthy discussions we are in a position to give an example of the grounds of this essential difference between the method of the scientist and that of the philosopher.

Every science seeks to reduce the complex to the more simple and to explain the former as a function of the latter. But we must understand the meaning of the term "simple." The nature of the simplicity to which one must reduce everything differentiates profoundly wisdoms. But it is easy to show that what we call simple in experimental science is quite opposed to what we call simple in philosophy. In experimental science the atom is infinitely more simple than a cell, the motion of the piston is much more simple than the leap of a panther onto its prey, and of all the beings that experimental science studies man is incontestably the most complex. But in philosophy quite the opposite is true. The animal is more simple than the plant, and of all the beings which the philosophy of nature studies it is man that is the most simple; much as in metaphysics the measure and cause of all being is the absolute simplicity that is pure act. In physics one measures an object by the *minima mensura*—time by atomic time, for example—in philosophy the measure is always richer and more comprehensive—time is measured by aeviternity, and that by eternity, which is identified with its measure.

In other words, experimental simplicity is inversely proportional to ontological simplicity. The philosopher will say that the scientist explains the higher by the lower, the perfect by the imperfect. Thus we can say in advance that in the measure that an experimental explanation of man is possible, it will consist in studying him in the perspective of that which is experimentally more simple than him, not in order to identify the complex and the elementary, but to derive the one from the other. It is therefore quite natural that the scientist seeks to derive man from animal, and animal from plant, and to see the whole hierarchy of natural species arranging itself in the direction of an organization always growing and more complex. The philosopher who denies the very possibility of an evolutionist theory denies the very essence of the scientific method. If he were logical, he would also deny the value of a measure of length. Let no one think he can escape this consequence by saying that the animal and plant are heterogeneous and rebel against a homogeneous measure. Can we not measure their duration with the same clock? Moreover, since existence is proportional to essence—*quantum unicuique inest de forma, tantum inest ei de virtute essendi*—the duration of cosmic beings is also more and more simple, less and less temporal; there exists thus a whole hierarchy of cosmic durations. But this ontological heterogeneity does not prevent physical time, which one defines by a description of its process of measurement, to link all spatio-temporal beings by what is homogeneous from the point of view of time. That common measure is grounded in the common genus of corporeity in which all natural beings are found. Physical time does not attain their depths (*bas-fond*) and touches them only from outside. Homogeneity being the basis of every quantitative measure, this common physical genus sufficiently explains the specific unity of experimental time, and why the heterogeneity of durations escapes the grasp of a metric calculated on homogenous exteriority. Experimental science takes its rise on the level where all natural beings touch and mingle. (The balance does not tell us if the object that registers 150 pounds is a rock or a human person. The graduated scale shows no difference between 150 pounds of bricks and 150 pounds of man.) If now physical time touched beings in their ontological and specific depth, if this time exhausted the real, if only from the point of view of duration, the different degrees of beings would be only epiphenomena of growing material complexity. But if these things are more than this "outside," this does not prevent the measure of their homogeneous exteriority from being common and true. These two perspectives are not contrary, they complete one another. Without knowing the experimental complexity of a thing, one cannot grasp the richness of its ontological unity. It is time for us philosophers, who so often arrogate to ourselves the right to confuse everything and to judge everything without knowledge of the cause, to rid ourselves of a homogeneous conception of the degrees of wisdom.

The language in which we express the infusion of the spiritual soul—do we not say that it *comes* to disposed matter?—gives rise to images that can falsify the idea. Is it not strange that the term toward which the entire cosmos tends should come to matter, and that the latter should *receive* this form from without? As if the Creator applied a form to matter in the same way that a stamp is to a properly addressed envelope? It is important to note that God does not act *on* things, but from *within*. Proceeding immediately from the Creator, the emanation of the spiritual soul is by that very fact more intimate, it comes more from within than the forms extracted from the potency of matter and which mark out the road to an emanation so profound that it must come immediately from the Universal Cause. In this perspective, it is rather material forms that come to and are from without.

12. The Cosmos as Impulse toward the Life of Thought

It is in man's intelligence that nature accomplishes its first definitive trajectory. We have seen in effect that the creature cannot realize his explicit return to God, his principle, except by thought. If God creates, necessarily He creates in order to manifest His glory outside, not to manifest it to Himself, as if by creation He could grow in His own regard. Creation is essentially a communication. His work must be capable of appreciating the gratuitous gift that communication is and that is achieved in the *person,* that is, in an intellectual creature who can give glory to his Principle. That is why God could not create a cosmos which was not essentially ordered to an intracosmic intelligence.[101] We have also seen in what sense matter is entirely at the service of spirit: either as nature and tendency toward man, or as subject of the proportioned spiritual form of human thought, a thought so attenuated that it cannot confront immaterial things.

Having studied the ontological mechanism of evolution, let us now consider this same process in the formal perspective of cosmic thought.

It is only in human understanding that the cosmos becomes a universe in the full sense. St. Thomas says,

> A thing can be perfect in two ways. In one way a thing is called perfect according to the perfection of his being, which perfection belongs to

> him according to his proper species. But because the specific being of a thing is distinct from the specific being of another thing, for this reason and in this precise respect, a created thing is purely and simply imperfect to the degree that it does not share in the perfection realized in other species; in this perspective the perfection of every created thing is imperfect, being only a part of the perfection of the whole universe, a perfection which flows from the coordination of particular things. But in order to compensate for this defect, there is found in some created things another kind of perfection; that by which the perfection which is proper to one thing can exist in another, and this is the perfection of the knower as knower, for we say of an object that it is known when it exists in a certain fashion in the knower. That is why it is said that the soul is in a way everything. And in this fashion the perfection of the entire universe can exist in one of its parts. For this reason philosophers have held that the ultimate perfection to which the soul can attain consists in embracing the whole order of the universe and its causes.[102]

> All the parts are evidently coordinated with an eye to the perfection of the whole; for the whole is not for the parts, but the parts for the whole. But intelligent natures have more affinity than the others with the whole, for each intelligent substance is in a certain way all things, in the sense that it can comprehend with its intelligence the whole of being, whereas the other substances participate in being only partly. Therefore it is in the order that God provides other beings because of intelligent substances.[103]

In order for the world to have a raison d'être, in order for it to be profoundly one and a universe, it is not enough that it be composed of parts and that these parts physically constitute a whole; it is also necessary that all the individual parts be oriented toward that one in which all together can exist, that each of the principal parts of the universe should be the entire whole, that each of these universes be in some fashion all the others.

In what sense can it be said that the soul is all things? Ought one not rather say that we have intelligence only to observe how obscure and impenetrable things are? We are so ignorant that it is impossible for us to know how ignorant we are. For the rest, if we knew the depth of our ignorance, we would be truly omniscient, for we would have to know what we do not know.

That is why God alone knows how much we do not know, for He alone knows everything.

Yet, to know that one does not know the whole of anything is a way of knowing the whole. When I say that I know nothing, I say that I am ignorant of everything. But how could I know that I do not know the whole, if I did not in some way know all things? I know that over and above the knowable whole there is nothing to know. There is then a way of not knowing the whole while knowing the whole. It is in this that the privilege of intelligence consists: it can say "nothing," "non-being," "impossible," which would be impossible if it did not in some way make a tour of being, if being were not transcendentally accessible to intelligence. Although this knowledge of being is infinitely indeterminate, confused, and implicit, it is nonetheless knowledge of all things as being. The progress of intelligence will consist in a growing explicitation of the confused and implicit content of being. But it suffices to have shown here in what sense every thought is necessarily open to all things, and unlimited, and in what sense it is made to live the whole universe.

We can then consider the maturation of the cosmos as a tendency toward the thought in which all its parts are united and lived; the cosmos thus tends to compenetrate itself, to touch itself in the intelligence of man, in which it can realize this explicit return to its First Principle.

Let us imagine the initial state of our universe as a pure exteriority. The world was so to say entirely outside, separated from itself, imprisoned in itself and its own obscurity. It is dead, empty, an abyss of division. But intelligence must appear. This demand is written in it from the beginning. Intelligence being a species of compenetration, it is necessary that the universe fall back in a certain way on itself, and that it close in on itself, that it interiorize, and it is just this interiorization that will permit it to open onto itself.

In the theory of the expansion of the universe, physics reveals to us a world which, beginning from an immense primitive atom, in which is found compacted all the energy now dispersed, an explosion occurs. We are in a universe which stretches itself and whose fragments are more and more dispersed. In the law of the degradation of energy, this same physics shows us an aging universe: energy, even while being quantitatively the same, is more and more irreversibly degraded. The world tends toward complete exhaustion, toward thermodynamic equilibrium.

In the theory of mutations, biology too sees life advance by successive explosions. But instead of the impoverishing dispersion of the physical world, life blossoms out by *dehiscence;* it always gets richer. The flower is a progress over its bud. The chick that breaks the shell of the egg by pushing from within provides us with a synthetic image of the manner in which life surges up in the cosmos. The physical world is like the shell of the egg.

Regarding these two inverse phenomena from the point of view of philosophy of science, we can say that it is the thrust of life which dismantles the universe under its physical aspect, which uses this universe and makes space grow. What is concentration from the physical point of view is separation from the biological point of view. When life travels toward an organization always more intense, the disorganization of the physical world is only a loss of a cosmos which is absorbed in life.

By this contraction the biosphere lifts itself above the fragmentation of space, the disappearance of time, which are only ashes and smoke of a world which glows with life. Absolutely speaking, it is life which, in the effort to touch itself in a consciousness, in a center of pure density, cuts through space-time as the prow of a ship cuts through the water.

Life travels against the grain of the diffusion of time: it is a species of triumph over the scattering of physical time. Thus, as we have already said, it is in the consciousness of animals and men that we find the most manifest sign of it, and most especially in memory. To the degree that a being is living, it is lifted above the conditions of space and of time which are separation. A knowing being is present to himself and intentionally assimilates his surroundings, whereas where space dominates, things are separated from one another and plunged into night.

The universe in expansion from the physical point of view rebounds on itself in life, constituting in these contractions more and more dense centers, more and more heterogeneous nuclei. It arrives finally at man in whom the world succeeds in uniting all the degrees of cosmic being, and in thought in which it touches and compenetrates itself. The world tends to join in man its extremities separated by space-time. In doing this, nature projects that whole hierarchy of species which the paleontologist and biologist study.

We said that the biosphere is lifted more and more above time. And this is not only a metaphor. Beings are perfected to the degree that they are intemporal; transcendence over the diffusion of time is a condition of life, of knowledge, of thought. If the vegetative species are hierarchized according as they approach animal species, and the latter in their turn as they approach man, it must be said that the vital thrust with which the cosmos is animated from outside since its origin, elicited from the potency of the matter of composites whose forms emerge more and more from matter; that is, essences more and more simple and one. *Quanto forma magis vincit materiam, tanto ex ea et materia magis efficitur unum.* But, since essence is proportional to existence, the duration of cosmic beings is also more and more simple, and less and less temporal. As has been said, they are specifically hierarchized in their existence as well as in their essence. The animal is less temporal than the plant.

This ontological perspective no doubt seems strange, since, from the experimental point of view, we use the same clock to measure the duration of all the specifically different beings. But, as we have seen in the preceding paragraph, these two perspectives are profoundly different.

It is understood that the diverse durations of natural beings are all temporal in the ontological sense, that is, successive and continuous. But some are less so than others. And when we consider this hierarchy of durations in the direction of their lower limit where they become experimentally measurable, we observe that these diverse durations incline to confuse themselves and evanesce in physical time to the point of erasing every distinction among *beings.* If the principle of the conservation of energy is true, and if the mass of the universe is constant, physical time is in this perspective absolutely one; in this perspective, which abstracts from the ontological cuts that divide the world into individuals, the diverse physical times proper to beings—the life of a cat, for example—are only local condensations of the same time which goes back to the origin. But if we consider ontologically, these same local condensations afflicted thanks to a transformation of energy are centers which gnaw at the physical world and consume it. And it is then the maturation of the biosphere, entailing in the physical line a degradation of energy, which gives birth to physical time and makes it enlarge; life, by dispersing the physical world whose disintegration is only the reverse of progressive biological organization, makes time. And here is a singular paradox. It is life itself that makes the time from which it distances itself. The fact of covering a distance suppresses it for the one who covers it. The inorganic world being the *terminus a quo* (A) of life in evolution (V), and the spiritual its *terminus ad quem* (B), the distance AV increases to the degree that the distance BV lessens.

Is not the inorganic world the most ancient, the most durable? Is it not absurd to say that the duration of living things is richer than that of the imperishable non-living?

It is here that the necessity of distinguishing the ontological and physical aspects of duration is clear. The quantity of time is a sign of a relaxed existence. While being quantitatively longer, the duration of the inorganic world is ontologically poorer. Considered in itself, it takes time to exist, *et peu s'y fait*—it *loses* time. This duration is diffused because it has little consistency. Homogeneous diffusion is a condition of quantitative measurability. A living being that existed only an instant would have an infinitely richer duration than that of the stars, although it would be infinitely shorter; it is infinitely closer to eternity than the aging inorganic world. It is again the notion of physical time, first in the experimental order, that makes us think quantity is a property essential to duration. And yet, the most simple duration does not mean the least duration.

In the order of homogenized, diffuse, and quantitatively measured, where the imperfect precedes the perfect, the ontologically more simple durations come after the more diffuse. In this perspective of progression in time, the world tends to reduce the quantitative measurability of beings, not by shortening this duration, but by intensifying it. This concentration can only be had at the expense of quantity. Death is necessarily a function of life. It is the uplift of life that is the cause of death.

We said earlier that the tendency of the world has as terminal point something immobile that does not have to pursue its existence, and if existence is successive insofar as it is composed of matter and form, this being is nonetheless above time because of the spirituality of its incorruptible form. If evolution could be completed in one leap, it would also realize at once an immortal cosmic being whose duration would be both quantitatively indefinite and ontologically simple. Subject to the resistance of matter, the world rejoins this end by projecting a whole hierarchy of intermediate composites in which it has not succeeded in establishing that equivalence of quantity and intensity of duration. Natural subhuman species should be considered as more and more audacious attempts to detach the world itself from the dispersion of time, in order to dominate it from outside, instead of being borne away by it. This ascent is made by sacrificing time from the point of view of quantity, as a man sacrifices his life in an heroic deed that makes him worthy of immortality. Evolution is a struggle against death, by means of death if necessary.

Our entire universe is troubled by a pitiless desire for immortality, a cosmic desire which takes on terrible proportions. The terrible thing essential to evolution is death.[104] Here below, generation always involves corruption. Elementary living things which multiply by dividing die in this generation. The unicellular living thing does not divide into two parts: it gives birth to two new individuals, and their birth is its death. The very fight to preserve life already involves death.

The maintenance of life is accomplished thanks to death. It is necessary for the animal to be nourished by organic substances. The biosphere eats itself in order to grow; it must destroy itself to the degree that it enriches itself. Tragedy is essential to cosmic life. The desire to reach man (and in humanity the desire to attain always higher cultural levels) knows no pity. To the degree that life becomes more noble and more intense in organization, death becomes more terrible and the fear of death takes on the most frightening proportions. We will come back to this point in the next section.

The expansion of space and the scattering of energy are in their turn only the reverse of a contraction in the ontological order. In the drive to produce more and more heterogeneous beings, nature is forced to overcome the homogeneity of space. The differentiation of parts which becomes more and more pronounced in living things is but an external sign of this.

In assimilating the other in sensible knowledge, the animal already breaks the barriers of a separating space; he extends himself to what is not himself: he can live the other. To the degree that animals are more perfect, the field of their knowledge becomes more vast; that is to say, the world compenetrates itself more and becomes more and more present to itself, more and more interior. This growing introversion blossoms into ontological simplicity in the human soul where intelligence embraces space without being mixed up in it, and transcends it. Not that the regard of this intelligence penetrates space and envelops it in the way that a pure spirit contemplates the world outside. Accidentally at least, the human spirit is tied to a corner of space like a tree, with this very profound difference that the corner can move itself. The immobility of human thought is thus intermediary between that of a pure spirit and that of a tree, conjoined in man thanks to local motion. That is the profound sense of the locomobility of knowers, a power that frees them from the shackles of their spatiality, and which in the final instance is at the service of the exploring intelligence. The intelligence, immobile in itself and transcending every place, must yet travel the world in order to assimilate it. The locomotion of living things is a species of the tendency toward ubiquity, toward a certain intentional omnipresence and a sort of immensity.

Although from the point of view of physics local motion from a material point is dispersion and total abandonment of the preceding position, by its displacement the conscious center gathers and enriches, living the preceding positions all together in the place where it finds itself for an instant. Man is a "microcosm," not only because in the ontological line he contains in himself all the degrees of being in nature, but above all because in the intentional line he is potentially all things. He uses the resources of art to draw to himself all the richness of the world diffused in space and time. The progress of navigation and aviation, the perfecting of telescopes, and the means of long distance communication supplied by modern technology are conquests for intelligence. The ultimate end of these emancipations is not control or the shipping of beans and bananas, nor weather prediction; it is more profoundly the exploration of the world with an eye to gathering it to a point, and contemplation.[105] Evolution is the world's effort to communicate with itself and thus to imitate its First Principle—*the Thought of Thought.* In the idea we make for ourselves of evolution, infrahuman beings are essentially in function of man, and fleeting: these natures thus are open to one another, constituting in their ascension toward him a more and more determined and powerful drive. But one should not conclude from this that this function is reduced to a pure canalization of the spiritual energy with which the cosmos is impregnated. This is too simplistic an interpretation. Necessarily a work of nature and a gift of self, so that evolution will be a gift of self *in the precise degree that it is a work of nature,* without which the concept of nature would become an exclusively passive principle.

It is true that inorganic nature, considered in itself, is only a passive principle of motion, and that such nature cannot actively give itself. But this creationist way of isolating inorganic nature is denaturing and factitious. Nature is only nature. Even inorganic nature is form and matter, although its form is not soul, that is, a principle of self-motion. But it is precisely this essential lack that opens the inorganic world to the spiritual universe, without the influx of which the inorganic would be deprived of its natural end, and thus contradictory. This essential need appeals to the spiritual world for the constitution of active nature; this need is logically anterior to the activity of nature.

And yet, taking into account the motive for this need—a motive inscribed in the inorganic by its ordination to life, which is its raison d'être—already the non-living begs to be given it: it gives out of its desire to be given by its natural appetite. And in this way is accomplished the generosity nature is. The non-living moves only insofar as it is moved, but it touches life at its two extremities like the paintbrush through which is filtered the thought of the artist.

While in the original eruption of life out of the inorganic the latter accomplishes the gift of self under the motion of a transcosmic agent; the plant, on the contrary, is already a certain self that affirms itself, which assimilates the non-living, which communicates its own life in the generation of similars, restoring thus to the world more than it received. Here already there is a gift of self by the self, that is, life.

When we consider the plant in the perspective of the ultimate end to be attained—a pure interiority—it seems a shallow vase; its feeble capacity makes it too swiftly overflow it; the fruit of its maturing detaches from it; deprived of all consciousness, it cannot communicate its own life, it lives in the night; it is completely exhausted by generation. *Non enim est in plantis aliquod nobilius opus vitae quam generatio.*

Let us listen to St. Thomas:

> The mode of emanation of beings varies following the diversity of their natures; and the more elevated the nature, the more what emanates from it is more intimate. . . . After inanimate bodies, plants come immediately, and in them emanation already proceeds from the interior insofar as the sap, which is in the plant, is changed to seed, and the seed given to earth produces a plant. That is the first degree of life, for living beings are those which can move themselves to act and those which on the contrary can move only by something extrinsic, are absolutely deprived of life; what reveals life in plants is that a principle inherent to them determines a certain kind of motor action. Still, the life of plants is imperfect because, although with them emanation proceeds from an

> intrinsic principle, however, which emanates from them, gradually leaving the interior ends by being completely extrinsic: for example, the sap in leaving the tree becomes first a flower, and then fruit which is distinct from the bark while remaining attached to it; when the fruit is fully developed, it is completely separated from the tree, and, falling to earth, produces another plant by the power inherent in the seed. Reflection enables one to see that even the first principle of this emanation is drawn with without, for the tree draws from the earth, through its roots, this intrinsic sap with which the plant is nourished.[106]

Let us note as well that the plant can assimilate the outside only by disintegrating it: nutrition entails corruption of the object assimilated; the plant cannot become the other objectively, that is, as other.

> Above the life of plants we find a more elevated kind of life, that of the sensitive soul, whose proper emanation, although its principle is extrinsic, nonetheless terminates in the interior; and the more one advances in emanation the more intimate it becomes, for the external sensible impresses its form on the external senses, when it passed to the imagination, and finally into the treasure house of memory. Moreover, at each step in this emanation, the principle and the term belong to different powers, for no sense power reflects on itself. This degree of life is thus so much superior to the life of plants that the proper operation of this kind of life is circumscribed in the intimacy of the being. Yet, is not an absolutely perfect life, since the emanation passes from one power to another.[107]

The animal has consciousness, but he does not know that he knows. He cannot express himself to himself, he does not compenetrate in the consciousness of self. "The highest degree of life is therefore the life of intelligence, because intelligence reflects on itself and can know itself. But . . . although human intelligence can know itself, it takes from outside that which constitutes the first principle of its knowledge, since it is incapable of knowing without images."[108]

Although our intelligence only knows itself in the grasp of an object other than self, it is nonetheless consciousness in the full sense of the word, since it is truly present to itself and touches itself. Man can say "*I* think," and to God, "*I* adore You."

In human intelligence the cosmos not only becomes present to itself, this presence opens on the whole of being and thus it can realize an explicitly lived return to the First Principle of being—God, who draws the world from Himself in order to 'speak' Himself by it, and which thus opens an abyss where He can make His abode.

13. Cosmic Desire as Thrust toward the Consubstantial Love and Liberty

Every thing is love, either insofar as it is ordered to an end, or insofar as it travels toward that end, or insofar as it rests in it. Whether it be distinct from the loving subject or identified with him, every being is good insofar as it is an object of love—*bonum est quod omnia appetunt.*

> The good is essentially an end, and while it is first in intention, it is the last in execution. With respect to execution or realization, the first thing is clearly what is produced above all in the being which tends to the end. But equally clearly every being which tends to an end must have an aptitude or proportion with respect to that end, for it is impossible that a being tend toward an end which is entirely disproportional to it. Second, comes the movement toward the end. Then, it is repose in the acquired end. But this aptitude, this proportion of appetite with respect to the end, is love, which is nothing other than delight in the good; the movement toward this good is desire or concupiscence; repose in the good acquired is joy or delight. And following this order, love precedes desire and desire precedes delight. But if we consider the order of intention, it is the contrary that emerges: the delight willed is the cause of desire and love; in effect, delight is rejoicing in the good, which is an end of sorts, like the good itself.[109]

Consequently, if we consider love as the aptitude or proportion of a thing to some other thing—as potency is aptitude to act—there is love in the inanimate and vegetative as well as in the knowing.

> Love pertains to appetite, because the one and the other have good for its object; the modes of appetite ought then serve us as a model for distinguishing love. There is an appetite which does not follow on the

> knowledge of the desirer but on that of someone else, and this is natural appetite in inanimate things, for they do not seek what befits them because of their own knowledge but rather the knowledge of the Orderer of nature. Next there is an appetite which follows apprehension, but necessarily, without free will: this is the sensible affectivity of the brute, although this appetite is also found in man along with some freedom, since it is subject to reason. Finally, there is an appetite that follows on apprehension with free will: this is rational or intellectual appetite which is called the will. In each of the appetites, love is the principle of movement toward the end sought. In natural appetite, the principle of this tendency is the connaturality of the subject to that to which it tends, what we can call natural love. . . . Similarly the coaptation between sensible affectivity or will is such or such a good, that is the complaisance with the good is called sensitive, intellective or reasonable love.[110]

In knowledge we become the thing known in an intentional way, we remain separated from its concrete being, we cannot be the very being in itself of the thing known. The latter is not itself in the faculty of knowledge but only according to resemblance. But we have seen that love is grounded on a certain conformity which carries the loving subject toward the loved object; by the intentional presence of the known object in the knower there is constituted a particular conformity which will bear the knowing subject toward the known object as it exists in itself, toward its concrete being. This conformity is the beginning, not the end. It is an end for knowledge but a principle of appetite. So much so that the knowledge by which the subject draws the universe to himself not only enlarges the subject in himself, this knowledge also opens on the concrete being of the other as on a good in which it could participate in a physical manner. While in knowledge the subject has only a resemblance of the other, by the inclination that follows apprehension of the other, he communicates with the other in the other.[111] Because of that the creature tends as much as he can to imitate the supreme Being in whom understanding and love are identical with one another and with their object.

Just as the faculty of knowing is not coextensive with either being or life—since one can be and live without knowing—so, too, love and knowledge are not as such coextensive. There is love in the plant but not knowledge. Even in animals knowledge remains subjugated by affectivity, since they cannot know for the sake of knowing, in which most of us seem to resemble them. On the contrary, in man taken purely as such, there is coextension between the object of intelligence and the object of love, since intellect grasps the mark (*ratio*) of the good. Indeed, the domain of intellect extends beyond the domain of love, for we can think of objects to which the will cannot tend as proper objects—mathematical entities, for example.[112] (If will were coextensive with intelligence, everything known would be willed, such that one could not know without loving, and thus God could not know the creature without loving it; and as His knowledge of every possible creature is necessary, He would also have necessarily to create it.) In intellectual being, the inclination which follows on apprehension is under the command of intelligence.

Let us note the paradoxical character of these ideas: on the one hand, the cognitive power is not coextensive with being, in the sense that not every being is knowing; on the other hand, only knowledge extends to all things. A thing is not possible, nor does it exist, without being known; if it cannot know, knowledge is still a condition of its being. (That is why that which is most profound in being is thought, and the life of thought is the formal constitutive of the divine nature.) There cannot be love without knowledge. The end toward which the non-knower is oriented and toward which it tends is neither really nor intentionally present to it. And yet, the end must be present to the subject that pursues it in order that the relation which is natural appetite be grounded. But this presence with respect to appetite can only be intentional. Therefore, it presupposes knowledge of the end in another subject.

In perfectible things, the imperfect precedes the perfect in time. Just as inanimate being precedes the living here below, so love precedes knowledge in the evolution of nature. Natural being will be more perfect insofar as its love proceeds rather from its own knowledge. The appetite that follows on intelligence which grasps the quiddity of being will carry toward being as toward its proper good. Just as intelligence is itself included in being and can reflect on itself, so the will, included in the idea of universal good and presented to it by intelligence, can love itself.

As God created in order to communicate, He is necessarily the Ultimate end of all things. Not having the character of good and desirable except as they participate in a divine likeness, every created being, in desiring any good whatever, be it an intelligent, sensitive, or natural desire, desires God as its end. But just as only intellectual creatures are capable of knowing God in an explicit manner, so, too, they alone are capable of loving Him in an explicit manner. All infrahuman things thus tend toward God by their tendency toward the human species to which they are immediately ordered and in which the trajectory of their desire is accomplished. They are love of and desire for man by their very tendency toward the explicit love of God.[113] Their desire, like their being, remains functional; the term cannot exist in the individual subject from which the desire emanates. What characterizes the love of irrational creatures is the incapacity to be loved in a radical fashion that presupposes the grasp of the universal idea of the good. As individual subjects, they cannot participate in the term of their desire. Seeking its individual good, the plant is exteriorized in generation: it is incapable of containing the fruit of its maturation. We are confronted here with a species of inverted altruism. As an individual it cannot love the good of another; as part ordered to the good of the whole, the pursuit of its proper good devolves on the other. It is in this sense that it is given to the other and that it is functional. Only the rational creature is able to give himself, in the measure that he is capable of possessing himself. The love of irrational creatures is substantial, but it cannot be consubstantial; lacking consciousness, they cannot be *with* themselves. Possession of oneself is a condition of the gift of self. And that is why God alone can give Himself in a full sense, for He alone possesses Himself in an absolute manner. His communication of self is even so profound that it is terminated in beings capable of imitating Him and giving themselves in their turn; although God is the absolute cause of the gift of self in all intellectual creatures.

Just as the cosmos seeks to compenetrate itself more through knowledge, so it tends to be united to itself and possess itself effectively in love. At the beginning it was so to speak entirely turned outside and separated from itself. But in the measure that it returns to itself in knowledge, it returns to itself in love. At the origin there was only natural appetite in the world, without knowledge in the subject and without intelligence. And yet the intrinsic ultimate end of the world is already inscribed in it as the term of its natural tendency. The goodness of man is so great that it extends itself to the very first instant of the existence of this universe that it draws to itself.[114] Every appetite presupposes in effect a certain conformity of the lover to the loved, either a conformity in act or a conformity by reason of potency as proportioned to the act to which it is essentially ordered—*secundum quod potentia habet similitudinem ad actum ipsum, nam ipsa potentia quodammodo est actus.* It is thus that matter is, in all its essence, a love of the human soul in which love becomes consubstantial. And it is just toward consubstantial love that the whole universe tends, that is, toward the love of self for itself, not doubtless as ultimate end, but as the pre-condition of the explicit return to the First Principle by love.

In the measure that the world approaches its term, its desire proceeds more and more actively from within, it becomes more and more elicited and a fruit of knowledge. In knowers, there is not only natural appetite, but also elicited appetite, that is, following on knowledge. And in the measure that this elicited appetite deepens, it approaches the human will.

There is cosmic love and desire, there is also a cosmic will which precedes that of man, and which is the active principle of the ascent of the world to its goal. Infrahuman living things are love for the higher forms of life, but this love cannot become desire without the cooperation of a sufficient cause, that is, of a cause at the level of the perfection of the goal pursued, and which in the final instance is nothing other than the spiritual agent (or agents) of which we have already spoken. The will by which this agent works the world and cooperates with nature in its ascent can be called *cosmic will* in the measure that it responds to the natural love in the world to become desire and conduct itself to its term. The ascent of life is thus a voluntary movement: *est voluntarius, quantum ad principium activum, et naturalis, quantum ad principium passivum.*[115] It is natural because of the passive principle, natural love, which tends to be released. Moreover, the principal goal of this motion is not to make use of the passivity of nature, but to increase love in it so that the desire might spring from a more and more profound interiority, proceed more and more from the within of nature by means of knowledge, and that love increase with consciousness, and in it, to arrive finally at a love reflected on itself, that the passion of living become more and more tense, the instinct of preservation more and more ferocious, and death more terrible. *Timor ex amore nascitur.*[116]

As knowledge increases in the world, elicited appetite extends to more things: the field of its good becomes more vast. But sensible knowledge remains necessarily on the surface of things, since it cannot grasp universal being nor reflect on itself; it follows that animals cannot grasp the very nature of the good, but this or that particular. Man, on the contrary, inclines to the good with the knowledge proper to intelligence which grasps the very nature of the good, which is identified with universal being; he inclines to the good, not under the impulsion of an alien cause, as is the case with beings deprived of knowledge, nor simply to the particular good, as is the case with beings having only sense knowledge, but to the universal: this elicited inclination is the will.[117] The cosmos thus touches will at its two extremities: the cosmic will which tends to rejoin the human will.

By the very fact that the cosmos tends toward intelligence and will, it also tends toward freedom. We find indeed a more and more profound vestige of freedom in the spontaneity of plants and animals, a spontaneity by which they participate extrinsically in freedom. If living beings were not endowed with spontaneity, things would go on as if the principle of their activity were entirely external and it would be impossible to distinguish them from the inanimate; the living being would be like a machine.

There is here a singular paradox. We said above that evolution consists in lifting up ever more determinate natures. But spontaneity and freedom are essentially indetermination. Is there not a contradiction? There are, however, two basically different types of indetermination. The indetermination of matter is indetermination by defect of being; spontaneity, on the contrary, is indetermination by surplus, by superabundance; it is a consequence of determination. The more perfect the intellectual being, the more free; the more natures are determined, the more spontaneous are the activities that spring from them.

Nothing equals the seriousness and pragmatism of the lower animals who do nothing useless. Higher animals, on the contrary, play. They have energy to dispense gratuitously. And if it is not perfectly disinterested, their play at least tends toward an activity exercised for themselves. Nothing prevents us from imagining that it is in play, which requires a quick adaption to new situations and sharp attention, that the higher animals have been progressively disposed and have called intelligence into the world. For the proper life of intelligence is above all play, a game within the principles of being and thought.

It is by the formation of hands that nature was freed little by little from the shackles of a determination due to defect of interiority; life directed by instinct tends toward one directed by reason. St. Thomas says, "The intellectual soul is in potency to an infinity of acts from the fact that it can grasp universal essences. It is not possible that instinctive judgments of a certain kind would be fixed for him, or even special means of defense and protection, as is the case with animals whose knowledge and activity are determined to certain particular ends. In place of all that, man by nature has reason and the hand, which is the *organ of organs*, because it enables him to fabricate tools of infinite variety and for an infinity of uses."[118]

Human nature is so rich that it needs nothing more. Man must create the means that he does not possess by nature. Art responds to a natural need and, in this precise respect, one can say that nature tends toward art, toward the *ars cooperativa naturae.* Let us take an example, in appearance extremely banal, the culinary art which in its deepest purpose is not for the preservation of health but responds to the refined taste of a sense at the service of intelligence. The most intelligent people, the most civilized, have the best cuisine.

Man has need of art not only to respond to the natural demands of a higher animal, but also for the operations of spirit, for the very life of speculative thought which depends on art. Logic is necessary for it. Mathematics is both a science and an art. And without art there would be no experimental science, for the procedures of measurement and mathematical construction of a theory from which derive the relations between number-measures are operations of art. Every language in which we express ourselves is a work of art.

This shows how false is the opinion of those who want what they call a return to pure nature. That would mean that man should fall back into the condition of the brute. It is quite paradoxical that naturists who pretend to live according to nature by the denial of all art are precisely those who deny nature since it is of the essence of very superior and very pure nature to prolong and fortify itself by art.

Although it could be explained as a reaction against the abuse of art—and let us admit that our times are victim of an art which has been pushed beyond its limits, which gets lost in the indefinite, and, in place of cooperating with nature, destroys it—there is nothing more anti-natural than naturism whether it is called anti-machinism, vegetarianism, the medicine of simples, nudism, or prohibition. All that is fundamentally perverse, in the measure that one considers the specific intervention of man in nature as an evil. It is a profoundly degenerate conception of man as well as of nature.

Naturism recoils from the effort required to impose the determination of reason in the constructs of art, just as it recoils from the measure that temperance in morality presupposes, where measure and determination are demanded by nature.

The moral order also is for us a condition of freedom. For those who do not confuse the indetermination of free will with the indetermination of prime matter, freedom is, in effect, the fruit of determination. Moral laws are not obstacles to freedom, they do not impose limits on it; they are essentially at the service of free agents. The possibility of choosing between good and evil is the case with an inferior will, of a will which is not master of its indetermination and which can succumb to the indetermination that is a defect of being. The virtues are determinations which free us from the shackles of that indetermination and by that very fact open for us the way to truly free action, which enables us to act with ease and promptness. It is the virtuous man who is free, not the man who does everything he likes. The just man is above the law in that he acts according to the law in a spontaneous manner without extrinsic constraint; it is the unjust who is under the law and deprived of true freedom.

It is remarkable that the useful arts, having attained a certain degree of perfection, tend more and more toward beauty. Let us not hesitate to consider a very ordinary case. An automobile is essentially a useful thing. But the more it is perfected mechanically and is adapted more to the demands of speed, endurance, comfort, it also becomes more beautiful. Let us say that a certain beauty was always aimed at, one that could only be realized by technical perfection that was not in the first instance meant to embellish it. At the beginning, a show was made of the mechanism. Today the entrails of cars are more and more hidden, and even if one did it exclusively to protect the mechanism, one would also have attained more aesthetic results in dissimulating all that is materially complicated and laborious. The artist imitates nature in doing this. At the beginning, life made a show of organs which in higher beings she has hidden. To the degree that immaterial interiority, physical and physiological, increase, the more hidden is the complexity and organization. Note moreover that that which is most fundamental in man envisaged from the point of view of experimental science is not found on the level of consciousness. We are not conscious of our atoms, our cells, our digestion. That which constitutes the dignity of a lower being becomes secondary and functional in higher beings. *Toute proportion gardée,* knowledge is superior to natural generation which remains a vegetative function. In man, sense knowledge is in function of intelligence. A work of sculpture is not a simple assembling of the members and organs of sensation, but above all the expression of the spirit of which they are the function, and the artist who would express man does well to bring them to the fore. In man considered in a state of ideal equilibrium it is not body which hides intelligence, but the opposite. Like nature, the artist tends to conceal what is purely useful in order to put it in its place, not to suppress or empty his work of the utility which is a precondition of its beauty. The chair must first of all be a chair and not an instrument of torture or an invitation to adventure. The beauty of the work in useful arts is a beauty by surplus which increases with the perfection proper to the work.

But the highest expression of human art is that found in the fine arts which are essentially pure and disinterested. They are not only the work of intelligence but also of the will which exteriorizes the work conceived, thus giving it its own being. The artist is truly the imitator of God the creator and of nature.

Natural things are in fact works of the divine art. Like creation, the fine arts are disinterested, and please the artist as if as a bonus. They derive all their value from their lack of utility, they are objects of contemplation and of the love of contemplation and they also have their own being. And just as a nature is perfect in the measure that it is an intrinsic principle of movement, so a work of art is perfect in the measure that it has a proper life, that it speaks for itself, and is independent and subsists in itself. The works of the divine art are perfect to the point of being natures. *Res naturales sunt quodammodo artificiata Dei.* Although human art cannot produces natures, it tends to give to its works an interiority like that of natures. Art imitates nature in the production as well as in the work. *Ars imitatur naturam*—an imitation which does not consist of making copies of nature, but of proceeding, on a properly human plane, as nature does, to produce works which, like those of nature, have their own interiority. The copy is false and hideous because it remains on the surface and is empty of all interiority, like a mannequin. What there is of a copy in a work of art is simply a point of departure, necessary but extrinsic, for a life which is lived within.

The fact that art is inferior to contemplation should not make us lose sight of its proper grandeur. Just as creation proceeds from the divine art, so the created work responds to the creator in imitating the proper activity which produced the creature. Just as creation is a free manifestation of the divine superabundance, so created art, considered at its summit—the praise that we formulate and that we address to God—is a work of art which springs from the superabundance of contemplation.

14. The Unity of the Cosmos

"The good of the universe is twofold: one is a separated good, namely God, who is like the head of an army; the other is in created things themselves, and this good is constituted by the order of the parts of the universe."[119] The proper perfection of the ensemble of the universe consists in the unity of the coordination of its parts.

Tending toward a greater perfection, the cosmos, whose ensemble in its turn is only a part of the universe,[120] also tends toward a greater unity. But we are tempted to think that the origin of the cosmos was constituted by a unique substance, or at the least by a very restricted number of substances, and that the multiple is simply of the accidental order. The multitude of substances and their diversity are the fruit of the work of propagation and maturing of the world. How to reconcile these apparently contradictory ideas? We must distinguish between the unity of perfection and the unity that is a defect of being. God is one by his own pure actuality, by his absolute determination; prime matter is one by its negative indetermination, by its pure potentiality: it is a unity which because of its imperfection cannot be differentiated and multiplied: it is one by negation. Consequently the multiplicity of substances that can be extracted from the matter of an original substance is a progress from the point of view of positive unity. And we thus see under what aspect the world can be more one, while being multiple, and in what sense the multiple can be a condition and consequence of unity. *Multitudo est quoddam unum.* The multiple is interior to the being whose unity is a transcendental property and so there is an analogy between the unity of creation and the unity of God. If unity were a univocal property of being, creatures would have to be less and less numerous as they approach the perfection of God. That was indeed the view of some Platonists who, ignoring or rejecting the distinction between *one* the transcendental property of being and *one* the principle of number, were then constrained to say that the multiple is purely and simply repugnant to unity, and that God could not be its cause. Applying this idea to the angels, they thought that they were less numerous as one ascended the hierarchy. And that came from their thinking that the more things approached the first principle, their number diminished, as numbers diminish as they approach one. Saint Thomas holds on the contrary that the more perfect things are in themselves, the more they have been created in great numbers. "*Quanto aliqua sunt magis perfecta, tanto in majori excessu sunt creata a Deo.*"[121]

> The distinction and plurality of things comes from the intention of the first agent who is God. God has given being to things because of His goodness which He wishes to communicate and represent in them. And because a single creature would not suffice for this, He has produced many and diverse ones, in order that what is lacking in one to represent the divine goodness would be supplied by another. Thus, the goodness which in God is simple and uniform is in creatures multiple and fragmented. In such wise that the entire universe participates in the divine goodness and represents it more perfectly than any one creature whatever.[122]

And yet the unity of the world is not achieved by the simple multiplication of beings. Thus as has already been said several times, the multiple could not be the end as multiple. The term of such an orientation would be the indefinite multitude, consequently unrealizable. The world would tend so to speak toward the confusion and formlessness of prime matter. "No agent proposes as an end for himself a purely material plurality, for a material plurality is without assignable term, as such it tends toward the indefinite, and the indefinite is repugnant to the idea of end."[123] That is why the multiplication of individuals within a species cannot be an end. The perfection of the universe could not then consist in a plurality of individuals of the same species, but in a plurality of species. "*Universi enim perfectio attenditur quantum ad species, non quantum ad individua.*"[124]

> It must be said that the wisdom of God, cause of the distinction of beings, is also cause of their inequality. And this is the reason. There is a twofold distinction in beings, the one formal, in specifically different

> things, the other material, in those which are only numerically different. But matter being in view of form, the material distinction is for the formal distinction. Thus we see that in incorruptible things (the pure spirits), there is only one individual to a species, for the species is preserved by one. In things subject to generation and corruption, there are many individuals of the same species, for the preservation of that species. Hence one sees that the formal distinction has more importance than the material distinction. But the formal distinction always requires inequality, for, as Aristotle explains in the *Metaphysics,* forms are like numbers whose species vary by addition or subtraction of units. That is why in natural things, species seemed ranked by degrees, the mixed more perfect than the elements, plants than minerals, animals than plants, and man than the other animals. In each of these orders of creatures, one species is superior to another. Therefore, just as the divine wisdom has caused the distinction of things in order that the universe be more perfect, so he is cause of inequality. For the universe would not be perfect if there were but one degree of goodness in things.[125]

Consequently, the unity of the ensemble of the universe is constituted by a heterogeneous plurality. An ensemble or whole is of two kinds. "There is the homogeneous whole, composed of similar parts, and the heterogeneous whole whose parts are dissimilar. In a homogeneous whole, the parts constituting the whole have the same form of being as the whole, as each drop of water is water. . . . On the contrary, in a heterogeneous whole, no part has the form of the whole: no part of a house is a house, and no part of man is a man."[126]

The ensemble of parts that compose the homogeneous whole constitute a material or accidental unity of order; the heterogeneous whole on the contrary constitutes a unity of the formal or *per se* order and is more perfect to the degree that it is more essential.

> Things which constitute a per se order participate in the order more than do those making up an accidental order. But it is evident that among individuals of the same species there is only an accidental order; they participate indeed in the same nature and only differ among themselves according to individuating principles and different accidents, both purely

> accidental with respect to the nature of the species. But in things which are different in species, there exists a per se order according to essential principles. In effect, in the hierarchy of species, the higher species contains the perfection of the lower species and surpasses them, much as in the series of whole numbers. But in inferior beings, which are generable and corruptible, which make up the lowest part of creation and which participate less in order, different things are not all arranged in a per se order; some among them make up only an accidental order, like the individuals of the same species. By contrast, in the upper regions of creation (in purely spiritual things) there does not exist any accidental order but only an order per se.[127]

But it is in this unity of a formal or per se order that the perfection of the universe consists. "The essential perfection of the universe consists in species; accidental perfection in individuals. And as the multiplication of souls takes place within the same species, it follows that the multitude of souls that God creates each day does not contribute to the essential perfection of the universe, but only to its accidental perfection."[128] The unity that results from numerical plurality is not profound enough to be of the very essence of the universe, material distinction being necessarily a function of something else.

This idea raises a great difficulty. On the one hand, we say that the world tends toward unity, and that this unity is more profoundly realized in heterogeneity, but we also said that the hierarchy of infrahuman living things is purely functional and provisory.[129]

This increasing variety of species is necessary in the world only insofar as it is found in a state of maturation. *Pertinent ad perfectionem universi sub motu existentis, non autem ad perfectionem universi simpliciter.*[130] Since the multiplication of individuals within a species is repugnant to the idea of an end, since the individuals of infrahuman living species are totally corruptible, it follows that the very existence of these species is naturally sacrificed to the human species, and that even the individuals of the latter cannot be infinitely multiplied. *Non autem potest esse finis multiplicatio animarum in infinitum, quia infinitum contrariatur rationi finis.*[131] This on the one hand the heterogeneity of species is essential to the perfection of the universe, and on the other hand the hierarchy of biological species will be suppressed in the definitive state of the world. How to explain this paradox?

That the infrahuman living things are destined to disappear presents no special difficulty. Their sole reason for being is to contribute to the establishing of the world in its ultimate perfection. The sculptor does not adorn the statue with the hammer and chisel he used to make it nor the debris of rock. If plants and animals had perfections such that they could contribute to the perfection of the world in its future and definitive state, unity would demand their perpetuation. But such is not the case, for they are by definition purely functional. The perfection of an ensemble does not consist in what it has of the multiple or in its pure heterogeneity, but in the unity constituted by the coordination of parts, and not vice versa. When one can suppress the multiple without harming unity, unity only becomes more one and more dense. But the unity constituted by the multitude and diversity of biological species is actually diffused in the world. This unity will be preserved in the future, not by its diffusion, but in the intense unity of man where all the perfections now diffused in the biological species will be united in a single species.[132] We said that the perfection of the universe consists in the coordination of parts. But it is important to distinguish two species of coordination: the objective coordination which is essentially perfection, and subjective coordination which is essentially imperfect. The former is a unity founded on the distinction of things, the latter is founded on their confusion.

Subjective coordination keeps things linked to one another in a more or less common subject by imposing on them their limitation. Thus natural things have a common matrix, the matter which makes them subjectively dependent on one another, and which is an obstacle to knowledge, that is, to objective presence. In this coordination things are prisoners of their subjectivity: *intus existens prohibet extraneum.* Knowers are perfect in the measure that their form emerges from matter. To know is to be the other as other. In the measure that natural things are subjectively coordinated, they are hidden from one another as objects: they communicate in the obscurity of matter, and not in form. So if we envisage natural forms, not in the sense that they emerge more from matter, but in the sense of their subjective coordination, this shades off into the homogeneity of prime matter which is pure limitation, negative indetermination, and one by defect of being.

But if we look at things in the perspective of their emancipation from matter, we observe that the more forms emerge from matter the more they are distanced from their common subject and the more that immateriality makes them present to themselves and to that which they are not; the more independent and separate they are, the more they have an object, and the more profoundly they are coordinated among themselves in an objective fashion. The less things are subjectively approached, the more they are objectively present one to the other.

In the evolution of the cosmos we must see a tendency to emancipate from the subjective and from potentiality, that is, a tendency toward an ever more pure act and consequently a more objective one. The world flees the unity of matter and subjective coordination for which is substituted a progressive maturation of the object and a more profound objective coordination. Subjective separation is a condition of objective union.

Note however that the objective coordination which opens beings to one another as objects is not perfect by the fact that it involves the multiple, but because of the unity that commands this multiple. The absolute objectivity that God is is negation pure and simple of subject, since He is pure subsisting thought. He is the absolute separation from all subjectivity. Consequently one cannot speak of coordination in the metaphysical sense, that is, insofar as coordination involves the idea of distinct parts of the whole and is opposed to the perfect, but uniquely of absolute identity. Just as, because of the imperfection of prime matter, there cannot be in it subjective coordination, so because of his pure actuality, there cannot be in God objective coordination, insofar as this still implies a multiplicity of beings.

Subjective coordination is only truly vanquished by intelligence which alone can attain true objectivity. Sense knowledge can never totally escape matter and subjectivity. "The most perfect of [cosmic] forms, that is, the human soul, which is the end of all natural forms, has an operation which totally leaves matter behind, and which is not exercised by means of a bodily organ, namely understanding."[133] Consequently it is also on the side of intelligence that one should seek the unity of the world: unity conditioned by the distinction of things according to form and not by confusion in matter.

The plurality of intelligences alone does not answer to the idea of an end. Although human individuals are all of the same species, there is a certain hierarchy among them, and we even see that the more perfect they are the more they differ from one another. There is the most striking example of this in those most superior men who are the saints. This diversity thus constitutes a unity of order which imitates obliquely the unity of essential order.

The inorganic world and the human species are alone part of the ultimate perfection of our cosmos. But their specific difference is not sufficiently profound to be of the essence of the universe. In corporeity they have a common natural genus. It is this insufficiency of unity of essential order that enables St. Thomas to formulate an argument for the existence of the angels who are specifically different from one another and exist outside any natural genus. Our cosmic universe is only the bottom rung of the whole of creation, of the universe in a full sense, where a pure and essential unity of order reigns. Like an isolated angelic species, our whole cosmos is only a degree, the lowest, of the universal hierarchy. It is only in the ensemble of the created universe, that is, in the ensemble constituted by all the specific universes that are the angels and the cosmos, that we find that pure hierarchy which is of the very essence of the work of God.

This shows how much our theory differs from monist and pantheist theories. Monism, in effect, wants to take everything back to homogeneous unity. Pantheism, under the pretext of reducing the multiplicity of things to the greatest unity, pretends that God and the world are one; God is only the sum total of what exists, or the sum total of what exists represents only an aspect of the divine substance. These systems are at bottom pancosmic: everything is at the level of cosmic reality, everything is within the cosmos.

If we abhor these conceptions, it is not because we would be partisans of unity. We reject these systems because they can only give us an absolute pluralism, that is, a pluralism pushed to the diffusion of the unity by defect of being. They seek the unity of the cosmos in the confusion of things, in a subjective coordination, in a substantial unity of which the different natural beings would be only accidental or superficial manifestations. They see things upside down and elevate into an ideal the least real; what is for them the perfect state of the cosmos is for us its most imperfect state. Closing the cosmos on itself as being the only reality, the pantheist thus puts the most imperfect aspect of the most imperfect part of the created universe in the place of God. The logical term toward which monist and pantheist philosophers tend is nothing else than the pure homogeneity of prime matter, and worse they have to understand it not as an appetite and tendency toward form, but as a term and ideal toward which forms are borne. They are obliged to embrace the theory of David of Dinant who maintained most stupidly that God was prime matter.[134]

By rejecting the multiplicity and substantial diversity in the cosmos one at the same time rejects what is most profoundly one: it is sufficiently one to give birth to multiplicity and diversity. Consider again this characteristic idea of pantheism according to which God is identified with things. Without any doubt it is necessary to place things as close to God as possible and to seek to find the profound coherence of beings. But it remains to know if the most intense unity will consist in the identity of all things, and if pantheism does not defeat its pretended desire for unity, the desire that animates it.

There is absolute unity in God alone: in His very unity He is absolutely distinct from every creature. But metaphysics also teaches us that by His immensity, God is more intimately in creatures than creatures are in themselves. It is because He is absolutely one and infinitely distinct from His creatures that He can be infinitely close to them. If He were confused with things not only would God be separated from Himself—which would be the negation of absolute unity—but He would not even exist profoundly in creatures. Putting aside the incomparable absurdity of this idea, things too would be deprived of their most intimate link, since God, their most profound principle of coherence, would be dispersed among them. The world would be like an army in disorder without a leader.

THREE

The Theological Point of View

The rational creature can know God in an explicit manner insofar as He is cause of all being, insofar as He is being in the full sense. But we also know that this knowledge is superficial, that God has properties which are absolutely His own, that the light in which He is seen and which is identified with Him surpasses absolutely the created light in which we know Him in the most inadequate way. We have thus a very confused knowledge of that which is hidden in God: we know of Him that we do not know. This ignorance does not apply only to the hidden life of God; there must be in created nature aspects, the most profound, which are only manifest to the sight of God and which remain hidden to every created light.

This very knowledge of our ignorance is nevertheless a sign of the amplitude of our intellect which extends to being where everything is confusedly given. But Revelation teaches us that, beside the gratuitous gift that the creation of nature already is, God has deigned to communicate another gift, infinitely more profound than the first, by which we can participate in His intimate and properly supernatural life. It is just the natural amplitude of intellect which makes it capable of receiving this gratuitous gift, whereas if God chose to make an irrational creature participate in His intimate life, He would first have to make it a rational creature. By contrast, the rational creature does not have to undergo any transformation of his nature to be capable of receiving grace: he is ready to receive it if God wishes to give it. By that gift the intellectual creature becomes capable of realizing an explicit return to God, not only under the general note of being, but under the proper notion of deity.

God can manifest Himself to creatures in three ways: He is manifested to us in the natural light of our intellect, in metaphysics which is a purely rational science; He manifests Himself to us in faith where we participate in God's own knowledge and will, but in an obscure fashion; and finally in the beatific vision of the blessed who see Him face to face.

Revealed truths are of three sorts: there are some which, absolutely speaking, can be known in the light of natural reason. "Even of that knowledge of God to which human reason can naturally attain it was needful that revelation come to our aid. Without revelation, knowledge of the truth on the subject of God would be had by a small number who would not themselves be able to arrive at it until after prolonged efforts and many errors."[135]

There are others which concern nature itself as nature but that we could in no way know by the light of reason; thus the fact that every intellectual creature is made in the image of the Blessed Trinity and that because of that our soul is naturally capable of being raised to the state of grace and glory is a truth that in no wise entails the necessity of such an elevation. Thus nature hides riches and passive potencies which are only open to the gaze of their supreme cause.

There is finally a third sort of revealed truths, to which the preceding are ordered, and which bear on the fact of our elevation to the supernatural order and on the means of attaining the salvation that God wishes to give us over and above any demand of our nature. We are destined to effect a return to God, not only under the note of being (*sub ratione entis*), but also under the very note of deity (*sub ratione deitatis*).

At the end of this discussion of the cosmos it is fitting to take at least a glance at a perspective infinitely more profound on this same cosmos, namely that of Sacred Theology, which, basing itself on the revelation in which God gratuitously communicates knowledge which is proper to Himself, permits us to see certain aspects of the world as God Himself sees them, in the feeble measure to which the obscurity of faith and the deficiency of our intellect permits us to see. I say 'Sacred Theology' because there is also a purely natural and philosophical theology which is a part of metaphysics and which proceeds consequently in the light proper to the human intellect, that is, *sub ratione entis*. Sacred Theology, on the contrary, is as an impression of the divine science itself on our souls—*velut quaedam impressio divinae scientiae.*

The diversity of sciences is founded on the differences of intelligible lights under which they are developed. Some proceed in the light proper to them, thus metaphysics studies things under the note of being; others borrow their principles from a higher science, as the physicist accepts principles furnished by the mathematician. Sacred Theology is an example of the latter, for it borrows its principles from a science which is proper to God and the blessed; it proceeds in the very light of deity, a light given us in the gift of faith.

In this brief part we will dwell on some revealed truths which concern the very nature of the cosmos, truths we could in no way know apart from faith. This does not mean that in nature considered as nature there are two different realities, one knowable by reason, the other by faith. It is the same nature that one studies in the two cases, but we regard it under absolutely different lights.

1. The Cosmos as the Work of the Trinity[136]

To create is not proper to one of the Persons but is common to the whole Trinity. To create is properly to cause the being of things and because every agent produces a resemblance of himself, the principle of action can be judged from its effect. That is why creating belongs to God by reason of His being. But His being is not, as is the case in creatures, distinct from His essence: it is identical with His essence. But the divine essence is common to the three Persons. Therefore to create is not proper to one or the other of the Persons exclusively, but common to the whole Trinity.

Nonetheless, there is another angle under which we can view the thing. God is cause of the creature by His intellect, which conceives it, and by His will by means of which He puts the creature into existence. Thus we can compare Him to the artist who conceives a work and who exteriorizes this conceived work by means of his will. The artist works with a mental word[137] that he conceives—for example, the conception of a tableau or a musical poem—and then he effects it outside himself by love of existence which is a good, thus giving a being proper to what he has conceived. His work as an intelligible construction is a work of intellect; as realized in a concrete fashion, this work is a good which proceeds from the will's love. But we know that there are in God two distinct processions, that of the Word who proceeds from the Father, and that of Love which proceeds from the Father and from the Word conceived. The procession of the Word is appropriated to the operation of intellect, and the procession of the Holy Spirit is appropriated to the operation of will. Therefore, like an artist, God the Father has realized the creature by His Word, who is the Son, and by His Love, which is the Holy Spirit. According to that, the processions of the divine Persons are the reason for the production of creatures, insofar as these processions include the essential attributes which are knowledge and will.

> Without doubt the divine nature is common to the three Persons, but it belongs to them in a certain order, for the Son receives it from the Father and the Holy Spirit from them both. Just so then, the creative power, although common to the three Persons, belongs to them in a certain order, that is, that the Son has it from the Father and the Holy Spirit from them. So much so that the quality of creator is attributed to the Father as to him who does not receive his creative power from another. Of the Son, it is said in St. John that *by* him everything has been made, because even while possessing the same power, he has it from another, for the preposition *by* usually indicates a mediate cause, a principle which itself has a principle. As for the Holy Spirit, who has the same power from the others, one attributes the governance as master and vivifying the creations of Father and Son.
>
> Also, there is a general reason for this attribution, drawn from the way in which the essential attributes of divinity are appropriated to the three Persons. As was said earlier, one attributes to the Father, by appropriation, the power which is manifested above all in creation, by reason of which he is called Creator. One appropriates wisdom to the Son by which the agent intellect acts, and that is why it is said of the Son that by him all things have been made. Finally, one attributes goodness to the Holy Spirit to whom belongs the governance conducting things to their fitting ends, and vivifying is attributed to him because life consists in a sort of inner movement, and because the prime mover of beings is the end or good.
>
> It is quite true that every effect of God proceeds from all these attributes; moreover, one refers each effect to that attribute with which it has a relation of fittingness by reason of its proper nature. Thus the order established among created things is referred to wisdom, the justification of the impious to mercy and goodness which display themselves in superabundance. As for creation, which is the production of the very substances of things, it is referred to power.[138]

2. The Vestige and Image of the Trinity in the Cosmos

Since every effect manifests in some way its cause, it is fitting to seek in creation traces of its higher cause insofar as this is the Trinity. But an effect can represent its cause in different ways. Thus smoke evokes fire, but although the smoke represents fire as cause, it does not represent the form of fire. When an effect represents only the causality and not the form of its cause, one calls it a *vestige.* A vestige (footprint) indeed shows that someone has passed by but without revealing his nature. But there are effects which represent their cause by offering a likeness of the very form of the cause, as the statue of Mercury represents Mercury, and the photograph the person photographed. In these cases there is an *image.*

"But the processions of the divine Persons relate to acts of intellect and of will, as has been said above; the Son proceeds as the intellectual Word, the Holy Spirit as the love of will. In consequence, in rational creatures endowed with intelligence and will, one will find a representation of the Trinity in the manner of an image, because one there finds a word conceived and a love which proceeds."[139]

As in God, so in the rational creature there is a certain circular motion in the operations of intellect and will. Indeed, the rational creature knows himself as knowing, and loves himself as loving. His intellect which springs from substance knows this substance by reflection—I know that I know and by "I" I mean not only the intellect *by* which I know other things as well as myself, but I mean by that my entire person which chiefly comprises my substance—just so the will loves the substance from which it proceeds, and it loves the intellect which shows it the substance. *Est ergo tam in nobis quam in Deo circulatio quaedam in operibus intellectus et voluntatis.*[140] But while God conceives His Word in knowing Himself, and conceives all things in knowing Himself—such that the circular motion is perfectly closed on Himself (*in Deo iste circulus clauditur in seipso*)—in the rational creature on the contrary the circular motion is not entirely closed, for intellect and will are distinct from one another and from substance, and they are moved by an object distinct from themselves, so that their circular motion always terminates in that which is external to them. Moreover, the circular motion of our thought and of our love in no way finds its term in itself; it is only a precondition of union with its true term which is God and is achieved in this union. By their natural desire created things love God more than themselves, and all knowers know God, at least implicitly, in any known object, for just as nothing is desirable save by its likeness to the supreme good, so nothing is knowable save by its likeness to the first truth.[141] Thus our thought and our love are only truly closed when they are joined explicitly to God as principal term of the union.

> Consequently, the representation of the Trinity is found in a more express manner in the soul insofar as it knows God than insofar as it knows itself; that is why the image of the Trinity is properly in the soul that knows God primarily and principally, and only in a secondary manner in the knowledge the soul has of itself, above all when it knows itself as an image of God and it is thus that this knowledge does not terminate in the soul itself but is raised up even to God.[142]

Rational creatures are not made to attain knowledge of being in general and to be conscious of themselves, but principally to know God. That is why knowledge of God moves and commands all other knowledge. It is because the soul should be able to elevate itself to God that it should have knowledge of being in general and consciousness of itself. That is why intellect and will are above all faculties of the divine, since by them the universe rejoins its creator in an explicit manner, thus accomplishing the ultimate end of all creation; they are faculties of the divine, because they are also *formally* in God, and not just in a virtual manner. One cannot say this of animal knowledge or sensible affectivity, but we must say that God is formally intellect and will. What saves the image of the Trinity in us is intellect and will which are also essential and formal attributes of the divine nature. Since we are made in the image of God, we represent Him in His form and species—*secundum formam et secundum speciem.*

> But in every creature there is a figuration of the Trinity in the form of vestige, for in all there is something which must be necessarily referred to the divine Persons as its cause. Indeed, every creature subsists in its being, has a form that places it in a species, and a relation to something else. Insofar as it is a created substance, it represents its cause, its principle, and thus reminds of the person of the Father, who is a principle

without principle. Insofar as it has a certain form, a certain species, it represents the Word, since the form of work comes from the conception of the worker. Finally, because it is ordered and oriented, it represents the Holy Spirit envisaged as love, for the orientation of an effect to another thing is the deed of a will that creates. That is what St. Augustine affirms when he says that a vestige of the Trinity is found in each creature insofar as it is some thing, is formed of a certain species, and has a certain order. To that too the three terms of the Book of Wisdom refer: the *number,* the *weight* and the *measure;* for measure refers to the substance of a thing limited to its proper elements and principles; number refers to the species, weight to the relation to order.—To that too are referred the three words employed by St. Augustine: the *manner, species* and *order,* besides those which he distinguishes in things 'that which constitutes, that which distinguishes, and by which they agree,' for each thing is constituted by its substance, is discerned by its form, and is fitting by its order.[143]

In all creatures there exists a certain likeness to God; nonetheless, only in the intelligent creature can this likeness be called an *image,* as we have said earlier; there is only a trace or *vestige* in other creatures. It is by his intellect or soul that the rational creature is raised above the others. From which we must conclude that, in the intelligent creature himself, the image of God is found only in the soul or spiritual part, whereas in the other parts, if they exist in the creature endowed with intellect or reason, there is only the likeness of vestige, as in the other bodies to which, moreover, the rational creature should be likened with respect to his material parts. The reason for this is easily grasped if we attend to the different ways in which image and vestige represent an object: the image represents it according to the likeness of species, as we have said, and the vestige represents it as an effect represents its cause, which cannot rise to the resemblance in species. The prints left by the passage of animals are called vestiges, ashes are the vestige of fire, and the desolation of the countryside of an enemy army. That then is the difference one can mark between rational creatures and the others, because in rational creatures is found expressed either the likeness of the divine nature or the likeness of the uncreated Trinity. As for the likeness of the divine nature, rational creatures rise, in a fashion, to the

> level of representation of species since they imitate God, not only under the aspect of being and life, but also under that of his intellectual nature. Other creatures are not endowed with intellect, although one sees a trace of the intellect that formed them if attention is paid to their structure. So too, just as in the Trinity the distinction of persons rests on this that the Word proceeds from Him who speaks, and Love from the one and other, one can say that rational creature in whom there is a procession of word according to intellect and procession of love according to will, is an image of the divine Trinity by the very representation of species. In the other creatures, there is neither the principle of a word, nor a word, nor love, but one can discover them there as an imprint of that which exists in the cause which produced them. By the simple fact that a creature has a molded and delimited substance, one cannot doubt that he comes from a principle, his species refers him to the Word that produced him, as the form of a house manifests the idea preconceived by the builder; the other that one notes there makes known love of which it is proper to order the effect with an eye to the good, as the use to which a building is destined makes known the will of the one who constructed it. Thus then the likeness of God, as image, is found in the soul, and it is as vestige in all the other parts of the human being.[144]

Vestige and image as we have spoken of them to this point are naturally in the works of God, although we would not have known it without the revelation of the Trinity and the creative cause.

Man is made in the image of God even apart from his actual ordination to the supernatural order. This image is called the *imago creationis.* The rational and abstract knowledge that we have of God could not alone go beyond the limits of nature. It is by grace and the light of glory that the image of the Trinity is carried to its summit.

> As it is by his intellectual nature that man is made in the image of God, this image is the more perfect in him as his intellectual nature imitates God the more. But intellectual nature imitates God above all in the knowledge and love that he has of himself. From which it follows that the image of God in man can be considered in a threefold way: first, in this that man has a natural aptitude to know and love God and

this aptitude is enclosed in the very nature of the soul, in that which, consequently, is common to all men. Second, insofar as man knows and loves God in act and in habit, but in an imperfect manner, and this image results from the conformity produced by grace. Third, finally, insofar as man knows and loves God actually in a perfect manner, and this image is what realizes in us the likeness coming from glory. That is why, on these words of the Psalmist, 'The light of the countenance has been sealed upon us, O my God,' the Gloss distinguishes a triple image, of *creation,* of *reconciliation,* and of *likeness.* The first is found in all men, the second only in the just, the third uniquely in the blessed.[145]

3. Vestige as Tendency toward Image

In his treatise on the Trinity St. Augustine says that God is so One that He is a Trinity, and such a Trinity that He is One. This unity and trinity are reflected in every creature. The more perfect the creature, the more he is one and simple. Man is more simple than an animal and more one; the animal is more simple and one than the plant, etc. But the more perfect and one creatures are, the more they are vestiges or images of the Trinity. Just as angels are more in the image of the Trinity than men,[146] so even the animal is a more profound vestige than the plant and the inorganic. Hence, infrahuman beings, in the measure that they tend toward man, tend as well, insofar as they are more or less profound vestiges, toward the image of the Trinity that is the human soul. From this point of view, we can consider the evolution of the cosmos as a maturation of vestiges which will terminate in an image of the Trinity. In evolution, the Trinity draws the world to itself in order to imprint on it its image.

Boethius says of God: *Mundum mente gerens, similique in imagine formans* (Carrying the world in his thought, he fashions it to his likeness and image).[147]

4. Generation of the Word and Natural Generation[148]

The procession of the Word in God is a generation in the most rigorous sense: *origo viventis a vivente a principio vitae conjuncto in similitudinem naturae:* the procession of a living being from a living being which is joined to it as principle of life assimilates it to its very nature in virtue of this very procession. This assimilation of the generator to the generated implies a perfect likeness of nature. Generation consists therefore in expressing a propagative likeness of its own nature.

Let us examine this distinction in the example of natural generation. The first part of the definition—the procession of a living thing from another living thing—designates the formation of one living being by another which is an efficient and living principle: thus the father is the efficient principle of his son. The second part—a living thing conjoined to it as principle of life—designates the material cause from which the engendered proceeds: the generator draws from his own substance the engendered in forming him. The third part—which assimilates him to his own nature in virtue of this very process—designating the likeness of nature between the generator and the engendered indicates both the final cause and the specifying formal cause of the generation. It designates the final cause, for the generator proposes to himself as end the propagation of his own nature. It designates the formal and specifying, for generation is specified by the form of the engendered insofar as that form is like that of the generator and expressive of it, such that the generative activity itself is essentially assimilating: it does not consist of similitude alone, but of the expression of the similitude and the very propagation of the nature.

The term 'generation' is not always taken in the strict sense. In a broad sense it can signify the passage from non-being to being, from the state of being potential to the state of being actual. Even when we use it to designate a process from a living being we do not always understand it in all its rigor, for there can be procession without similitude between the engendered and the generating principle. Thus the hair and beard are not the result of a generation properly speaking: a man is not a father because he grows a beard and his beard is not his child. Just any similitude won't do. The mutations by which evolution progresses are not generations in the strict sense, for the similarity between the mutant and the species from which he proceeds is not perfect. Mutations are equivocal generation where the terms do not communicate in the same species. In order for there to be generation in the strict sense, the being which proceeds must show in his very nature the likeness of the species from which he derives, as when a man proceeds from a man and a horse from a horse.

And thus the generation of beings which pass from potential life to actual life, like man and animal, is at once a generation in a broad sense and a generation in a strict sense: it is a passage from non-being to being, but there is a likeness between the generator which causes the engendered to come to be and the engendered himself. Natural generation departs from the perfect type of generation in the measure that it necessarily involves a passage from potency to act. In natural generation there are at bottom three elements: the generator who is the active principle; potentiality whence the engendered is drawn, potentiality which is a passive principle, a subject; and the engendered itself which is also an act, not as principle, but as term. The second element, the passive principle is consequently cause of imperfection: the assimilation of the generator and engendered will be defective in the measure that they are separated by the potentiality of an intermediate term.

But let us suppose a living being which does not proceed from potency to act, which proceeds immediately from the activity alone of the generating principle: he will have the second sort of generation without the first, that is, without the imperfection that an intermediate element introduces, namely, the potentiality from which the engendered is drawn. There will be a generation in the full sense: there will be perfect similitude in the very assimilation and in the source; there will be both propagation of nature and absolute identity of nature: the nature will be expressed in itself.

It is thus that the Word is enclosed in His procession from the Father, all the characteristics of generation taken in the full sense. He proceeds by an intelligible act which is a vital operation; He comes from a principle to which He is conjoined as principle of life: the divine nature with which He is identified; He contains a perfect likeness of His principle of which He is the conceived and consubstantial image; He shares the nature of principle from which He takes His origin, since essence and intellect in God are identical. So it is that the procession of the Word is called generation in the Holy Trinity, and the Word Himself takes the name of Son.

The generation of the Word is thus linked to the plenitude of the divine nature which is communicated to itself in expressing it in the Word's identity. It is the very perfection of knowledge to be manifestative and expressive of the thing known; this fecundity is essential to intellectual nature. The opposition between the Person of the Father and the Person of the Son is thus born from the fecundity of the divine nature. And this perfect distinction of Persons is only possible in a perfect numerical identity of nature. Knowledge, in effect, has the property of drawing to itself the object known: it is thus a procession toward the inner: *processio ad intra.* Consequently, the more perfect knowledge is, the more the knower is united with the known. Since in God knowledge is absolutely perfect, the divine Word must be absolutely one with the principle from which He proceeds and without diversity of nature. The similitude of Father and Son is not a common similitude—like the similitude between a human father and son by reason of their common species which transcends them—but a similitude in the identity of one and the same form which entails the diversity of Persons.

This enables us to see the infinite distance that separates natural generation, even the most perfect, from divine generation, of which it is nonetheless a profound vestige. Divine generation, indeed, has its source in the absolute plenitude of the divine nature. Natural generation, on the contrary, makes up for the imperfection of cosmic natures. Such natures have to propagate in order to perpetuate and preserve the species: generation makes up for their corruptibility. Thus this propagation of nature is possible only by reason of prime matter which is pure potency. Cosmic natures express themselves by multiplying numerically. Natural generation cannot itself be a term, it is a pure means, for the pure multiplication is repugnant to the notion of end. Even pure resemblance cannot be the ideal in the propagation of cosmic natures. Humanity does not aim at the reproduction of perfectly similar and homogeneous individuals. Its imperfection is made up for by a certain variety. And we even see that the more perfect individuals are, the more they differ from one another.

And yet, it must not be thought that natural generation is a pure and simple imperfection. It, too, is a real fecundity, but a functional one; it is a means to attain the end, for nature a perfection to make use of this means. Matter, indeed, which makes natural generation possible, is not a pure negation: it is for the perfection of form. If the form were perfect in its species, natural generation would be impossible. The angels, naturally subsistent forms, cannot be engendered. Even human generation, because of the spirituality of the soul, requires the special intervention of a principle transcending nature: besides the father, the natural active principle and the potency of the matter, there must be a creative principle of the substantial form which is spiritual. Moreover, because generation must be judged by its term, the son who is made in the likeness of the father, this generation is more perfect than that of infrahuman natures where the engendered are already given entirely in the potency of the created nature.

The term of the divine generation is a Word. We of course see that the mental word which is born in us by the intimate act of our thought is not a child and that its production is not a generation. Indeed, our mental word is not of the substance of our self; there is no similitude of nature. Intelligence in us, as in every intellectual creature, is distinct from our substance, and the mental word is not intelligence itself. If our knowledge of ourselves is in a sense consubstantial, substance is the root of intelligence and intelligence can know substance, yet, intelligence and substance are really distinct.

[*Here the text breaks off. The page proofs and accompanying notes make it clear that De Koninck intended to advance the argument beyond the point that he had reached. For all that,* The Cosmos *shows a young philosopher already immersed in his sources and capable of taking them into areas undreamt of by the authors on whom he relies, chiefly St. Thomas Aquinas.—Ed.*]

NOTES

1. Eddington gives a speed of 23,300 miles per second (*New Pathways in Science,* 209). Here is his humorous description of a nebula: "The following is a recipe for making galaxies: Take about ten thousand million stars. Spread them so that on the average light takes three or four years to pass from one to the next. Add about the same amount of matter in the form of diffused gas between the stars. Roll it out flat. Set it spinning in its own plane. Then you will obtain an object which viewed from a sufficient distance, will probably look more or less like the spiral nebula. . . ."

2. Georges Lemaître, *L'Univers en Expansion* (Louvain: Revue des Questions Scientifiques, 1935), 357–75.

3. 'Force" is a Newtonian term that one has to abandon in relativity physics, but that we use here for reasons of convenience.

4. A state that gives us an image of the universe as conceived by Einstein before the work of Lemaître.

5. Lemaître, *L'Expansion de l'éspace* (Revue des Questions Scientifiques, 1931), 391–410.

6. Lemaître, *L'Univers en Expansion,* 369 ff.

7. Ibid., 371. See, too, Eddington, *The Expanding Universe* (Cambridge, 1935), chap. x.

8. See James Jeans, *The Universe around Us* (Cambridge, 1933).

9. "I feel inclined to claim that *at the present time* our race is supreme; and not one of the profusion of stars in their myriad clusters looks down on scenes comparable to those which are passing beneath the rays of the sun" (Eddington, *The Nature of the Physical World* [Cambridge, 1931], 178).

10. See ibid., chap. iv.

11. Lemaître, *L'Expansion de l'éspace,* 408.

12. This question has importance only in the debate between the determinist and the indeterminist. The indeterminist recognizes to a certain limit the objectivity of the statistic character of the second law of thermodynamics. It seems to me that a non-mechanist conception of life should maintain this objectivity.

13. This law is far from being universally true. Thus, mushrooms feed themselves like animals, that is to say from already formed organic substances. So, too, it is most often difficult to determine if one is dealing with a plant or an animal. But these exceptions and difficulties do not prevent us from tracing the grand characteristic lines. The number of deviations and failures of nature is moreover unlikely.

14. I know that this way of seeing the matter can only be justified by objective indeterminism. Every other conception is either mechanist or parallelist.

15. This is not to say that everything in man comes about freely. But the simple fact that I can raise my arm when I wish justifies this affirmation. It is equally true that the behavior of masses does not elude statistics. We will see later that liberty admits degrees.

16. That biology cannot attain to the rigor of experimental physics is perhaps seen in the fact that biological laws are far more statistical than physical laws.

17. *Flore Laurentienne* (Montreal, 1935), 63.

18. J. B. P. A. de Lamarck, *Histoire Naturelle des Animaux sans Vertèbres* (Paris, 1825), t. I, pp. 151–52.

19. "None of the facts cited in favor of this conception can resist an objective critique. Multiple causes of error: the heterogeneous nature of the population one studies, incertitude about what concerns the real action of the internal actors, retention more or less lasting of modifications wrongly taken as hereditary variations, account for the illusion to which have fallen victim those who thought themselves to have observed the heredity of non-congenital particularities" (Emile Guyénot, "Le mecanisme de l'evolution et l'experience," Première Semaine Internationale de Synthèse, Premier Fascicule, L'Evolution en Biologie [Paris: Alcan, no date]).

20. Charles Darwin, *The Origin of Species* (New York: Harvard Classics, 1909), 79.

21. ". . . according to the theory of natural selection an interminable number of intermediate forms must have existed, linking together all the species in each group

by gradations as fine as are our existing varieties" (op. cit., p. 502). "If we look to long enough intervals of time, geology plainly declares that species have all changed; and they have changed in the manner required by the theory, for they have changed slowly and in a graduated manner" (p. 505).

22. Guyénot, "Le mecanisme de l'evolution," 41.

23. Ibid., 47 ff.

24. Marie-Victorin, *Flore Laurentienne,* 65.

25. Ibid., 64.

26. See the summary exposition in Guyénot (p. 39 ff.). By a general theory I mean one that extends to all vital phenomena. We will speak of spontaneous generation in Part Two.

27. Note to students of physics: I do not mean that the 'trail' in question is a continuous trajectory having always a value simultaneously spatio-temporal. Its identity is nonetheless safeguarded by the principle of conservation.

28. *Q.D. de potentia,* q. 4, a. 1, c.

29. We intentionally go around the considerable difficulties that the substance and accidents of mobile being imply. By *mobile being* we understand both the mobile substance and mobile accidents. (See Cajetan, *De subjecto philosophia naturalis.*) Nevertheless, I must make precise here that whatever be the mobility that one takes for point of departure, being is of the accidental or of the substantial order, one arrives at exactly the same conclusions. For mobility in the proper sense in the accidental order presupposes one in the substantial order. The whole mobile being necessarily composed of substance and accidents, and the substance being the root of accidents, it is in the substance that the two principles must be placed, and again it is the matter, an essential principle, which will explain mobility in the accidental order. One can therefore take as point of departure, to demonstrate the thesis of hylomorphism, any entity whatsoever that presents a mobile aspect, or any two real entities of the purely accidental order, providing that they are homogeneous: one must find the root in substance.

30. See Aristotle, *Metaphysics,* II, 2, 994b26.

31. Moreover, temporal duration is not considered as such, but only as implying a real successive continuity. One does extend *this* particular case to others—all the others are implied in advance.

32. If it is *natural* for the human form to inform matter, this is not natural in the strict sense, not have been *nata,* it was not generated. Nevertheless the human composite can be said to be generated, and in this respect the composite is a natural being.

33. ". . . appetitus formae non est aliqua actio materiae sed quaedam habitudo materiae ad formam, secundum quod est in potentia ad ipsam" (*Q.D. de potentia,* q. 4, a. 1, ad 2). But above all see *In I Physic.,* lectio 15, nn. 9–10, where it is shown that this is not a matter of metaphor.

34. "Est autem considerandum quod alio modo intentio naturae fertur ad corruptibiles et ad incorruptibiles creaturas. Id enim per se videtur esse de intentione naturae quod est semper et perpetuum; quod autem est solum secundum aliquod tempus, non videtur esse principaliter de intentione naturae, sed quasi ad aliud ordi-

natum, alioquin, eo corrupto, naturae intentio cessaretur" (Ia, q. 98, a. 1, c.). ". . . nullum agens intendit pluralitatem materialem ut finem: quia materialis multitudo non habet certum terminum, sed de se tendit in infinitum; infinitum autem repugnat rationi finis" (Ia, q. 47, a. 3, ad 2).

35. *Q.D. de potentia,* q. 3, a. 18, ad 5.

36. IIaIIae, q. 2, a. 3, c.

37. "Quum vero . . . perfectum . . . sit unumquodque in quantum fit actu, oportet quod intentio cujuslibet potentiae sit ut per motum tendat in actum. Quando igitur aliquis actus est posterior et magis perfectus, tanto principalius in idipsum appetitus materiae fertur. Unde oportet quod in ultiorem et perfectissimum actum quem materia consequi potest tendat appetitus materiae quo appetit formam, sicut in ultimum finem generationis.

"In actibus autem formarum, gradus quidam invenitur. Nam materia prima est in potentia primum ad formam elementi; sub forma vero elementi existens, est in potentia ad formam mixti, propter quod elementa sunt materia mixti; sub forma autem mixti considerata, est in potentia ad animam vegetabilem; nam talis corporis anima actus est. Itemque anima vegetablis est in potentia ad sensitivam, sensitiva vero ad intellectivam; quod processus generationis ostendit; primo enim in generatione est foetus vivens vita plantae, postmodum vero vita animalis, demum vero vita hominis. Post hanc autem formam non invenitur in generabilibus et corruptibilibus posterior forma et dignior. Ultimus igitur generationis totius gradus est anima humana, et, in hanc tendit materia sicut in ultimam formam. Sunt ergo elementa propter corpora mixta, haec vero propter viventia, in quibus plantae sunt propter animalia, animalia propter hominem; homo enim est finis totius generationis. . . .

". . . Si igitur motio ipsius coeli ordinatur ad generationem, generatio autem tota ordinatur ad hominem sicut in ultimum finem hujus generationis, manifesum est quod finis motionis coeli ordnatur ad hominem sicut in ultimum finem in genere generabilium et mobilium" (III *Summa contra gentes,* 22).

38. Ia, q. 98, a. 1.

39. "Posset etiam dici, quod vis generationis ab imperfectioribus ad perfectiora pervenitur, et hoc ordine quod *quae imperfectiora sunt, prius ordine naturae producuntur. In via enim generationis quanto aliquid perfectius est, et magis assimilatur agenti, tanto tempore posterius est; quamvis sit prius natura et dignitate.* Et ideo, quia homo perfectissimum animalium est, ultimo inter animalia fieri debuit" (*Q.D. de potentia,* q. 4, a. 11).

40. *In I de anima,* lectio 1.

41. It is in that very exploration that we discover the ontological cuts that divide the world into distinct substantial beings. Already having the metaphysical notion of substance, it is easy to identify a substantial being. Substance is that which is *of itself, subject of accidents.* But I perform these acts that are mine, I act freely, I enjoy independence with respect to my surroundings, and can oppose them. Concomitant signs enable me to recognize other independent lives. But I have no *direct* knowledge of my substance, still less of that of others. I am obliged to reconstitute them by means of signs.

42. This way of looking at it astonishes at first blush. We here dissect a process which comes about spontaneously, but which nonetheless follows the path we have just described. The most solid arguments put forth by modern Thomists are along these lines. See, for example, Joseph Gredt, *Elementa Philosophiae,* vol. 1, n. 437: "Si animal est substantia una vivens vita vegetativa et sensitiva seu informata anima, quae simul est vegetativa et sensitiva, etiam planta est substantia una vivens vita vegetativa seu informata anima vegetativa; nam phaenomena vegetativa in animali: nutritio, augmentatio, generatio, eodem modo essentialiter contingunt sicut in planta neque differunt nisi valde accidentaliter. Quare si haec phaenomena in animali vitalia sunt, etiam in planta ita explicari debent. Atqui animal est substantia una vivens vita vegetativa et sensitiva. Ergo.

"*Probatur minor.* Animal est substantia una sentiens (id quod est in homine, in animali rationali, ex testimonio sensus communis et tactus constat et in ceteris animalibus ex modo, quo se gerunt, ostenditur), quae simul ostendit phaenomena vegetationis, seu cuius diverse partes ad invicem agunt ad totam nutriendum et evolvendum; atqui substantia una sentiens, cuius diversae partes ad invicem agunt ad totum nutriendum et evolvendum, est substantia una vivens vita vegetativa et sensitiva. Ergo."

43. Vital activities cannot be called movements in the strict sense of the term, for every movement in the cosmological sense essentially involves matter, whereas life already supposes a certain degree of emergence from matter. See on this subject Yves Simon, *Introduction à l'Ontologie du Connaître* (Paris: Desclée De Brouwer, 1934). I do not know a better exposition of this question.

44. "Omni potentiae passivae respondet potentia activa; potentia enim propter actum est, sicut materia propter formam. Non potest autem ens in potentia consequi quod sit actu, nisi per virtutem alicujus existentis in actu. Otiosa esset ignitur potentia nisi esset virtus activa agentis quae eam in actu reducere possit, quum tamen nihil sit otiosum in rebus naturae; et per hunc modum videmus quod omnia quae sunt in potentia materiae generabilium et corruptibilium, possunt reduci in actum per virtutem activam quae est in corpore caelesti, quod est primum principium activum in natura. Sicut autem corpus caeleste est primum agens respectu corporum inferiorum, ita Deus est primum agens respectu totius entis creati" (II *Summa contra gentes,* 22).

45. "Non differt autem, quantum ad praesentem intentionem, utrum corpus caeleste moveatur a substantia intellectuali conjuncta quae sit anima ejus vel a substantia separata, et utrum unumquodque corporum caelestium moveatur a Deo, vel nullum immediate, sed mediantibus substantiis intellectualibus creatis, aut primim tantum immediate a Deo, alia vero mediantibus substantiis creatis; dummodo habeatur quod motus caelestis est a substantia intellectuali" (III *Summa contra gentes,* 23).

46. "*Non igitur motus caelestis principium est sola natura. Oportet igitur quod principium motus ejus sit per apprehensionem moventis.*

"Non tamen est negandum motum caelestem esse naturalem. Dicitur enim esse aliquis motus naturalis, non solum propter activum principium, sed etiam propter passivum; sicut patent in generatione simplicium corporum, quae quidem non potest dici naturalis ratione principii activi. Movetur enim id naturaliter a principio activo cujus principium activus est intra; natura enim est principium motus in eo in quo est. Principium autem activium in generatione simplicis corporis est extra. Non est igitur naturalis ratione principii activi, sed solum ratione principii passivi, quod est materia, cui inest naturalis appetitus ad formam naturalem. Sic ergo motus caelestis corporis, quantum ad activum principium, non est naturalis, sed magis voluntarius et intellectualis; quantum vero ad principium passivum, est naturalis; nam corpus caeleste habet naturalem aptitudinem ad talem motum" (ibid.).

47. It is precisely against this kind of evolutionism, according to which "species inferior et onorganica extiterit quasi causa *principalis, et non instrumentalis tantum,* sui progressus suaeque in speciem superiorem transformationis," to which theologians object. See Mgr. A. Paquet, *Disputationes Theologicae, de Creatione,* Disp. V, q. 4, a. 1 (third edition).

48. Not that my substance itself acts, but it is the root of the faculties which are the immediate subject of operations, which arise from essence as their principle. See Ia, q. 77, a. 6: "Utrum potentiae animae fluant ab ejus essentia."

49. The formal subject of experimental science is thus an inferred subject. And yet this inference is not of the epistemological order. The mediate character of the magnitude fabricated in scientific experience—the number-measure one reads on the graduated scale of a given instrument and which only translate objectively this experiment—is *objectively mediate.* A number-measure which was not defined by the description of a concrete operation which furnishes it would be deprived of sense. It does not suffice to see the symbol, one must first know what it signifies. It is an objective trace.

50. Nonetheless, if the sensation of heat can be neither the formal subject nor point of departure of experimental science, I am more sure of my sensation of heat than any of the formally scientific properties known mediately by measurements and deductions. A physics established on *proper sensibles* would be perfectly imaginative and subjectivist, like the qualitative physics of the ancients. This does not mean that proper sensibles are illusory, but that they are not fecund in experimental science, even if they condition our contact with the external world. Experimental science is possible only with respect to the metric aspect of the universe, an aspect gained in the realm of *common sensibles* all of which involve quantity—*quae omnia reducuntur ad quantitatem*—and which are perfectly independent of a particular sense. I can *see* the temperature and know the length by touching it. *Sentiri potest sensibili commune sine proprio.* Quantity is only known through measure, *quantitas est id quod mensura cognoscitur.* Hence experimental knowledge will be scientific only to the degree that it is physico-mathematical. That is as true of experimental psychology as it is of experimental physics. We do not imagine that we have explained the proper sensible heat when we know that heat is the disordered motion of molecules. The kinetic energy of the molecules is not what provokes in us a sense of heat: it is only its metric aspect. Heat, an alterating quality, is absolutely indefinable and irreducible. I can call it an alterating quality moreover only by leaving in shadow its specific difference. Still the proper sensible is the indispensable extrinsic condition for any experimental science.

"[I]n the end we must trust to our perceptions to tell us the result of the experiment. Even if the apparatus is self-recording we employ our senses to read the records" (Eddington, *New Pathways in Science,* 3).

51. Exception must be made for the philosophy of science, the sapiential function of mathematics, and the philosophy of nature, which operates with formally scientific data.

52. Even the philosophy of science presupposes a philosophy-science already constituted.

53. An ideal body would be a mass in every point of view absolutely homogeneous, an entity which is no more ideal than the material point of mechanics.

54. Is there any need to say that the *soul-form,* no more than *form* tout court, has absolutely nothing to do with figure, configuration, or form in the vulgar sense? A scientist as distinguished as Dastre gave this strangely stupid interpretation of Aristotelian form. "Natural history," he wrote, "contented itself with the morphological consideration; it studied the Form, the word being understood in its extensive sense and comprising the external configuration and the internal configuration or structure. Zoology and botany have been until now anatomical or morphological sciences, that is, exclusively attached to the description of forms. For the ancients, for Aristotle, the living thing is entirely its form" (A. Dastre, *La Vie et la Mort* [Paris: Flammarion 1920], xiii).

55. ". . . licet in litera dicitur quod forma fit in materia, non tamen proprie dicitur. Forma enim proprie non fit, sed compositum. Sicut enim dicitur forma esse in materia, licet forma non sit, sed compositum per formam: ita etiam proprius modus loquendi est, ut dicamus compositum generari ex materia in talem formam. Formae enima proprie non fiunt, sed educuntur de potentia materiae, inquantum materia quae est in potentia ad formam fit actu sub forma, quod est facere compositum" (*In VII Metaphysic,* lectio 7, n. 1423). "Sicut forma est quodammodo causa materiae inquantum dat ei esse actu, quodam vero modo materia est causa formae, inquantum sustentat ipsam; ita etiam quodammodo ea quae sunt ex parte formae, sunt priora his quae sunt ex parte materiae, quaedam vero e converso; et quia privatio se tenet ex parte materiae, ideo remotio privationis est prior introductione formarum naturaliter, secundum ordinem quo materia est prior forma, qui dicitur ordo generationis; sed introductio formae est prior illo ordine quo forma est prior materia, qui est ordo perfectionis" (*Q.D. de veritate,* q. 9, a. 3, ad 6; *Q.D. de potentia,* q. 3, a. 8, c.).

56. ". . . cum anima sit actus corporis organici, ante qualemcumque organizationem corpus susceptivum animae esse non potest" (*Q.D. de potentia,* q. 3, a. 12 c.).

57. ". . . sicut dispositio in via generationis praecedit perfectionem, ad quam disponit, in his quae successive perficiuntur; ita naturaliter perfectionem sequitur quam aliquis jam consecutus est; sicut calor, qui fuit dispositio ad formam ignis, est effectus profluens a forma ignis jam praexistentis" (ibid., a. 13, ad 2).

58. "Perfectibile autem non unitur formae nisi postquam est in ipso dispositio, quae facit perfectibile receptivum talis formae, quia proprius actus fit in propria potentia: sicut corpus non unitur animae ut formae, nisi postquam fuerit organizatum et dispositum" (*Q.D. de veritate,* q. 8, a. 3, c.).

59. "... hoc stare non potest, *primo* quidem quia nulla forma substantialis recipit magis et minus; sed superadditio majoris perfectionis facit aliam speciem sicut additio unitatis faciat aliam speciem in numeris. Non est autem possibile ut una et eadem forma numero sit diversarum specierum. *Secundo* quia sequeretur quod generatio animalis esset motus continuus paulatim procedens de imperfecto ad perfectum, sicut accidit in alteratione. *Tertio* quia sequeretur quod generatio hominis aut animalis non sit generatio simpliciter, quia subjectum ejus esset ens actu. Si enim a principio in materia prolis est anima vegetabilis, et postmodum isque perfectum paulatim perducitur, erit semper additio perfectionis sequentis sine corruptione perfectionis praecedentis; quod est contra rationem generationis simpliciter" (Ia, q. 118, a. 2; IaIIae, q. 52, a. 1).

60. "Oportet namque in materia quaelibet esse aptitudinem ad formam. Non enim quodlibet artificiatum potest fieri ex qualibet materia, sed ex determinata. Sicut serra non fit ex lana, sed ex ferro" (*In VII Metaphysic.,* lectio 8, n. 1437). "... non enim materia quocumque modo se habens potest subesse formae, quia proprium actum in propria materia oportet esse. Cum ergo est materia in dispositione quae non competit formae alicui, non potest a principio incorporeo, a quo forma dependet per se, eam consequi immediate; unde oportet quod sit aliquid transmutans materiam; et hoc est aliquod agens corporeum, cujus est agere mutando. Et hoc quidem agit in virtute principii incorporei, et ejus actio determinatur ad hanc formam, secundum quod talis forma est in eo, actu (sicut in agentibus univocis), vel virtute (sicut in agentibus aequivocis)" (*Q.D. de potentia,* q. 5, a. 1).

61. However, when this unique cell constituting the new being is broken into two parts, into two new cells, thus beginning the development of the embryo, this bipartition does not touch the substances as in the case of bacteria. One does not have to do with two new beings, but to a growth by partition of the same being. Whereas bacteria born in strangling of the mother-cell will lead a independent life from then on, the cells of the embryo are only parts. I do not say that the interdependent coordination of parts is *always* the sign of ontological individuality. These *signs* can be more or less manifest, and often insufficient.

62. "Via enim quae est in simplicter non ens, quam dicit (Aristoteles) esse corruptionem simpliciter, non potest intelligi in id quod est omnino nihil: quia omnis naturalis corruptio fit per resolutionem in aliquam materiam. Similiter etiam non potest intelligi non ens simpliciter, quod sit privatio pura sine forma: quia materia nunquam denudatur ab omni forma, ita quod sit sub sola privatione. Ergo oportet per non ens in quod tendit corruptio simplex, intelligi privationem quae est adjuncta alicui formae" (*In I de generatione et corruptione,* lectio 8, n. 3). See John of St. Thomas, *Cursus philosophicus,* Philosophia Naturalis, III p., q. 2, a. 1: "Quomodo differat corruptio in ratione mutationis a generatione et ab annihilatione. Corruption is opposed to generation, whereas annihilation is opposed to creation."

63. "Et ita non sequitur quod id quod corrumpitur secedat a tota rerum natura: quia quamvis fiat non ens hoc quod est corruptum, remanet tamen aliquod aliud, quod est generatum. Unde non potest materia remanere quin sit subjecta alicui formae: et

inde est quod uno corrupto aliud generatur, et uno generato aliud corrumpitur: et sic consideratur quidam circulus in generatione et corruptione, ratione cujus habet aptitudinem ad perpetuitatem" (*In I de generatione et corruptione,* lectio 7, n. 6). But whereas Aristotle thought that corruptible beings pursued the perpetuation of their species as an end, St. Thomas opposes this view. The philosophical foundation of this divergence is exposed, not in the place cited (*quod tamen fides catholica non supponit),* but in *Q.D. de potentia,* q. 5, a. 5 and in *In I de coelo,* lectio 20, n. 12: "Ea vero quae [a Deo] sic producta sunt ut in sempiternum sint, habent potentiam et virtutem ad semper essendum, et nullo modo ad hoc quod aliquando non sit. Quando enim non erant, talem potentiam non habebant: quando autem jam sunt, non habet potentiam respectu non esse quod prius fuit, sed respectu esse quod nunc est vel erit; quia potentia non respiciat prateritum, sed praesens vel futurum." This idea flows logically from the Aristotelian adage: *in perpetuis non differt esse et posse.*

64. See John of St. Thomas, *Cursus philosophicus,* Philosophia Naturalis, III p., q. II, a. 3: "Ad ultimum respondetur generationem et corruptionem dari in eodem instanti temporis, sed in diversa prioritate naturae."

65. "In actionibus naturalibus formae substantiales non sunt immediatum actionis principium, sed agunt mediatibus qualitatibus activis et passivis sicut propriis instrumentis, ut dicitur in II de Anima, quod calor naturalis est, quo anima agit; et idea qualitates non solum agunt in virtute propria, sed etiam in virtute formae substantialis. Unde actio earum non solum terminat ad formam accidentalem, sed etiam ad formam substantialem, et propter hoc generatio est terminus alterationis. Hujusmodi autem virtutem instrumentalem recipiunt eo ipso, quod a principiis essentialibus causantur" (*In IV Sent*,, d. 12, q. 1, a. 2, sol. 2). "Corpus agit et ad formam accidentalem, et ad formam substantialem. Qualitas enim activa, ut calor, etsi sit accidens, agit tamen in virtute formae substantialis sicut ejus instrumentum; et ideo potest agere ad formam substantialem, sicut et calor naturalis, inquantum est instrumentum animae, agit ad generationem carnis; ad accidens vero agit propria virtute. Nec est contra rationem accidentis quod excedat suum subjectum in agendo, sed quod excedat in essendo; nisi forsitan [*sic*] quis imaginetur, idem accidens numero defluere ab agente in patiens, sicut Democritus ponebat fieri actionem per defluxum atomorum" (Ia, q. 115, a. 1, ad 5).

66. ". . . alteratio primo et per se est in qualitatibus tertiae speciei, mediantibus quibus ex consequenti fit alteratio etiam in aliis; sicut per aliquam alterationem calidi et frigidi mutatur homo de sanitate in aegritudinem aut e converso, et per alterationem mollis et duri perducitur ad aliquam figuram" (*In I de generatione et corruptione,* lectio 10, n. 2). "In eodem instanti quod primo est dispositio necessitans in materia, forma substantialis inducitur. Cum enim generatio sit terminus alterationis, oportet in eodem instanti alterationem terminari ad dispositionem quae est necessitans, et generationem ad formam substantialem. Sed quia alteratio est motus continuus, ideo principium alterationis et medium quod materia disponitur ad forma substantialem, tempore praecedunt introductionem formae substantialis" (*In II Sent*,, d. 5, q. 2, a. 1, c.). See, too, IaIIae, q. 52, a. 1, ad 3.

67. "In qualibet enim generatione vel mutatione est duos terminos invenire; scilicet terminum a quo et terminum ad quem . . . quandoque vero sunt duo termini ad quem, quorum unus ad alium ordinatur, sicut patet in alteratione elementorum, cujus terminus unus est dispositio quae est necessitans, alius autem ipsa forma substantialis" (*Q.D. de veritate,* q. 9, a. 3, c.). ". . . dispositio proprie dicitur illud quod se habet ut incompletum in motu ad perfectum, quod est terminus motus; sicut qui addiscit, habet dispositionem scientiae, qua perficitur in termino motus disciplinae. Contingit autem terminum motus esse duplicem: quia vel ejusdem generis; vel alterius. Verbi gratia, alterationis terminus est qualitas sicut ejusdem generis; sed forma substantialis sicut alterius generis. Si ergo dispositio comparatur ad id quod est terminus motus ejusdem generis, sic constat quod dispositio potest fieri illud quod disponit, sicut calor imperfectus fit calor perfectus; si autem accipiatur terminus alterius generis, hoc nunquam fit forma substantialis ignis" (*In II Sent.,* d. 24, q. 3, a. 6, ad 6); see, too, *Q.D. de virtutibus,* a. 1, ad 3; *Quaestio quodlibitalis,* VII, a., c.

68. "Nec est mirum si tota generationis transmutatio, non est continue, sed sunt multae generationes intermediae, quia hoc etiam accidit in alteratione et augmento; *non enim est tota alteratio continua* neque totum augmentum; sed solum motus localis est vere continuus, ut patet in octavo Physicorum" (*II Summa contra gentes,* cap. 89). See Sylvester of Ferrara on this passage, and John of St. Thomas, *Cursus philosophicus,* Philosophia Naturalis, III p., q. 3, a. 3.

69. ". . . quidquid movetur, jam quantam ad aliquid motum est. Et eadem ratione quicquid fit, jam quantum ad aliquid factum est, licet enim factio in substantia quantum ad introductionem formae substantialis sit indivisibilis, tamen si accipiatur alteratio praecedens cujus terminus est generatio, divisibilis est, et totum potest dici factio. Quia igitur quod fit quantum ad aliquid factum est potest aliqualem operationem habere quod fit ejus ad quod terminatur factio; sicut quod calefit potest aliquomodo calefacere, licet non perfecte, sicut id quod jam factum est calidum" (*In IX Metaphysic.,* lectio 7, nn. 1853–1854).

70. "Dispositio se habet ad perfectionem dupliciter, uno modo sicut via ducens ad perfectionem; alio modo sicut effectus a perfectione procedens: per calorem enim disponitur materia ad suscipiendam forma ignis; quae adveniente calor non cessat, sed remanet, quasi quidam effectus talis formae" (IIIa, q. 9, a. 3, ad 2). ". . . dispositio in via generationis praecedit perfectionem, ad quam disponit in his quae successive perficiuntur; ita naturaliter perfectionem sequitur quam aliquis jam consecutus est; sicut calor, qui *fuit* dispositio ad formam ignis, est effectus profluens a forma ignis jam praexistentis" (ibid., q. 7, a. 13, ad 2). "Et est simile in rebus naturalibus de dispositone quae est ad formam, quae quodammodo praecedit formam substantialem, scilicet secundum rationem causae materialis. Dispositio enim materialis ex parte materiae se tenet: sed alio modo, scilicet ex parte causae formalis, forma substantialis est prior, in quantum perficit et materiam, et accidentia materialia" (*Q.D. de veritate,* q. 28, a. 8, c.). " . . . dispositio subjecti praecedit susceptionem formae ordine naturae; sequitur tamen actionem agentis, per quam etiam ipsum subjectum disponitur" (IaIIae, q. 113, a. 8, ad 2). "Ridiculum autem est dicere quod ideo corpus non agat quia accidens non transit de

subjecto ad subjectum. Non enim hoc modo dicitur corpus calidum calefacere quod idem numero calor qui est in calefaciente corpore transeat ad corpus calefactum; sed quia virtute caloris qui est in calfaciente corpore, alius calor numero fit actu in corpore calefactor, qui prius erat in eo in potentia; agens enim naturale non est traducens propriam formam in alterum subjectum, sed reducens subjectum quod patitur de potentia in actum. Non igitur auferimus proprias actiones creatis, quamvis omnes effectus rerum creatarum Deo attribuamus quasi in omnibus operanti" (*III Summa contra gentes,* cap. 69).

71. The importance of the role of the transmitted disposition is manifest in the Thomist doctrine of original sin. ". . . *peccatum originale* dicitur peccatum totius naturae, sicut peccatum actuale dicitur peccatum personale; unde quae est comparatio actualis ad unam personam singularem, eadem est comparatio peccati originalis ad totam naturam humanam traditam a primo parente, in quo fuit peccati initium et per cujus voluntatem in omnibus originale peccatum quasi voluntarium reputatur. Sic ergo originale peccatum est in anima traducitur a parente in filium per traductionem carnis, cui postmodum anima infunditur; et ex hoc infectionem incurrit quod fit cum carne traducta una natura. Si enim non uniretur ei ad constituendam naturam sicut Angelus unitur corpori assumptio, infectionem non reciperet" (*Q.D. de potentia,* q. 3, a. 9, ad 3).

72. ". . . cum necessitas corruptionis sit necessitas absoluta, utpote proveniens ex ipsa materia non ex fine, sequitur quod unumquodque communicet perpetuitate secundum quod potest" (*In II de anima,* lectio 7, n. 317).

73. ". . . qui ponit infinitum in causa finali destruit finem et naturam boni. Pertingere enim quod infinitum est, impossibile est. Nihil autem movetur ad in quod impossibile est ipsum consequi" (*Q.D. de potentia,* q. 5, a. 5, c.).

74. "Oportet ergo finem motus coeli ponere aliquid quod coelum per motum consequi possit, quod sit aliud a motu, et eo nobilius. Hoc autem dupliciter potest poni. . . . Alio modo potest poni finis motus coeli aliquid extra coelum, ad quod pervenitur per motum coeli; quo cessante illud potest remanere; et haec est nostra positio. Ponimus enim quod motus coeli est propter implendum numerum electorum. Anima namque rationalis quolibet corpore nobilior est, et ipso coelo. Unde nullum est inconveniens, si ponatur finis motus coeli multiplicatio rationalium animarum: non autem in infinitum, quia hoc per motum coeli provenire non posset; et sic moveretur ad aliquid quod consequi non potest; unde relinquitur quod determinata multitudo animarum rationalium sit finis motus coeli" (ibid.).

75. ". . . corruptio seminum et omnis defectus sunt contra naturam particularem hujus rei determinatae per formam, quamvis sit secundum naturam universalem, cujus virtute reducitur materia in actum cujuslibet formae ad quam est in potentia, et uno generato necesse est aliud corrumpi" (*Q.D. de malo,* q. 5, a. 5, c.). See above all John of St. Thomas, *Cursus philosophicus,* Philosophia Naturalis, III p., q. 2, a. 3: "Utrum corruptio sit naturalis et per se intenta a natura."

76. When we speak of the divine nature, or of angelic nature, we do not take the term 'nature' in its proper sense. See John of St. Thomas, *Cursus philosophicus,* Philosophia Naturalis, III p., q. 9, a. 2: "In quibus ratio naturae invenitur."

77. "Quod autem dicitur quod *in sempiternis non differt esse et posse,* intelligendum est secundum potentiam passivam, non autem secundum activam. Potentia enim passive actui non conjuncta, corruptionis principium est, et ideo sempiternitati repugnat: effectus vero activae potentiae actu non existens, perfectioni causa agentis praejudicium non affert, maxime in causis voluntariis. Effectus enim non est perfectio potentiae activae sicut forma potentiae passivae" (*Q.D. de potentia,* q. 3, a. 14, ad 5). And Sylvester of Ferrara, *Com. In Summum Contra Gentes,* II, c. 91, n. IV, 3, and n. VIII; St. Thomas, *In IV Physic.,* lectio 22, nn. 2 and 5.

78. Time, taken formally, is deprived of efficacy, it is rather loss, cause of corruption rather than of generation. ". . . tam generatio quam corruptio fit in tempore. Et ideo quidam attribuebant generationes rerum tempori, ut disciplinam et hujusmodi, dicentes tempus esse sapientissimum, propter hoc quod generatio scientiae fit in tempore. Sed quidam philosophus, Paro nomine, de secta Pythagoricorum, posuit e converso, quod tempus est penitus indisciplinabile, quia scilicet per longitudinem temporis accidit oblivio. Et in hoc rectius dixit: quia ut prius dictum est, [lectio 20, n. 5] tempus per se magis est causa corruptionis quam generationis" (*In IV Physic.,* lectio 21, nn. 2 and 5).

79. To avoid what is called *latitatio formarum.*

80. ". . . anima sensibilis cum non sit res subsistens, non est quidditas, sicut nec aliae formae materiales, sed est pars quidditatis, et esse suum est in concretione ad materiam; unde nihil aliud est animam sensibilem produci, quam materiam de potentia in actum transmutari" (*Q.D. de potentia,* q. 3, a. 11, ad 11). ". . . proprie loquendo, materia non habet ideam, sed compositum, cum idea sit forma factiva. Potest tamen dici esse aliquam ideam materiae secundum quod materia aliquo modo divinam essentiam imitatur" (ibid., a. 1, ad 13).

81. ". . . anima mensuratur tempore secundum esse quo unitur corpori; quamvis prout consideratur ut substantia quaedam spiritualis, mensuretur aevo" (ibid., a. 10, ad 8).

82. ". . . formae substantiales differunt secundum perfectius et imperfectius. Quod autem est perfectius, potest quidquid potest imperfectius, et adhuc amplius" (*In I de generatione et corruptione,* lectio 10, n. 8). "*Similitudo effectus in causa quidem univoca invenitur* uniformiter; in causa autem aequivoca invenitur excellentius" (Ia, q. 6, a. 2, c.); also q. 4, a. 2, ad 3; q. 104, a. 1; q. 115, a. 3; q. 110, a. 2.

83. "Nihil enim secundum propriam speciem agens, intendit formam altiorem sua forma; intendit enim omne agens sibi simile. Corpus autem coeleste, secundum quod agit per motum suum, intendit ultimam formam, quae est intellectus humanus; qui quidem est altior omni formam ut ex praemissis [c. 22] patet. Corpus igitur coeli non agit ad generationem secundum propriam speciem, sicut agens principale, sed secundum speciem alicuius superioris agentis intellectualis, ad quod se habet corpus coeleste sicut instrumentum ad agens principale. Agit autem coelum ad generationem secundum quod movetur. Movetur igitur corpus coeleste ab aliqua intellectuali substantia" (*III Summa contra gentes,* 23).

84. ". . . cum generatio unius est corruptio alterius, quod ex corruptione ignobilorum generentur nobiliora, non repugnat primae rerum institutioni" (Ia, q. 72, art. un., ad 5).

85. St. Thomas along with the ancients thought he recognized in the celestial bodies the instrument used by the spiritual substance directing the cosmos. ". . . corpora caelestia etiamsi non sint animata, moventur a substantia vivente separata, cujus virtute agunt, sicut instrumentum virtute principali agentis; et ex hoc causant in inferioribus vitam" (*Q.D. de potentia,* q. 6, a. 6, ad 10). ". . . corpus caeleste, in quantum movetur a substantia spirituali, est instrumentum ejus; et ita movetur in virtute substantiae spiritualis ad causandam vitam in istis inferioribus, sicut serra agit in virtute artis ad causandam arcam" (*Q.D. de spiritualibus creaturis,* a. 6, ad 12). ". . . supposito secundum fidem nostram quod caelum est corpus inanimatum, nihilominus tamen ponimus quod motus ejus sit ab aliqua substantia spirituali sicut motore: et cum motus sit actus motoris et mobilis, oportet quod in motu non tantum relinquatur virtus corporalis ex parte mobilis, sed etiam virtus quaedam spiritualis ex parte motoris: et quia motor est vivens nobilissima vita, ideo non est inconveniens, si motus caelestis, inquantum est in eo intentio et virtus motoris, per modum quo virtus agentis principalis est in instrumento, est causa vitae materialis, qualis est per animam sensibilium et vegetabilium" (*In II Sent.*, d. 18, q. 2, a. 3, ad 3); and also Ia, q. 70, a. 3, etc. And if St. Thomas makes exception for the higher animals of which the first ought to be directly formed by a special intervention of God, although natural (as in the case of the creation of the human substantial form), it is still for pure experimental reasons that he departed from the tradition of the Fathers. ". . . *videmus enim sensibiliter,* quod aliquis debilis effectus producitur ab agente remoto; sed fortis effectus requirit agens propinquum" (*Q.D. Malo,* q. 16, a. 9, c.). (See the important work of Ernest Messenger, *Evolution and Theology* [New York: Macmillan, 1932].) ". . . quanto aliquid est imperfectius tanta ad ejus constitutionem pauciora requiruntur. Unde cum animalia ex putrefactione generata, sint imperfectiora animalibus quae ex semine generantur, in animalibus ex putrefactione generatis sufficit sola virtus caelestis quae etiam in semine operatur, licet non sufficiat sine virtute animae ad producendum animalia ex semine generata: virtus enim caelestis corporis in inferioribus corporibus relinquitur in quantum ab eis transmutatur, sicut a primo alterante. Et proter hoc dicit Philosophus in libro De animalibus quod omnia corpora inferiora sunt plena virtutibus animae. Caelum autem licet non sit simile in specie cum hujusmodi animalibus ex putrefactione generatis, est tamen similitudo quantum ad hoc quod effectus in causa activa virtualiter praeexistit. . . . Corpus caeleste etsi non sit vivum, agit tamen in virtute substantiae viventis a qua movetur, sive sit Angelus, sive sit Deus . . . virtus substantiae spiritualis moventis relinquitur in corpore caeleste et motu ejus, non sicut forma habens esse completum in natura, sed per modum intentionis, sicut virtus artis est instrumento artificis" (*Q.D. de potentia,* q. 3, a. 12, ad 12–14). If we are today incapable of identifying that instrument, we are no less obliged to affirm its existence.

86. *Casus* and *fortuna* are often confused in debates on indeterminism. "Ostendit (Philosophus) in quibus maxime casus differt a fortuna. Et dicit quod maxime differt in illis quae fiunt a natura; quia ibi habet locum casus, sed non fortuna. Cum enim aliquid fit extra naturam in operationibus naturae, puta cum nascitur sextus digitus, tunc non dicimus quod fiat a fortuna, sed magis ab eo quod est per se frustra,

idest a casu. Et sic possumus accipere aliam differentiam inter casum et fortunam, quod *eorum quae sunt a casu, causa est intrinseca,* sicut eorum quae sunt a natura; eorum vero quae sunt a fortuna, causa est extrinseca, sicut eorum quae sunt a proposito" (*In II Physicorum,* lectio 10, n. 10). "Omne quod est a fortuna est a casu, sed non convertitur" (ibid., n. 2). "Casus non solum est in hominibus, qui voluntarie agunt, sed etiam in aliis animalibus, et etiam in rebus inanimatis" (n. 7) ". . . id quod est in pluribus est causa entis per accidens" (*In VI Metaphysic.,* lectio 2, n. 1187). And these deviations must necessarily happen. "Si enim non fieret aliquando id quod est in paucioribus, tunc id quod est in pluribus numquam deficeret, sed est semper et ex necessitate, et ita omnia essent sempiterna et necessaria, quod est falsum" (ibid., n. 1186).

87. Unforeseeability is essential to chance, as it is to every contingent as such. It is clear that one can predict a chance phenomenon if one starts from knowledge of the direction that causal lines have already taken before their intersection, which constitutes the phenomenon of chance. But that is not knowledge of the *cause* of chance, which is as such perfectly undetermined. Hence the impossibility even for a pure created spirit to know future contingents.

88. ". . . unio animae et corporis non est propter corpus, sed propter animam; non enim forma est propter materiam, sed e converso. Natura autem et virtus animae deprehenditur ex ejus operatione, quae etiam quodam modo est finis ejus. Invenitur autem corpus nostrum necessarium ad aliquam operationem animae, quae mediante corpore exercetur, sicut patet in operibus animae sensitivae et nutritivae. Unde necesse est tales animas unitas esse corporibus propter suas operationes. Est autem aliqua operatio animae quae non exercetur corpore mediante, sed tamen ex corpore aliquod adminiculum tali operationi exhibetur; sicut per corpus exhibentur animae humanae phantasmata; quibus indiget ad intelligendum. Unde etiam talem animam necesse est corpori uniri propter suam operationem, licet contingat ipsam separari" (Ia, q. 70, a. 3, c). See, too, q. 89, a. 1, c.; q. 55, a. 2, c.

89. ". . . corpus non unit eam et continet, immo magis anima continet corpus. Videmus enim quod egrediente anima a corpore, corpus deficit et marcescit. Si autem aliquid aliud continet eam, tunc illud erit maxime anima, quia animae est continere et regere" (*In I de anima,* lectio 14, n. 206). ". . . magis anima continet corpus, et facit ipsum esse unum, quam e converso" (Ia, q. 75, a. 3, c.).

90. "Ostendit (Philosophus) quod anima est causa, ut finis. Et quod sit causa, ut finis, viventium corporum, sic ostendit. Sicut enim intellectus operatur propter finem, ita et natura, ut probatur in secundo Physicorum (lectiones 13 et 14), Sed intellectus in his quae fiunt per artem, materiam ordinat et disponit propter formam; ergo et natura. Cum igitur anima sit forma viventis corporis, sequitur quod sit finis ejus. Et ulterius non solum anima est finis viventium corporum, sed etiam omnium naturalium corporum in istis inferioribus: quod sic probat. Videmus enim quod omnia naturalia corpora sunt quasi instrumenta animae, non solum in animalibus, sed etiam in plantis. Videmus enim quod homines utantur ad sui utilitatem animalibus; plantae autem rebus inanimatis, inquantum scilicet alimentum et juvamentum ab eis accipiunt. Secundum autem, quod agitur unumquodque in rerum natura, ita natum est agi.

Unde videtur quod omnia corpora inanimata, sint instrumenta animatorum, et sint propter ipsa. Et etiam animata minus perfecta, sint propter anima magis perfecta" (*In II de anima,* lectio 7, nn. 321–23).

91. ". . . ex quo materia intelligitur constituta in esse quodam substantiali, intelligi potest ut susceptiva accidentium quibus disponitur ad ulteriorem perfectionem, secundum quam materia fit propria ad ulteriorem perfectionem suscipiendam. Hujusmodi autem dispositiones praeintelliguntur formae ut inductae ab agente in materiam, licet sint quaedam accidentia impropria formae, quae non nisi ex ipsa forma causentur in materia, unde non praeintelliguntur in materia formae quasi dispositiones, sed magis forma praeintelligitur eis, sicut causa effectibus. Sic igitur cum anima sit forma substantialis, quia constituit hominem in determinata specie substantiae, non est aliqua forma substantialis media inter animam et materiam primam; sed homo ab ipsa anima rationali perficitur secundum diversos gradus perfectionum, ut sit scilicet corpus et animatum corpus, et animal rationale. Sed oportet quod materia secundum quod intelligitur ut recipiens ab ipsa anima rationali perfectiones inferioris gradus, puta quod sit corpus, et animatum corpus, et animal, intelligatur simul cum dispositionibus convenientibus, quod sit materia propria ad animam rationalem, secundum quod est forma dans esse, non habet aliquid aliud medium inter se et materiam primam" (*Q.D. de anima,* a. 9, c.).

92. ". . . quod aliqua forma non subito imprimatur subjecto, contingit ex hoc quod subjectum non esset dispositum, et agens indiget tempore ad hoc quod subjectum disponat. Et ideo videmus quod statim cum materia est disposita per alterationem praecedentem, forma substantialis acquiritur materiae. . . . Quod enim agens naturale non subito possit disponere materiam, contingit ex hoc quod est aliqua proportio ejus quod in materia resistit, ad virtutem agentis" (IaIIae, q. 103, a. 7, c). See as well John of St. Thomas, *Cursus philosophicus,* Philosophia Naturalis, III P, q. 1, a. 7: *Quomodo ultima dispositio causetur, vel causet generationem substantialem.* Evidently, there is no question here of conditional necessity (*ex suppositione*). See *I Summa contra gentes,* c. 83 et seq. One might object that in adultery man necessitates the creation of a soul, and that God thus responds to a perverse will. To this, St. Thomas replies that the evil is not in nature, but in the will of those who commit it. "Deum vero adulteris cooperari in actione naturae, nihil est inconveniens; actio autem quae est ex virtute seminis ipsorum est naturalis, non voluntaria; unde non est inconveniens si Deus illi cooperatur, ultimam perfectionem inducendo" (*II Summa contra gentes,* c. 89).

93. *II Summa contra gentes*: "Nec est inconveniens si aliquid intermediorum generatur, et statim postmodum interrumpitur, quia intermedia non habent speciem completam, sed sunt ut via ad speciem; et ideo non generantur ut permaneant, sed ut per ea ad ultimum generatum perveniatur. Nec est mirum si tota generationis transmutatio non est continua, sed sunt multae generationes intermediae, quia hoc etiam accidit in alteratione et augmento; non enim est tota alteratio continua neque totum augmentum, sed solum motus localis est vere continuus, ut patet in octavo Physicorum (cc. 7, 8 et 9). Quanto igitur aliqua forma est nobilior et magis distans a forma elementi, tanto oportet esse plures formas intermedias quibus gradatim ad forma ulti-

mam veniatur, et per consequens plures generationes medias; et ideo in generatione animalis et hominis, in quibus est forma perfectissima, sunt plurimae formae et generationes intermediae, et per consequens corruptiones, quia generatio unius est corruptio alterius. Anima igitur vegetabilis, quae primo inest quum embryo vivit vita plantae, corrumpitur, et succedit anima perfectio quae est nutritiva et sensitiva simul, et tunc embryo vivit vita animalis; hac autem corrupta, succedit animal rationalis ab extrinseco immissa, licet praecedentes fuerit virtue seminis."

94. See *III Summa contra gentes,* c. 69.

95. "Anima autem rationalis cum sit pars humanae naturae, non habet naturalem perfectionem nisi secundum quod est corpori unita. Unde naturaliter habet esse in corpore, et esse extra corpus est ei praeter naturam; ideo non fuisset conveniens anima sine corpore creari. Sustiniendo ergo opinionem Augustini de operibus sex dierum, dici potest, quod *sicut in illis sex diebus corpus primi hominis non fuit formatum et productum in actu, sed in potentia tantum secundum rationes causales;* ita et anima ejus non fuit producta tunc in actu et in se ipsa, sed in suo simile secundum genus; et sic praecessit in illis sex diebus non in actu et in se ipsis, sed secundum quamdam similitudinem generis, prout convenit cum Angelis in intellectuali natura. Potest autem opere quo Deus creaturam primo conditam administrat, fuit simul anima in actu cum corpore formato producta" (*Q.D. de potentia,* q. 4, a. 2, ad 20). "Ante ergo quam actu orientur (opera sex dierum) super terram facta sunt causaliter in terra. Confirmatur etiam hac ratione; quia in illis primis diebus condidit Deus creaturam causaliter vel originaliter vel actualiter opere a quo postmodum requievit, qui tamen postmodum secundum administrationem rerum conditarum per opus propagationis usque modo operatur. Producere autem plantas in actu ex terra, ad opus propagationis pertinet: quia ad earum productionem sufficit virtus caelestis tamquam pater, et virtus terrae loco matris; ideo non fuerunt plantae terta die producta in actu, sed causaliter tantum; post sex vero dies fuerunt in actu secundum proprias species et in propria natura per opus administrationis productae; et ita antequam causaliter plantae essent productae, nihil fuit productum sed simul cum caelo et terra productae sunt; similiter pisces, aves et animalis in illis sex diebus causaliter, et non actualiter producta sunt" (ibid., ad 28).

96. It is understood that there could not be in matter considered as in itself pure potency seminal reasons in the Augustinian sense. The three determining causes (final, exemplary and efficient) must be attached before we can speak of "reasons." To speak absolutely, these reasons are rather in the intelligence of the spiritual agent who conceives more or less determinate prefigurations of the intermediary forms which, in this intelligence, rise up from a synthesis of the initial composite given at the origin with the ultimate end of the cosmos which they are going to link. These prefigurations are cosmic ideas: "etiam formae corporales a substantiis spiritualibus deriventur, non tamquam influentibus formas, sed tamquam moventibus ad formas. Ulterius autem reducuntur in Deum, sicut in primam causam etiam species angelici intellectus, *quae sunt quaedam seminales rationes corporalium formarum*" (Ia, q. 65, a. 4). It can be seen that the Thomist does not reverse from top to bottom the central idea of Platonism. "Ad secundum dicendum quod formae participatae in materia reducuntur non ad

formas per se subsistentes rationis ejusdem, ut Platonici posuerunt, sed ad formas intelligibles vel intellectus angelici, a quibus per motum procedunt; vel ulterius ad rationes intellectus divini, a quibus etiam formarum semina sunt rebus creatis indita, ut per motum in actum reduci possint." See, too, *III Summa contra gentes*, c. 24.

97. "Etsi enim detur quod corpus hominis formetur priusquam anima creetur [*sic*], aut e converso, non sequitur quod idem homo sit prior seipso; non enim homo est suum corpus neque sua anima. Sequitur autem quod aliqua pars ejus sit altera prior, quod non est inconveniens; nam materia tempore est prior forma; materiam dico, secundum quod est in potentia ad formam, non secundum quod actu est per forma perfecta; sic enim est simul cum forma. Corpus igitur humanum, secundum quod est in potentia ad animam, utpote quod nondum habet animam, est prius tempore quam anima, tunc autem non est humanum actu, sed potentia tantum; quum vero est humanum actu, quasi per animam humanam perfectum, non est prius neque posterius anima, sed simul cum ea.

"Neque etiam sequitur, si anima ex virtute seminis non producitur sed solum corpus, quod sit imperfecta operatio tam Dei quam naturae, ut septima ratio procedebat. Virtute enim Dei utrumque fit, et corpus et anima, licet formatio corporis sit ab eo mediante virtute seminis naturalis, animam autem immediate producat. Neque enim sequitur quod actio virtutis seminis sit imperfecta, quum perficiat hoc ad quod est.

"Neque etiam, si formatio corporis animam humanam praecedit, sequitur quod anima sit propter corpus, ut duodecima ratio inferebat. Est enim aliquid propter alterum dupliciter: Uno modo propter ejus operationem sive conservationem vel quidquid hujusmodi est quod sequitur ad esse, et hujusmodi sunt posteriora eo propter quod sint, sicut vestimenta sunt propter hominem, et instrumenta propter artificem; alio modo est aliquid propter alterum, id est propter esse ejus, et sic quod est propter alterum est prius tempore et natura posterius. Hoc autem modo corpus est propter animam, sicut etiam omnis materia propter formam. Secus autem esset, si ex anima et corpore non fieret unum secundum esse, sicut dicunt qui ponunt animam non esse corporis formam" (*II Summa contra gentes*, c. 89).

98. ". . . si similitudo ad Deum in causando est finis motus caeli, praecipue attenditur haec similitudo secundum causalitatem ejus quod a Deo immediate causatur, scilicet animae rationis, ad cujus causalitatem concurrit caelum per motum suum materiam disponendo. Et ideo probabilius est quod finis motus caeli sit numerus electorum quam assimilatio ad Deum in causalitate generationis et corruptionis, secundum quod philosophi ponunt. Et ideo concedimus quod motus caeli complete numero electorum finietur" (*Q.D. de potentia*, q. 5, a. 5, c. ". . . licet generabilia et corruptibilia sint viliora caelo, tamen animae rationales sunt corpore coeli nobiliores, quae tamen a Deo pruducuntur ad esse in materia disposita per motum caeli" (ibid., ad 5).

99. ". . . totus homo egreditur de femore generantis, propter hoc quod virtute seminis de femore egredientis operatur ad unionem corporis et animae, *disponendo materiam ultima dispositione, quae est necessitans ad formam*, ex qua unione homo habet quod sit homo; non autem ita quod qualibet pars hominis per virtutem seminis causetur" (*Q.D. de potentia*, q. 3, a. 9, ad 2). ". . . pro tanto in homine non est duplex

esse, quia non est sic intelligendum corpus esse a generante et animam a creante; sed quia creans dat esse animae in corpore et generans disponit corpus ad hoc quod hujus esse sit particeps per animam sibi unitam (ad 20). ". . . duo agentia omnino disparata non possunt hoc modo se habere quod actio unius terminetur ad materiam, et alterius ad formam; hoc tamen contingit in duobus agentibus ordinatis, quorum unum est instrumentum alterius. Actio enim principalis agentis se extendit quandoque ad aliquid ad quod non potest se extendere actio instrumenti. Natura autem est sicut instrumentum quoddam divinae virtutis. . . . Unde non est inconveniens, si virtus divina sola faciat animam rationalem, actione naturae se extendente solam ad disponendum corpus" (ad 21). See, too, Ia, q. 118, a. 2, ad 3; *III Summa contra gentes,* c. 89.

100. ". . . licet anima rationalis non sit a generante, unio tamen corporis ad eam, est quodammodo a generante, ut dictum est. Et ideo homo dicitur generari" (*Q.D. de potentia,* q. 3, a. 9).

101. Doubtless there are authors who do not want to admit the absolute impossibility of a cosmos that is not essentially ordered to man, nor that subhuman beings are absolutely unintelligible, that is, contradictory, outside of their relation to humanity, although such a creation appears to be repugnant to Divine Wisdom. But this understood, the distinction between divine Omnipotence and Wisdom is vain. "Quidam theologi," writes Billuart, "praescindentes omnipotentiam divinam a caeteris attributis, dicunt statum naturae purae, attenta divina omnipotentia sic praecisa, esse possibilem; attenta autem divina omnipotentia ut conjuncta divinae sapientiae, bonitati et iustitiae, non esse possibilem. Verum haec metaphysica praecisio videtur futilis et absona; quod enim est contra Dei sapientiam, bonitatem, justitiam aut quod vis aliud ejus attributum, debit censeri simpliciter et absolute impossibile; Deus enim, ut ait Apostolus 2 Tim. 2: *Seipsum negare non potest,* neque facere quod repugnat divinis suis perfectionibus: 'Nihil potest esse in divina potentia,' inquit Auctor, 'quod non possit esse in voluntate justa ipsius et in intellectu sapientiae ejus'" (F. C. Billuart, *Summa Sancti Thomae* [Paris: Letouzey], t. 3, dissert. 2, a. 2.).

102. *Q.D. de veritate,* q. 2, a. 2, c.

103. *III Summa contra gentes,* c. 112.

104. I take the word 'terrible' in its Aristotelian and Thomistic sense. Thus, the object of the virtue of courage is the *terribile,* and of the *terribilia* death is the most frightening. "The most terrible of bodily evils is death, which takes away all goods. This caused Saint Augustine to say that the claim of the body not to be beaten or tormented inspires the fear of pain and grief; and in order that it be neither shaken nor broken, it makes the soul tremble with the terror of death. The virtue of courage thus has for object the fear of mortal dangers" (IIaIIae, q. 123, a. 4, c).

105. Lest these be thought the mere reveries of a philosopher, I allow myself this long citation drawn from a book by the wife of the Aviator, Mrs. Anne Morrow Lindbergh, *North to the Orient* (New York: Harcourt Brace, 1935): "One could sit still and look at life from the air; that was it. And I was conscious again of the fundamental magic of flying, a miracle that has nothing to do with any of its practical purposes and will not change as they change. It is a magic that has more kinship with what one

experiences standing in front of serene Madonnas or listening to cool chorales, or even reading one of those clear passages in a book—so clear and so illuminating that one feels the writer has given the reader a glass-bottomed bucket with which to look through the ruffled surface of life far down to that still permanent world below.

"For not only is life put in new patterns from the air, but it is somehow arrested, frozen into form. There is no flaw, no crack in the surface. Looking down from the air that morning, I felt that stillness rested like a light over the earth. The waterfalls seemed frozen solid; the tops of the trees were still; the river hardly stirred, a serpent gently moving under its shimmering skin. Everything was quiet: fields and trees and houses. What motion there was, took on a slow grace: the crawling cars, the rippling skin of the river, and birds drifting like petals down the air; like slow-motion pictures which catch the moment of outstretched beauty—a horse at the top of a jump—that one cannot see in life itself, so swiftly does it move.

"And if flying, like a glass-bottomed bucket, can give that vision, that seeing eye, which peers down to the still world below the choppy waves—it will always remain magic."

106. *IV Summa contra gentes*, c. 11.

107. Ibid.

108. Ibid.

109. IaIIae, q. 25, a. 2; q. 26, a. 2.

110. IaIIae, q. 26, a. 1; Ia, q. 59, a. 1; *Q.D. de veritate*, q. 22, a. 1, etc.

111. Ia, q. 59, a. 2; q. 27, a. 4.

112. The intelligence as such is a certain concrete nature, it is a natural appetite of its proper object, the intelligible. Being, considered as the term of this appetite, has beauty as a transcendental property. That is to say that every being, as an object of intelligence, is beautiful. Consequently, although mathematical being, being only a being of reason, does not at all participate in goodness, and cannot be an object of will, nevertheless it participates in beauty. And thus, like every object of intelligence, mathematical being can be indirectly an object of will insofar as will desires the concrete good of intelligence. In effect, one can distinguish a twofold good of intelligence: the good of the object considered as term of the desire to know for the sake of knowing, which is beauty—*pulchrum proprie pertinet ad rationem causae formalis*—but it is also the good of the concrete act which entails knowledge in intelligence taken as nature, and this act is an object of will and causes in it this characteristic joy which is as a complement to contemplation. Without being essential to the beauty which is formally in contemplation, delight is a *quasi per se accidens*. The enjoyment proper to beatitude which consists in contemplation is consequently an enjoyment of the object of intelligence as object of intelligence; this enjoyment, which one can call aesthetic, is the most noble of all pleasures.

113. *Q.D. de veritate*, q. 22, a. 2, and also *In II Sent.*, d. 1, q. 2, a. 3.

114. "Bonum dicitur diffusivum sui, eo modo quo finis dicitur movere" (Ia, q. 5, a. 4, ad 2). See as well *III Summa contra gentes*, c. 24 and, above all, *Q.D. de veritate*, q. 21, a. 1, ad 4.

115. *III Summa contra gentes*, c. 23.

116. "... materia dicitur appetere formam, in quantum est in ea forma in potentia. Et ideo, quanto ista potentia magis est perfecta et propinquior est actui, tanto causat vehementiorem inclinationem" (*Q.D. de veritate*, q. 22, a. 1, ad 3).

117. Ia, q. 59, a. 1, c.

118. Ia, q. 76, a. 5, ad 4. See, too, q. 91, a. 3, ad 2. "The soul, Aristotle says, is analogous to the hand; just as the hand is indeed the instrument of instruments, so intellect is the form of forms" (*In III de anima*, lectio 13).

119. *Q.D. de spiritualibus creaturis*, a. 8, c.

120. Our cosmos and the angels (each angel being unto itself a universe more perfect than the cosmos) constitute together the total creation, the created universe in the full sense. When we speak of the superiority of the angels we put ourselves on a uniquely natural plane. In the supernatural order it is otherwise.

121. Ia, q. 50, a. 3. See as well q. 11, articles 1 and 2. This position, while very certain is also very paradoxical, but we cannot dream of justifying it here. Let us note only that in the measure that one ascends to the higher regions of creation, the demands of unity are greater: the pure spirits are not only more and more different, this increasing perfection requires at the same time a greater multitude. Let us add in passing that if it were otherwise, there would be the possibility of a creature so one and unique that God could not have created a more perfect, which is manifestly absurd.

122. Ia, q. 47, a. 1.

123. Ia, q. 47, a. 3, ad 2. *Q.D. de potentia*, q. 5, a. 5: "Qui ponit infinitum in causa finali destruit finem et naturam boni. Pertingere enim quod infinitum est, impossibile est."

124. *II Summa contra gentes*, c. 84.

125. Ia, q. 47, a. 2, c.

126. Ia, q. 11, a. 2, ad 2.

127. *Q.D. de spiritualibus creaturis*, a. 8, c.

128. *In II Sent.*, d. 17, q. 2, a. 2, ad 6.

129. See *Q.D. de potentia*, q. 5, a. 9; *IV Summa contra gentes*, c. 97.

130. *Q.D. de potentia*, q. 5, a. 9.

131. *IV Summa contra gentes*, c. 97.

132. *Q.D. de potentia*, q. 5, a. 9, ad 11: "in ipso homine continuatio quaedam naturarum apparebit; in quantum in eo congregatur et natura corporis mixti et natura vegetabilium et animalium."

133. *Q.D. de spiritualibus creaturis*, a. 2, c: "Perfectissima autem formarum, id est *anima humana, qui est finis omnium formarum naturalium*, habet operationem omnino excedentem materiam, quae non fit per organum corporale, scilicet intelligere."

134. Ia, q. 3, a. 8: "qui stultissime posuit Deum esse materiam primam."

135. Ia, q. 1, a. 1, c.

136. Ia, q. 45, a. 6; *In II Sent.*, Prolog.

137. To understand the word 'word' (verbum), we must note that the vocal sound is the external sign of that which we speak inwardly in the soul. That is why we

call what we speak with the soul and express outwardly by speech a word. The mental word is the very cause of the word uttered vocally.

138. Ia, q. 45, a. 6, ad 2 et ad 4.

139. Ibid., a. 7, c.

140. *Q.D. de potentia,* q. 9, a. 9, c.

141. Ia, q. 60, a. 3 et a. 5; *Q.D. de veritate,* q. 22, a. 2, ad 1.

142. *Q.D. de veritate,* q. 10, a. 7, c.

143. Ia, q. 45, a. 7, c.

144. Ia, q. 93, a. 6, c.

145. Ia, q. 93, a. 4, c.; *Q.D. de potentia,* q. 9, a. 9, c.

146. Ia, q. 93, a. 3.

147. Cited by St. Thomas, Ia, q. 93, a. 2.

148. Ia, q. 27. See, too, John of St. Thomas, *Cursus theologicus,* ed. Vivès, t. 4, q. 27, disp. 12, a. 6.

The Problem of Indeterminism

1935

Let me first of all say how conscious I am of the honor that your learned President has done me in asking me to present a paper to this Academy. What both moved me and gave me unease is the confidence shown in me by so learned a Thomist and an authority so authentic as the Theologian of Canada. Neither my experience (Aristotle says that experience only comes with age) nor authority can justify this confidence. I have neither the one nor the other. And when, in the paper presented I propose the attitude a Thomist ought to take toward the difficult philosophical problem which the indeterminism of modern physics poses, I feel embarrassed, for it is not a question of elaborating principles already established and then developing them within philosophy so much as insinuating their possibilities in the domain of philosophy of science, and to suggest how we could apply them to the essentially moving aspect of the world, to that 'outside' of our universe which can only be attained in the experimental sciences and which never stops raising ever new problems of which our masters in the past could not have dreamt.

The experimental sciences cannot attain immutable and eternal truths, and that is how they differ from the [philosophical] disciplines. If—what is impossible—the world on which they base themselves had a necessary structure like that of an angelic essence, the method to which the scientist is confined would never allow him to grasp it in its necessity; the science of that necessity would be found at infinity, as mathematicians say. The knowledge which bears on this real aspect of the cosmos is never completely separate from individual matter; it can only furnish us concepts whose very genesis is never terminated; it demands of intellect a constant recourse to the senses immersed in the flux of time and for that reason in the contingent which is resistant to complete abstraction. New experiences can modify to a greater or lesser degree all the concepts suggested by preceding experience, or at least their relations. That is why history is of the very essence of every experimental science, whereas the pure sciences are only accidentally engaged in history.

My undertaking is all the more risky in that it has led me to results which, on many points, differ from conclusions reached by a good number of scholastics whose authority gives me pause. It would have been better to refrain from suggesting another point of view if I did not think it based on the letter of St. Thomas and his great commentators. Indeterminism as it is professed by the new generation of scientists has already been consigned to the great aberrations of modern times, somewhat as Einsteinian relativity was a few years ago. Those who condemned the latter are back today arguing against the objectivist interpretations of quantum mechanics. As one says in Flemish, "It is an old cow I am pulling from the ditch." But be assured. My intention is not to propose achieved perspectives that I regard as definitive. Moreover I would warn you that emphatic passages could very well be the most problematic.

For that matter, it is always well to be on guard against the philosopher who talks science. His proper preoccupations differ from those of the scientist. If we think of the ways they tend to approach the real, the two go off in different directions. The one explains by mathematizing, the other strives to attach this elaboration to ontological causes. The situation of the philosopher of science is strangely paradoxical; he must rejoin the real by passing through a science which is successful to the degree that it distances itself from the ontological mode of knowing. He has misgivings which the scientist ignores, and sometimes scoffs at, a custom that has thankfully become less and less fashionable. The one has evidence that the other seems not to know. The *material* point of classical mechanics was for a long time evidence of the first order. Philosophical facts imposed themselves on some minds, whereas for others these same facts and the problems they raise are chimerical. Was there not a time when physicists mocked philosophical speculation which concluded in the absurdity of space-time-milieu? In different respects, both were right. On the one hand, abstract speculation contributes nothing to the solution of physical problems, whereas, on the other hand, the image of an absolute time and absolute space in which things are plunged proved to be fecund in classical mechanics. When experience finally obliged scientists to abandon this image and to substitute another apparently closer to ontological space-time, philosophers were astonished by the procedure followed and have yet to stop protesting against an established fact.

The evolution of this methodology which provides us with the rules necessary for experimental science is itself conditioned by material progress which takes place in time. The methodological principle of relativity, a principle definitively established even if the experimental principles were found faulty, is of recent discovery, at least with respect to its practical consequences. Despite his proverbial phlegm, the philosopher is impatient with time which he wishes to regard in the perspective of eternity, whereas slow maturing is essential to time: he is tempted to kill the goose that lays the golden eggs. His haste and the ontological motives which interest him in that always provisory knowledge expose him to misunderstandings of the sense and value of scientific terms which he cannot fit into his system without forcing them. And the day when he seems obliged to toss overboard all the rapprochements that he has made, often at the price of deep misgivings and compromise, he is infuriated at the instability of the scientist. If, on the one hand, philosophers begin to take themselves less seriously in these *excursus*—we have to admit that it is close to certainty that many scholastics lack a sense of humor—and if all scientists had the humor of an Eddington, there would be less of this futile indignation, let alone ridicule. Isn't it a fact confirmed by history that the philosopher and scientist are like the coordinates of an electron? Nature seems incapable of bringing them together. In order to appease the indignation this comparison might raise, I hasten to add that its value depends on the ideas one has of the philosopher and the scientist. Since in fact we all hold our own system of reference privileged, it is not astonishing that we cannot agree and together recognize an invariant.

If one can believe what he hears and reads, the first and indemonstrable evidences are not the same for all men. If it were truly a matter of first principles, any discussion of contradictory evidence would be apriori impossible. We would be dupes of a naive illusion if we thought we could weaken the apriori certainty of a man who pretends to see physical determinism implied by the principle of identity. The complacency of such an individual is by definition unshakable; one can even understand how impossible it would be for him not to be amused by those who do not enjoy his strange privilege. We address ourselves only to those who see in indeterminism a matter of understanding and not of intuition.

Finally be assured that if it were shown that any of the ideas I submit to your judgment go contrary to the spirit of Thomism—given the subject and length of the work, what is more likely?—I repudiate them with promptitude. For I hope to know St. Thomas sufficiently well so as always to be a disciple who believes in his master.

Let us consider first of all the problem of indeterminism as it is presented in scientific methodology.

I

One has to admire the good intentions which animated the ingenious attempts made by scholastics to reconcile the determinism of classical mechanics and liberty, but these attempts strike me as more crafty than profound. They have had, per accidens, some pragmatic value, but then so did Cartesianism. What can be regretted is that Thomists, by admitting rigorous determinism in phenomena where no free agent intervenes, adopted a position in part Stoic and frankly Suarezian, and had recourse to a Leibnitzean interpretation of the distinction between absolute and hypothetical necessity, an interpretation St. Thomas had already rejected, even in the same terms. Thomists could not have made such compromises without reversing the whole Aristotelian doctrine of hylomorphism and of the contingency in nature that follows necessarily from matter. Do we not find in the works of modern Thomists that contradiction in terms that is the hypothetical necessity of the laws of nature? The spirit of conciliation has even led them to say, with Vasquez, that natural future contingents are perfectly foreseeable. Isn't that to abandon an absolutely fundamental Thomist position?

What is meant by physical determinism? One knows that in classical mechanics, the coordinates of a material point, its energy and its quantity of motion deduced from its speed and defining its state, have at every instant a rigorously determinate value. Knowing the field of force to which it is subject, we know implicitly its future position. Applied to the electron, for example, this would mean that its future is already completely given in it and in what surrounds it. It is impossible that its future position not be already given except by removing from it a present determination, which is by definition excluded. Note well that the determinist does not say that the future will be determined, but that the future is already determined. The consequent is completely in the antecedent. From a logical point of view, they are completely convertible with one another. The future is part of the definition of the present. If what will be were not already determined, its new determination would have repercussions on the past, would modify the past. An objectively uncertain future would lead to a contradiction in the present where indetermination is excluded in advance.

This logical identity between the future and the present is implicated in what customarily is called in physics the principle of causality or of determinism. It supposes that the cause is as implicated in the effect as the effect in the cause. In other words, we have to do here with what Aristotle called absolute necessity.

It is clear that this principle excludes in advance the possibility of a free intervention in the course of phenomena, for a free action in the present would be meddling with the past. A movement of the arm freely determined would modify that which is no more. That is why the distinction between necessity of right and necessity of fact is here absolutely devoid of sense. Applied to physical determinism it would mean neither more nor less than that *the past was determined by the future only if it is not going to be.* Eddington, who has seen all the consequences of this position, was perfectly right to maintain that it is impossible to make compromises. Those who suggest that distinctions must be made always forget to tell us how to translate them into physical terms without making contradictory a principle whose very definition excludes any restriction.

It is evident that these deductions are valuable only if one abstracts from a time that leaves the future open to events which will not be mere logical derivatives from the past. But it is just that kind of future that determinism is constrained to exclude, because of the logical identity of future and past implied in the values at each determined instant of a material point. Future existence cannot bring on the logically new which would have no repercussions on the past. The coordinate of time, in classical mechanics, makes sense only if it abstracts from such existence. Present and future existence are only a shadow of the past. To introduce into the world something new would be to change the shadow without changing the object that projects it.

Laplace, in a celebrated passage, formulated the ideal of scientific determinism in the following words:

> We must therefore see the present state of the universe as the effect of its anterior state and as cause of the state that is going to follow. An intelligence which, for a given moment, would know all the forces with which nature is animated and the respective situation of the beings that compose it, if moreover it were vast enough to submit its data to analysis, would embrace in the same formula the motions of the greatest bodies of the universe and those of the smallest atom; nothing would be uncertain for it and the future like the past will be present to his eyes. The human spirit offers in the perfection that it has been able to give to astronomy, a feeble sketch of that intelligence. . . .[1]

Henri Mineur, a contemporary astronomer, tells us how astronomical phenomena have been the springboard of determinism, and in what sense they provide an absolute evidence for it.

> Astronomy was the first to teach us, as Henri Poincaré said, that natural laws are ineluctable, one does not compromise with them. It is indeed an observation of a completely elementary order to observe that the rising of the stars, or the coming of an eclipse, for example, are phenomena that could not not have come about at a fixed moment and conditions. It is also when one has been able to give a mathematical expression to astronomical phenomena, that is, when from the observation of the stars, one was able to deduce laws, that this character of astronomical laws has clearly appeared.[2]

The rigorous laws that are supposed to govern the real universe are called primary laws or laws of nature by contrast with statistical laws whose uncertainty betrays our ignorance and never achieves an objective indetermination. That is why thermodynamics was for a long time regarded as the least scientific branch of physics. Thus, the second law of thermodynamics allows us to predict only with a certain probability, a probability which increases, it is true, by reason of the number of elements of the ensemble; it can take enormous proportions but never achieves rigorous certitude. In order to eliminate every vestige of uncertainty about the future state of any system whatever, that is, such that the probability would be zero, the elements of the system would have to be infinite in number or the future state to be predicted is found at infinity. Once the statistical method is adopted, it is impossible to get absolute certainty with it. If there is determinism in nature and we can know it, some other access to it must be found.

No need to say that we would have to find an access analogous to that which allows us to formulate the primary and necessary laws. But such laws, we know today, have never been discovered. Eddington has indeed demonstrated that the apparently absolute and ineluctable laws of the theory of relativity are not true laws, that is, that they do not govern the behavior of things and the course of events; that they express identities; they are pure truisms when we are referred to the cycle in order to understand the constitution of beings subject to it. In that they are analogous to the laws of the celestial mechanics of the ancients as the Peripatetics interpreted them. The movement of the stars constituted cycles perfectly closed on themselves. Necessity was defined by the identity of the cycle, but the direction of the celestial bodies was measured by *aevum* and not by time. All the laws of behavior presently known, and they are the only ones that deserve the name 'law,' are statistical. But it is important to know that all modern physicists are in accord on that point, none among them pretends to formulate an ineluctable law *experimentally.*

Determinism takes its point of departure from regularity observed at the macroscopic level. But it is also clear that this point of departure is not itself manifestly determinist; it can suggest determinism. It is not a proof. In fact, this regularity could only be defined as determinist if one knew that for each of the microscopic elements considered individually there exists no alternative. Failing that macrocosmic determinism could only be an appearance. The future result of six thousand throws of a die, a relatively large number, already involves a good deal of probability which assures a fairly equal distribution of the six sides despite the sixfold alternative equally probable for each individual throw. In order to demonstrate that the behavior of large numbers [*ensembles*] is determinist, it would be necessary to define in an experimental way the determinism of the parts taken individually. If one could do that, he would have demonstrated that the laws that ensembles of this sort obey are at bottom only the laws of parts: in reality there would be no laws proper to ensembles.

On the one hand, the material point and its properties such as these are defined in classical mechanics would only be identified in an ensemble of infinite size; on the other, they could be applied to a microscopic element only if that element gave us an experimental certitude equal to that we would have with an ensemble of infinite size. Since a real infinite size actually given is contradictory, physical determinism could only be verified in the elements.

But it is just this necessity to verify experimentally in the elements the physical meaning of the determinist concept that is contested by some authors. The verification, they hold, consists not in demonstrating a determinism evident of itself, but to identify the elements that we know in advance to be entirely determined. In fact, is not to exist to be somewhere, that is, at a determined place and moment? If a corpuscle ceased to be determinately somewhere, it ceases to exist, and vice versa; since it is always, we must always know the follow-up to the trace: it is necessary that its trajectory have simultaneously determinate values of space and time, its trajectory must be continuous and its speed constant. It cannot have one or the other in isolation without ceasing to exist. Consequently, if we cannot in fact determine both the position and speed of a corpuscle, if we cannot simultaneously measure the initial values which enable us to determine its state at a given moment, that is because our knowledge of this corpuscle is still insufficient and we have not yet succeeded in identifying its absolute properties.

It is indeed this impossibility to determine at the same time the position and energetic state of a corpuscle that modern physics is up against.[3] The electron can have a determinate position, it can have a determinate speed, but it cannot have the two simultaneously. In knowing the one determinately we do not know the other. We are uncertain of the one to the degree that we are certain of the other. To the symbol of a value determinable by observation is joined a symbol one cannot determine. One could attribute this indetermination to errors of observation if it did not itself and in its fashion have a rigorously determined value, that namely of Planck, h, the quantum of action. In fact, when we take a couple of partner symbols, each of which is known with a certain determination, the product of the two indeterminations is constant. That is, if q is a coordinate, and p the quantity of motion, our uncertainty about q multiplied by our uncertainty about p is of the order of magnitude of h. Therefore this ignorance does not constitute an imperfection. In order to suppress the margin of indetermination totally, h would have to be nil. But Planck's constant is a definite and indivisible amount: 6.55 x 10 – 27 erg-seconds.

As Dirac says,

> It is generally supposed that in paying attention we can indefinitely reduce the disturbance that our observation entails. The concepts of *large* and *small* are then purely relative and refer to the delicacy of our means of observation as well as to the object described. To give an absolute value to size, such as is required by every theory concerning the ultimate structure of matter, it becomes necessary to suppose that there exists a limit to the finesse of our means of observation and to the smallness of the concomitant interference—a limit which is inherent in the nature of things and which could never be surpassed by a more perfect technique or by the greater ability of the observer.[4]

We can be surprised at having attained a limit, but there is no cause to be deceived. If the indetermination in question is purely subjective, how to explain that the product of the errors of two conjoined variables should be invariant—invariant as we know already by other procedures? Taking into account the size of *h*, we understand that they are negligible at the macroscopic scale of ordinary experience, but this does not prevent indetermination from being essential at the microcosmic level.

The determinist is thus frustrated at the two antipodes of the universe of the possibility of identifying his ideas. To identify determinism at the macrocosmic level, he would need an ensemble of infinite size. If he has recourse to the microscopic level as his last refuge, he would then need a quantity infinitely small in size. From the experimental point of view, the principle of physical causality is consequently a pure postulate whose justification requires impossible conditions.

We have already said that this principle completely abstracts from real time because it presupposes a perfect symmetry between the coordinates of space and the coordinate of time, which renders impossible any future that is not already determined. Whatever the moment in which one looks at the universe, be it in the past or toward the future, it is always identical with itself. The perspective changes nothing, such that time has no privileged direction; as Eddington says, there is no arrow. Such symmetry immobilizes the universe.[5]

But if time really advances, if there is a unique direction, there could not be perfect symmetry. Not only is the witness of our consciousness opposed to this indifference of direction, but the unique direction of time is experimentally defined in the degradation of energy. But it is to be noticed that if we remove from the second law of thermodynamics its statistical character, we also take from time its arrow, and entropy no longer has any objective meaning. There is then no choice between the statistical objective and the witness of consciousness. Moreover, if time could flow backward—something the physicist can only say is quite improbable—we would still say that the world *progresses* backward, that it *advances* into the past. If the determinist is right, this inversion is not absurd.

As a final refuge, the determinist could still say that the flow of the universe empties into an infinity of time in the past and in the future. Thus he would exclude the possibility of contradicting his fundamental postulate. But if, which is impossible, it were thus, it would follow that the extremities separated by an infinite time meet in the present. In this way one would obtain a universe whose duration would be comparable to that of the spiritual universe—a duration at once instantaneous, unlimited, without boundaries.

The hypothesis of a universe which is dissolving always and a future indefinitely remote is moreover contradicted by experience. This indefinite is excluded by the individual grains of energy engaged in the process of the world's degradation, the quanta, and by the impossibility of an infinite expansion of space. It would have to be the case that these grains of energy were infinite in number and that space was infinitely extended. If what we think are the ultimate constituents of the universe were indefinitely divisible, their limit would be zero; if space stretched to infinity, it tends toward infinity as a term to be reached, and it would also tend to zero. By whichever end one takes the universe, it empties into nothing: for it is important to remark that the zero savior of the proposed hypothesis is efficacious only if it represents a real value. If it is only a convenient symbol, it cannot serve the argument.

Moreover, if we have recourse to an accordion-universe which alternately dilates and contracts, which recommences indefinitely the process of organization and disorganization, we again lose ourselves in the same indefinite which incessantly takes away the definite term sought. Isn't it significant that determinism can only be established by that which it rightly wants to avoid: the undetermined that is the indefinite?

We have given an example of some of the concrete difficulties that determinism faces. It is customary today to say that if one must abandon it, it nonetheless had its value as a working hypothesis. But being given on the one hand the inevitable disastrous consequences that it entails in domains other than that of physics, and on the other hand that a hypothesis does not deserve the name of scientific except by at least the remote possibility of being verified by experience, one can ask in what sense this hypothesis was legitimate. If the value of absolute determinism depends on an impossible experience, how can we call it a working hypothesis?

No one would wish to contest, without making certain distinctions, "that a natural phenomenon, whatever it be, being given, the experimenter would never be able to admit that there is a variation in the expression of this phenomenon unless at the same time certain new conditions had advened in its manifestation." When one knows to what order of phenomena Claude Bernard applies this principle, one would have to be a charlatan to cast doubt on it. That is because the modern experimenter takes into account that it had been possible to recognize a variation in the expression without new conditions advening. But when Bernard adds, "moreover, [the experimenter] has apriori certitude that these variations are determined by rigorous and mathematical relations," and that he wants to extend this to every observable phenomenon, one must ask whence comes this certitude?[6] And if he has said "the doubter is the true scientist," where did he get the evidence for the universal value of absolute determinism for every natural phenomenon? The true scientist is reputed to have apriori consciousness. And it must be admitted, too, that if experimental science is an absolute science, it should also follow that its principles and the matter on which they bear are absolute. But how can we know that experimental science is an absolute science? That is the problem that cannot be supposed to be resolved apriori. The true scientist seeks the absolute where he can find it. He has no doubt *about science,* but he should ask himself if the matter studied conforms to the demands of absolute science. If mathematics is absolute, if it has a hypothetical necessity, how can we know if the stuff of the world is adjusted to that necessity? Isn't that the whole problem of determinism? Let us add that if an individual has a certitude apriori and unreasoned of the transcendental value of the principle of physical causality, it is clearly useless to discuss it. There remains only for him to rejoice in what he ought to consider his fatal superiority.

It is just because the transcendental range of this principle is not evident apriori that it must be submitted to experience. And if this experience is impossible, in what sense is its transcendence a scientific hypothesis? The most convinced modern determinists agree in affirming that the experimental truth of the principle of physical causality cannot be demonstrated by abstract arguments; they await its experimental confirmation.[7] But it is the possibility of that experimental confirmation that we question.

Absolute determinism proposes to submit to experience the hypothesis that the truth of the future is entirely present. But it is not the known present that can confirm it. If the future was entirely present to us, the principle of physical causality would serve for nothing. For it to have sense, it is necessary that the present truth of the future be future with respect to us. If the truth of the future were manifestly present, the principle would have no need of being confirmed by present experience. That is to say that, on the one hand, the value of the principle which affirms the present truth of the future depends on a non-present future whose truth aimed at by the principle is known for certain only if this future is effectively present; and, on the other hand, as soon as this future is present with respect to us, it does not meet the conditions necessary for the confirmation which would render the principle valuable for every future. Presence is not of itself evidence about the future. It is as future that the future was not present, and not as effectively present.

The experimental demonstration of physical causality should therefore consist in suppressing the future by the future, to make the future evident in the present by the non-evident future.

It is indeed time that rebels against determinism. Even if the entire past had realized its hopes, the future will still be uncertain, although the determinist will no doubt have acquired the habit of certitude. It is against an acquired habit and not against evidence that one must battle even in the most remarkable of contemporary physicists who are unable to resign themselves to the facts. One can see this clearly when indeterminism in quantum mechanics is discussed. There are those who pretend that one could only abandon the principle of physical causality if the principle of indetermination permitted a complete description of phenomena. This involves multiple beggings of the question. It supposes that universal determinism has been sufficiently confirmed, or that it can be confirmed in the future; that the principle of indeterminism is admissible only if it is a principle of determinism; that a complete description of phenomena is a strictly causal description. There can be no question of abandoning a position which has never been established, and could not be. An indeterminist description of phenomena is complete only if phenomena are in themselves absolutely determined, which is not susceptible of being demonstrated.

As Eddington says, it is determinism, postulating more than is necessary to explain phenomena, which ought to be justified, not indeterminism. It is the determinist who pretends to omniscience, since he claims to know what we cannot know. How indeed does he know that the indeterminist passes the limit in affirming that, even if there were ineluctable laws in nature, the method to which experimental science is restricted would never enable him to know them? Isn't it because he pretends to a determined knowledge of the unknown? Should science be resolving problems that cannot be posed?

It would be ridiculous to say that indeterminism abandons truth to the caprices of the scientist, as if one meant that ignorance on our part corresponds to an indetermination in nature. This generalization made by certain philosophers sufficiently shows that they do not understand the question.

If the greatest regularity that we can observe is susceptible of being explained by statistics, why ask for more? Is it not just rigor that forbids us to postulate more than is absolutely necessary to explain phenomena? Is it not determinism that is insufficient because it is too demanding?

To use the analogy of cause, it is indeed in the statistical explanation that we attain the cause of phenomena, since it permits us to *construct* a regularity, a determination tending toward the absolute from undetermined elements. It is a way of entering into the intimacy of phenomena and comprehending them. Determinism, on the contrary, is not constructive but tautological; it keeps us on the surface of things and it poses apriori an irrational which prevents us from penetrating into the reason of phenomena.

This idea might appear paradoxical. Isn't it by positing indetermination that we posit the irrational? And doesn't determinism suppose a pure intelligibility on the side of things? No Thomist would be surprised by this paradox. Into transcendentally intelligible being the pure indetermination of prime matter enters, at once intelligible and unintelligible depending on the angle under which one regards it. To say that it is in itself purely intelligible would be to turn it into an absolute, as did David of Dinant; it would be to deny at the same time the intelligible and to posit an absolute materialism. To say that it is absolutely irrational would be to identify it with nothing, that is, with the impossible. By contrast, if we regard it in the perspective of the act to which it has a transcendental relation, it is in being, and intelligible in its order to act; matter is nothing else but this order. That is why the opinion that maintains the possibility of a subsistent matter implicitly maintains the possibility of the impossible.[8]

It has been claimed that statistics supposes on the side of the elements of the ensemble a rigorous determinism. I have never understood this objection. So I cannot pretend to refute it. I will nonetheless seek to put forward an incontestable fact which could relate to the difficulty. One cannot quarrel with the success of statistical predictions. And note that it is a question of predictions and not of observations after the fact. Before throwing the die, I do not know which facet will appear each time. But that ignorance does not prevent me from predicting that out of six thousand tosses, the six facets will be rather equally distributed. All I have to know beforehand is the number of alternatives, the equiprobability of these alternatives, and the independence of individual throws. If my prediction is not verified within certain limits, I will conclude that the die is loaded rather than suspect the calculus. If the alternatives are not equiprobable, that is, if there is not perfect indetermination in the limits of the determinate number of alternatives, my prediction will be false. The regularity predicted is thus conditioned by the indifference of the individual elements that enter into play. If I arrive at a determination despite my ignorance, why couldn't nature gain this determination despite the indifference of each try taken singly? In doing so, she would be acting quite reasonably.

Isn't this coincidence due to chance? Isn't it chance that would have to be taken away if there were no coincidence? Speaking strictly, the laws of chance are not laws of chance. When the probability is not realized, then chance comes into play. The law of large numbers could not apply to the elements unless these elements are indifferent. Thus it presents an analogy with free will whose determination presupposes indifference. But I will not press an analogy which has already caused so many misunderstandings and which would need to be clarified in a special study.

In the way we have described it in its formula and consequences, it is sufficiently clear that the principle of physical causality is far from being synonymous with causality as we speak of it in philosophy. It seems to me that the causality of which one should speak in philosophy of science apropos of the experimental sciences uniquely resembles the formal causality that we find in a pure state in mathematics. It expresses only the metric coherence of phenomena. In indeterminism, this coherence is not rigorous; it tends toward rigor and the symmetry of space-time. Not only does the determinist conceive it as rigorous and mathematical, but he converts it into a species of efficient cause; he substitutes a causality that can have no sense in experimental science, no more than final causality can.[9]

We have also remarked that the determinist speaks of physical entities as of things entirely determined in themselves; he gives them, as do the majority of modern scholastics, a directly ontological sense. But we forget that the things of experimental science can only be attained if they are registered in number-measures. For that in the things which permits this registering—and it is important not to forget the distance that separates that which permits and the result—is not the whole of the thing: it is only its measurable aspect. From metric cuts one cannot conclude to ontological cuts. The sun and the moon are not two substantial beings because distant and separated from one another by a void. The distance and the void as defined in experimental science are not susceptible of an immediate ontological transposition. In this way one would arrive at an atomistic philosophy of nature. The fundamental entities of physics symbolize only metric cuts in things of which they represent only an aspect. It is absurd to consider an atom as a thing. These entities are real only in the manner of a smile. It is as senseless to speak of the hylomorphic composition of body as understood in physics as to speak of the hylomorphic compositions of a smile, even if the smile finds its ultimate cause in rationality, and that presupposes matter and form; it is as absurd as to ask if the counterpoint realized in the execution of a symphony is composed of prime matter and form.

But it is time to turn to the strictly philosophical problem of indeterminism as it arises in metaphysics and philosophy of nature.

II

We have seen that the physicist envisaged purely as such can never formulate experimentally determinist laws even if they exist in nature. But if this principle is unverifiable in experience, could one not have recourse to another method to demonstrate its at least theoretical value? Haven't scholastics admitted determinism in nature, putting aside evidentially the intervention of free agents in the course of the phenomena?

This is what Suarez and Vasquez, among others, maintain. They agree in affirming that, if one abstracts from the intervention of a free agent, all of nature comes about with necessity, even chance, such that every event is perfectly foreseeable by an intellect which knows sufficiently the ensemble of natural causes that enter into play.[10] For Suarez, chance phenomena—as opposed to fortuitous phenomena—are not contingent in the strict sense, but only in an extrinsic and relative (*secundum quid*) manner. The initial constellation of the world prolongs itself in accidental encounters which are contingent in the same way as the constellation itself. There is contingency there, either because God could have not created it, or because he could have created another. But once given "such a constellation, the accidental encounters are as necessary as the constellation in which they are already given. Whether God acts freely or with absolute necessity, the necessity of these accidental crossings of per se causal lines would not have been affected."[11] These encounters are *accidents by accident,* being contingent only with respect to their proximate causes and not with respect to the total constellation of nature. This contingency is extrinsic, because it does not come from the intrinsic power of the natural agent, but from an outside obstacle.[12]

Vasquez distinguishes two species of future contingents: "some which come entirely from the natural cause" and these are perfectly necessary and foreseeable; others "which first and proximately, or at least remotely depend on free will" are neither necessary nor foreseeable by a created intellect, even when they are determinately true.[13]

No need to point out that this position leads logically to the Occasionalism of Malebranche, the preestablished harmony of Leibnitz and his distinction between the absolutely necessary and the hypothetically necessary applied to natural contingency.

It seems to me that the majority of contemporary Thomists see nothing strange in these ideas, provided that they are only applied to the contingency in nature. Do they not say that the laws of nature are hypothetically necessary, meaning by that that they are necessary only if no obstacle arises? If the obstacle is not due to a free agent, there is both contingency and necessity—that is, that there will be future contingents predetermined in their causes and foreseeable.

These odd concessions take us a long way from Aristotle and St. Thomas. One could say that, in order to make them up to date, we sometimes forget the most elementary and fundamental principles.

The doctrine of St. Thomas, which was inspired directly by Aristotle, is constant on this point: a contingent effect is an effect which was not predetermined in its cause. When this cause determines itself to the effect, it is free; when the effect has no cause per se, it is fortuitous if the accidental cause is a free agent, it is chance if the agent is purely natural. We call an effect fortuitous or by chance when it is not one, per se. If it has only accidental unity, its cause is necessarily undetermined.

Everything that comes from such undetermined causes is a future contingent and absolutely unforeseeable, as opposed to necessary futures which are entirely determined in their causes and which nothing can impede.

There is therefore no compromise possible. If there are natural future contingents, such futures are neither necessary nor foreseeable. If a future effect is necessary, consequently foreseeable, it is not contingent.

But, it may be objected, a cause and an effect can be at once necessary and contingent. This is the case with every creature. Even the necessary future, being finite, will be contingent. Therefore there are some necessary future contingents. *Nihil enim adeo est contingens, quin in se aliquid necessarium habeat.*

Let us distinguish first of all absolute necessity and conditional or hypothetical necessity. We call absolutely necessary that which in its very nature is determined only to be. Thus God is absolutely necessary, but there is also absolute necessity in creatures.

> Although everything depends on the will of God, as on its first cause, which, apart from the hypothesis of an anterior design, acts without necessity, it must not be denied, for this reason, that there is absolute necessity in creatures; which would lead us inevitably to say that all beings are contingent. What might make us adopt this opinion, is the fact that beings do not come from their causes in virtue of absolute necessity, since there are contingent effects which proceed from their cause without necessity.
>
> Among created beings, there are some whose existence is simply and absolutely necessary. Indeed, one can say simply and absolutely that those things must exist of which it is impossible that they not exist. God has given existence to things which, by reason of their nature, can not exist, and that comes from the matter which is in them and is in potency to another form. Therefore, beings in which there is no matter, or those whose matter is not in potency to another form, are such that it is impossible for them not to exist. Therefore it is simply and absolutely necessary that they exist.[14]

It is absolutely impossible that things with a simple essence be corruptible, absolutely impossible that this man not be a rational animal, that my soul should be mortal, that when Socrates runs he is not running. We see here how this necessity is attached to duration. Excluded are all beings whose substantial duration is successive and continuous and which are not measured by *aevum*—the duration that measures things changeless in their being. The example of Socrates is based on his presence. That he runs does not mean that he ran or will run.

There is hypothetical necessity in God as well as in creatures. For, although God wills nothing absolutely and necessarily with respect to the effects He produces, He cannot now not will that which it is supposed He has willed, since His will is immutable and His act is measured by eternity. Therefore He could never not will anything that He wills. *Numquid potuit non velle quidquid voluit.* So it is hypothetically necessary that He has willed all that He has willed and will will.[15] Or, if one wishes, it is absolutely necessary that if He wills, this will is hypothetically necessary. Hypothetical does not mean here that this will could have been not necessary—if He wills, it is absolutely necessary that He wills—but that God does not will the creature by a necessity of nature, that He could have not willed him, that since all eternity He has freely decreed that the creature be. This necessity is also opposed to the possible, in this sense that it is impossible that a hypothetical necessity not be necessary.

This insistence will seem strange to a reader who is not aware of the meaning nowadays assigned to these two necessities. One speaks, in effect, of hypothetically necessary futures: these would be futures which are necessary only if certain conditions are realized. But this is a contradiction in terms. For if the conditions are not necessary, the future tied to them participates in their contingency. If the conditions are given in fact, and if the future is necessarily linked to them, it is absolutely necessary with respect to those conditions; hypothetically, because with respect to the non-necessary cause in which these conditions were not determined. The hypothetical refers to the remote antecedent cause which was neither necessarily determined to this effect (the divine freedom), and not to the proximate determined cause (the determined divine will). *If* God wills, the willed follows of absolute necessity; it is absolutely impossible that the will of God not be realized. The hypothetical necessary refers in no way to the present or to the future, considered as such. With respect to this proximate cause, the future is either absolutely necessary or contingent; there is no intermediary. The hypothetical is inseparable from the necessity. With respect to the determined divine will, all futures are absolutely necessary, which, as we know, does not in any way destroy the contingency of certain futures with respect to created non-necessary causes.

Hypothetical necessity is an authentic necessity opposed to the possible as well as to the impossible, and not a necessity which could be non-necessary, or that is necessary only in certain conditions; we might as well say that if these conditions are not realized, the necessity is not necessary. Therefore the necessity depends on conditions and as long as they are not given, there is no necessity; if a thing is necessary in such conditions wherein it is absolutely necessary in those conditions which, moreover, might not be given and it is with respect to the non-necessary cause of the conditions, whence it was possible before being necessary at least with logical anteriority that the thing linked to those conditions is only hypothetically necessary. When that which is now hypothetically necessary with respect to this remote cause was not, it had no hypothetical necessity. It is absolutely necessary that this dog be mortal, but it is only hypothetically necessary that it exist, otherwise it could not not exist. But to say that the death of the dog is only hypothetically necessary is either to utter the truism, "the death of this dog is not absolutely necessary, because if he had not existed he could not die," or "the death of this dog is only hypothetically necessary because it could not die"—which is a contradiction in terms, for if it could not die, this is because it is not necessary that it die, that is, the hypothesis "this dog will die" is not necessary. But what is hypothetical is the existence of the dog; but once he exists, it is absolutely impossible that he not die. And if we say that death is only hypothetically necessary, we mean that it would be rather difficult to die if he did not exist.

There is a possibility that is opposed uniquely to the impossible and which is implied in the necessary. "There is a possibility that necessity itself presupposes. In fact, that which exists necessarily *can* exist, for it is impossible that that which cannot exist, exist, and that of which it is impossible to exist necessarily does not exist. Therefore (if one denies this possibility implied by necessity), that which ought necessarily to exist, necessarily does not exist; but that is absurd. Therefore it is repugnant that the existence of a thing be necessary and that, moreover, this thing could not exist. Therefore, necessity of existence supposes its possibility."[16] In this way, all existent beings are possible.

Like the necessary, the possible is opposed to the impossible, but there is a possibility which is opposed to the necessary. Such is the possibility of creatures insofar as God can will them. Creatures are necessarily possible, but this possibility does not entail necessity of the existence which depends on the divine will. It is with respect to the possibility opposed to the necessary that creatures are called contingent, and necessary by hypothesis only. This contingency is therefore not opposed to necessity *tout court*, but only to absolute necessity. And thus a thing can be both contingent and necessary, that is, necessary without being absolutely necessary.

There is, finally, a possibility that is opposed both to absolute necessity and to hypothetical necessity, that is, to necessity as necessity, namely that a being can exist and not exist: *prout dicitur possibile quod potest esse et non esse.* Beings which have in their essence this *possibilitas ad non-esse* are called contingent in the strict sense. But when we say that a thing is possible or contingent in this sense, this is not only, as some suppose, because it is sometimes in potency and sometimes in act, for in that way even the necessary could be possible and contingent: every future would be contingent. On this hypothesis, the necessarily corruptible would not be necessarily corruptible.

The possible or contingent opposed to all necessity has the characteristic of not being necessary while it is not yet, and that because such an effect does not proceed necessarily from its cause, because it is not predetermined in its cause. So it is that we say that it is contingent that Socrates will sit, but he will die necessarily, for the reason that the second effect results with all necessity from its cause, and not the first. Thus when we say that Socrates will die, the possibility or contingency opposed to necessity disappears.[17]

It is insufficient to say therefore that the necessary is that which will always be—this distinction has no value because it is a posteriori: it is not because a thing is or has been that it was necessary—for a thing is not necessary because it will always be, but it will always be because it is necessary. Nor is it sufficient to distinguish the necessary and the possible according to extrinsic obstacles (*secundum exteriora prohibentia*) which would impede the necessary from being necessary; for a thing is not necessary because it encounters no obstacles, but because it is necessary it cannot be impeded.[18]

That is why it is absurd to apply to the contingent thus understood the hypothetical necessity which is a posteriori. One cannot say of a thing that it was necessary because it is now necessary.

The hypothetical necessity of which Aristotle speaks[19] goes from consequent to antecedent, and not vice versa. If the consequent is given, it is now necessary that the antecedent has been and that it has caused. The foundation of this necessity which binds the antecedent to the consequent comes not from the antecedent; it is extrinsic to it; the necessity goes from the consequent to the antecedent. *Quod habet necessitatem ab eo quod est posterius in esse, est necessarium ex conditione.* If there were conversion of terms, if the proximate cause was necessary, there would be an absolutely necessary reciprocal relation. *Necessitas quae dependet ex causis prioribus, est necessitas absoluta. Quod habet necessitatem ex causa formali, vel ex causa efficiente, est necessarium absolute.*[20]

That is why hypothetical necessity never concerns the future; for the future which proceeds from a proximate principle with necessity comes about with absolute necessity. It is in relation to a remote principle that the future is only hypothetically necessary. Once given its hypothetically necessary proximate principle, the future which comes from it necessarily is, with respect to this principle, absolutely necessary.[21] Let us consider a concrete case to bring out the paradox implicit in this idea. It is absolutely necessary that, if there exists a universe of space-time, men will one day exist, without whom a material universe is contradictory; moreover, this universe, abstraction made from man, is only hypothetically necessary. How can a hypothetical necessity entail absolute necessity? And how can this same absolute necessity entail, under another aspect, the absolute necessity of that which is only hypothetically necessary? That is the whole difficulty of the necessity conditional on the end. It must be resolved by the distinction between the order of intention and the order of execution. In the order of intention, the end is primary. Made determinate by intention, this end is hypothetically necessary with respect to its free cause, but absolutely necessary with respect to the will which is hypothetically necessary with respect to the hypothetically necessary will of this cause. But he who wills the end wills the means necessary for the end. In this perspective, the means are absolutely necessary with respect to the hypothetically necessary end. But in the order of execution, the end is realized last. This time, it is the means that are hypothetically necessary; that is, if the means are not realized, the end will not be. But once given the means in the order of execution, the realization of the end will follow with absolute necessity; if not, the given means are impossible. In neither of the two perspectives does hypothetical necessity involve the future. With respect to the end fixed in intention, the means are absolutely necessary; with respect to the means realized, the end to be executed is again absolutely necessary.

From a strictly philosophical point of view, "laws of nature" means either the natures as measured by eternal law, or these same natures as measures of the activity by which natural beings achieve and accomplish their end. It is the latter meaning that occupies us now, one in which the laws of nature are called laws only by analogy—unlike the natural or moral law.

Let us note right off that if eternal law—that is, the *ratio gubernationis rerum in Deo sicut in principe universitatis existens*—is changeless, its immutability does not exclude from things the contingency opposed both to the absolutely necessary and to the hypothetically necessary. No need to insist here on this compatibility characteristic of the divine causality which sustains Thomistic metaphysics. But, as soon as it is a question of the participated laws in the universe which are identified with natures—and note that nature is not law insofar as intrinsic and thus necessary measure, but as measure of the motion distinct from it of which it is the principle and cause—it is impossible that they necessitate the activities which spring from the nature without nature ceasing to be nature and the laws becoming contradictory. In fact, if these laws necessitated activities, they would no longer be laws, for necessity considered in itself is above the law—*necessitas non subditur legi.* If natures could infallibly attain their ends only by means of activities entirely predetermined in their causes, they would be forms and matters entirely determined *ad unum,* they could not be intrinsic causes of motion—motion being taken here in its proper sense. An entirely determined form is not a nature; a totally actuated matter is contradictory. If future activities were perfectly predetermined in the nature, they would no longer be *ordinanda,* but *ordinata;* the nature would be the intrinsic measure of these activities and would no longer be law. To be sure the nature-measure is perfect insofar as it is itself determined *ad unum,* insofar as the operations are more intimate and immanent, but if they could attain to that species of identity toward which their increasing interiorization obliquely tends, natures would cease to be laws and natures. They aspire to a determination more and more one, to necessity, to repose in an immobile activity. Works will be called natural in the measure of their unity and according to how they enclose themselves within the limits of determination; they will be contingent insofar as they exceed these limits, that is, insofar as they escape laws and nature is not the cause.[22]

The expression which is so abused, "the hypothetically necessary laws of nature," can mean two things: that necessarily they conduct universal nature toward its end, or that the laws which lead to this end are necessary in the sense that they rigorously measure the concrete by which nature relates to its term—they would thus be analogous to the postulates of mathematics. In the first case, non-necessary laws could lead the world to its end, unless its intrinsic end was not the best possible—if it is necessary to build a house, it is not necessary to use bricks. In the second case, only the necessitating laws could lead to this end—it would be necessary to use bricks and not wood or stone.

In its turn, "hypothetically necessary" could signify that *some* laws are necessary, if the end willed is posed, that is, that there must be natures; or that the laws given in the order of execution will lead the world to its end with hypothetical necessity. Taken in this latter sense, "hypothetically necessary laws of nature" is a contradiction in terms. For if the laws aim at the future with necessity, this necessary can only be absolute. Therefore, it would be necessary to say rather that the laws of nature are absolutely necessary.

This expression could only make sense if it designated the eternal law and the hypothetical necessity of the divine decrees in which the future is absolutely determined. There, it will be said, is a hypothetical necessity that governs the future. But this necessity is eternal and consequently is ahead (*devance*) of the future from which it draws infallibly every determination without necessitating it. It does not have to rejoin in the future whose truths will add nothing to the truth of the decrees, although in natures not every future is determinately true unless one recommends the doctrine according to which the future contingent is determinately true. For the rest, the necessity of eternal law could never justify a hypothetical necessity of the laws of nature. That would presuppose in the secondary causes, where this end would be subjectively predetermined, an immediate transposition of the intrinsic end of the world as eternally fixed in the immutable will of God.

Just as the necessity of willing happiness in general does not deprive us of liberty, and that this does not prevent us from attaining infallibly an absolutely determined end, so the laws of nature, without being absolutely necessary, necessarily conduct to its end. There are then determined limits, but within these limits there is play; these laws then are neither purely contingent nor absolute. They are, consequently, truly natural, that is, never perfectly determined *ad unum*. As has been said, the being whose form is entirely determined in itself is not natural.

That is why speculative reason cannot deduce the concrete laws which are nothing but individual natures, where matter is never sufficiently subjected to assure the efficacy of the measure. Let us not join those who with indiscreet zeal allow the principle of identity to be breached: if no intrinsic or extrinsic obstacle were opposed to the nature, it would necessarily be efficacious. There is for that same idea a more happy formula which displays the truism: if nature is efficacious, it cannot not be efficacious. What else does the following series of words mean: a natural cause produces its effect necessarily providing it encounters no obstacle? If that made sense, one could say of every future contingent that it is hypothetically necessary. For example, if Socrates does not die tomorrow, it is necessary that tomorrow he live.

Let us pass on now to another point of view. As we have already indicated, St. Thomas distinguishes necessary forms from contingent forms. Necessary forms are entirely determined and constitute themselves essences, the pure spirits, and forms which determine their matter sufficiently so as to be inseparable from it, the celestial bodies of a surpassed astronomy, and those of men in the future definitive state of the universe. The forms of corruptible beings are contingent forms. Among these we can distinguish those which are entirely corruptible *secundum totum et secundum partem,* and those which are partially corruptible—like men, in the present state of the world. Thus we have absolutely contingent forms and forms contingent *secundum quid.* Natural beings are contingent because there is in them a real potency to non-being, prime matter.

What exactly do we understand by contingency of the form? In fact, a form is not contingent because its essential co-principle is for it the possibility of non-being; the composite is corruptible because its form is contingent. It is the contingency of the form that is the intrinsic reason for the precariousness and uncertainty of existence. That is why we can conceive a form which would not be contingent despite its union with matter, the human form after the resurrection when the composite will be incorruptible.

Thus it remains that the form is contingent because it is not sufficiently determined in itself. Moreover, it is the defect of determination and incapacity to individuate itself that calls for matter, and which ultimately causes the essential complexity of mobile being. The existence of the cosmic essence will be in its manner complex, that is, successive and continuous. In fact, the nature of existence is measured by the nature of the essence. *Quantum unicuique inest de forma, tantum inest ei de virtute essendi.* If the form is not necessary, its existence cannot be totally assured.

This need that form has for matter introduces into it an irreducible obscurity. We cannot have a distinct idea of the cosmic form independent of the idea of the composite; even the separated human form implies a relation to matter. And the matter that enters into this idea is not determined without signifying as well determinability with reference to an infinity of other forms. A non-subsisting form is not a quiddity in the strict sense. That is to say that the different sub-species, the species of dog, the species of elephant, cannot be absolutely opposed as are the species-individuals which are the pure spirits; that is to say as well that definition will include the notion of matter. If they were determined in matter, there would be an independent idea of matter for each of them, and that would no longer be pure potency; there would be a *latitatio formarum* or all forms would advene *ab extrinseco,* such that the existent varieties are analogous to the divisions made in the continuum which are determinately true only a posteriori. Consequently, the determination that is a material form is yet to be so far as determination goes. If it were completely given in advance, generation for example would be a pure releasing into existence of a form already determined in the matter.[23]

Two neighboring angelic forms are infinitely close in this that they admit no intermediary species; they are as infinitely remote insofar as a transition from one species to another is impossible, for they communicate in no physical genus: they are absolutely heterogeneous. On the contrary, natural sub-species are infinitely close because of their common natural genus, and infinitely distant by the real possibility of an infinity of other intermediary sub-species. Thus the vegetable realm has no absolute extreme limits. Between the most perfect of plants that exists and the lowest animal, there is the possibility of an infinity of more perfect plants and of less perfect animals, even if this infinity is incompossible from the point of view of existence. Natural species should be conceived as zones of probability. No given natural and individual form is an absolute type of a sub-species, nor any sub-species of its natural species. The dog, the carrot, are statistical entities like the French and the English. None of the elements exhausts the essence of its class. (That is why racism which erects nations into absolute entities, and its contrary, atomism, are forms of determinism. The satirical poet was right to say that "All men are fools, despite their cares, they only differ as more and less." For rational man, too, is only a statistical entity.)

All corruptible forms are contingent, but compared with one another they are not contingent in equal measure. A form is determined *ad unum* depending on its perfection and to the degree that it responds to the appetite of matter. But the more perfect a determination, the more unique it is. The pure spirit whose essence is entirely determined is absolutely unique as species and individual. In the same manner, natural forms approach necessity to the degree that they emerge more from matter. Perfection is refractory to subdivision and diffusion. The more perfect a species, the more demanding it is, the easier mistakes. Nature thus tends toward essential necessity, toward a quidditative determination more and more heterogeneous. That is why the wise (*sapientes*) are both rare and more different among themselves than the run of men (*homines ut in pluribus*); that is to say that with respect to the species they are more probable, but by contrast when we attend to individuals, the wise are extremely improbable.[24]

The more one rises in the hierarchy of species, the more forms become necessary and consequently intelligible. *Quanto magis distant a materia, tanto magis necessariae.* But only the human form will have a totally assured existence, because it is spiritual and because its duration, putting aside the time entailed by its union with matter, is eviternal.

Consequently, an intelligence subjected to time and which contemplates the universe in its beginnings, or whose vision is bounded by lower natural forms, could see or predict with absolute certitude the human form alone. Its knowledge of intermediate sub-species would be always more or less conjectural. All the sub-species were, at a certain moment in the existence of the world and in a more or less greater degree, future contingents. This spirit could predict infallibly vegetative and animal life, but it would not know determinately all the ways they would be realized.

Thus we see in what sense there is necessity in nature and in the maturation of the world, and in what sense there is contingency. There is necessity because of the end; there is a necessity of means, as in the case of freedom. But the means that will be effectively engaged in the order of execution are not rigorously predetermined in the original sketch of the world.

The problem of contingency in the world is not there limited to that of chance and fortune, which are extreme cases and are accidental causes, that is, entirely undetermined. There is contingency where the cause is natural and per se, because a natural cause is never determined to the point of rendering its effect absolutely certain, but only in the majority of cases, *ut in pluribus.* The contingency of chance is possible only because of the contingency of nature. If nature were necessary, chance would be impossible. "In his enim quae in minori parte accidunt dicuntur esse fortuna et casus. Si autem non provenirent aliqua in minori parte, omnia ex necessitate acciderent; nam ea quae sunt contingentia ut in pluribus in hoc solo a necessariis differunt quod possunt in minori parte deficere." Events which proceed from nature are events "quae *contingunt* ut in pluribus." They are contingent because before they are given, there is always the possibility of an accident. *Contingens est quod potest deficere.* That is why, with Aristotle, we must distinguish the contingency of nature from the contingency of chance.

> To be contingent has two senses: on the one hand that which arrives more often but without necessity is called contingent; for example, greying in man, the fact of growing and declining and, in a general fashion, whatever proceeds from nature. In fact, none of that has a constant necessity, for man does not live always (the duration of his life is not determined). But if man exists, that will necessarily come about, or at least most often. In another sense, the undetermined is called contingent, that is, that which can be or not be; for example, an animal walks, and while he walks there is an earthquake, or in a general way, all that happens by chance. For none of that is destined by nature to take place in one way rather than in another. (*Prior Analytics,* I, 12)

Frequency is a sign of a determinate reason and orientation, of a constancy in the cause and of unity. For it does not suffice that a phenomenon be produced outside the intention of the agent in order to be by chance or fortuitous. For example, a man drinks wine with a view to pleasure he finds in it; if that drink inebriates always or frequently, drunkenness will not be fortuitous or by chance; on the contrary, it will be an accident only if it happens rarely.[25]

> Fortune and chance are accidental causes in things susceptible of producing neither absolutely nor frequently, and beside susceptible of being produced with a view to an end. But they differ in this that chance has more extension; indeed every effect of fortune is by chance, but not

> everything that is by chance is fortuitous. Indeed, there is fortune and effects of fortune to whatever happy fortune can be attributed and in general practical activity. So there is fortune necessarily in the objects of practical activity. A proof is that one considers good fortune as identical, or almost identical, with happiness; but happiness is a certain practical activity since it is achieved practical activity. And so beings which cannot act practically cannot moreover produce any fortuitous effect. Whence it results that no inanimate being, no beast or infant, is the cause of fortuitous effects, because it has not the faculty of choosing; no more are they susceptible of happy fortune or misfortune, unless metaphorically. . . . As for chance, it belongs to animals and to many inanimate beings; thus one says that the arrival of a horse is by chance when that by that arrival he achieves safety without having had safety in view. Another example: the fall of a tripod is by chance if after its fall it is upright and can serve as a seat. Thus one finds it in the realm of things which take place absolutely in view of an end, when things happen without having been the intended result and having their final cause outside of it, then we speak of effects of chance; and of effects of fortune in all those effects of chance which, belonging to the genus of things susceptible of being chosen, attaining beings capable of choice [free]. (*Physics*, II, 5 and 6)

St. Thomas expresses the foundation of this distinction in the following terms: *eorum quae sunt a casu, causa est* intrinseca, *sicut eorum quae sunt a natura; eorum vero quae sunt a fortuna, causa est extrinseca, sicut eorum quae sunt a proposito.*[26]

Chance and fortune are accidental causes, that is, undetermined. The reason given is analytic: *omne quod est per se, habet causam; quod autem est per accidens, non habet causam, quia non est vere ens, cum non sit vere unum.*[27] Socrates the architect is the determinate cause of this house; that he has a pimple on his nose might have a determinate cause, but that the cause of the house has a pimple on his nose, that is accidental, for it is not in the nature of the architect to have a pimple on his nose. Otherwise, the architect could not construct a house without having a pimple on his nose. Therefore, this meeting of two determinate causes in the construction of a house could not have a determinate cause unless pimples were essential to architecture and architecture to pimples. The reason for this conjunction is undetermined.

"The per se cause is determined, the accidental cause indefinite, for the multitude of possible accidents is an infinite thing."[28] "It follows that it is matter, which is susceptible of being other than what it is, which is the cause of the accident." Just as when a man chooses to do something, and it happens that another thing comes about that is not necessarily linked to that choice, this conjunction is fortuitous. The cause will be undetermined, namely the imperfection of his act of will which cannot extend to a number of deeds sufficiently large nor control all the concomitant circumstances. Only the divine will is above all fortune.

If the effect truly has no unity, it is impossible to track it back to a determinate cause, it is impossible that it be predetermined. If it was not determined in its cause, it was unforeseeable. One can indeed trace the series of determined causes which enter into play to a certain point, but not indefinitely; in the absence of that, nature as nature will be chance, and the determined will will be fortune.

> For example, the living will necessarily die, for it already carries within it the condition of its death, namely the presence of contraries in the same body. But in reality, be it by sickness or a violent death, one knows not, it will be only if some other event comes about. It is therefore clear that it is taken back to a principle, which is reduced to no other. That will be the principle of all that is due to chance; this principle will not itself have been produced by any other cause. (*Metaphysics,* VI, 3)

Because of the matter that it does not succeed in subjecting to itself, nature exists in danger. That is why St. Thomas considers the existence of every natural form as the result of a victory over matter. "In quibus vero forma non complet totam materiae potentiam, remanet adhuc materia in potentia ad aliam formam; et ideo non est in eis necessitas essendi; sed virtus essendi consequitur in eis victoriam formae super maeriam."[29] St. Thomas can speak of a victory here for the nature is the *intrinsic* principle of motion and rest. This manner of speaking would be absurd in the geometrical conception which Suarez and Vasquez advocate on the subject of contingency. For Suarez, as for the Stoics, "extrinsece dicitur effectus contingens, quando carentia necessitatis quae in illo est, solum est ab extrinsecis impedimentis" (*Disputationes Metaphysicae,* paragraph 4). But if, on the one hand, that which can be impeded can necessarily be impeded, and if extrinsic impeding be produced necessarily, this encounter is necessary and the effect foreseeable: "Talis effectus consideratus in ordine ad totam seriem et collectionem talium causarum, non habet contingentiam, sed necessitatem" (ibid., paragraph 5). On this hypothesis, the cosmic drama of St. Thomas is pure anthropomorphism for he is going to have to substitute the bees under the jurisdiction of a more sober Malebranche, and a providence which now is at rest after having made for us round heads with a view to berets. This solution evidently has the advantage of being clear, and quite finely extended by *thinkers ut in pluribus*—at least as more scientific than that of Aquinas who would be astonished to see clearly that which is unintelligible in itself.

We know already that St. Thomas explicitly rejects this kind of necessity and contingency. The case cited by Suarez is moreover an example of necessary violence which has nothing to do with contingency formally understood. For St. Thomas there can only be perfect necessity in the works of nature if we abstract from matter—at once the principle of individuation and of contingency[30]—which enters into every work of nature and without which nature would not be nature. Not only form is called nature, but matter and the composite are as well. In beings where form alone is the principle of activity, this form is not called nature, and its activity is not motion, but quality. Nature is determined *ad unum*, but if it were absolutely so, it would no longer be nature: it could not be generative. That is why *id quod est ut in pluribus est causa entis per accidens.* Chance is nothing other than unsubjected matter insofar as it is the undetermined cause of an accidental coincidence. *Defectus ejus quod est ut in pluribus, est propter materiam, quae non subditur perfecte virtuti agenti ut in pluribus.* There can only be chance in an agent that is already contingent, that is, defectible. *Solum in contingentibus potest esse ens per accidens.* If there is fortune in the angelic universe, chance is unthinkable there.[31]

But if nature, principle and intrinsic cause, is not absolutely determined *ad unum*, natural effects cannot be absolutely predetermined in their cause, otherwise neither the cause nor the effects would be natural. Consequently, to eliminate all uncertainty on the subject of effects is to suppress nature. The chance-cause, which is nothing other than the margin of indetermination which exceeds every natural form, is always present.

As St. Thomas remarks in his commentary on the *Perihermeneias* of Aristotle, matter can be the root of contingency only if there is a defect of determination on the side of the active cause: "possibilitas materiae ad utrumque, si communiter loquamur, non est sufficiens ratio contingentiae, nisi etiam addatur ex parte potentiae activae quod non sit omnino determinata ad unum; alioquin si ita sit determinata ad unum quod impediri non potest, consequens est quod ex necessitate reducat in actum potentiam passivam eodem modo."[32] If matter is totally subject to form, it is still form that is the reason.

This indicates the essential role that undetermined matter plays in the Thomist conception of natural contingency. This role is totally neglected by Suarez. Indeed, he seems to agree with Vasquez who refuses to call matter nature.[33] In our conception, if matter were not nature, this would be because form in no way determined it. If the form determined it in no way, a proper act would have to be assigned to matter, and indetermination would only be a word. Everything is contained by these systems.

If each nature, taken individually, always implies a certain dose of indetermination, how could the ensemble of nature—*natura universalis*—totally compensate for this defect? For Suarez, this difficulty does not exist since the obstacle that enters into play in a phenomenon of chance is purely extrinsic.

To substitute a necessity due to the ensemble for the uncertainty that individual natures entail is to deny individual nature, which is the intrinsic principle of motion. To be sure, the ensemble can involve a certitude that is not verified in individual natures taken separately. But this certainty, founded on the ensemble, does not remove the uncertainty from each individual taken separately.

But for all that, the difficult question remains. Even Cajetan thought for a long time that if we abstract from the intervention of a free agent in the course of events, there would be no contingency in nature. But in his profound commentary on the *Prima pars,* q. 115, a. 6, he takes it back.[34]

The hypothesis of the absolute necessity of the causality of celestial bodies does not diminish the difficulty of the problem. As St. Thomas says in the body of the article: "Sed nullum tale principium invenitur in rebus naturalibus, quod habeat libertatem sequendo vel non sequendi impressiones caelestes. Unde videtur quod in talibus, ad minus, omnia ex necessitate proveniant: secundum antiquam quorundam rationem, qui, supponentes omne quod est causam habere, et quod posita causa, ex necessitate ponitur effectus, concludebant quod omnia ex necessitate contingent."

The solution is simple enough. "Impressiones enim causarum naturalium recipiuntur in effectibus secundum recipientium modum. Haec autem inferiora sunt fluxibilia et non semper eodem modo se habentia, propter materiam, quae est in potentia ad plures formas, et propter contrarietatem formarum et virtutum. Non igitur impressiones corporum caelestium recipiuntur in istis inferioribus per modum necessitatis."[35]

Cajetan insistently demonstrates that the obstacle which explains the phenomena of chance always goes back, directly or indirectly, to matter. "Impedimentum enim duo dicit: scilicet rem quae impedit; et relationem ad aliud ex qua denominatur impedimentum."[36] We must distinguish the *impedimentum ex parte agentis, vel ex parte recipientis actionem* from that which is nothing other than the *possibilitas materiae.*[37] The entirely determinate agent is not an obstacle considered in itself but with respect to that which can be impeded. But the reason for the possibility of being impeded is the insufficient determination of the form; because of that it is vulnerable to be unexpectedly swallowed up by the matter.

The concourse of several causes is called accidental when the undetermined matter, and not matter-nature, is cause of it. Because the cause of the concourse is undetermined, the concourse is unforeseeable. As Cajetan says: "Et sic impedimentum ex parte materiae, et hic concursus est omnino idem." But once the concourse is determinate, whatever further results from it can be foreseen.

Some authors confuse the plurality that is the chance-cause with the plurality of the determined agents which come into play in the production of the phenomenon of chance, whereas the plurality in question here is nothing other than the undefined in the matter. Socrates has the possibility of dying of hunger, by falling from a tree, from this sickness or that, of some poison or other, of old age, and so on and on. If one takes into account all the given circumstances, his future death is more or less a zone of probability. It is these real indefinite possibilities which make the concourse of several determined causes possible. Since none of these possibilities is absolutely privileged, the concourse based on them is not predetermined.

Here is a recipe for giving the illusion of being able to predict a chance phenomenon. First, confuse the chance-cause, *casus,* and the effect of this cause, the *casuale.* Then mix plurality-of-chance-causes with the determined causes which accidentally come together. Apply the result of this mixture to the following case, a certain gentleman's dog is killed by a falling tree. You can now give determinate reasons for this accident. The dog was chasing a cat who took refuge in the tree. At the moment that the dog arrived at this spot near the tree, the tree fell. But the tree had to fall at that moment. It had been infested with insects and rotting beside so as to be sure to fall in a wind of such a velocity adding its weight to the branch. But all these determinate conditions were fulfilled. Their convergence ended in the intersection of the tree and the poor dog. Therefore, you have there foreseen a future contingent. Lest anything be lacking in your delight, suppress the Thomist idea that chance was the cause of this determinate convergence, and that beginning with this constellation there is no more contingency, but a determinate happening which is prolonged in a determined intersection of determined factors.[38]

It is evident that we most often attribute to chance phenomena which are in fact natural and not contingent. In a certain respect, the progress of science consists in unmasking the appearances of chance. As for the philosopher of nature, he cannot attribute determinately an effect to chance unless he knows sufficiently the natures to which it happens. That is the case in the example given. It is certain that a tree does not fall in order to kill dogs; it is equally certain that canine forms can be reduced to the potency of matter by an infinity of other causes.

Whatever be the power of an intellect obliged to foresee phenomena, effects which are objectively by chance are absolutely unforeseeable. It is the same with works of nature, in the measure that they cannot be absolutely determined *ad unum.* "In istis causis effectus futuri non habet cerititudinem absolutam, sed quamdam, inquantum sunt magis determinatae causae ad unum quam ad aliud; et ideo per istas causas potest accipi scientiae conjecturalis de futuris, quae tanto magis erit certa, quanto causae sunt magis determinatae ad unum; sicut est cognitio medici de sanitate et morte futura, et judicium astrologi de pluviis et ventis futuris."[39]

It is evidently impossible to transpose these ideas directly to the experimental sciences. However that may be, the Thomist will not be surprised by the testimony of scientists. He knows in advance that there should be some play in the limits of nature. How does this suppleness manifest itself from the experimental view? It is not for the philosopher to say. But it is certain that once instructed by the scientist, he can engage in fecund reflections on this aspect of things. The most competent of scientists, de Broglie, Dirac,

Heisenberg, Jordan, Eddington, and the like, have even preceded on this path the suspect race that one calls professional philosophers, who seem interested in science only in order to find errors. In 1927, Eddington put us on guard against too much precipitation. "It would probably be wiser to nail up over the door of the new quantum theory a notice: 'Structural alterations in progress—No admittance except on business,' and particularly to warn the doorkeeper to keep out prying philosophers."[40] But Sir Arthur soon succeeded in corrupting the doorman and engaged in certain reflections, one might say premature, which show today how farsighted was this man with the flair of genius. In experimental science, above all in physics, many things have happened in the space of eight years and one can wonder if Eddington would not be disposed to replace the warning of 1927 with a simple, "Philosophers, watch your step."

I will not undertake to give examples of such reflections in this already too long essay. I have touched on this general problem of contingency in nature only to suggest that it cannot be impossible for Thomists to take a more open attitude toward the ideas of this genial race of modern young physicists, not so much for their sake, as for our own—for there are some of them who find droll and bizarre the worlds we must scrutinize and weigh before being able to say, "That works—that works very well." At bottom, what have they gained? But I would be unjust if I did not add that this new generation interests itself in strangely useless philosophical considerations that we are disposed to believe. The race of scientists is dying, and the more living among them are now philosophers.

It is in no way a question of compromises. Because of compromises with schools much more dangerous for us because they are easy and use the same vocabulary, we are no longer able to recognize ideas inherent to the logic of our vision of the world.

III

Let us bring these considerations to an end with a view of the whole that will permit us to situate this contingency proper to nature in the universal hierarchy.

Nothing would be more disappointing for absolute determinism, which seeks pure intelligibility in the most obscure corner of reality, than truly pure intelligibility. For the absolute and transcendental determination that is God is at the same time his freedom to create. Every creature participates in some way in that indetermination that is positive by superabundance. In intellectual creatures there is always freedom; in material living things, spontaneity; the inorganic participates in it by its active principle which is a spiritual agent; this agent is outside inorganic nature, but without it, it could not act. There exists then a constant relation between the degree of essential determination and the degree of positive indetermination.

But there is also found in every creature a negative indetermination, by defect of being, which consists in the absolute non-necessity of its existence. *Ipsa natura vel quidditas est possibilis respectu esse quod a Deo habet.* This indetermination is not a positive reality in the finite. It is not opposed to the actual existence by which the essence is determined to be, but to the absolute necessity of its remote principle—God considered in Himself and not in His determined will—in which the finite is not determined to be. It is in that that the contingency of every creature consists, contingency in hypothetical necessity. In this respect, all finite beings as finite are equally contingent. But if we compare them with one another, they are not such to an equal degree. For the more simple the essence of a being, the more intimate to it is its existence, the closer to eternity is its duration, the more it is one. *Quanto aliquid est propinquius Deo, tanto magis recedit a non-esse.* And in this perspective, the lesser angels are more contingent than the higher. The more simple the angelic forms, the more necessary they are.

We can therefore establish an inverse proportion between the degree of positive indetermination and the degree of negative indetermination. The more an angel is determined, the more simple his intellect and the more free he is. *Libertas a necessaria coactione nobilius invenitur in Deo quam in angelo, et in uno angelo quam in alio, et in angelo quam in homine.*

Let us think in the sense of its degradation the hierarchy of the angelic universes each of which constitutes unto itself a complete and individual subsistent species outside of any natural genus. To give a direction to this perspective it is important to note that if this hierarchy cannot have any ultimate possible upper limit, there is nonetheless a lower limit, as in the case of whole numbers; a limit one cannot breach without establishing a new order of generically different essences—an order of essences that will communicate in the same physical genus.

Looked at in the direction of this lower limit, we foresee in the spiritual hierarchy itself the prefiguration of a new species of negative indetermination. Spiritual essences, always simple, are less and less one, less and less determined. There is there something like a tendency toward the disintegration of essence, toward a real intra-essential indetermination. The substantial duration of the angels, while remaining simple, is less and less intense. The present tends to diffuse itself into a *prius et posterius.* This degradation of spiritual durations prefigures the complex existence of the composite cosmic essence; it prefigures the successive and continuous duration that is time properly speaking; it prefigures the mobile and a substantial future—the world of *fluxibilia.*

The intuition of essence in the angel becomes poorer following the imperfection of its essence and its intellect; in order to know other beings, it has need of more and more numerous ideas, its activity is more and more fragmented; the discrete time constituted by the discontinuous suite of thoughts and willing is more and more atomized; there is more and more of a future. The pure spirits are more and more removed from themselves and from what they are not. All that prefigures an intellect turned outside itself, a blank slate; a non-intuitive intellect which will need to seek gropingly for its object outside, which presupposes both homogeneous exteriority and passive experience in the knowing subject (since intellect is impassible), that is, it will need matter and senses immersed in the flow of things which ceaselessly disappear and that these senses cannot experience without vanishing with them. (That is the deep sense of *rational animal.* To have the daylight of discursive intelligence, there must be the night of the 'outside' and of animality; the shadows are born from a need for light.) Abandoned to his natural powers alone, the human intelligence cannot confront things which are in themselves light and hidden from its regard in the measure that they are present, changeless, intelligible in act; its proportioned object will have to be a moving and opaque thing such that the intellect itself must make the intelligibility of it, drawing it to itself in giving itself to it. That is how the life of our thought retains a certain analogy with the vegetative life which grows and is maintained thanks to decomposable things, for although intellect is objective and does not cause disintegration of the object proportioned to it as is the case with nutritive assimilation, it can only grasp forms immersed in that obscure subjectivity of matter which ceaselessly empties mobile things into the past.

To the degree that the perfection of pure spirits diminishes, their heterogeneity also diminishes; they more and more resemble one another. This tendency toward a homogeneity of persons symbolizes a plurality of individuals of the same species. The growth in complexity in the interior of an individual pure spirit is equally, in the perspective we are taking, like a tendency that prefigures the intra-individual homogeneous exteriority of predicamental quantity.

This perspective reveals in the angelic hierarchy a prefiguration of the spatio-temporal world; a prefiguration analogous to that of the circle toward which tends an inscribed polygon whose sides are multiplied.[41] Whichever of the points of view of those we have considered one adopts, we are always given a glimpse of matter as pure negative indetermination. It is by matter that the individuation of non-subsistent forms is explained, and passive experience, time, space, motion. But it entails as well a new species of contingency, unknown in the spiritual universe, and which is essential to nature.

Happily, the perspective followed does not indicate the real orientation of things. The movement of universal nature is an ascending one. Animated by a spiritual impetus thanks to which the nature elicits more and more heterogeneous composites from the potency of matter, our universe becomes more and more present to itself and interior to itself. *Quanto forma magis vincit materiam, tanto ex ea et materia magis afficitur unum.* The works executed are more and more determinate, the forms more and more victorious. The diffusion of time and space is little by little vanquished by the interiorization of life and of knowledge. And to the degree that essences are more determinate, life is freed from the shackles of matter into a growing spontaneity. Thus determination becomes cause of always greater suppleness. To future contingents due to the indetermination by defect of being are added future contingents which proceed from an indetermination of superabundance. What is always only chance tends toward fortune. We would be wrong to see in this only a defect. Not that they are themselves fecund, but in causing chance or fortuitous encounters, they are in the presence of natures which open on one another. Natures are so to speak at once too rich and too poor to follow their determinate ways. Whether it impedes particular natures from closing on themselves in a premature and sterile introversion, or reunites need and profusion that fatally it separated, indetermination itself thus becomes a function of universal superabundant nature. In the whole there is a good that is more than the sum of its parts. In this absolute perspective, chance and fortune are the redundance of an essentially free richness to which no particular nature has an individual right. It would be an evil for the universe, St. Thomas says, if there were not accidental causality; this would be contrary to divine Wisdom, and Providence would not exist if necessity presided over all. It would be equally destroyed if nothing in the world is a work of chance and fortune.

> That which does not exist can cause nothing; from which it follows that the aptitude of a thing to become a cause is in direct ratio to its relation to being. Therefore, the different degrees in the order of causes should correspond to the different degrees in the scale of beings. But the perfection of the universe requires, not only that there exist beings that are such by essence, but also that there be accidental beings, for those whose substance is not as perfect as possible must achieve a kind of perfection by way of accidents, and the accidents multiply in proportion as these beings are more removed from the simplicity of God. As soon as several accidents are joined in a subject, that being exists by accident, for the subject and the accidents, and even two accidents inherent in a subject, are one thing only accidentally: for example, a white man, or a man who is both white and a musician. Therefore the universe would be imperfect if there were no accidental cause. Now whatever comes from a cause accidentally is attributed to chance and fortune. So it is not repugnant to Providence, which preserves the perfection of things, that some effects come about fortuitously and by chance.
>
> The order of divine Providence requires that causes be coordinated and graduated. The more elevated the cause, the greater its power of action, and, consequently, its causality extends to a greater number of effects. But no natural cause seeks to surpass the bounds of its power of action, for it would do so in vain. Therefore the activity of a particular cause cannot extend to all possible effects. But the fortuitous is that which comes about outside the intention of agents. Therefore it enters into the order of divine Providence that chance and fortune take place in the world.[42]

Let us not forget that natural things are works of the divine art—*artificiata ipsius Dei.* Nature is like a musical poem deployed in time. All the more determinate insofar as they are unforeseen, occasional harmonies are essential to nature in which creative thought is interiorized as in the composition of a fugue. The image is invoked by a mathematician. "To my mind," says Sir James Jeans, "the laws which nature obeys are less suggestive of those which a machine obeys in its motion than of those which a musician obeys in writing a fugue, or a poet in composing a sonnet."[43]

In this immense effort, sustained and instigated by the intellectual substance which cooperates in the work of nature, the world disposes matter little by little to receive the ultimate act of which it is the desire, the human soul: *in quam tendit materiam sicut in ultimam formam.* That effort has to succeed, otherwise matter would not have been able to exist. But the way to be followed was not predetermined in matter. The work of execution consists just in marking out the paths. It is impossible that the road leading to man should have been quite direct and laid out in advance. That would be to say that the determination of the world was already given in its origin. If it had been given, this could only be in matter. But once matter is disposed, and it is so by determination, it has a proportioned act: *ultima dispositio necessitat formam.* Unless we imagine that there is not room enough in the universe for all those things ready to emerge, or that efficient causes are lazy or capriciously make us wait, one would have no reason for the slowness of the work of propagation. In Suarez' hypothesis, the potentiality of matter is absolutely deprived of sense, and there is no reason why all things do not actually exist from the origin of the world.

The ascent of the world consists in vanquishing indetermination—by means of indetermination if it must. The checks, the *peccata naturae,* the vain detours, the diffusions in quantity, none of that surprises once given matter and excellence of the end. Directed and certain as it is, the spiritual causality that nature experiences—*quodlibet opus naturae est opus alicujus substantiae intelligentis*—is received *ad modum recipientis.* For the necessity that is in the active cause depends on the disposition of the agent and patient.

We are in a universe which is at the state of maturation; one can compare it to an immense embryo.[44] In the process the world is exhausted little by little. The certainty of life is paralleled by a growing uncertainty that in physics is called very vaguely matter. The degradation of energy will end by suffocating the life that it sustained and by which it desegregates itself.

But we also know that all this is provisory, that this agitation and the shape of the present world are only a shadow of that which in it is truly made for a definitive future where there will be no more history; we know that meanwhile there has been infused in matter a life which cannot be extinguished—forms henceforth absolutely necessary—and that these forms, separated for a time, must rejoin and this time fill up matter, as did the form of the celestial bodies of a surpassed astronomy. Keats expressed the deep word of nature in saying: "I will clamber through the Clouds and exist."

NOTES

1. Cited by Eddington, "Sur le problème du Déterminisme," trans. E. Neculcea, in *Actualités scientifique et industrielles* (Paris: Hermann et Cie., 1934), 5.

2. Laplace, *Science et Loi,* 5th Semaine Internationale de Synthèse (Paris: Alcan, 1934), 51.

3. See the excellent overview and precise summary by André George, "Les conséquences générales de la physique contemporaine," *Revue des Questions Scientifiques* (20 Sept. 1933): 173–97.

4. P.A.M. Dirac, *The Principles of Quantum Mechanics,* 2nd ed. (Oxford: Clarendon Press, 1935), 3–4.

5. Eddington, *The Nature of the Physical World* (Cambridge, 1928), chaps. IV and V. This paper was finished when there appeared *New Pathways in Science* (Cambridge, 1935). See chap. III. No one has treated the methodological problems of indeterminism more profoundly than Sir Arthur in these two works.

6. Claude Bernard, *Introduction à la médicine expérimentale* (Paris: Bailliere et Fils, 1865), 92 ff. Let no one take my remarks as a general disapprobation of a work whose value is ever present to those for whom it was destined. Compare with Dirac, *Principles,* 13: "When an observation is made on any atomic system that is in a given state, in general the result will not be determinate, i.e. if the experiment is repeated several times under identical conditions several different results may be obtained. It is a law of nature, though, that if the experiment is repeated a large number of times, each particular result will be obtained in a definite fraction of the total number of times, so that there is a definite *probability* of its being obtained. This probability is what the theory sets out to calculate. Only in special cases when the probability for some result is unity is the result of the experiment determinate."

7. See the views of Planck, Einstein, and Rutherford, cited by Eddington, *New Pathways in Science,* 295 ff. Among indeterminist physicists one can cite Heisenberg, de Broglie, Dirac, Bohn, Eddington, Jeans, Weyl, Compton, Thomson, Schrodinger, Jordan, Millikan, LeMaître, Reichenbach, etc. In the final instance, the principal rea-

son that Planck and Einstein cannot resign themselves to indeterminism is that they want experimental science to be an absolute science. Planck, for example, would always prefer "weil eine bestimmte Antwort auf eine Frage immer wertvoller ist, als eine unbestimmte" (*Wege sut physikalischen Erkenntni* [Leipzig, 1933], 201). But it remains to know if nature accords with our preferences and if our determined questions always make sense.

8. It is in this sense that Eddington and Jeans must be understood when they think they see in indeterminism a confirmation of their idealism, an idealism which consists in affirming the transcendental intelligibility of the real, and which is perfectly compatible with what we call realism, although for these authors realism is synonymous with materialism. See Jeans, *The New Background of Science* (Cambridge, 1933), 308 and 398: "Broadly speaking, the two conjectures are those of the idealist and realist—or, if we prefer, the mentalist and materialist—views of nature." Jeans has a penchant for mathematicism, above all in *The Mysterious Universe,* while Eddington is clearly opposed to this view. See, for example, *The Nature of the Physical World,* 209; *New Pathways in Science,* 323 ff.

9. Fernand Renoirte, "La théorie physique," *Revue Néoscolastique* (1924): 360: "The law expresses only the numerical relation between several measurements. This functional relation indicates what will be the amount of one of these measures for all possible other values. If the measure of time comes into the law, this is simply because the size of the other properties varies with time. The antecedent follows the consequent, but the law does not tell us that it causes it since one can also deduce the second from the first. To express the law in a causal form is to make a metaphor or to interpret it in a manner foreign to physics." This conversion of terms is not verified in objective statistics, but there is no question of physical causality there.

10. "Effectus qui est contingens respectu causae proximae naturaliter operantis, si comparetur ad totum ordinem et seriem causarum universi, et in his causis nulla intercedat libere agens, saltem ut applicans alias causas, vel removens impedimenta, non habet contingentiam, sed necessitatem" (Suarez, *Disputationes Metaphysicae,* disp. 19, sect. 10, par. 5). St. Thomas and Sylvester of Ferrara (*Summa contra gentes,* c. 10) are cited as authorities for this position. Here is the text of St. Thomas: "Sicut ex causa necessaria sequitur effectus certitudinaliter, ita ex causa contingenti *completa* si non impediatur." Suarez seems to have overlooked the word "completa." Among effects there are some that are natural, that is, have a per se cause—for example, this dog. There are others that have an undetermined cause—for example, the death of this dog by the falling of a tree. The first effect was foreseeable in the measure that it was determined in its cause. Once given, that is, *causa contingenti completa,* we can take it back determinately to this per se cause. As we will see, every corruptible cause is contingent in this sense. By contrast, the second effect can in no way be taken back to a determined cause; there is certitude only in the present act of this accidental cause, as will be developed later.

11. "Prima autem causa, sive Deus, solum dici potest prima radix hujus contingentiae, sicut est prima causa omnium effectuum universi; quia nimirum tales causae

secundae ab ipsa fuerunt et creatae, et ita dispositae et ordinatae, ut ab eis hujusmodi effectus contingentes provenirent. Ad hoc autem, formaliter loquendo, nil refert, quod prima causa libere haec omnia produxerit; eadem enim contingentia sequeretur etiam si ex necessitate creasset haec, omnia dummodo eodem modo illa ordinasset, et postea cum illis concurreret" (*Disputationes Metaphysicae,* par. 13). The initial constellation could thus be compared with an old Ford with a flat tire, of which we could say that from now on it will run determinately on three tires. This is how determinists explain the disorder in the world from determined causes.

12. Suarez, Opusc. II: *De scientia Dei futurorum contingentium absolutorum,* c. 1: "Contingentia vero illa dicitur esse secundum quid, quia est tantum respectu unius causae, ut impediri potest ab alia; non vero respectu totius collectionis occurentium causarum. Dicitur etiam extrinseca et per accidens, quia non proveniat ex intrinseca virtute causae per se agentis sed ab extrinseco impediente."

13. *Commentariorum ac disputationum in Prima Partem Sancti Thomae,* t. 1 (Antverpiae: Belleros, 1621), disp. 64, c. 1: "Alia vero sunt futura contingentia: sed hace adhuc dupliciter dicuntur: quaedam omnino proveniunt a causa naturaliter, quae tamen impeditir potest ab alia aut libera aut naturali. . . . Haec autem licet ab hominibus non ita certo cognoscantur, ut in eorum cognitione decipi non possint, ab Angelis tamen certo, et evidenter sciuntur, ut ostendemus disp. 207, quoties in his eventibus solum intervenit concursus et occursus causarum naturalium, et nulla cause libera aliquod modo intercedit. . . . Est deinde alterum genus effectuum contingentium, qui primo et proxime, aut saltem remote ex libero pendent arbitrio. . . ." Molina in *Concordia Liberi Arbitrii* (Lethielleux, 1876) makes an exception for the future contingents that have their source in animal spontaneity: "Si secludas liberum arbitrium tam hominum quam angelorum, atque appetitum sentientem bestiarum ad actus quosdam in quibus cernitur vestigium libertatis, posita constitutione mundi universi qua nunc est. Deumque nihil agere supra communem concursum, ordinemve inditum rebus, tollitur contingentia ab effectibus omnibus causarum secundarum, omniaque fatali quadam necessitate opus est evenire" (disp. 47, p. 277).

14. St. Thomas, *II Summa contra gentes,* c. 30: *Licet autem omnia . . .*

15. *I Summa contra gentes,* c. 83; *Summa theologiae,* Ia, q. 19, a. 3; q. 82, a. 1.

16. *III Summa contra gentes,* c. 86, "Si autem aliquis forte dicat . . ."

17. Ibid.

18. *In I Perihermeneias,* lectio 14, n. 8; *In IX Metaphysicorum,* lectio 9, n. 1873. Compare Suarez, *Disputationes Metaphysicae,* disp. 19, sect. 10, pars. 4 and 5.

19. *Physics II, 9; De generatione et corruptione,* II, chap. 11. See O. Hamelin, *Le systèms d'Aristote* (Paris: Alcan, 1920), the 15th lesson. His interpretation, excellent as far as I can judge, differs notably from that which one finds in Gomperz, Mansion, and Ross. The last attributes to Aristotle a conception like that of Suarez, although the latter was convinced he differed from Aristotle on this point. Neither St. Thomas nor Cajetan (*Commentarium* Ia, q. 115, a. 6) seem to think themselves unfaithful to the text of Aristotle on this question of chance.

20. *In II Physicorum,* lectio 15, n. 2.

21. *II Summa contra gentes,* c. 30: "Sciendum est itaque quod, si rerum creatarum universitas consideretur, prout sunt a primo principio, inveniuntur dependere ex voluntate, non ex necessitate principii, nisi necessitate suppositionis. *Si vero comparetur ad principia proxima,* inveniuntur necessitatem habere absolutam; nihil enim prohibet aliqua principia rerum non ex necessitate produci; quibus tamen positis, de necessitate sequitur talis effectus. . . ."

22. Is it necessary to say how different is the indeterminism of contingentism of which certain manuals of apologetics speak? Indetermination is in effect within certain determined limits according to the case studied. But contingentism, *as these manuals interpret it,* seems to imply that the improbable is as probable as the probable, and that there is equal indifference at every level; that there is regularity by chance; even that it is not impossible that a die with six facets should reveal a seventh, that a mouse be suddenly transformed into an elephant, or into two elephants, etc. If in fact the scientist never even get to the point of defining experimentally an impossibility where there is manifestly ontological impossibility, would it not be better to recall that experimental science is not the only science of nature rather than reject a method on which we want to load all the consequences of our own confusion? Since when has probable knowledge been opposed to every form of certitude?

23. By varieties of existence I mean the sub-species contained within the limits of absolute natural species. Note however that a sub-species which in fact constitutes a limit of a natural species is never the absolute limit of that natural species. It tends toward a limit which is found at infinity. In the final instance, the absolute character of natural species is founded on matter insofar as it is essentially ordered to its ultimate act, to its ultimate end—the human form, which is formally and in an eminent way at once sensitive, vegetative, and form of corporeity.

24. "Bonum proportionatum communi statui naturae, accidit ut in pluribus; et defectus ab hoc bono, ut in paucioribus. Sed bonum quod excedit communem statum naturae, invenitur ut in paucioribus; et defectus ab hoc bono, ut in pluribus. Sicut patet quod plures homines sunt qui habent sufficientem scientiam ad regimen vitae suae, pauciores autem qui hac scientia carent, qui moriones vel stulti dicuntur: sed paucissimi sunt, respectu aliorum, qui attingunt ad habendam profundam scientiae intelligibilium rerum. Cum igitur beatitudo aeterna, in praecipue secundum quod est gratia destituta per corruptionem originalis peccati, pauciores sunt qui salvantur. Et in hoc maxime misericordia Dei apparet, quod aliquos in illam salutem erigit, a qua plurimi deficiunt secundum communem cursum et inclinationem naturae" (*Summa theologiae* Ia, q. 23, a. 7, ad 3). See John of St. Thomas, *Cursus Theologicus,* t. 1, p. 322, par. 41.

25. *III Summa contra gentes,* c. 6; *Q.D. de malo,* q. 1, a. 3, ad 17.

26. *In II Physicorum,* lectio 10, n. 10.

27. *In I Perihermeneias,* lectio 14, n. 11; *In VI Metaphysicorum,* lectio 3; *Summa theologiae* Ia, q. 115, a. 6, c.

28. *Physics,* II, 5.

29. *II Summa contra gentes,* c. 30: "Uno quidem modo. . .".

30. *Summa theologiae* Ia, q. 86, a. 3, with the commentary of Cajetan.

31. *In VI Metaphysicorum,* lectio 3. For the distinction between *casus* and *casuale, fortuna* and *fortuitum,* see John of St. Thomas, *Cursus Philosophicus,* t. 2, p. 510.

32. *In I Perihermeneias,* lectio 14, n. 9.

33. *Commentariorum, In Primam secundae,* disp. 25, c. 3, p. 167.

34. See Bañez in the same place, "Cajetanus super hunc articulum acutissime et eruditissime loquitur, mutatque sententiam suam quam olim habuerat negans contingentiam in rebus ad quas non se extendit hominis operatio libera." Cajetan gives an example which Suarez takes up and from which he concludes necessity without making the least allusion to Cajetan, who, after having recognized *et haec ratio multo tempore me vinctum tenuisse videtu,* gives us such profound and convincing solutions that it is difficult to understand how they could have been forgotten.

35. *III Summa contra gentes,* c. 86, and *II,* c. 30: *Ex praedictis igitur patet. . .*

36. Cajetan, *Commentariorum,* n. 17.

37. St. Thomas, *In II Sent.,* d. 3, q. 3, a. 3, ad 4.

38. John of St. Thomas, *Cursus Theologicus,* t. 2, p. 40: "Nec distinguit inter contingentiam, et indifferentiam seu indeterminationem, ut aliqui faciunt: quia contingens dicitur aliquid ex causa indifferenti ad utrumlibet in actu primo, et antequam de facto producat; ergo antequam effectus producatur, ex eadem parte, ex qua habet contingentiam, habet indeterminationem, scilicet ex causis: extra causas autem nondum aliquid habet determinate, et ibi amittet contingentiam ubi habet determinationem."

39. *In I Sent.,* d. 38, q. 1, a. 5, c. St. Thomas in this text touches on the ontological foundation of the distinction to be made between the *disciplines* and experimental sciences. Their *ratio intelligibilis* will be profoundly different, for in the former case one studies the necessary and the contingent insofar as it is necessary, in the latter one approaches things in their very contingency. Here must be applied the distinction Aristotle makes between the *scientificum* and *ratiocinativum.* The physico-mathematical method has changed nothing in such principles, quite the contrary. See *Q.D. de veritate,* q. 15, a. 2, ad 3; *Summa theologiae* Ia, q. 79, a. 9, ad 3; *In III de anima,* lectio 16.

40. Eddington, *The Nature of the Physical World,* 211.

41. Lest this image arouse a scruple, it might be useful to add that the more imperfect the spiritual species are, the less numerous they are within determined limits. Beginning with the last lower degree, the progression is so to say spiroidal. Thus complexity is inversely proportional to the multitude of species within the given limits.

42. *III Summa contra gentes,* c. 74.

43. Jeans, *The Mysterious Universe* (Cambridge, 1931), 123–24.

44. *III Summa contra gentes,* cc. 22–24.

Reflections on the Problem of Indeterminism

1937

I

Contemporary Thomists who oppose the very idea of objective indeterminism as it is maintained by the new generation of scientists seem to be in complete agreement with Suarez who holds that an effect "which is contingent with respect to the proximate cause operating naturally, if compared to the whole order and series of the causes of the universe, no free agent intervening, at least as applying other causes or removing impediments, has not contingency but necessity."[1] If this were the case, every science of nature that would have a finite understanding knowing sufficiently the initial constellation of the universe would be a hypothetico-deductive science and as absolutely rigorous as mathematics until the arrival of one who, on the speck of sand that he inhabits, would be able to introduce by his free will unforeseeable determinations. From the origin of the world and until the intervention of free agents, everything would be given once for all, and the future would await only a lazy existential determination. We say that every science would be *hypothetico*-deductive, if one admits that the initial constellation could be other than in fact it had been and in this it would be comparable to mathematical postulates; but once such a constellation is given, everything would follow rigorously until the arrival of the disturbing gentleman.

Since Suarez is obliged on this point to contradict Aristotle, and since this position results logically from principles most absolutely contrary to those of Thomism, one ought at least ask whether we should make this concession. For Suarez, the phenomena of chance (by opposition to those of fortune) are not *future contingents*[2] but future necessaries, coming predetermined from the causes of the universe and foreseeable. Natural contingency would be only extrinsic and *secundum quid.* "Prima autem causa, sive Deus, solum dici potest prima radix hujus contingentiae, sicut est prima causa omnium effectuum universi; quia nimirum tales causae secundae ab ipsa fuerunt et creatae et ita dispositae et ordinatae, ut ab eis hujusmodi effectus contingentes provenirent. Ad hoc autem, formaliter loquendo, nil refert, quod prima causa libere haec omnia produxerit; eadem enim contingentia sequeretur etiam si ex necessitate creasset haec omnia dummodo eodem modo illa ordinasset, et postea cum illis concurreret."[3] I do not see how this extrinsicist conception of contingency can be reconciled with that of St. Thomas who attributes every chance phenomenon as such to an intrinsic cause: eorum quae sunt a casu causa est intrinseca sicut eorum quae sunt a natura, which is how chance differs from fortune whose cause is extrinsic.

The solution of this purely ontological problem cannot be applied just as such to the problem of indeterminism in the experimental sciences. This is what I will try to show in the second section of this essay, where we will adopt the viewpoint of the philosophy of science. These reflections provide only 'approaches'—scattered and often quite indeterminate—which could contribute to a systematic and in-depth study of the problem. I hope moreover to show that the unbridgeable chasm that separates the Thomist school from schools of Suarezian inspiration involves not only the summits of creation, free agents, but also the unforeseeable leaps of electrons.

Positive and Negative Indetermination. Let us distinguish at the outset two completely different species of indetermination. The freedom of God with respect to the finite is a necessary consequence of His absolute necessity. In other words, absolute determination is the root of a positive indetermination which is essentially perfection. Only in God do we find fully realized the determinist ideal. But at the same time, nothing could more disappoint the determinist, since this pure actuality grounds the possibility of the finite and the liberty God has to bring it into being.

Every finite being participates in this indetermination by perfection, according to the degree of indetermination of its essence. The essential determination of the higher angels is the root of superior intelligence and consequently of greater liberty. As the intellection of the angels becomes more and more complex, there is a proportional positive decrease.[4] And just as there can be cognition that is not intelligence, so there can be positive indetermination without liberty. The plant and animal participate in this positive indetermination in their spontaneity and to the degree that their behavior involves unforeseeability. No doubt there is no spontaneity in the inorganic world, considered as such. But to consider the inorganic world 'in itself' is to make a partial abstraction, for it is not a whole closed on itself like the living. Speaking ontologically, there is no inorganic world 'as such' in the way that there are plants and animals 'as such' because the active principle 'quod' is totally exterior to it. But at the same time, without this principle, which is at least living—by which the non-living participates in spontaneity—the inorganic world is contradictory.

Thus there is a constant relation between the degree of essential determination and the degree of positive indetermination. In the finite order, this indetermination is always of an accidental order. Even in living things this indetermination by increase is the root of an uncertain future, of future contingents. Otherwise, it could not be known if they act, and if the active principle of their movement is truly theirs, at least in part, according to their degree of perfection; it would be impossible to distinguish a robot from a living thing; there would be no essential difference between two stags confronting one another and two toy soldiers that collide. In fact, setting aside greater complexity, their behavior would be absolutely the same—whether the active principle were extrinsic or intrinsic—and Descartes would have been perfectly right.

But in every finite creature there is also found another kind of indetermination, this one negative, which is essentially imperfection. To the liberty that God has to cause the finite to exist there answers in the finite an indetermination due to defect of being: it can be or not be. The existing essence cannot be its existential determination. The contingent is necessary when it exists, but it does not derive this necessity from its present condition; that comes from the one who gives it existence. In its present necessary condition, it is also necessarily of a contingent nature. *Ipsa natura vel quidditas est possibilis respectu esse quod a Deo habet.* And in this sense it can have contingency within necessity, on condition that we are talking of the present, not the future.

So all finite beings are equally contingent insofar as they are finite, compared to one another, some are less so than others, according to the perfection of the essence which receives more or less intimately the proportioned existence. In this perspective, the lower angels are more contingent than the higher, man less contingent than the brute, and so on.

What pure spirits have that is quite specific by opposition to cosmic beings is simplicity and perfect determination of essence. Hence the simplicity of their non-successive and invariable substantial duration. The essence is given in its entirety once and for all. It has no past or future. There is on the other hand something irreducibly obscure in the composed angelic substance, because its essence is not its existential determination. This obscurity is proportional to the imperfection of the essence. From this point of view, one can say that one angelic essence is less determined than another even when there is no indetermination in the essence considered in itself. There is contingency here only in the relation of essence to existence.

Let us consider for a moment the direction of degradation in this hierarchy of the angelic universe, each of whom constitutes in itself a complete species subsisting outside any natural common genus. To provide a direction to this perspective, it is important to note that if this hierarchy cannot have an ultimate higher possible limit there is however a lowest possible limit (as in the analogous case of the series of whole numbers) that could not be surpassed without entering into a new order of essences generically different. More precisely, an order of essences sharing in the same physical genus. Looked at in the direction of this lower limit, we observe in the spiritual hierarchy itself the prefiguration of a new species of negative indetermination. The essences, always simple, are less and less one, less and less determined. There is as it were a tendency to disintegration of the essence, toward a real and intra-essential indetermination. The substantial duration of pure spirits is less and less intense. The present tends to disintegrate. This degradation of spiritual durations prefigures the existence of the physical and composed essence; it prefigures the successive and continuous duration that is time properly speaking. In other words, it prefigures the true future. The intuition of the essence in the angels is impoverished according to the imperfection of the essence and understanding; in order to know other beings, it has need of more and more numerous ideas, its activity is more and more fragmented; the discrete duration constituted by the continuous suite of thoughts and acts of will is more and more dispersed, there is, so to say, more and more of a future. The angels are more and more removed from themselves and from what is outside themselves. All this prefigures an intelligence turned outside itself, a blank slate, and which will have need of the passive experience of the subject. To the degree that the perfection of the pure spirits diminishes, their heterogeneity is attenuated, they resemble one another more and more: they give an intimation in this way of a plurality of individuals of the same species and quantitative and spatial homogeneity.

This perspective reveals in the angelic hierarchy a prefiguration of the cosmos, analogous to that of the circle toward which the inscribed polygon whose sides are multiplied tends. Whichever of the points of view just suggested be chosen—that of essence, that of duration, of understanding, of individuation—it enables us to foresee matter, pure negative indetermination. It is by this that the individuation of non-subsistent forms is explained, passive experience, time, space, etc. But it also entails a new species of contingency unknown in the spiritual universes, which is proper to the nature which results from the hylomorphic composition of essences.

Contingency in Nature. This problem is very intimately linked to that of duration. What is it in fact that impedes cosmic essences from being given all at once and to endure without succession if not the indetermination of matter? It is not only the complexity of the essence which entails as well a certain complexity of existence. One of the principles of the essence must be pure indetermination, without which the essence could not be an "unum per se." This indetermination is not only the root of a duration which flows, but to the degree that it is in play, it makes a totally assured existence impossible: it is the cause of the uncertainty of becoming. This uncertainty does not have absolutely precise conditions, since it arises from a real indetermination. We find ourselves confronted here by a contingency in the very interior of duration that one does not find in the pure spirits which have no substantial becoming and whose existence is assured in the identity of an eviternal present. *In perpetuis non differt esse et posse.*

Natural beings are busy in the pursuit of existence, and lose time in doing so. But the pursuit of an always remote existence cannot be the ultimate end. This diffusion of time must be progressively arrested by the quidditative perfection of the world. From this point of view, our universe is a tendency toward a duration ever more simple, ever less diffuse, finally terminating in the spiritual form of man, whose existence, abstracting from the matter of the composite, is eviternal. In his present state, man already realizes this aspiration of the world, but in a provisory way, since he is always in part corruptible.

What prevents this ultimate and intrinsic end of the cosmos from being realized from the beginning? From the beginning, matter is essentially ordered to man, to this intelligence that has need of passive experience, therefore of sensation and animality which entail vegetative life and corporeity; it is in the human species which by the possibilities of matter compensates for the defect of unity in the multiplication of individuals. If matter does not have this act right away this is because originally it is not sufficiently disposed and first much must be done, a work which consists in eliciting ever more simple quidditative determinations. The cause of this resistance of the world is nothing other than the indetermination of matter.

Still, it is impossible that the entire future should be really predetermined in the past or present state of the universe. If it were, since matter is something real and not a pure logical possibility, the future would already exist; everything really possible in matter would exist simultaneously and eviternally; the pure potentiality of matter would be wholly deprived of any real meaning. And if the future is not predetermined in the present, then there is uncertainty, the future contingent.

If the term of this cosmic ascension (the human species) is very certain, without which matter would be really contradictory, the ways that lead there cannot be absolutely predetermined, otherwise matter would be determined in advance to all the forms which in fact lead to this term. So we must see in matter cause both of certitude and incertitude. Hence the absolutely irreducible role of contingency in the maturation of the world.

This contingency touches even the structure of natural forms which cannot be entirely determined "ad unum" like the angelic form. It is just this lack of determination and incapability of individuating itself that calls for matter. This need for matter introduces into the form itself an irreducible obscurity. One cannot have a distinct idea of a cosmic form independent of the idea of the composite.[5] And the matter which enters into this idea is not determined without signifying as well its determinability with respect to an infinity of other forms. A non-subsisting form is not a quiddity in the strict sense.[6] That means that the different (I do not say diverse) natural forms cannot be absolutely opposed as are those of pure spirits, because their definition includes the notion of matter, that is, the possibility of an infinity of other forms which can be extracted from this matter, so much so that the existing varieties are analogous to the segments of a continuum determined *a posteriori*.[7] In this sense they are contingent, always *quidditatively new*. Between any two given natural forms there is an indefinite possibility of other forms. These forms are purely potentially in matter and consequently the determination that any material form is must come to be *insofar as it is determination*. One must keep to this language in order to avoid any *latitatio formarum*. Too often the birth of natural compounds is thought of as the release of already given determinations.

The different natural forms are not contingent in all respects however. This contingency affects only the sub-species, but, since the infra-human natural species are only realized in sub-species, one can see the range of this contingency.

Let us suppose, in order to illustrate this idea, a finite intelligence contemplating the universe at a moment when it contains no actual living thing. This intelligence would be able to foresee with infallibility the coming of man into the world and also everything that conditions absolutely the determination of matter in view of the human composite: it would foresee the plant, the brute, but it would be impossible for it to foresee all the concrete ways in which natural species are realized. These species, which are *quasi-genera* with respect to sub-species, are apriori certain because they constitute irreducible degrees of being: there is no intermediary between 'being,' 'living,' 'knowing,' and 'understanding.' The absolute character of this gradation moreover has its ground in the idea of man whose soul is formally sensitive, vegetative, and the form of corporeity. Because man's soul is all that, not only eminently but formally, these degrees of being are susceptible of being directly realized outside him. The inorganic, the plant and animal are certain limit-species. But it is impossible that the proper determination of the sub-species which realizes in a particular manner these natural species should participate in this certitude. If it did, the ways in which the animal or plant can be realized would be determined in advance in matter; or again, the matter included in the idea of man would explicitly signify all possible forms: that is, that matter would not only be an idea, but determinate ideas.

The intelligence we have imagined would know with certainty that matter will receive the human form, but the same could not be said of intermediate forms. The multitude of possible sub-species is indefinite—between the highest of vegetative forms and the lowest of given animal forms there is still an indefinite number—and consequently it involves what is not compossible. If one wants to progress, one would have to span the intermediate forms, each leap constituting a clear rupture with an actual intermediary. No doubt the structure of the scale will be to a certain degree determined by the material given at the outset and by the end. But the number and distance of degrees could not be given in advance. The number of steps it takes to travel a road does not depend exclusively on the length of one's legs but also on the quality of the road. The surprises matter has for us are indefinite. One could not see in the initial composite (or composites) a rigorous plan of the hierarchy to be established, as if the universe were a multiplication table, or matter a subject which receives forms coming from without, as the Platonists would have it.

There is then the unforeseeable in the order of *natural determinations:* all sub-species were at one moment of the existence of the world future contingents. The hierarchy of these species is irreversible. So one can see why the sub-species 'cow' as cow is philosophically indefinable. It has determinate truth only *a posteriori,* like the actual cuts of a continuum. (The Flemish proverb "True as a cow" to designate a truth at once evident and obscure is to the point.) The problem of contingency in nature is not limited to that of chance and fortune, even if these two forms of contingency are the most evident.[8]

The fixity of sub-human forms is thus only a counterfeit fixity. We are naturally metaphysicians: hence the need to see the necessary and to liken in this instance the cosmic hierarchy to the series of whole numbers or to the immobile hierarchy of pure spirits, when there is only an analogy between them. If we are manifestly metaphysicians in our search for the necessary and the purely intelligible, we deceive ourselves and we reveal ourselves as undemanding when we think it is everywhere realized. And it is precisely in an era of metaphysical sterility that physical determinism was born.

To say that all the sub-species are contingent in their very structure is not to say that they all are so in the same fashion. A natural form is determined "ad unum" according to its degree of perfection, to the degree that it responds to the appetite matter is. The greater a determination, the more unique it is. The pure spirit, whose essence is totally determined, is absolutely unique as a species and as an individual. Material forms approach necessity to the degree that they emerge from matter. Nature tends toward essential necessity as it tends toward an ever greater positive indetermination, which is realized in the highest degree in human freedom. The more one ascends the natural hierarchy, the less contingent in their structure are forms, the more heterogeneous. Of all cosmic species only man cannot have sub-species, just because his form is spiritual, and in that the immobile determination toward which nature tends is realized. Moreover, even here, determination attains only the species and not the multitude of extremely various individuals through which the defect of determination due to matter is compensated.

The path that leads nature to its term becomes more and more straight, and when one considers the situation of the lineage of anthropoids one observes that the departures from the principal current are more and more easy and profound: the possibilities lessen because of the extreme determination required for man.

It is for experimental science to tell us how this world of "fluxibilia" is fashioned. This role devolves on experimental science precisely because one could not make of this domain rigorous deductions in function of the necessary. By its research it tries first of all to reconstitute the concrete path or paths which nature has in fact followed. But it also tries—and this is its principal role as 'science'—to find the essential limits within which the world should progress in order to arrive at man. Between these limits there is play. It is precisely this orientation of nature, very determined with respect to the final end, relatively undetermined with respect to the prior developments, which grounds the possibility of a science in this domain.

Let us now place ourselves in the point of view of nature taken in the strict sense of "principium et causa motus et quietis ejus in quo est primo et per se et non secundum accidens."

Natura determinata est ad unum. This is a principle that is ceaselessly abused. Habitually one fashions too homogeneous an idea of nature, as if all natures were equally natures. Ought one not rather say that there is nature only to the degree that matter and form are determined? If the form had perfect determination of itself, it would no longer be nature. Notice that not only is form called nature but also the matter of the composite. In beings where form alone is principle of activity, the form is not called a nature nor its activity movement.[9]

If natural beings form a hierarchy according to the degree of determination of their forms, they constitute a hierarchy of natures. There will be a gradation in the order of activity: effects will not be lawfully determined in their cause only to the degree of the perfection of nature. And if they are perfectly determined in their causes, neither the causes nor their effects will be natural. Taking into account the important distinction between indetermination by defect of being and indetermination by excess, it appears that in a higher nature the effect will be more assured in the cause and at the same time that the emanation will have less necessity, either because of spontaneity or because of freedom. The certitude grounded in the determination of nature is matched by an incertitude due to the very perfection of the cause.

Regarded under the aspect of negative indetermination, every future natural effect can be uncertain, not only because it cannot respond to the inclination of nature but also because none of the *intended* effects is sufficiently predetermined in its cause. Each future effect, taken individually, involves uncertainty. Only an absolutely determined cause can exclude the contingency of the future. It is false to think that in a natural cause certain effects are perfectly determined to be, others predetermined not to be or not to respond to the intention of nature. This is due to forgetting that matter is potency and that it is precisely its indetermination which is the cause of uncertainty, and that matter enters into play in every natural causation. "Est autem unumquodque contingens ex parte materiae: quia contingens est quod potest esse et non esse; potentia autem pertinet ad materiam. Necessitas autem consequitur rationem formae: quia ea quae consequuntur ad formam, ex necessitate insunt. Materia autem est individuationis principium. . . ."[10] But matter can be the cause of contingency only because there is a defect of determination even on the side of the agent cause. "Unde dicendum est quod possibilitas materiae ad utrumque, si communiter loquamur, non est sufficiens ratio contingentiae, nisi etiam addatur ex parte potentiae activae quod non sit omnino determinata ad unum; alioquin si ita sit determinata ad unum quod impediri non potest, consequens est quod ex necessitate reducat in actum potentiam passivam eodo modo."[11] There is play in the very interior of the determination of nature, to the degree that this can be entirely determined ad unum. The absence of necessity in the form entails an absence of necessity in the effects. "Quoniam entia necessaria, ut sic, abstrahunt ab omni tempore et mutatione, cum sint impossibilia aliter se habere: ac per hoc, cum ista sint consequentia materiam necessaria, quanto magis approprinquant ad materiam, tanto minus sint necessaria. Entia vero contingentia e converso se habent."[12] Taking into account this idea in the order of activity, it is evident that every natural generation involves uncertainty. If uncertainty were entirely eliminated, this would be because the form is entirely determined. But then generation itself would become impossible.

As in the case of form, this uncertainty affects the very structure of the effect and not only its existence. A child is not said to be defective because he is not a perfect reproduction of its parents. It can be particularly successful because he is different; which does not prevent its being a natural effect. Uncertainty does not suppress nature, it is the elimination of all uncertainty that suppresses nature.

If each nature taken individually always implies a certain dose of indetermination, how could the ensemble of natures totally compensate for this defect?[13] The whole of the universe does not permit us to abstract from the consequences of matter, as Vasquez did, or to a purely extrinsicist conception of the contingency in nature, with Suarez, who follows very close the Stoics of whom Thomas said, "dixerunt haec (possibile et necessarium) secundum exteriora prohibentia."[14] One can also see what are the effects of so profound a divergence from the doctrine concerning the principle of individuation.

To substitute for the uncertainty entailed by individual natures a necessity due to the ensemble is to deny the individual nature which is the intrinsic principle of movement. Even by adopting the surpassed hypothesis according to which the movement of the heavenly bodies was taken to be necessary, the works of lower nature would not have been: on the one hand, this movement communicated to lower agents, even if in itself necessary, was received according to the mode of the lower agents whose form is not wholly determined; on the other hand, the effect does not relate directly to the necessary cause, but mediately to the lower agent of which it bears the mark. That is, in causation one must take into account the non-subjected (*non-soumise*) matter.[15]

No doubt it does not suffice to consider an effect exclusively in its relation to the proximate cause to determine whether it is absolutely natural or not. It is the intention of universal nature which is primary and principal, and in this perspective the corruption of individuals and species is natural. But the birth of new species is also natural, although they are superior to the natures that precede them. It is not a matter of considering the particular end of individual agents or species, since these can be essentially ordered to something else and make sense only in the perspective of the universal order. Thus, the reproduction of similar individuals cannot be the final end of infra-human species, since this multiplication shades off into an unrealizable indefinite. Something else more perfect must result. Moreover, here below, every generation is essentially provisory. (This is what fixists forget when they attribute to natural generation properties which belong to generation only in God.) Lower natures are a function of universal nature even in generation. Still, when a higher nature is elicited from the potency of a lower nature by equivocal generation, this eliciting is still natural, not with reference, no doubt, to the lower agent considered in itself as lower—generatio est origo viventis a vivente *in similitudine naturae*—but it is always natural in the degree that it responds to the desire of the lower nature as ordered to the good of universal nature and to the ultimate intrinsic end of the world. And if the constitution of the hierarchy of cosmic species is an "opus naturae," the irregularity of this scale, as shown to us by experimental science, is perfectly explained.

Therefore there could only be perfect necessity in the works of nature if abstraction were made from matter—at once the principle of individuation and of contingency—which enters into every work of nature and without which nature is not nature. And when we speak of hypothetically necessary laws, we mean to say that an effect is certain to the degree that the form dominates matter. In other words, the laws of nature would be necessary if matter were neither nature nor the principle of contingency, if in the work of nature form alone were nature. The expression "hypothetically necessary" is therefore subject to a caution. It applies in no way to future contingents save in their relation to the divine intelligence and will.

Natural causes attain their effects in the majority of cases. But this must be understood. We say that the majority of human generations are successful, since the majority of men are also normal. But the majority of men are also mediocre. Yet mediocrity cannot be the intention of nature. In what sense can it be said that men are *naturally* mediocre? Because it is quite natural that mediocre generators produce mediocre children. What is astonishing is that they sometimes produce superior men. Moreover, it is the wise who are *de primaria intentione naturae,* and in this regard, the majority of men are nature's gaffs. It does not suffice then to consider an effect in its relation to the ultimate end in order to determine whether or not it is natural. For in this perspective, nature succeeds only exceptionally and this can be more natural than the *ut in pluribus.* It is not sufficient that a thing be exceptional and unforeseeable in order that it be due to chance. There is chance only when it is in the intention neither of the proximate cause nor in the intention of universal nature, because as long as it remains in these two orders, there are more or less determinate causes. Chance is an entirely undetermined cause.

The Accidental Causality of Nature

Consider a dog killed by the fall of a tree. We say that its accidental death is due to chance. What allows us to say this? Wasn't the tree determined to rot and fall with such and such a speed? And was not the dog pursuing such and such a cat that had hidden in the tree? Is it not natural for a dog to chase a cat and, being mortal, to be killed by such a weight? All that can be perfectly determined, therefore foreseeable. But if chance is the cause of essentially unforeseeable future contingents, how can we attribute this coincidence to chance?

Whatever the number and remoteness of the factors which enter into play in the phenomenon, it is absolutely certain that it was unforeseeable in its proper cause. One cannot deny it without denying nature. Let us interpret this example in the light of the fundamental principles of the theory of chance of Aristotle and St. Thomas.

a) *Virtus naturae se habet ad unum; quod autem est per accidens non est unum.*[16] The proposition, "the fall of a tree killed a dog" has only an accidental unity: there is no essential connection between the fall of a tree and the death of a dog. Otherwise, a tree could not fall without killing a dog, and the dog could only die by being crushed by a tree. But a natural cause is one and determinate. Therefore, such an effect can only have an indeterminate cause.

b) *Id quod est ut in pluribus est causa entis per accidens.* "Ens ut in pluribus est causa et principium quod aliquid sit per accidens. In rebus enim quae sunt semper, non potest esse aliquid per accidens; quia solum quod est per se potest esse necessarium et sempiternum. . . . Unde relinquitur, quod solum in contingentibus potest esse per accidens."[17] It is the insufficient determination of nature that makes possible events which exceed the very limits of nature, limits within which there is play. So much so that the contingency proper to chance presupposes a contingency, a *mutabilitas* in the natural cause. Whatever the perfection of the form, there always remains a margin of indetermination in the composite which exceeds it and can cause it to lack, or to achieve, an effect in no way predetermined in the nature, neither particular nor universal, since this margin exists for the entire universe.

c) *Chance is a cause and not an effect.* "[E]x quo non quodlibet quod fit habet causam per se, palam, quod in futuris contingentibus, effectus futuri reductio ad causam per se vadit usque ad aliquod principium; quod quidem principium non reducitur in aliquod principium adhuc per se, sed ipsum erit cujus causa 'erit quodcumque evenit,' idest *causa casualis,* et illius causae casualis non erit aliqua alia causa. . . ."[18] If chance were an effect, it would remain to ask what is its cause, and so on to infinity. One must accordingly distinguish between *casus* and the *casuale.* Between chance and the phenomenon produced by chance there is all the distance between indetermination and determination. So there is no distinction to be made here between contingency and indetermination. The effect is determined and as such is not contingent. "Nec distingui debet inter contingentiam et indifferentiam seu indeterminationem, ut aliqui faciunt," says John of St. Thomas, "quia contingens dicitur aliquid ex causa indifferenti ad utrumlibet in actu primo et antequam effectus producatur, ex eadem parte, ex qua habet contingentiam, habet indeterminationem, scilicet ex causis: extra causas autem nondum aliquid habet, vel si aliquid habet determinate, ibi amittet contingentiam ubi habet determinationem."[19] Once we know the direction taken by two causal lines, we can evidently predict their intersection. As soon as there is a determinate orientation, there is no more chance. When we see an ensemble of converging accidental causes, before they intersect, we are already in a determinate order where there is no longer contingency properly speaking. True contingency and chance are anterior to the direction which will terminate in the intersection: the prediction in question is not made from the side of the proper cause of this phenomenon, but from an effect henceforth determined which will end in the intersection; it is not the prediction of the effect from a indeterminate cause, which would be impossible. The death of our dog therefore is not due to chance in the measure that it is already determined in this constellation produced by cat, dog, tree, wind, etc., but in the measure that this constellation itself has no determinate cause.

d) "Causa per se est finita et determinatam; *causa autem per accidens est infinita et indeterminata, eo quod infinita uni possunt accidere.*"[20] The dog can die of old age, from sickness, from the fall of a tree; it can do it either by pursuing a cat or burying a bone, etc. The tree can fall because it is rotten, or because of the wind, or a thunderbolt, etc. It can rot because of age, because of insects, etc.

e) *Natural chance is opposed to fortune.* "Omne quod est a fortuna est a casu, sed non convertitur. . . . Casus non solum est in hominibus, qui voluntarie agunt, sed etiam in aliis animalibus, et etiam in rebus inanimatis. . . . Ostendit (Philosophus) in quibus maxime casus differt a fortuna. Et dicit quod maxime differt in illis quae fiunt a natura; quia ibi habet locum casus, sed non fortuna. Cum enim aliquid fit extra naturam in operationibus naturae, puta cum nascitur sextus digitus, tunc non dicimus quod fiat a fortuna, sed magis ab eo quod est per se frustra, idest a casu. Et sic possumus accipere aliam differentiam inter casum et fortunam, quod *eorum quae sunt a casu, causa est intrinseca, sicut eorum quae sunt a natura;* eorum vero quae sunt a fortuna, causa est extrinseca, sicut eorum quae sunt a proposito."[21] The death of our dog is therefore a chance event, but not a fortuitous one.[22] Chance is also opposed to art, not only because the principle of the latter is extrinsic, but because it involves finality, and in that art differs from fortune.[23] It is also distinct from the violent, "quod est a principio extrinseco vim passo non conferente." The violent can enter into a chance phenomenon, but it is not as violent that it is cause of accident, since it is a determinate and extrinsic cause.[24] Finally, chance and 'the vain' must be distinguished, since chance involves a determinate effect.[25] It is not insofar as it is violent that the tree is the cause of the dog's *accidental* death, and it would not have fallen in vain if it did not kill the dog.

f) "[H]ujusmodi causae (quae ordinantur ad suos effectus non ex necessitate sed ut in pluribus), non deficiunt in minori parte, *nisi propter aliquam causam impedientem. . . .*"[26] But if this cause is determinate, how can we speak of chance? Must we not say with Suarez, "sicut naturalis causa proxima non impedita et habens materiam aptam sufficienter applicatam, necessario producit proportionatum effectum, ita si eadem causa sit omnino impedita, eadem necessitate nihil operabitur, vel si non omnino, sed ex parte impedita est, eadem necessitate faciet imperfectum et monstruosum effectum; ergo si causae omnes tam agentes quam impedientes ex solo naturali ac necessario cursu ita conveniunt, et singulae etiam cum necessitate operantur suo modo, id est, quae impedit, necessario impedit, et quae materiam applicat, necessario, et sic de aliis; ergo talis effectus consideratus in ordine ad totam seriem et collectionem talium causarum, non habet contingentiam, sed necessitatem"?[27] In this case, chance would be reduced to a pure encounter, it is no longer an intrinsic cause, it is no longer truly contingent: "extrinsece dicitur effectus contingens, quando carentia necessitatis quae in illo est, solum est ab extrinsecis impedimentis."[28] These principles being given, Suarez is perfectly right in saying that chance is contingent only secundum quid, and that in this domain there cannot be any future contingents. But that is the great difference between the Stoics and St. Thomas. "Stoici vero distinxerunt (possibile et necessarium) secundum exteriora prohibentia. Dixerunt enim necessarium esse illud quod non potest prohiberi quin sit verum; impossibile vero quod semper prohibetur a veritate; possibile vero quod potest prohiberi vel non prohiberi. (Haec) autem distinctio videtur esse incompetens . . .

(quia) assignatio est ab exteriori et quasi per accidens; non enim ideo aliquid est necessarium, quia non habet impedimentum, sed quia est necessarium, ideo impedimentum habere non potest."[29] With these words, St. Thomas rejects the distinction between the necessary of fact and the necessary by right applied to the contingency of nature. "Et ideo alii melius ista distinxerunt *secundum naturam rerum,* ut scilicet dicatur illud necessarium, quod in sua natura determinatum est solum ad esse; impossibile autem quod est determinatum solum ad non esse; possibile autem quod ad neutrum est omnino determinatum, sive se habeat magis ad unum quam ad alterum, sive se habeat aequaliter ad utrumque, quod dicitur contingens ad utrumlibet."[30]

If chance is an intrinsic cause, there is an analogy with divine causality in our exercise of freedom and its causality in chance, which is also in a certain manner in nature as liberty is in our will. But in the conception of Suarez, God is immediately and exclusively cause of chance. For any given constellation selected necessarily entails such interferences predetermined in that constellation. These interferences would not be due to chance save insofar as God could have chosen another constellation.[31] For St. Thomas, on the contrary, it is the indetermination that any constellation involves which is the cause of the effects of chance: future and contingent encounters have their cause, not in the constellation insofar as it is determinate, but in the indetermination, the indefinite margin of matter exceeding form.

Let us note that the hypothetical necessity of which Aristotle speaks (*Physics* II, 9; *On Generation and Corruption,* chap. 11) goes from the consequent to the antecedent, and not vice versa. If the consequent is given, the antecedent was necessary in order for the consequent to be given. The necessity of the antecedent is grounded in the consequent, and not vice versa. The antecedent is only hypothetically necessary: "Quod autem habet necessitatem ab eo quod est posterius in esse, est necessarium ex conditione, vel suppositione; ut puta si dicatur, necesse est hoc esse si hoc debeat fieri; et hujusmodi necessitas est ex fine et forma inquantum est finis generationis. Quaerere igitur utrum in rebus naturalibus sit necessarium simpliciter aut ex suppositione, nihil aliud est quam quaerere utrum in rebus naturalibus necessitas inveniatur ex fine, aut ex materia."[32] When we say that, a certain constellation being given, certain effects are hypothetically necessary, we reverse the order. We should rather say: such effects being given, such a constellation was hypothetically necessary. If the effects are accidental they necessarily have a determinate cause. One could also say: given the margin of indetermination that the constellation involves, some future contingents—and not this or that future contingent—are hypothetically necessary; which means that the contingency, that is to say, the non-necessity, cannot be impeded. For even hypothetical necessity excludes the possibility of an impediment. If the initial constellation were absolutely determined, effects would be absolutely necessary, and there would be a conversion of terms. In this case, the constellation is no longer hypothetically necessary, but absolutely. And thereby we destroy time. "For that which is necessarily is also, at the same time, what always is, since what is necessary cannot not be. It follows that, if a thing exists necessarily, it is eternal, and if it is eternal, it is necessary. Therefore if the generation of something is absolutely necessary, it is necessarily circular and returns to its point of departure."[33] If the point of departure and the term coincide, we have an identity that makes the hypothetical impossible.

If chance is an intrinsic and indeterminate cause, and if this cause has no power to determine itself in one direction rather than another, how can it be in anything other than a purely passive fashion? The casual is a determined phenomenon. There must be a passage from indetermination to determination. Thus it is necessary that "tam casus quam fortuna reducuntur ad genus causae moventis: quia casus et fortuna vel est causa eorum quae sunt a natura, vel eorum quae sunt ab intelligentia . . . ; unde cum natura et intelligentia sint causae ut unde est principium motus, etiam fortuna et casus ad idem genus reducuntur. Sed tamen, quia casus et fortuna sunt causae per accidens, eorum multitudo est indeterminata."[34] A passive potency—and such is the case with chance—can only be actuated by a cause in act. In other words, how can chance be an intrinsic and undetermined cause without liberty? And if the determined impediment is cause of the casual, there is no more chance and the casual is only a metaphor. St. Thomas addressed this difficulty perfectly: "Sed nullum tale principium invenitur in rebus naturalibus, quod habeat libertatem sequendi vel non sequendi impressiones caelestes. Unde videtur quod in talibus, ad minus, omnia ex necessitate proveniant: secundum antiquam quorumdam rationem, qui, supponentes omne quod est causam habere, et quod, posita causa, ex necessitate ponitur effectus, concludebant quod omnia ex necessitate contingunt" and if moreover "ipsum impedimentum talis causae (impedibilis) ex necessitate contingit," how can the effect be contingent?[35]

One must distinguish between the "impedimentum ex parte agentis, vel ex parte recipientis actione," and the latter is nothing other than the *possibilitas materiae*.[36] There are active obstacles and passive obstacles. The former is determined. But it is not an impediment insofar as it is determined, but in relation to that which can be impeded or not because of the matter: "Impedimentum enim duo dicit," Cajetan observes, "scilicet rem quae impedit; et relationem ad aliud ex qua (relatione) denominatur impedimentum."[37] And one must also distinguish in the passive obstacle the indisposition due to other determinate causes (if the dog had not eaten, it would have been quicker) and the natural indisposition one finds in every corruptible thing because of matter. The latter is the cause of the casual effect. One also sees how, in the final account, every obstacle that enters into play in the phenomenon of chance is grounded in indetermination: "potentia defectiva quocunque defectu, ad potentiam passivam reducitur."[38]

Let us note that the margin of indetermination which exceeds the form and this form itself are incommensurable, since matter is indetermination. Suarez speaks of the one and the other as if their conjunction permitted us to establish in advance what will result: "si non omnino, sed ex parte impedita sit, eadem necessitate. . . ." The form is definite, but the margin of indetermination always remains indefinite, even if its range diminishes according to the perfection of the form. To say that "there no longer remains but a *certain* quantity of indetermination" is to suppress indetermination. All we can say is that, given the perfection of the form, there will be that much more probability that it will conquer the matter. That matter should play no role is not determined in advance.

The effect of chance is characterized by its lack of unity: it does not have sufficient determination to be an *unum per se*. Under this aspect, it is something privative, a determination which fails from the point of view of intention. I say from the point of view of intention, since the fact of finding a bone while running after the cat is a happy coincidence for the dog. Chance then is not a determinate cause, but a cause of insufficient determination, a cause of the absence of unity. We ought not therefore have recourse to a power which determines itself to one direction rather than another in order to explain the phenomena of chance.

g) *Talis concursus non habet causam inquantum est per accidens*.[39] It is often said that chance is brought on by the encounter of a plurality of causes and that because these causes are not ordered per se to this encounter, their intersection is only accidental. It is clear that in this hypothesis the phenomenon of chance is perfectly foreseeable, for it would suffice to know the orientation of these determinate causes. Unfortunately, this suppresses the very idea of a cause per accidens. The plurality of which Aristotle and St. Thomas speak is indefinite as the *possibilitas materiae,* and as soon as a determination (orientation) is introduced, there is no longer plurality. In the example we have been using, the plurality is not constituted by the dog, the cat, the tree, the wind, etc. There is a plurality in the dog that can die and in the tree that can fall for quite other reasons. As soon as the death of the dog is determined by the ensemble of factors constituting this constellation, there is no longer plurality, while there are always several causal series: for it is neither these determined causal series or their accidental orientation, nor their encounter, which causes the effect as effect of chance. The accidental concourse, *as it is habitually understood,* is not the cause of the casual: it is already an effect. This concursus so understood is accidental because it has no determinate cause. "Et propter hoc, id quod ex tali concursu sequitur, non reducitur in aliquam causam praeexistentem, ex qua ex necessitate sequatur," because the concourse itself, as accidental, is not a determinate cause.[40]

h) "Haec enim contingentia, *si ulterius in causam caelestem deducantur, multa horum invenientur non esse per accidens.*"[41] Who does not see that we often attribute to chance what is quite natural? Does not progress in science consist precisely in eliminating more and more this appearance of chance? No doubt. But then what allows me to say that chance is the cause of the death of the dog? This is because we have chosen a particularly privileged example. We know sufficiently what is a dog and what a tree to judge the proposition "the death of the dog is caused by the fall of the tree" has only accidental unity, therefore an indeterminate cause. It is only when the terms of the proposition are not sufficiently known that it is impossible to choose between nature and chance. Let us repeat again that the factors that permitted me to foresee the coincidence are not the cause of the accident, even if this convergence has been determined for ages. It is one thing to establish that a phenomenon is due to chance, and another to determine the moment from which this phenomenon was predetermined. And if the effect truly lacks unity one can say in advance that it is impossible to remount indefinitely the series of per se causes. If one could do that, this is because the series of natural causes would be contradictory among themselves insofar as determined ad unum.

"[T]amen etiam hac reductione facta, inveniuntur esse aliqua per accidens."[42] There are phenomena which are absolutely unforeseeable, whatever the perfection of the intelligence in play. (I see 'unforeseeable' such that if God could only know effects in their causes, he would not know future contingents.) Let us not say that it could *foresee* for extrinsic reasons, for to the degree that extrinsic reasons determine the future, this future is no longer contingent, but necessary and knowable because it is already present. "[F]utura, secundum quod habent determinationem in causis suis, accedunt ad rationem *praesentium,* inquantum jam quodammodo sunt determinata in causis suis"; ". . . quia contingentia futura non sunt determinata in causis suis, sed facta determinatione causarum efficiuntur in actu praesentia; et ideo eorum, quamdiu futura sunt, cognitionem (angeli) non habent."[43]

It is evident that the pure spirits already see futures which appear contingent to us: "quaedam quae contingentia *videntur.*"[44] Their intelligence surpasses ours "in hoc quod contingentiam *determinatorum is suis causis* plura et certius novit."[45] One cannot find any text of St. Thomas in which he does not take into account this quite essential nuance. Even when he treats of destiny (fatum) he ascribes to Providence the necessity of natural future contingents: "ea quae hic per accidens aguntur, *sive in rebus naturalibus* sive in rebus hunanis, reducuntur in aliquam causam praeordinantem, quae est providentia divina."[46] Suarez, on the contrary, can speak of fatal necessity in natural things untroubled by the intervention of free agents; and he can do it because in this domain he rejects future contingents.[47]

When St. Thomas refutes the Stoics—"qui posuerunt fatum in quadam serie, seu connexione causarum, supponentes quod omne quod in hoc mundo accidit habet causam; causa autem posita, necesse est effectum poni. Et si una causa per se non sufficit, multae causae ad hoc concurrentes accipiunt rationem unius causae sufficientis; et ita concludebant quod omnia ex necessitate eveniunt"—he makes appeal not only to human liberty, but even "in aliis corporalibus effectibus rerum corruptibilium, in quibus multa per accidens eveniunt" to created causes which, whatever be their necessity cannot introduce the necessary.[48]

i) *The fecundity of chance and fortune.* "[C]asus dicitur ex hoc quod consequitur aliquid aliud quod non intendebatur."[49] When the dog in pursuing the cat finds a bone, this was not in his intention; however, it is pleasant and it coincides with another intention, more constant no doubt than that to pursue cats: to chew a bone. The bone enters per se in the intention. But that this intention be accomplished by realizing another, that is accidental. One sees here how chance can rejoin finality with respect to per se causes. If natural causes were to succeed always, being given as well the restrictions due to their very determinations, many happy combinations would be eliminated by that very fact. And if Mr. Kwabberbil had not had the good fortune of meeting Sophie with whom he fell in love when he went to the inn for a glass of beer, all the little Kwabberbils issued from their marriage as per se effects would never have been.

Chance is in no way the proper cause of the natural result of these casual coincidences, but the fact that the encounters arise from per se causes: "id quod est per accidens reducitur ad per se, in quantum accidit ei quod est per se, sicut musicum accidit Socrati, et omne accidens alicui subjecto per se existenti. Et similiter omne quod in aliquo effectu est per accidens consideratur circa aliquem effectum per se: qui quantum ad id quod inest ei per accidens non habet causam per se sed causam per accidens. Oportet enim effectum proportionaliter referre ad causam suam."[50]

Just as a free act can involve happy consequences in no way intended in its determination, so matter has reserves that the determined nature can exploit. Universal nature is not only the sum of particular natures: the whole has its own superabundance that the parts do not. Chance and fortune are in their way necessary for the finality of the world. However this necessity does not predetermine the determined encounters which will take place any more than the necessity of willing happiness deprives us of free will.

One also sees the sense in which we can speak of *creation of possibles.* (Evidently, creation is taken in a large sense here.) And this idea applies not only to chance and fortune but even to nature. We have already said that the infra-human cosmic species are not absolutely certain with regard to their structures, nor true apriori. Each species is new in its structure. Once established, it constitutes a determined point of departure for other species in which the determination of their strain will be in a certain fashion prolonged: this determination has opened the world to essential structures that could not possibly have been determinately possible without it.

II

Before taking up the problem of indeterminism as it is posed for us by the experimental sciences, there must be precision about the sense and value of scientific entities and formally scientific laws.

Every science seeks to reduce the complex to the most simple and to explain it as a function of it. But the meaning of the term 'simple' must be understood. The nature of the simple to which it leads back will profoundly differentiate the sciences. It is easy to show that what we call simple in experimental sciences is quite opposed to what we call simple in philosophy. In experimental science a rock is infinitely more simple than a cell; the movement of a piston is more simple than the leap of a panther onto its prey; of all the beings experimental science studies man is incontestably the most complex. But in philosophy quite the opposite is true. The animal is more simple than the plant, and of all the beings that philosophy of nature studies, it is man who is the most simple; so too in metaphysics the measure and the cause of every being is the absolute simplicity of Pure Act. In physics one measures by the *minima mensura,* time by atomic time, for example; in philosophy the measure is always rich and comprehensive, time is measured by eviternity, and both by eternity.

In other words, experimental simplicity is inversely proportional to ontological simplicity. The philosopher will say that the scientist explains the higher by the lower, the perfect by the imperfect. Thus we can say in advance that to the degree that an experimental explanation of man is possible, it will consist in studying him in the perspective of that which is experimentally simpler than he is, not in order to identify the complex and elementary with one another, but to derive the one from the other. It is thus quite natural for the scientist to seek to derive man from the animal, and animal from plant, and to see the whole hierarchy of natural species arise in the direction of an ever increasing and more complex organization. The philosopher who denies the very possibility of an evolutionist theory denies the very essence of the scientific method. If he were logical, he ought also deny the value of the measure of length. Nor can one hope to escape this consequence by saying that the animal and plant are heterogeneous and resist a homogeneous measure. Can we not measure their duration, and the quantitative measure from which it proceeds by the same clock? Moreover, since existence is proportional to essence—quantum unicuique inest de forma, tantum inest ei de virtute essendi—the duration of cosmic beings is also more and more simple, less and less temporal; thus there exists a hierarchy of cosmic durations. But this ontological heterogeneity does not prevent physical time which one defines by its procedure of measurement from embracing all spatio-temporal beings by what is homogeneous in them from the point of view of duration. This common measure is founded on the common genus of corporeity in which all natural beings agree. Physical time attains only their background (bas-fond) and touches that only from without. Homogeneity is the basis for every quantitative measurement; this common physical genus sufficiently explains the specific unity of experimental time and why heterogeneity of durations escapes the grasp of a metric calculated on homogeneous exteriority. Experimental science begins there where all beings come together and are one: the graduated scale on the balance shows no difference between 150 pounds of man and 150 pounds of bricks. If physical time touched beings in their ontological and specific ground, if this time exhausted the real, if only from the point of view of duration, the different degrees of being would be only epiphenomena of growing physical complexity. Even if things are more than their outsides, this does not prevent the measure of their homogeneous exteriority from being common and true. These two perspectives are not contraries, they complement one another. Without knowing the experimental complexity of a thing one cannot grasp the richness of its ontological unity.

Confined from the outset to the domain of common sensibles which are all reducible to quantity, having for *formal subject* the measurable aspect of things *as measured,* and the quantitative measure from which it proceeds being found on homogeneous exteriority, experimental science can only touch nature from without and can never go behind what is outside. Being able to attain its object only by means of an artful operation—the scientist *makes* experiments[51]—it can only arrive at a concept based on the measurements effected by the repetition of experiences. It takes its proper point of departure in a work of art, the result of a certain procedure of measurement effected in determinate circumstances, and defined by the description of that procedure.[52] The following passage from Eddington expresses this idea very clearly: "The physical quantity so discovered, is primarily the result of the operations and calculations; it is, so to speak, a *manufactured article*—manufactured by our operations."[53] It is the *known quantities*, defined as such, that enter into science. But between the number-measures determined by the graduated scale of an instrument and the *material subject*, there is the fabrication from which one cannot abstract without falling into subjectivism.[54] Let us not confuse the prescientific given with the number-measure which is not an immediate and adequate translation of that given. It is not the object in the balance dish that is the proper point of departure of scientific elaboration, but the number on the graduated scale on which the needle rests. Once I have defined the property, I cannot apply it as such to the object, as if the balance were a species of screen and in weighing one peeked 'behind' the balance to surprise the bare object. (And that is indeed what one thought he was doing prior to the Einsteinian criticism of the measurements of space and time, forgetting that the very circumstances of measuring are part of the definition and that different circumstances qualitatively change the definition. To say that the quantitatively different definitions of length *ought* to have the same quantitative value is to fall into the relativism from which Einstein has freed us.) Let us not say that the concepts of science rest by definition on a distortion of the world and that thus the documents of the physicists are from the start forged and betray reality. But of course one ought not be abused by this distortion. The documents are faithful in their fashion and only deceive when one gives them a meaning to which they do not pretend. Is light an evil demon who toys with us when a stick plunged in water looks bent? No more than my radio is responsible if my children think there is a monster hidden in the cabinet.

The only things that science can attain are those which can be registered in number-measures. But that in things which permits this—and never forget the distance separating what permits this and the result—is not the whole of the thing: it is only its measurable aspect. And if this measurable aspect is all quite real, that does not mean that one can consider it as existing apart. One cannot derive ontological cuts from metric cuts. The sun and moon are not two substantial beings because they are distant and separated from one another by a certain void. The fundamental entities of physics are only cuts in the metric aspect of things, things from which moreover the physicist wholly abstracts. It is absurd to consider the atom to be a thing. Such entities are real only as a smile is. It is as senseless to speak of the hylomorphic composition of bodies taken in the sense of physics as to speak of the hylomorphic composition of a smile, even if the smile finds its ultimate reason in rationality, and rationality presupposes prime matter. It is also without meaning to ask if the counterpoint realized in the execution of a symphony is composed of matter and form. Contemporary scholastics who indulge in such absurdities—and who manage to amaze their confreres—are legion. A flock of false problems are created in this way. One asks if a molecule of water is an individual, or Siamese twins, *vel aliquid hujusmodi.*

Experimental science can never rid itself of a certain nominalism and never arrives at concepts independent of experience in their structure. It is not a "discipline." It defines its concepts with reference to concrete experience from which it never completely abstracts, because this experience itself is never complete. The truth of propositions is not justified by their logical coherence; still it is necessary that these propositions are really true, for every experimental science, in the measure that it attains the level of science, is *physico-mathematical.* Newtonian space was three dimensional, Euclidean. That is what experience seems to show. When Einstein arrived, one noticed that the majority of physicists had forgotten the experimental foundation of this idea. They thought that one could now separate the ideal of experience from that which had formulated it, forgetting that the idea has no experimental sense apart from its genesis.

This is because every formally scientific concept is grounded on an incomplete induction indefinitely perfectible—*inductio per descensum* can never rejoin experience to the point of closing the concept and making it a universal properly speaking: its very genesis is never terminated. In other words, experimental science can never attain the first degree of abstraction. But just as nature tends to an ever greater determination, experimental science tends toward the first degree of abstraction.

This is not to call into question the rigor of scientific reasoning nor to contest the logical coherence of a theory. It is when it is a matter of the real value of deductions from a theory that one observes their inadequate character. Let a determinist mechanics be as necessary and absolute as one wishes, is it really true? Or can one at least imagine experiences which would confirm it? If not, in what sense can it be called physical? If the confirmation of a principle has to await a future indefinitely remote, it loses by that very fact its experimental character: it is methodologically false.

But that is the case with what is called the principle of causality in experimental science. According to this principle the entire future will be rigorously predetermined in the present, and a sufficiently powerful intelligence, etc. We know the hypothesis of Laplace.

The principle will be immanent in every law of behavior. (Excluded by this fact are the laws of identity—and perhaps the transcendental laws of atomicity—since they abstract from the relation of the present to the future.[55] Thus the law of the conservation of energy is by definition invariable—which is not to say that it is really true.) The character of the second law of thermodynamics will be purely subjective. The impossibility of inserting the fundamental entities of the physical world into a space-time scheme always and rigorously determined will be due to our ignorance, or even to the accidental or essential defectiveness of our means of observation.

Moreover, no modern scientist pretends to formulate experimentally a law of rigorous behavior. All the known laws are statistical, which does not prevent their explaining sufficiently the observed regularities. But there is no agreement on the future of these laws. Some think that one day this statistical character will be replaced by absolute rigor; others are convinced that it is necessary to reject definitively the determinist ideal, and that even if there is determinism in the world, we could never know it.

The principle of determinism deserves to be called physical only if it can be verified in experience. Everyone agrees on that, even the determinists.[56] But one can demonstrate that this principle postulates an impossible experience.

Let us suppose a super-physicist contemplating a finite spatio-temporal world from its beginning to its end. (One must indeed close this universe even from the point of view of time if we posit as condition a complete experience.) When the farce has been thus enacted, he has observed that all phenomena have unfolded with perfect regularity and are inserted in the differential equation that he originally formulated. Could one deduce from this that this universe has been ruled by absolutely rigorous laws? That is probably what he would do if he lacked imagination. But if he wants to explain what has happened, if he is not content to write natural history, he will show that even if the behavior of isolated microscopic entities had been undetermined, being given their large number, the development of this universe would have been sensibly such as it has been. He would never be able to say that the development could not have been other than it has been. In order to be certain, he would have to make everything rebegin indefinitely. And then?

We should not say that experience would be sufficient only if this universe had realized all possible cases. But if we must imagine as matter of ideal experience a universe where all possible cases are realized, it would be easy to imagine a super-physicist and have him await the end of the development: such a universe would be by definition determinist; knowledge of the initial constellation would be sufficient, and if it was sufficient, there would be no need to await the outcome.

One calls this a *petitio principii.* The determinist posits a principle which allows him to predict the future absolutely, but whose value depends on the future. If the future were present, the principle would no longer make sense. But to show that it makes sense, it is necessary that the future be present. As Eddington would say: the determinist can make prophecies only after the accomplishment of facts. Note that he cannot demonstrate it apriori. If demonstration there be, it could only be philosophical. He could say: every effect has a cause. But effect and cause have a quite different sense in philosophy; moreover, the effect is proportioned to the cause: every effect requires only an equally determined cause. This proportionality is necessary in virtue of the ontological principle of causality itself. And after making the transposition of this principle to the experimental order, he would notice that in physics there is question only of a certain formal, not efficient, causality: it only expresses a metric coherence of phenomena. What could be more natural, since his science is physico-*mathematical.*

At bottom, it is time that rebels against the physical principle of causality and is the enemy of the determinist. Even if the entire past had realized his hopes, the future will still be uncertain, unless he can demonstrate that the future is present and that he suppresses time. In this case the principle of causality becomes absolutely useless—there is no longer anything to predict.

Not only does he do metaphysics in conceiving physical entities as things entirely determined in themselves: he spatializes time. To exist, he tells himself, is to be somewhere at a certain moment. If a particule ceases to be somewhere, it ceases to exist, and vice versa. Since it is always, we must be able to follow its trace; its trajectory must be simultaneously a spatial value and a temporal value: it cannot have the one in isolation without ceasing to exist. Still, if we cannot determine both the position and the velocity of an electron, this is because our knowledge of this phenomenon is still insufficient. As in reality the two are determined together, the scientist ought to seek to know them experimentally as such.

Such reasoning would be troublesome if their terms had an ontological meaning. But if one sets philosophical prejudices aside, if one holds to their purely physical meaning, no difficulty is presented. The contradiction only appears at the moment when we confuse the two domains, at the moment where we give to space, to time, and to the corpuscle a directly ontological meaning. Evidently, if one claims the right to confuse, the confusion poses an insoluble problem. But note, too, that the beings of which we speak in the philosophy of nature are from the metric point of view macroscopic ensembles for which this question does not arise. With what right does one attribute the properties of the ensemble to each of its constituents individually taken?

Certainly, it is not experience that allows us to affirm that there exists on the microscopic scale a perfect symmetry between space and time. This symmetry only appears on the macroscopic scale and it is perfectly compatible with a dissymmetry in the components. The uncertainty of the individual throws of a die does not impede us from making predictions about a large number of throws, predictions whose certainty augments with the size of the ensemble. The ensemble has a determination that the parts do not.

It has been pretended that the certitude that bears on an ensemble presupposes a determinism on the side of the components. This affirmation is at the least strange. One cannot all the same contest the outcome of the predictions. I do not know which facet will be presented in the individual throws, but this ignorance does not impede me from predicting that in six thousand throws, the facets will be equally distributed. If this prediction is not verified, I would have suspicions about the die and not about my calculation. The only thing I have to know at the outset is the number of alternatives, the equiprobability of these alternatives, the independence of the individual throws and their number. If the alternatives are not equiprobable, that is, if there is not perfect indetermination within the limits of the determined number of alternatives, my prediction will be false. Macroscopic determinism is conditioned by microscopic indeterminism. Moreover, the kind of determinism in question cannot be absolute, for that would presuppose an actual infinite of constituents, that is, a contradiction.

Time should not embarrass the determinist since his principle denies it in advance. For to establish a perfect symmetry between time and space is to deny time, it is to immobilize the universe from the point of view of duration and render it absolutely reversible.

Let us consider for a moment the astronomical hypothesis of Father Lemaitre. There seems to exist between the law of the degradation of energy and the expansion of the universe a constant relation: the entropy of the universe is proportional to its volume. "The augmentation of entropy which characterizes the direction of evolution is the progressive fragmentation of the energy which exists at the beginning in a unique package."[57] The scattering comprises a growth of the world. For growing disorder takes more and more space, or rather, disorder makes more and more space. An assembled toy cannot be inserted in its box save on condition that all the parts are put in good order. The initial state and the present state of the universe are comparable to a valise which at the outset is well ordered and at the end of the trip cannot be closed without being sat upon. While the expansion of a man comes about thanks to borrowing from his milieu, the expansion of the universe—since it is not in a milieu but itself constitutes the milieu—cannot take place at the expense of the milieu. For it there exist no reserves of time and space: it cannot borrow from volume for its volume. It cannot snowball. It must inflate from its own substance like a soap bubble. The collapse of the world should lead to the new—a new which must be drawn from within the universe. This new cannot be spatio-temporally determined in the present world: otherwise the new would be always present and time would not advance. The new of the future can be true only in the present possibility of a future disorder. The fading away of the present order is a condition of the new. Let us not say that disorder can be determinately foreseen in all respects, since that would suppose that it already has a determinate spatio-temporal value. But in what would the progression of time then consist? It is indeed necessary that there exist in the present a certain dose of indetermination with respect to the future. The direction of time is only true and objective if a certain indeterminism exists in the world. That is to say that tomorrow can only be true on condition that it is not entirely today. By this indeterminism of the microscopic order we can explain the novelty necessary if the direction of time is to have a real value, and the regularity of the macroscopic order where a determinism bordering on necessity and certitude can reign.

What is so reprehensible in the following affirmation: If at instance t' the electron e is in the orbit b, that does not mean that at the instant t it was determinately true that at instant t' it will be in the orbit b? For Heisenberg could it not be said that the question of knowing whether a complete knowledge of the past can predict the future does not arise, since a complete knowledge of the past implies a contradiction? Does not the philosopher also say: "Si enim similiter se habet veritas et falsitas in praesentibus et futuris, sequitur ut quidquid verum est de praesenti, etiam fuerit verum de futuro, eo modo quo est verum de praesenti . . . ergo si ante unum diem verum fuit dicere quod erit album sequitur quod semper fuit verum dicere de quolibet eorum quae facta sunt, quod erit. . . . Sequitur ergo ex praemissis quod omnia, quae futura sunt, necesse est fieri. . . . Ergo est falsum scilicet quod omne quod est verum esse, verum fuerit determinate dicere esse futurum."[58] It is right to cite this text since the difficulties raised against the proposition are purely philosophical.

Let us not say that if there exist equal alternatives for the fundamental entities of physics, the macroscopic order is a result of chance, the universe is ruled by the laws of chance. Let us not be duped by words. Since a statistical law expresses a regularity, one ought not give the current expression "law of chance" a philosophical meaning. If a comparison must be made, should not "chance' be translated as improbable? As for the law of large numbers that the universe follows from the physical point of view, is not this tendency toward unity just a sign of nature? But rapprochements are dangerous in this domain and require a more profound study which we will have occasion to give elsewhere.

Too univocal rapprochements between physical indeterminism and the indeterminism we encounter in experimental biology have been made, as if the one were a reenforcement of the other. The spontaneity of microscopic entities is spoken of as if it were of the genus of life. If this were only a simple analogy, I see nothing reprehensible in it. But if one takes the term 'spontaneity' in its rigorous sense the assimilation cannot be admitted.

All the beings that we encounter are composed of atoms: the inorganic world, potatoes, rats, professors, etc. All are composed of purely physical elements. Yes, but while all beings are covered by the physical point of view, this point of view does not cover the whole of these beings; it is neither exclusive nor exhaustive. Nothing among the living goes against the principle of the conservation of energy—supposing this principle to be true and that the degradation of energy is objectively statistical. The atoms of a man are as truly physical atoms as those of a rock. But the atoms are not parts of beings as bricks are of a house. The physical world is only one of the metric aspects of the universe. How should we distinguish the world of experimental biology from that of physics? Life is not inserted into the physical world like a coin. They are not distinct like things juxtaposed or superimposed. A living being is not opposed to a physical being but to a non-living being. Most authors seem to confuse the physical world with the inorganic world. But this confusion can be explained. While from the experimental point of view physical laws sufficiently explain inorganic phenomena, these same laws, even while being verified of the living being, do not suffice to explain the whole of the metric and experimental aspect of the living. Phenomena present themselves which, without being contrary to physics, oblige us to formulate laws proper to living things: formally biological laws.

Let us adopt a more restricted point of view that will make this opposition clearer. Whereas the physicist observes in the world a greater and greater disorganization and diffusion, the biologist encounters living islands, on the way to a higher and higher organization, toward a more intense concentration. Like a trout or salmon mounting rapids, life seems to progress against and despite the current of degradation that carries the physical world toward extinction. Nutrition which is assimilative and enriching from the biological point of view is combustion from the physical point of view. And the higher forms of life eat the lower. Life is organized by disorganizing. The universe, in expansion from the physical point of view, rebounds on itself in life, thus constituting centers of density ever more heterogeneous. To employ an image: just as a toy to be assembled is not made in order to remain neatly stored in its box, but to make marionettes, the physical universe also serves a higher goal which it approaches by losing its initial state of organization. The universe unpacks its matter in view of a higher construction. It is like the eggshell which breaks in order to free the chick.

Let us now apply this distinction to the question of indeterminism. The physical world, even living things, tends toward disorder. From the physical point of view, there is more and more chance in the world. The more loosed and scattered, the more difficult is it to predict the behavior of physical entities. Let us say that on this scale unpredictability is proportional to the degree of entropy, entropy being the measure of disorder. (One could object that the universe, in approaching the state of thermodynamic equilibrium, becomes, in this way, more and more determined, and that predictability ought to increase in proportion. But that would be to forget that this equilibrium is characterized by the absence of time and of a future to foresee.)

The biologist observes an analogous phenomenon. But for him predictability is proportional to the degree of organization: the more organization there is, the more spontaneity, a spontaneity which, like chance, escapes the grasp of metric rigor. Arrived at man, who presents a maximum of organization, characteristic behavior involves the absolutely unforeseeable: his liberty gives him a degree of spontaneity that entirely escapes the grasp of the metric. In living things spontaneity emanates from the subject, it results from an interior integration, it is the measure of the degree of interiority.

I well know that these considerations will not interest the biologist. This classification of living things according to their degree of spontaneity would even make most of them laugh, so much more so since a good number of them are still mechanists. Even while admitting spontaneity, it is extremely difficult to know in what measure the margin of indetermination is due to our ignorance and in what measure it is objective. But I do not think I will scandalize biologists by saying that the behavior of a dog is more spontaneous than that of infusoria.

In philosophy of science these considerations are capital. Between the opposition we have just introduced and that between positive and negative indetermination, a symmetry evidently suggests itself. The ontological opposition is manifestly the root of the first. Let it suffice to say here that when one speaks of spontaneity in the physical world, one uses this term in a completely improper sense.[59]

Here is another philosophical reflection that can appear ridiculous in the eyes of the biologist. In the domains where one can observe them, mutations are produced with a certain frequency, but by chance. Taking account of the particular characteristics of each species which determines this frequency, these hereditary variations seem to appear according to the law of large numbers. It is for genetics to provide an experimental explanation of this phenomenon. How might one interpret it in philosophy? Let us say immediately that this interpretation is completely devoid of sense in experimental biology. The philosophy of nature teaches us that the infra-human living species are purely functional. They exist only as a provisory state of the universe and are made to disappear. The multiplication of their individuals cannot be itself its end: it must be essentially ordered to something else which transcends the species. It should signify a qualitative enrichment of the species without which it would be a pure diffusion in quantity. This enrichment has no place in the individuals taken in isolation, it is a quality of the ensemble. In this multiplication the ensemble must become more and more determined and certain. Since this numerical increase cannot lose itself in the indefinite, it must have an approximative term, determined by the nature of its own species. This term will be the mutation. It will be produced by chance, that is, no individual of the species taken in isolation is especially disposed to undergo it. The regressive or indifferent character of most mutations and the weak probability of their persistence takes nothing away from the value of this explanation: they are quite simply signs of the resistance of matter. It is only in the rarest of exceptions that universal nature attains its term. We have only to think of humankind.

III

The consequences of hylomorphic composition are thus the objective foundation of the distinction between the experimental sciences and the disciplines. Philosophy of nature, being *scientia certa per causas,* can only attain what is essential and necessary to nature, such as the hylomorphic composition of natural substances, the contingency this composition entails, the necessity of evolution, the necessity of humanity as the ultimate end of this ascension of the world, etc. In short, what one can establish with rigor are what Maritain calls *philosophical facts.*

Experimental science, on the contrary, to the degree that it does not confine itself to pure truisms and tautologies, to the degree that it is an explanatory science, can only give us a probable knowledge of things. I am not speaking of particular observations which can be perfectly certain, but of the laws of behavior and of theories. These probabilities can achieve enormous proportions, they can provide what we call practical certitude, to the point where they create the illusion of absolute certitude. But one can never lead them back to the principle of contradiction as can be done in the disciplines.[60] The scientist can think that this indefinitely achieved character of his science derives exclusively from the method he must employ. He can believe that the margin of incertitude is purely subjective. In fact, the progress of the sciences consists in reducing this margin of subjectivity. That is why, from the point of view of experimental research, it is rather indifferent whether a scientist be a determinist or an indeterminist, although the determinist exposes himself to getting lost in impasses created by his philosophical prejudices which cause him to postulate more than is necessary to explain known phenomena—even knowable, the indeterminists would say. Notice, moreover, that in philosophy of science we must distinguish between the methodological principle of indeterminism according to which it is impossible to formulate other than statistical experimental laws, even if there is determinism in nature, and an experimental principle of indeterminism, such as Heisenberg's relation of uncertainty. If in the future the latter is proved defective, the first would remain intact. It is the same with the methodological principle of relativity and experimental principles.

St. Thomas underscores many times the ontological cause of this uncertainty: "in istis causis effectus futuri non habet certitudinem absolutam, sed quamdam, inquantum sunt magis determinatae causae ad unum quam ad aliud; et ideo per istas causas potest accipi scientia conjecturalis de futuris, quae tanto magis erit certa, quanto causae sunt magis determinatae ad unum; sicut est cognitio medici de sanitate et morte futura, et judium astrologi de ventis et pluviis futuris."[61] Because there are more or less contingent fluctuations in nature and degrees of spontaneity, the analytic method of the philosophy of mobile being cannot furnish an adequate and comprehensive knowledge of the cosmos. The philosopher of nature becomes a dialectician in the pejorative sense as soon as he considers his method to be exhaustive and extends it to that aspect of the world which is never totally separable from individual matter, which is resistant to complete abstraction and which can only be followed by the sense appropriate to the contingent. This measurable outside of the real moving thing, this domain where perfect certainty is impossible, is the necessary consequence of mobility. Abstracting from the margin of subjective uncertainty, the distinction we make between two degrees of knowledge, between these two modes of defining, does not derive exclusively from a partitioning necessitated by our psychological structure—it derives as well from the very nature of things. The same cause explains both the abstractive and rational character of our understanding and the fundamental opposition between these two degrees of knowledge—matter. The opposition designated for us exists as well for intelligences which do not know by experience. (There is no reason why a pure spirit should be able to predict the future position of an individual electron.)

It is in philosophy of science, the sapiential function of the philosophy of nature, a role which it shares with mathematics, that we combine these two modes of definition. For the philosophy of nature is both science and wisdom.[62] Metaphysics is wisdom because it has being as its formal subject, because it makes the tour of being and because of that can reflect on itself in explaining itself by its chief subject, God, and in defending against the natural doubt of human intelligence. But metaphysics, by the very fact that it makes a tour of being and can reflect on itself, includes as well in a certain fashion all the sciences inferior to it. It can judge them, defend them, use them, and explain them in its fashion. Reflecting on mathematics, it becomes philosophy of mathematics. For the philosophy of mathematics is formally metaphysical; it is in the third degree of abstraction. Making use of formally mathematical data it is itself only materially mathematical since it judges them in its proper light. Metaphysics plays the same sapiential role with respect to the philosophy of nature: there is a metaphysics of the philosophy of nature. It is just this need to reflect metaphysically on the content of the philosophy of nature that explains why so many modern scholastics have adopted the Wolfian division of philosophy.

It is by this sapiential function in which metaphysics departs from itself as science while still remaining in the domain of nature that philosophy of nature participates. It cannot be wisdom with respect to itself as metaphysics can, since it cannot touch on the absolute ground of its subject, mobile being: the being that it grasps only under the angle of mobility. But this very mobility comprises two aspects: the one necessary which it treats insofar as it is a science, the other which escapes *cognitio certa per causas,* but which characterizes the experimental sciences which move in the chiaroscuro of this world which tends to necessity.

Just as the quidditative intuition of the divine essence by the blessed does not yield a comprehensive knowledge of this essence and its indefinite participability, so metaphysics which attains the quiddity of being cannot tell us all the ways it can be realized, and so, too, the philosophy of nature cannot tell us all the ways in which the mobile, that *fluxibile et non semper eodem modo se habens propter materiam,* can be fashioned. But once this aspect that escapes us is disengaged by the experimental sciences, it can reflect on it without leaving the domain of mobility which is always its. It can judge, defend, and use the experimental sciences, but it can do so only in the measure that the sciences are first closed on themselves and are autonomous.

NOTES

1. ". . . qui est contingens respectu causae proximae naturaliter operantis, si comparetur ad totum ordinem et seriem causarum universi, et in his causis nulla intercedat libere agens, saltem ut applicans alias causas, vel removens impedimenta, non habet contingentiam, sed necessitatem" (*Disputationes metaphysicae,* disp. 19, sect. 10, par. 5).

2. Opusc. II: *De scientia Dei futurorum contingentium absolutorum,* c. 1. "Contingentia vero illa dicitur esse secundum quid, quia est tantum respectu unius causae, ut impediri potest ab alia; non vero respectu totius collectionis occurentium causarum" (par. 1). Compare John of St. Thomas, *Cursus Theologiae,* ed. Solesmes, t. 2, p. 410: "In causis autem creatis non possunt cognosci futura contingentia, quantumcumque causae accumulentur: quia illae omnes contingentiam non sufficiunt exhaurire, nisi forte causae istae sumuntur ut determinatae a Deo, et subjectae ipsi decreto sic causanti determinationem futuritionis." Vasquez, *Com. Ac Disput. In Iam Partem* (Anvers, Belleros) in disp. 64, c. 1, p. 338, and in disp. 207, p. 515. "(An futura contingentia ex aliis causis naturalibus provenientiae, ab angelo cognosci possunt) makes a clear distinction between future contingents necessary by nature and thus foreseeable, and non-necessary and unforeseeable future contingents, founded in liberty."

3. *Disputationes metaphysicae,* disp. 19, sect. 10, par. 13. It is important to note that Molina (*Concordia Liberi Arbitrii*) makes an exception for the spontaneity of animals, "Si secludas liberum arbitrium tam hominum quam angelorum, atque appetitum sentientem bestiarum ad actus quosdam in quolibet cernitur vestigium libertatis, propositis constitutione mundi universi qua nunc est" (q. 14, art. 13, disp. 47).

4. "Libertas a necessaria coactione nobilius invenitur in Deo, quam in angelo, et in uno angelo quam in alio, et in angelo quam in homine" (*In II Sent.,* d. 25, q. 1, a. 4).

5. John of St. Thomas, *Cursus Theologicus,* t. 2, p. 575, n. 15.

6. "Anima sensibilis, cum non sit res subsistens, non est quidditas, sicut nec aliae formae materiales, sed est pars quidditatis, et esse suum est in concretione ad materiam. . ." (St. Thomas, *Q.D. de potentia,* q. 3, a. 11, ad 11).

7. Sertillanges, O.P., *Saint Thomas d'Aquin,* 4th ed., t. 2, pp. 20 ff.

8. Aristotle, *Prior Analytics* I, c. xii (xiii) (ed. Didot): "Contingere *aliquid* dici duobus modis; uno quidem, quo ut plurimum fieri aliquid, non tamen necessario, *dicitur;* ut canescere hominem, aut augeri, aut corrumpi, aut omnino, quod natura esse potest (hoc enim non continuam necessitatem, quum homo non semper vivat [*ad justam aetatem perveniat*]; si autem vixerit, aut ex necessitate *canescit, augetur, minuitur,* aut ut plurimum *ut id fiat* contingit); altero autem modo *contingere dicitur* indefinitum, quod et sic et non sic esse potest; ut animal progredi, et progrediente *animale terrae motum fieri,* aut omnino in quod fortuito fit. Nihil enim magis sic *fieri* natum est, quam ratione contraria."

9. John of St. Thomas, *Cursus Philosophicus,* ed. Reiser, t. 2, pp. 180 ff.

10. St. Thomas, *Summa theologiae,* Ia, q. 86, a. 3. See Cajetan's commentary.

11. *In I Perihermeneias,* lectio 14, n. 9.

12. *Summa theologiae,* Ia, q. 86, a. 3, c. See Cajetan's commentary n. 9.

13. *III Summa contra gentes,* c. 86: "Adhuc, ex multis contingentibus non potest fieri unum necessarium, quia, sicut quodlibet contingentium per se dificere potest ab effectu, et omnia simul. Contat autem. . . ."

14. *In I Perihermeneias,* lectio 14, n. 8.

15. *III Summa contra gentes,* c. 86: "Impressiones enim causarum naturalium recipiuntur in effectibus secundum recipientium modum. Haec autem inferiora sunt fluxibilia et non semper eodem modo se habentia, *propter materiam,* quae est in potentia ad plures formas, et propter contrarietatem formarum et virtutum. Non igitur impressiones corporum caelestium recipiuntur in istis inferioribus per modum necessitatis."

16. *In I Perihermeneias,* lectio 14, n. 14.

17. *In VI Metaphysicorum,* lectio 2, n. 1182.

18. Ibid., lectio 3, n. 1201. John of St. Thomas, *Cursus Philosophicus,* t. 2, p. 510.

19. John of St. Thomas, *Cursus Theologicus,* t. 2, p. 420. Ibid., p. 410: "Neque enim contingentia rei consistit nisi in ordine ad futurum, quia quod jam est praesens vel praeteritum, extra contingentiam est in eo quod jam est; solum autem est contingens in eo in quo deest, et quod futurum restat. Si ergo contingens fundat de se futuritionem contingentem et impedibilem, ergo indeterminatum; et ita quandiu est in statu futuritionis, est in statu indeterminationis."

20. *In II Physicorum,* lectio 8, n. 8.

21. Ibid., lectio 10, passim. *Q.D. de malo,* q. 16, a. 7, ad 16.

22. However, in the degree that living things are endowed with spontaneity, they participate extrinsically in fortune.

23. *In VI Metaphysicorum,* lectio 2, n. 1185; *In VI Ethicorum,* lect. 3, n. 1159.

24. *In V Metaphysicorum,* lectio 6, nn. 829 ff.

25. *In II Physicorum,* lectio 10, n. 9.

26. *Summa theologiae,* Ia, q. 115, a. 6, c.

27. *Disputationes Metaphysicae,* disp. 19, sect. 10, par. 5.

28. Ibid., par. 4.

29. *In I Perihermeneias,* lectio 14, n. 8. See as well *III Summa contra gentes* 86: "Si autem aliquis forte dicat. . . ."

30. Ibid.

31. Suarez, *Disputationes Metaphysicae,* disp. 19, sect. 10, par. 13.

32. *In II Physicorum,* lectio 15, n. 2.

33. *On Generation and Corruption,* II, c. 11, 357a35. The celestial mechanics of the ancients was determinist just because they conceived the paths of the stars to be cycles completely closed in on themselves. Necessity was defined by the identity of the cycle, and the duration of celestial bodies was measured not by time, but by the *aevum.* Nowadays we would say that they reduced all astronomical laws to laws of identity which abstract from the progression of time and are by definition inviolable.

34. *In II Physicorum,* lectio 11, n. 11.

35. *Summa theologiae* Ia, q. 115, a. 6, c. See the profound commentary of Cajetan in which he avows "Et haec ratio multo tempore me vinctum tenuisse videtur."

36. *In II Sent.,* d. 3, q. 3, a. 3, ad 4.

37. Cajetan, Ia, q. 115, a. 6, c, n. xvii.

38. Ibid, n. vii. Suarez seems to say the opposite, and it is this that explains his whole position. "Sed hoc non proprie dicitur, nam casus non significat materialem causam, sed efficientem, respectu cujus mullus est effectus ad utrumlibet contingere, nisi in causis liberis. Nam naturales sunt determinatae ad unum; in liberis autem talis effectus non est casualis ex eo capite, sed liber; erit autem casualis si sit praeter intentionem, quod non invenitur proprie nisi in eis quae raro conjunguntur effectibus per se intentis. Indifferentia autem potentiae materialis nihil refert, ut effectus dicatur casualis, tum quia non sequitur effectus ex vi illius; tum etiam quia ex parte ejus non est effectus per accidens aut praeter intentionem; nam hoc proprie pertinet ad causam efficientem ut per se constat."

39. *Summa theologiae,* Ia, q. 115, a. 6, c.

40. Ibid. See Cajetan nn. xvii and xx.

41. *In VI Metaphysicorum,* lectio 3, n. 1211. See for example n. 1206.

42. Ibid., n. 1212.

43. *II Sent.,* d. 6, q. 2, a. 2, ad 2; d. 3, q. 3, a. 3, ad 4. *In XI Metaphysicorum,* lectio 8, n. 2282.

44. *Q.D. de veritate,* q. 8, a. 12.

45. Ibid, ad 6. *Q.D. de malo,* q. 16, a. 7, c.: "Ea vero contingunt ut in pluribus, possunt cognosci in causis suis non per omnimodam certitudinem, sed per conjecturalem quamdam cognitionem; certius tamen ab angelis bonis et malis, quam ab hominibus. Considerandum tamen quod cognoscere futurm in causa sua, nihil est aliud quam cognoscere praesentem inclinationem causae ad effectum; unde hoc non est proprie cognoscere futurum, sed praesens." Ad 11: "Et quae futura sunt, praecesserunt quidem in saeculis praeteritis secundum aliquam similitudinem, non tamen quantum ad omnia; sed forte unus effectus futurus assimilatur diversis effectibus praeteritis quantum ad diversa. Et tamen cognitio quae ex similibus procedit de rebus contingentibus, non habet ceritudinem propter transmutabilitatem materiae, sed est cognitio conjecturalis." See as well *Q. Quodlibet.,* VII, a. 3, ad 1.

46. *Summa theologiae,* Ia, q. 116, a. 1, c.

47. *Disputationes Metaphysicae,* sect. xi, par. 9.

48. *In I Perihermeneias,* lectio 14, nn. 10 ff.

49. *In I Physicorum,* lectio 10, n. 9. But let us add "quod non omne quod est praeter intentionem oportet esse fortuitum vel casuale, ut prima ratio proponebat. Si enim quod est praeter intentionem sit consequens ad id quod est intentum vel semper vel sicut frequenter, non eveniet fortuito vel casualiter, sicut in eo qui intendit dulcedine vini frui, si ex potatione vini sequitur ebreitas semper vel frequenter, non erit fortuitum vel casuale; esset enim casuale, si sequeretur ut in paucioribus."

50. *In I Perihermeneias,* lectio 14, n. 13.

51. Even the comparisons that we effect directly by the senses fall into the category of art as much as those effected by means of manufactured material instruments. "There is no essential distinction between scientific measures and the measures of the senses. In either case our acquaintance with the external world comes to us through material channels; the observer's body can be regarded as part of his laboratory equipment, and so far as we know, it obeys the same laws" (Eddington, *Space, Time and Gravitation* [Cambridge, 1929], chap. 2, p. 31).

52. See the very precise study of Fernand Renoirte, *Physique et philosophie* (Revue Neoscolastique, 1936), 51 ff.

53. Eddington, *The Mathematical Theory of Relativity,* Introduction. Above all, see *The Nature of the Physical World,* chap. 12.

54. It is altogether incredible that Eddington has been accused of subjectivism when it is by awareness of this mediate character of physical quantities (grandeurs) that he reestablishes their objective character; only one who confuses these two separate terms of an operation is deceived.

There is a well-known passage in John of St. Thomas on the distinction between the natural sciences and the true disciplines: "Omnis nostra speculatio dependet ab inductione, sicut dependet a sensu et experientia. Unde si propositiones universales alicujus scientiae non sint ita abstractae et communes, quod ex quocumque individuo manifestari possit ipsarum veritas, sed ex plurimum numeratione et experientia pendeat, sicut scientiae naturales, non sint ita certae sicut aliae scientiae abstractiores et communiores, ut metaphysica et mathematicae, quorum principia etiam in uno individuo habent totam certitudinem, ut 'Quolibet vel est vel non est'" (*Cursus Philosophicus,* t. 1, p. 200). Perhaps John of St. Thomas has not drawn all the methodological consequences of this for his own philosophy of nature, but what seems to me certain is that he never abandons these fundamental theses as being *minus certae.* Moreover, one can easily disengage them by applying the principles stated in the passage. In another passage in this same logical treatise, we read: "Experimentalis cognitio non dicit abstractionem intelligibilem, qua cognoscitur res per suam quidditatem praesertim quia apud nos experientia semper dependet ab aliquibus sensibilibus. Et sic *est diversa abstractio a scientia,* quae procedit a priori, quantum est ex se" (p. 828).

55. Eddington, *The Mathematical Theory of Relativity,* 117 ff, 222. *The Nature of the Physical World,* 237 ff.

56. Eddington, *New Pathways in Science,* 295 ff. Rutherford, Einstein, and Planck are cited.

57. Lemaitre, "L'expansion de l'Espace," *Revue des Questions Scientifiques* (1931): 408.

58. *In I Perihermeneias,* lectio 13, n. 10.

59. "The indeterminist is sometimes said to postulate 'something like free will' in the individual atoms. *Something like* is conveniently vague; the various mechanisms used in daily life have their obstinate moods and may be said to display something like free-will. But if it is suggested that we postulate psychological characters in the individual atoms of the kind which appear in our minds as free-will, I deny this altogether. We do not discard one rash generalization only to fall into another equally rash" (Eddington, *New Pathways in Science,* 66).

60. "Objectum autem intellectus est quod quid est, ut dicitur in III de anima, et propter hoc, actio intellectus extenditur quantum potest extendi virtus ejus ad quod quid est: per hanc autem primo ipsa principia cognita fiunt, ex quibus cognitis ulterius ratiocindando pervenitur in conclusionum notitiam: et hanc potentiam quas ipsas conclusiones in quod quid est nata est resolvere, Philosophus scientificum appellat. Sunt autem quaedam in quibus non est possibile talem resolutionem facere ut perveniatur usque ad quod quid est, et hoc *propter incertitudinem sui esse;* sicut est in contingentibus in quantum contingentia sunt: unde talia non cognoscuntur per quod quid est, quod erat proprium objectum intellectus, sed per alium modum, scilicet per quamdam conjecturam de rebus illis de quibus plena certitudo haberi non potest" (*Q.D. de veritate,* q. 15, a. 2, ad 3).

61. *In I Sent.,* d. 38, q. 1, a. 5, c. See, too, Aristotle, *Metaphysics* VII, c. 3, 1078a8–15.

62. See Maritain, *Science et sagesse,* 67 ff.

Are the Experimental Sciences Distinct from the Philosophy of Nature?

1941

1. It seems that they are quite distinct. The philosophy of nature is in effect presented as a very definite body of doctrine whose conclusions do not need to be confirmed by experience. By experimental science, by contrast, one commonly means today a knowledge which takes its proper principles from sense experience, but these principles themselves are such that the conclusions derived from them must be in their turn verified by experience. If despite the goodness of a formal consequence a conclusion is not sufficiently guaranteed, this is because the principles from which it derives are not themselves certain, and one can still question them. For this reason the experimental sciences fall into the genus of dialectics, whereas the properly demonstrative knowledge questions only its conclusions.[1] The suppositions of the experimental sciences ought to be neither true nor false; it suffices that they save appearances. In philosophy of nature, on the contrary, it seems that propositions must be true.

2. Moreover, it indeed seems that the experimental sciences better realize the end the ancients themselves proposed for the study of nature, which is achieved in the *Meteorology*, the treatises on the animals, and the *Parva Naturalia*; the earlier treatises such as the *Physics* and *De anima* remain in generality and confusion.

3. It is also said that "ancient physics was constructed by virtue of intelligibles ordered to the intelligibility of being (or to metaphysical abstraction)," whereas "physics studies the real of experience in all its manifestations independent of the activities of living things (as such)."[2]

4. If one wants the philosophy of nature to be based on experience, can it be anything more than a general reflection on the acquisitions of the experimental sciences, at the same time reestablishing the unity compromised by specialization? Grounding ourselves in experience this time, we could rejoin the philosophy of nature in very general considerations analogous to those of the ancients.

5. Moreover, Aristotle himself marked the difference of his treatise *On the Parts of Animals* from the treatises written "according to philosophy."[3]

In the Aristotelian conception, the philosophy of nature is distinguished from other sciences by its mode of defining: natural definitions imply sensible matter. Insofar as it is a work of reason, the science of nature follows a certain order.

> The natural way of doing this is to start from things which are more knowable and obvious to us and proceed towards those which are clearer and more knowable by nature; for the same things are not 'knowable relatively to us' and 'knowable' without qualification. So in the present we must follow this method and advance from what is more obscure by nature, but clearer to us, towards what is more clear and more knowable by nature. Now what is to us plain and obvious at first is rather confused masses, the elements and principles of which become known to us later by analysis. Thus we must advance from generalities to particulars; for it is a whole that is best known to sense-perception, and a generality is a kind of whole, comprehending many things within it, like parts.[4]

And also not to have to say again with respect to each thing studied that which it has in common with other things, one first treats what natural beings have in common, descending then by degrees toward the species in their particularity. Studying first of all the property common to every mobile being, one descends toward the most common species of motion. After having treated each species in general, one studies each species, first of all in its most common applications: first local motion, the most common of motions in a treatise which will have for its subject the material universe as a whole; then motion according to quality in a treatise on generation and corruption which will press on to the study of the elements (the *Meteorology*); in the last place, motion according to quantity or vital growth, first in general, in the *De Anima,* where one treats in the first place the principle that all living things have in common, to descend then to the most common species of the principles of life. This very general treatise is followed by treatises in which one passes to the application of the principles, the *Parva Natu-*

ralia and the treatises on the animals. Here one will always study in the first place the more general, such as the generation of animals, then the generation of certain kinds of animals, the ultimate term being the generation proper to each ultimate species, as far as possible.

But, for a reason that neither the text of Aristotle nor those of the great commentators can explain, one understands this manner of proceeding in an idealist sense. To the philosophy of nature one assigns only the most general considerations, the *De Anima,* for example, or the *De Incessu Animalium,* because in the most general considerations that are found in the manuals, one better attains the essence and substance of things; the philosophy of nature will have a more profound knowledge of things insofar as it embraces them in the greatest universality. In the *De Anima* one would have attained the very substance of the soul, flies and elephants being the study of the accidental modalities of the brute. In short, like Hegel, the general would be substance, the species a phenomenal mode, a later elaboration of the substance, each species not concerning philosophy which halts at the profound essence of things. That means that, according to the Aristotelians, the more known and more clear for us will also be the more essential, the more known and clear in itself. He who knows the genus will know the substance of the species. One makes precise that the scholastic ideal, pushed to its limit, will consist in deriving by a play of logical concepts the trunk of the elephant by beginning with the substance of animal, and experience will be only a profane confirmation of the powers of logical thought.

This interpretation is contrary both to the principles and to the way of proceeding of the Peripatetics. It attributes to Aristotle a position he never ceased opposing.

> Lack of experience diminishes our power of taking a comprehensive view of the admitted facts. Hence those who dwell in intimate association with nature and its phenomena grow more and more able to formulate, as the foundation of their theories, principles such as to admit of a wide and coherent development: while those whom devotion to abstract discussions has rendered unobservant of the facts are too ready to dogmatize on the basis of a few observations. The rival treatments of the subject now before us will serve to illustrate how great is the difference between a 'scientific' and a 'dialectical' method of inquiry. For whereas

> the Platonists argue that there must be atomic magnitudes because otherwise 'The Triangle' will be more than one, Democritus would appear to have been convinced by arguments appropriate to the subject, i.e. drawn from the science of nature.[5]

> [The Pythagoreans] are not asking for theories and causes to account for observed facts, but rather forcing their observations and trying to accommodate them to certain theories and opinions of their own.[6]

The whole first book of the treatise *De Partibus Animalium* is devoted to a justification of research into the ultimate differences of animals and their parts, as well as their proper Why, by experience. The Philosopher defends himself against those who do not think it worthy of the sage to explore the entrails of beasts. "If any person thinks the examination of the rest of the animal kingdom an unworthy task, he must hold in like disesteem the study of man. For no one can look at the elements of the human frame—blood, flesh, bones, vessels, and the like—without much repugnance."[7]

And earlier he had written:

> We proceed to treat of animals, without omitting, to the best of our ability, any member of the kingdom, however ignoble. For if some have no graces to charm the sense, yet nature, which fashioned them, gives amazing pleasure in their study to all who can trace the links of causation, and are inclined to philosophy. Indeed, it would be strange if mimic representations of them were attractive, because they disclose the mimetic skill of the painter or sculptor, and the original realities themselves were not more interesting, to all at any rate who have eyes to discern the causes. We therefore must not recoil with childish aversion from the examination of the humbler animals. Every realm of nature is marvelous: and as Heraclites, when the strangers who came to visit him found him warming himself at the furnace in the kitchen and hesitated to go in, is reported to have bidden them not to be afraid to enter, as even in that kitchen divinities were present.[8]

Is not this treatise *De Partibus Animalium* preceded by the *Historia Animalium* in which Aristotle recounts pure facts of observation which will serve as principles of the later treatise? Why must he return more and more to experience, drawing from it ever new principles? Is this manner of proceeding an anomaly in the natural doctrine of Aristotle?

Is it not in conformity with the necessity to go as far as possible, even to the elements, and never to define without sensible matter? Isn't it for that reason that definitions by form alone, such as 'the desire for revenge' as definition of 'anger', are purely dialectical, because they remain common and distant from the proper matter?[9] Only experience can give us the natural definition. The knowledge that we acquire in the earlier treatises, although it is quite determinate to the subject of the common as such, when it is considered in relation to species, remains dialectical.[10]

It is by an ever deepening experience that the mind emerges little by little from this dialectical condition. In this respect, the treatises nowadays designated as properly constituting the philosophy of nature are at bottom only an introduction to knowledge of nature properly speaking.

The philosophy of nature seeks to know what natural things are, not in a confused manner, but in their proper concretion. The unity of that end is not broken by the diversity of means employed. On the contrary, it is the same end that governs them, provided that they enable us better to know. Even the use of mathematics in which the physicist subalternates himself to the mathematician in order to know things in their quantitative aspect and by way of that aspect which first presents the common sensibles—number, size, shape, motion, time, situation, place, all of which are connected with quantity—does not divide natural doctrine radically. For, although the subject of the physico-mathematical sciences—such as the composite of *line* and *sensible*—is one only according to reason, although the sciences are formally mathematical insofar as they borrow their proper principles from mathematics and consequently their arguments are both hypothetical and proceed by form alone, these sciences remain principally natural since they terminate in the natural things that it is their goal to know better.[11] Doubtless knowledge of the reach of these instruments, of their fecundity and proper perfecting, will be linked to the historical evolution of the sciences. Aristotle did not foresee the amplitude that physico-mathematical science would attain, which for him remained confined to astronomy, optics, acoustics, and mechanics, nor the breadth of the use of logical doctrine, of dialectics, and of practical artifacts in the investigation of nature.

But it remains true that he best characterized these types of knowledge and of the instruments which have since been fashioned.

But the reproach brought against Aristotle is that he considered definitive many principles which were only provisory hypotheses, such as the perfect uniformity of the movement of the heavenly bodies, the four elements, etc. To take one example, in the *De Coelo*[12] Aristotle gives the principal basis for grounding his theory of the absence of all change from the heavenly bodies except local motion.

> The mere evidence of the senses is enough to convince us of this, at least with human certainty. For in the whole range of time past, so far as our inherited records reach, no change appears to have taken place either in the whole scheme of the outermost heaven or in any of its proper parts.

On this St. Thomas remarks,

> Nevertheless, this is not necessary, but only probable. In fact, the longer the duration of a thing, the more time is needed to perceive its change; thus the change that takes place in a man is not perceived in a lapse of two or three years as that which takes place in a dog over the same time, or of an animal of even briefer life. Therefore one could always say that although the heaven is naturally perishable, it is of such long duration, that all the time of which we have memory does not suffice to perceive its change.[13]

Let us cite that other well-known passage where St. Thomas remarks that Aristotle granted truth to hypotheses invented only to save the sensible appearances. It concerns the motion of the planets: "Astronomers have had recourse to diverse ways of explaining this motion. But it is not necessary that the suppositions they have imagined are true, for perhaps the appearances that the stars present could be saved by some other mode of motion still unknown to men. Aristotle, however, uses such suppositions relative to the quality of the movements as if they were true."[14] But we should not forget that Aristotle himself had already said that "we regard the zeal of one whose thirst after philosophy leads him to accept even slight indications where it is very difficult to see one's way, as a proof rather of modesty than of overconfidence."[15]

It is appropriate to recall here, as others have,[16] that those we are now accustomed to honor as the first to employ the true method of the experimental sciences, Copernicus, Kepler, Galileo, held a position on the subject of physical and astronomical hypotheses, and that in principle and in the most resolute manner, which we would be wrong to attribute to Aristotle.

Consider first his position of principle. "The science which is knowledge at once of the fact and of the reasoned fact, not of the fact by itself without the reasoned fact, is the more exact and the prior science."[17] Indeed, if we know the reason, we then know the fact by its proper reason which is as such prior to it.[18]

"A science such as arithmetic, which is not a science of properties qua inhering in a substratum, is more exact than and prior to a science like harmonics, which is a science of properties inhering in a substratum; and similarly a science like arithmetic, which is constituted of fewer basic elements, is more exact than and prior to geometry, which requires additional elements."[19] If we consider the philosophy of nature in its tendency toward things as concretized in matter, it depends more and more on matter and experience; its principles become more and more numerous. It does not derive the subjects and their proper principles from one another as is done in mathematics; and when it tries to derive species from one another, the derivation presupposes direct or indirect experimental knowledge of the species. It has as its goal to lead the multiplicity of principles gained from experience back to as small a number of principles as possible, as one does nowadays in the theory of evolution. But this reduction will not be to confused generic principles, but to principles which allow us to descend to the species in their very diversity. The *History of Animals* is only a vast collection of facts (principles for us) gathered from observation, facts for which one must go on to seek the principles of the order as such, and of species and their parts.

From this one sees why the first parts of philosophy of nature can be more certain than the following. We rest in what is most certain and clear to us, that is, the general and confused. It is not hard to speak with certainty as long as one remains in the common and does not wish to say much. "Therefore, since the truth seems to be like the proverbial door, which no one can fail to hit, in this respect it must be easy, but the fact that we can have a whole truth and not the particular part we aim at shows the difficulty of it."[20] This house burned, but what is burning and why did this house burn? With respect to the later treatises, the first, the *Physics* and *De Anima,* give us only a superficial knowledge of things, and that is why they are more certain for us. So it is right to reproach those who are content with this kind of consideration as if they had attained the ultimate causes, their air of false profundity, unless one calls the confused and undetermined profound.

Must one not conclude from this position that the *De Incessu Animalium* is from the point of view of the philosophy of nature more important than the treatment of the intellectual soul in *De Anima III*? It is true that in the former one attains a greater concretion, but it remains that the subject of the latter is more noble and worthy of consideration, more important for us and also more certain. In this respect it ranks above all the other treatises. It seems that with this distinction we touch the root of the historical conflict that burst out in the trial of Galileo.

But isn't it true that the best modern physicists ignore almost all the questions studied in the first parts of the philosophy of nature? Would they be better physicists if they knew the definition of motion, or that the comparison of different species of motion supposes a predication of identity and a dialectical movement of thought? One can answer with a question: Would the bricklayer be a better bricklayer if he were an architect? The writings of modern scientists on the "more philosophical" aspects of their science sufficiently show the perils of the bricklayer who wants to be an architect insofar as he is a bricklayer. They do violence to the order we must follow in knowing if we wish to come to see the order of the part in the whole. They have neglected considerations logically prior to their proper subject, a negligence which makes itself felt when they seek to go on from there. To do violence to the order, if only to that which is imposed on us by the very nature of intelligence, is to do violence to wisdom, and to the science of nature insofar as it is philosophical.

If the prior parts of the philosophy of nature remain in that which is more known to us and do not arrive at the causes more known and determinate in themselves, why is it that they are less accessible to a greater number than the others? When we say "more known to us" we already put ourselves in the point of view of intelligence and not of sensation. If "more known to us" comprised the sensible singular, the object of sense as such, this sensible is more known to us than the sensible universal.[21] To the degree that the sciences which bring us close to things in their concretion depend more and more on sense, inasmuch as one wishes to attend to the part without regard for the whole, a facility results which is due to the proximity of the sensible singular.[22] It is also true that mathematics, independent of experience in the proper elaboration, is the science in the proper sense which is most proportioned to our intelligence. These two facts explain the possibility of mathematical physics so far without regard to the whole.

The responses to the positions advanced at the outset of this article will enable us to be more precise.

Ad 1. If by philosophy of nature is understood a science in a quite rigorous sense, that defined in *Posterior Analytics,* I, 1, and if by experimental sciences we mean those branches of the knowledge of natural things which remain in a condition of dialectical movement because they cannot sufficiently detach themselves from the singular and whose generalizations will thus always be tentative and provisory, it is understood that the two are quite distinct. Nevertheless, they bear on the same subject, their principles have a common origin, sensible matter; their term is the same, knowledge of natural things as much as possible in their proper principles. In this respect, the experimental sciences are only a continuation of the properly demonstrative science of nature. But this continuation requires the use of another method, not only in the search for principles, but for the choice and positing of the principles themselves.[23] We will have occasion to give more of an explanation on this subject in a note soon to appear. It suffices to have indicated that it is the same inspiration that drives the philosophy of nature from the first book of the *Physics* to the fact and the explanation of the elephant's trunk.

Ad 2. From the fact that the experimental sciences go farther in the direction of concretion one cannot conclude that they can be substituted for the philosophy of nature of the ancients. To identify the philosophy of nature with the experimental sciences which are only the dialectical extension of it is to destroy it in its root, to deny the most certain part of our knowledge of nature, as well as its most noble natural subject. For that reason, the identification of the two [philosophy of nature and experimental sciences] is the most complete missing of the point of the ancients and of wisdom.

Ad 3. The physics of Aristotle, from the *Physics* to the *De Incessu Animalium,* never abstracts from sensible matter, unless one means by sensible matter, individual sensible matter. If, as is said, he constructed it in virtue of intelligibles ordered to the intelligibility of being, he would have denied the proper subject of physics which in its very nature is inseparable from matter, both with respect to being and with respect to understanding. And if the author identifies physics with mathematical physics, even in Aristotle the use of mathematics in astronomy, for example, was ordered, not to the intelligibility of quantity as separated by mind, but always to mobile things in their concretion in sensible matter. And if it is sometimes a question of *substance* and *accidents* in philosophy of nature, we must not conclude that Aristotle is using metaphysical concepts. We forget that even the science of natural things presupposes logic, and in particular the categories.

Ad 4. If the philosophy of nature were only an extension of experimental sciences as this is understood in the first position, it is understood that it would be purely dialectical, even more conditioned and provisory than scientific theories. Let us remember that even the first parts of the philosophy of nature are based on experience, although their principles are very general and still confused. It seems that the very widespread position that we consider here is only an expression of the desire to go to the most universal principles and causes in the order of concretion, and in this respect, provided that one has not neglected or denied the parts logically prior to the experimental sciences, this attempt responds to the ultimate aim of the philosophy of nature. When the scholastics say that in the experimental sciences are sought the most proximate causes of things, whereas the philosophy of nature seeks the ultimate causes, they are quite right, provided that by ultimate causes one means, not causes most universal in their predicable community (as is the case with the principles considered in the earlier treatises insofar as they are prior to the treatises dealing with things in greater concretion), but the ultimate causes which are first by reason of causality, and which we do not know save by way of the more proximate causes. And if one often confuses the two, this is because the properly ultimate causes can be known only in a confused way. So it is that in the *De Anima* we can demonstrate that man is the natural end of all natural species. But this knowledge, although certain, remains very confused. Theories of evolution are only an attempt to rejoin this end in the order of concretion. It is only by means of the latter that we can attain the ultimate cause in itself absolutely. But we have recalled that the experimental sciences remain in a state of motion toward a term that one approaches nearer and nearer without every attaining it in itself. Thus, the reflections of the philosophy of nature, insofar as they are based on the experimental sciences, themselves remain in a state of dialectical movement toward a term which is no less the ultimate aim of all our knowledge of nature.

Ad 5. This treatise is less philosophical insofar as it is less scientific, taking *science* in the strict sense of the term. We will explain ourselves on that point in a commentary on the *De Partibus Animalium,* I, 1, 640a, where Aristotle opposes natural science to speculative sciences. For the present, it is enough to indicate that it is the philosopher who pursues the subject of that same treatise, as is said later, c. 5, 645a5.

NOTES

1. St. Thomas, *In I Posterior Analytics,* lectio 21, n. 3.
2. J. Dopp (Louvain), "Physique ancienne et physique moderne: Leurs conceptions de l'intelligible," *Travaux du IXe Congrès International de Philosophie* (Paris: Hermann, 1937), t. 5, 172–73.
3. *De Partibus Animalium,* I, c. 1, 642a5.
4. *Physics* I, c. 1, 184a15–25.
5. *De Gen. et Corr.,* I, c. 2, 31615–15.
6. *De Coelo,* II, 13, 293a25.
7. *De Partibus Animalium,* I, c. 5, 645a25.
8. Ibid., 645a5–23.
9. *De Anima,* I, c. 1, 403a25 ff.
10. We use the term 'dialectical' in the two senses defined by St. Thomas in the *De Trinitate,* q. 6, a. 1. (Cf. John of St. Thomas, *Cursus Philosophicus,* t. 1, p. 278a19 ff.) It is not therefore always synonymous with probable.
11. *Posterior Analytics,* I, c. 13; *Physics,* II, c. 2.
12. *De Coelo,* I, c. 3, 270b10.
13. *Comm. In de Coelo,* I, lectio 7, n. 6.
14. Ibid., II, lectio 17, n. 2. Cf. Duhem, *La théorie physique* (Paris: Riviere, 1914), 54 ff.
15. *De Coelo,* II, c. 12.
16. Duhem, *La théorie physique,* 58 ff.

17. *Posterior Analytics,* I, c. 27, 87a30.

18. Note that Aristotle is not speaking here of facts of experience, but of those of which we know by reasoning either their existence alone or a remote explanation.

19. Ibid. That is why we seek to arithmetize geometry.

20. *Metaphysics,* II, c. 1, 993b.

21. St. Thomas, *In I Physic.,* lectio 1, n. 8.

22. No doubt this is what M. Maritain means when he says that the empirical sciences put the accent on the *sensible.*

23. *Topics,* I, c. 16.

Index

CHARLES DE KONINCK

was on the faculty of Québec's Université de Laval and was Director of Laval's philosophy faculty from 1939 to 1956. He determined the course of philosophy at Laval and in much of French Canada through his publications and his connections with the Roman Catholic Church. He lectured frequently in the United States, as well as in Latin America, Europe, and Canada.

www.ingramcontent.com/pod-product-compliance
Lightning Source LLC
Chambersburg PA
CBHW060301100726
47907CB00002B/231

9780268026226